THE REAL GUIDE

W9-DDE-146

PARIS

New and Revised

THE REAL GUIDES

OTHER AVAILABLE REAL GUIDES

CALIFORNIA AND THE WEST COAST • SAN FRANCISCO
NEW YORK • MEXICO • GUATEMALA & BELIZE • BRAZIL
PERU • FRANCE • CZECHOSLOVAKIA • SPAIN • PORTUGAL
AMSTERDAM • HOLLAND, BELGIUM, AND LUXEMBOURG
IRELAND • ITALY • VENICE • GREECE • SCANDINAVIA
GERMANY • BERLIN • HUNGARY • POLAND • YUGOSLAVIA
TURKEY • HONG KONG • KENYA • MOROCCO • NEPAL
and WOMEN TRAVEL

FORTHCOMING
FLORIDA • EUROPE • BARCELONA

PARIS REAL GUIDE CREDITS

Editing: Mark Ellingham and Greg Ward
Proofreading: Kate Berens
Production: Susanne Hillen, Kate Berens, Gail Jammy, and Andy Hilliard
Typesetting and Design: Greg Ward
Series Editor: Mark Ellingham

We'd like to thank all the readers who have helped us revise and update this guide by sending information, comments, and criticisms. Thanks in particular to Rosie Ayliffe and Matthew Yeomans for their
work on the *Basics* section, and to Margaret Doyle for additional US text editing. Many thanks also to
Oristelle Bonis, Hélène Rouch, Catherine Henrigou, and Thomas Moutel for help, sustenance, and
encouragement while researching this new edition, and to Peter Polish for support throughout.

Illustrations in Part One and Part Three by Ed Briant.
Basics and Contexts illustrations (pages 1 and 281) by Henry Iles.

Typeset in Linotron Univers and Century Old Style to an original design by Andrew Oliver.
Printed in the United States by R.R. Donnelley & Sons.

The publishers and authors have done their best to ensure the accuracy and currency of all the information in
Paris: the Real Guide; however, they can accept no responsibility for any loss, injury, or inconvenience
sustained by any traveler as a result of information or advice contained in the guide.

Published in the United States by
Prentice Hall General Reference
A division of Simon & Schuster Inc.
15 Columbus Circle
New York, NY 10023

No part of this book may be reproduced in any form without permission from the publisher except for the
quotation of brief passages in reviews.

PRENTICE HALL and colophon are registered trademarks of Simon & Schuster Inc.

© Kate Baillie and Tim Salmon 1987, 1988, 1989, 1992

Library of Congress Cataloging-in-Publication Data

Baillie, Kate
    The Real Guide. Paris / written and researched by Kate Baillie and Tim Salmon.
    322p. (The Real Guides)
    Includes bibliographical references (p.297) and index.
    ISBN 0–13–766676–4: $13
    1. Paris (France)—Description—1975—Guide-books. I. Salmon, Tim. II. Title. III. Series.

914.4'3604839—dc20
                                                               91–16342
                                                                   CIP

THE REAL GUIDE

PARIS

New and Revised

Written and researched by

KATE BAILLIE and **TIM SALMON**

PRENTICE HALL TRAVEL

NEW YORK LONDON TORONTO SYDNEY TOKYO SINGAPORE

HELP US UPDATE

We've gone to a lot of effort to ensure that this new edition of *Paris: The Real Guide* is up-to-date and accurate. However, Paris information changes fast: new bars and clubs appear and disappear, museums shift round their displays and opening hours, restaurants and hotels change prices and standards. If you feel there are places we've under-praised or overrated, omitted or ought to omit, please let us know. All suggestions, comments, or corrections are much appreciated and we'll send a copy of the next edition (or any other Real Guide if you prefer) for the best letters.

Please write to:

Kate Baillie and Tim Salmon,
The Real Guides, Prentice Hall Travel, 15 Columbus Circle, New York, NY 10023.

CONTENTS

Introduction viii

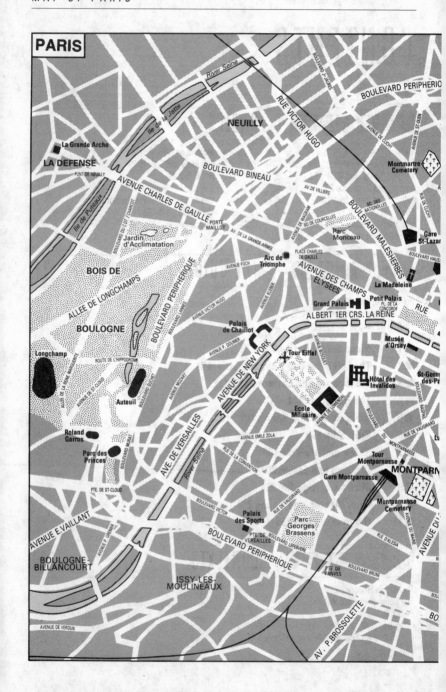

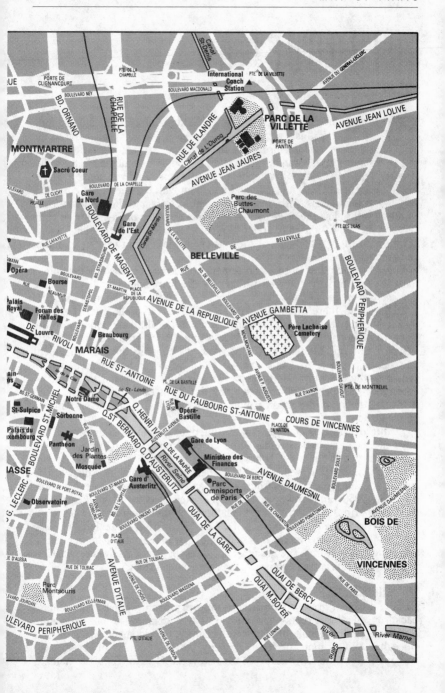

INTRODUCTION

Pre-eminent as the center of French cultural, intellectual, and commercial life, **Paris** is a self-conscious and assertive city. You see it in the grandiose architecture of both past and present—in Mitterrand's projects of La Grande Arche and La Villette, as much as in the Eiffel Tower, Napoléon's Arc de Triomphe, or Notre-Dame. And you sense it, above all, in the people. Often arrogant and impatient with outsiders, but entertaining, too, the Parisians, with their attachment to style and the figure they cut in the street, reflect the pride of the city where so much of life is carried on in public. The animation and variety of **street life** makes just strolling along, browsing with eyes and ears at the café-pâtisserie level of existence, one of the greatest Paris pleasures.

For natives of other large urban centers, the **compactness** of Paris comes as a novelty. Strictly confined within the 78-square-kilometer limits of the *boulevard périphérique*, the character and contrasts of the different *quartiers* are sharp and more intensely experienced. You can walk from the calm, village-like atmosphere of Montmartre and parts of the Latin Quarter to the busy commercial centers of the Bourse and Opéra or to the aristocratic mansions of the Marais; vast subterranean shopping and entertainment complexes compete with tiny *coins de quartiers* in the poorer areas where textiles and teapots from North Africa are piled high behind narrow counters; cars can cross the city in minutes along the Right Bank expressway, while below, on the *quais*, the classic panoramas of the Louvre and Cité fall within a single glance.

Ethnic diversity is an important, if contentious, element in the weft of the city's life. Long a haven and magnet for foreign refugees and artists, Paris in this century has sheltered Lenin and Ho Chi Minh, White Russians and Iranians (Khomeini as well as the Shah's eldest son), dissidents from Eastern Europe, disillusioned writers from the US, and a host of assorted expatriates. Since the 1950s immigrants from the ex-French colonies of southeast Asia, west and north Africa, have come to fill the labor shortages for the worst-paid jobs, and made the run-down areas of the city home from home. Finally, there are the students from every corner of the globe, whose access to higher education is no different from the French, and who support themselves by working in the restaurants and enterprises of their own compatriots.

Some Highlights

Paris is a city of great **art and contemporary architecture**. The general backdrop of the streets—part of the city's glamor—is predominantly Neoclassical, the result of nineteenth-century development. Each period since has added, more or less discreetly, novel examples of its styles—**August Perret, Le Corbusier, Mallet-Stevens, Gustav Eiffel**, to name a few of their authors. And in the last two decades the architectural contributions have taken on a scale that has made a dramatic difference to the city, producing new and major landmarks, and recasting down-at-heel districts into crucial centers of cultural and consumer life. **Beaubourg**, **La Villette**, **La Grande Arche**, the **Bastille Opéra**, the **Louvre pyramid**, the **Institut du Monde Arabe**, have expanded the dimensions of the city, pointing it determinedly towards the future as well as to the past.

The **museums and galleries** are probably the finest in western Europe, and, with the tradition of state cultural endowment very much alive, certainly the best displayed. The art of conversion—the **Musée d'Orsay** from a railway station, the **Cité des Sciences** from abbatoirs, and spacious well-lit exhibition spaces from mansions and palaces—has given the city's great collections unparalleled locations. The Impressionists at the **Musée d'Orsay**, the **Orangerie**, and **Marmottan**; the moderns at **Beaubourg** and the **Palais de Tokyo**; the ancients in the **Louvre**; **Picasso** and **Rodin** with their own individual museums: all these could keep the dedicated follower of art busy for a month of Sundays. In addition, there's the contemporary scene in the **commercial galleries** that fill the Marais, St-Germain, and the area round the Champs Élysées. Other areas of human action—science, history, decoration, and performance art—have equal status with fine arts in the ever-expanding range of Parisian museums.

As for more hedonistic pleasures, few cities can compete with the thousand and one **cafés**, **bars**, and **restaurants**—ultra-modern and designer-signed, palatial, traditional, scruffy, and homely; and for every pocket—that line each Paris street and boulevard. The choice is not just French, but a tempting range of cuisines and social culture from every ethnic origin that the city's population represents. Where **entertainment** is concerned, the city's strong points are movies and music. Paris is the **movie** capital, and the **music** encompasses excellent jazz, top quality classical, avant-garde experiment, West African and French Caribbean groups, Algerian raï, and folk, both French and foreign. If you want to hear world dance rhythms, Parisian clubs are exciting grounds to discover.

When to Go

When to visit is largely a question of personal taste and time. The city has a more reliable **climate** than points farther north in Europe (London, for example), with uninterrupted stretches of sun (and rain) all year round. For anyone crossing the Atlantic, there are hints of a southern climate, but it is definitely not Mediterranean. Winter temperatures drop well below freezing, with sometimes biting winds. If you're lucky, the spring and fall will be mild and sunny—in summer it can reach the high 20s° C (80s° F).

In terms of pure aesthetics, winter sun is the city's most flattering light, when the pale shades of the older buildings become luminescent without any glare, and the lack of trees and greenery has no relevance. By contrast, Paris in high summer can be choking: the fumes of congested traffic trapped by the high narrowness of streets, and the city's parks too parched and hemmed by roads to be a haven; while the reflected light in open spaces is too blinding to enjoy.

What is perhaps most important is **when not to go**. If you visit during the French summer vacation, from July 15 to the end of August, you will find large numbers of Parisians have fled the city. It's quieter but a lot of stores and restaurants will be closed, and the people who remain can be more ill-humored than usual. There is, too, the commercial calendar to consider—fashion shows, trade fairs, etc. Paris hoteliers warn against September and October, and **finding a room** even at the best of times can be problematic. Given the choice, early spring, fall if you make reservations, or the midwinter months are most rewarding.

AVERAGE TEMPERATURES IN PARIS

Jan	Feb	March	April	May	June	July	Aug	Sept	Oct	Nov	Dec
7.5	7.1	10.2	15.7	16.6	23.4	25.1	25.6	20.9	16.5	11.7	7.8

All temperatures are in ° **Centigrade**: to convert to **Fahrenheit** multiply by 9/5 and add 32.
For a recorded **weather forecast** you can phone the Paris forecasting office on ☎45.55.91.09
(☎45.55.95.02 for specific inquiries).

PART ONE

THE

BASICS

GETTING THERE

It's not at all difficult to reach Paris from the United States; there are direct flights from most major cities, with scheduled connections from all over the continent. Several different airlines operate flights, making Paris one of the cheapest destinations in Europe. In fact, only London can offer more discounted flights; and the price difference is rarely sufficient to make a stopover in London a money-saving idea. Paris' two main airports, Roissy-Charles de Gaulle and Orly, are roughly equidistant from the city center; see p.33 for details on their relative accessibility.

DIRECT FROM THE UNITED STATES

The most comprehensive range of flights from the US is offered by *Air France*, the French national carrier, which flies direct to Charles de Gaulle from six locations across the country—**New York JFK**, **Newark**, **Chicago**, **Miami**, **Houston**, and **Washington DC**—in most instances daily. *Air France* is expensive, however; low to high season prices range from $682 to $844 for the New York route, while from the Midwest flights tend to be around $100 more than that. The major American competitors tend to be cheaper, but offer fewer routes. *United* flies daily non-stop to Charles de Gaulle from New York (JFK), Washington DC, and San Francisco; *American* flies to Orly from New York, Chicago, and Raleigh-Durham NC; *Pan Am* and *TWA* link JFK and Charles de Gaulle daily. The cheapest way to take any of these scheduled flights is with a non-

refundable APEX fare, which normally entails booking 21 days in advance of flying, traveling midweek, and staying for at least seven days.

The best guarantee of a cheap flight is to contact a travel agent specializing in discounted fares. Restrictions on such tickets are often not all that stringent; you need not assume that youth or student fares are the best bargain, nor worry if you're not eligible for them. *STA Travel* and *Council Travel* are two of the most reliable agents, but for Paris the best bet is *Nouvelles Frontières*, which offers a high-season round-trip fare of around $500 flying from JFK to Orly. Addresses of local offices are given on p.4. The travel sections of the *New York Times*, *Washington Post*, and *Los Angeles Times* advertise discounted fares to Paris which will always be cheaper than booking with the airlines directly. Make sure that you are dealing with a reputable travel agent before you hand over any money.

Rebel Tours (25050 Avenue Kearney #215, Valencia CA 91355; ☎805/294-0900 or ☎1-800/227-3235) provides discounted flights from both **Los Angeles** and **San Francisco** to Paris for about $700 (with a one-hour stopover in Newfoundland).

If you're prepared to travel light and at short notice, it might be worth acting as a **courier**. *Now Voyager* (☎212/431-1616) arranges courier flights to Europe from JFK, Newark, and Houston. Flights, which cost as little as $380, are issued on a first-come, first-served, basis, and there is no guarantee that the Paris route will be served at the specific time you want.

DIRECT FROM CANADA

The strong links between France and Québec's Francophone community ensure regular air services from Canada to Paris. *Air France* flies four times a week from Toronto and Montréal, varying from around $850 high season to around $700 in the summer. *Air Canada* and *British Airways* flies direct to London from Toronto and Montréal, with frequent onward connections to Paris. Once again, *Nouvelles Frontières* is the most likely source of good-value discounted tickets, from Montréal, Toronto, and Québec; call for details as flights vary from season to season. *Travel Cuts* also sells cheap seats on non-stop flights from all major Canadian cities.

COUNCIL TRAVEL IN THE US

Head Office: 205 E. 42nd St., New York, NY 10017; ☎212/661-1450

CALIFORNIA
2486 Channing Way, Berkeley, CA 94704; ☎415/848-8604
UCSD Price Center, Q-076, La Jolla, CA 92093; ☎619/452-0630
1818 Palo Verde Ave., Suite E, Long Beach, CA 90815; ☎213/598-3338
1093 Broxton Ave., Suite 220, Los Angeles, CA 90024; ☎213/208-3551
4429 Cass St., San Diego, CA 92109; ☎619/270-6401
312 Sutter St., Suite 407, San Francisco, CA 94108; ☎415/421-3473
919 Irving St., Suite 102, San Francisco, CA 94122; ☎415/566-6222
14515 Ventura Blvd., Suite 250, Sherman Oaks, CA 91403; ☎818/905-5777

COLORADO
1138 13th St., Boulder, CO 80302; ☎818/905-5777

CONNECTICUT
Yale Co-op East, 77 Broadway, New Haven, CT 06520; ☎203/562-5335

DISTRICT OF COLUMBIA
1210 Potcmac St., NW Washington, DC 20007; ☎202/337-6464

GEORGIA
12 Park Place South, Atlanta, GA 30303; ☎404/577-1678

ILLINOIS
1153 N. Dearborn St., Chicago, IL 60610; ☎312/951-0585
831 Foster St., Evanston, IL 60201; ☎708/475-5070

LOUISIANA
8141 Maple St., New Orleans, LA 70118; ☎504/866-1767

MASSACHUSETTS
79 South Pleasant St., 2nd Floor, Amherst, MA 01002; ☎413/256-1261
729 Boylston St., Suite 201, Boston, MA 02116; ☎617/266-1926
1384 Massachusetts Ave., Suite 206, Cambridge, MA 02138; ☎617/497-1497
Stratton Student Center MIT, W20-024, 84 Massachusetts Ave., Cambridge, MA 02139; ☎617/497-1497

MINNESOTA
1501 University Ave. SE, Room 300, Minneapolis, MN 55414; ☎612/379-2323

NEW YORK
35 W. 8th St., New York, NY 10011; ☎212/254-2525
Student Center, 356 West 34th St., New York, NY 10001; ☎212/643-1365

NORTH CAROLINA
703 Ninth St., Suite B-2, Durham, NC 27705; ☎919/286-4664

OREGON
715SW Morrison, Suite 600, Portland, OR 97205; ☎503/228-1900

RHODE ISLAND
171 Angell St., Suite 212, Providence, RI 02906; ☎401/331-5810

TEXAS
2000 Guadalupe St., Suite 6, Austin, TX 78705; ☎512/472-4931
Exec. Tower Office Center, 3300 W. Mockingbird, Suite 101, Dallas,TX 75235; ☎214/350-6166

WASHINGTON
1314 Northeast 43rd St., Suite 210, Seattle, WA 98105; ☎206/632-2448

WISCONSIN
2615 North Hackett Avenue, Milwaukee, WI; ☎414/332-4740

NOUVELLES FRONTIÈRES

In the United States
NEW YORK 12 East 33rd St, New York, NY 10016 ☎212/779-0600
LOS ANGELES 6363 Wilshire Blvd., Suite 200, Los Angeles, CA 90048; ☎213/658-8955
SAN FRANCISCO 209 Post St., Suite 1121, San Francisco, CA 94108; ☎415/781-4480

In Canada
MONTREAL 800 East Blvd. de Maison Neuve, Montréal, Quebec (☎514/288-9942)
QUEBEC 176 Grande Allée Ouest, Québec, P.Q. G1R 2G9; ☎418/525-5255

STA IN THE US

BOSTON
273 Newbury St., Boston, MA 02116; ☎617/266-6014

HONOLULU
1831 S. King St., Suite 202, Honolulu, HI 96826; ☎808/942-7755

LOS ANGELES
920 Westwood Blvd., Los Angeles, CA 90024; ☎213/824-1574

7204 Melrose Ave., Los Angeles, CA 90046; ☎213/934-8722

2500 Wilshire Blvd., Los Angeles, CA 90057; ☎213/380-2184

NEW YORK
17 E. 45th St., Suite 805, New York, NY 10017; ☎212/986-9470;☎ 800/777-0112

SAN DIEGO
6447 El Cajon Blvd., San Diego, CA 92115; ☎619/286-1322

SAN FRANCISCO
166 Geary St., Suite 702, San Francisco, CA 94108; ☎415/391-8407

TRAVEL CUTS IN CANADA

Head Office: 187 College St., Toronto, Ontario M5T 1P7; ☎416/979-2406.

ALBERTA
MacEwan Hall Student Centre, Univ. of Calgary, Calgary T2N 1N4; ☎403/282-7687.

10424A 118th Ave., Edmonton T6G 0P7; ☎403/471-8054.

BRITISH COLUMBIA
Room 326, T.C., Student Rotunda, Simon Fraser University, Burnaby, British Columbia V5A 1S6; ☎604/291-1204.

1516 Duranleau St., Granville Island, Vancouver V6H 3S4; ☎604/687-6033.

Student Union Building, University of British Columbia, Vancouver V6T 1W5; ☎604/228-6890.

Student Union Building, University of Victoria, Victoria V8W 2Y2; ☎604/721-8352.

MANITOBA
University Centre, University of Manitoba, Winnipeg R3T 2N2; ☎204/269-9530.

NOVA SCOTIA
Student Union Building, Dalhousie University, Halifax B3H 4J2; ☎902/424-2054.

6139 South St., Halifax B3H 4J2; ☎902/494-7027.

ONTARIO
University Centre, University of Guelph, Guelph N1G 2W1; ☎519/763-1660.

Fourth Level Uni-centre, Carleton University, Ottawa, K1S5B6; ☎613/238-5493.

60 Laurier Ave. E, Ottawa K1N 6N4; ☎613/238-8222.

Student Street, Room G27, Laurentian University, Sudbury P3E 2C6; ☎705/673-1401.

96 Gerrard St. E, Toronto M5B 1G7; ☎ (416) 977-0441.

University Shops Plaza, 170 University Ave. W, Waterloo N2L 3E9; ☎519/886-0400.

QUÉBEC (Known as *Voyages CUTS*)
Université McGill, 3480 rue McTavish, Montréal H3A 1X9; ☎514/398-0647.

1613 rue St. Denis, Montréal H2X 3K3; ☎514/843-8511.

Université Concordia, Edifice Hall, Suite 643, S.G.W. Campus, 1455 bd de Maisonneuve Ouest, Montréal H3G 1M8; ☎514/288-1130.

19 rue Ste. Ursule, Québec G1R 4E1; ☎418/692-3971.

SASKATCHEWAN
Place Riel Campus Centre, University of Saskatchewan, Saskatoon S7N 0W0; ☎306/975-3722.

TOLL-FREE AIRLINE NUMBERS

Access International ☎212/465-0707

Air Canada ☎1-800/776-3000

Air France ☎1-800/237-2747

American Airlines ☎1-800/433-7300

British Airways ☎1-800/247-9297

Pan Am ☎1-800/221-1111

TWA ☎1-800/221-2000

United Airlines ☎1-800/241-6522

Virgin Atlantic ☎1-800/862-8621

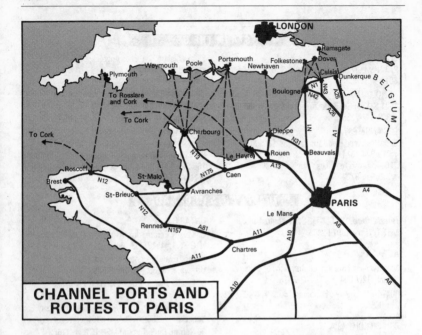

CHANNEL PORTS AND ROUTES TO PARIS

Although flying to London has long been considered the cheapest way of reaching Europe, price differences these days are minimal enough for there to be little point traveling to Paris via London unless you've specifically chosen to visit England as well. Having said that, you may well be able to pick up a London flight at an advantageous rate; *United* and *American Airlines* have recently acquired certain of *Pan Am* and *TWA*'s London routes, and as a result the competition between the major airlines is hotting up.

In recent years, *Virgin Atlantic* has offered the best fares from New York year-round, and has now added flights from Los Angeles, Miami, and Boston to its schedules. *British Airways* has entered the fray with a series of rival offers. In the summer, the savings are bound to be less, but shop around as there may yet be some European bargains. As well as JFK and Newark, *British Airways* has regular non-stop flights from Philadelphia, Detroit, Boston, San Francisco, and Los Angeles.

Once you're in Britain, the quickest way of reaching Paris is by air, although only from London can you expect any kind of cheap deal.

The rail- or road-and-sea routes are significantly more affordable, but can be uncomfortable and tiring, involving a journey of up to nine hours.

LONDON–PARIS FLIGHTS

Deals on **flights** from London to Paris change all the time, so it's well worth shopping around, and checking out newspaper ads. In particular, **students** and anyone **under 26** should look out for special discount fares, such as *STA*'s current return price to Paris (Charles de Gaulle) of £66 ($108). *Campus Travel* runs a student/youth charter to **Beauvais**, open to all if bought in conjunction with accommodation. Round-trip fares to Paris start at £55 ($90), flights plus two nights accommodation start at £79 ($129). The drawback is the distance of the airport from the city, although the 70km bus ride into town is included in the ticket. *Air UK* offers seven daily return flights to Charles de Gaulle for £75 ($122).

Other alternatives include a **charter**—*Nouvelles Frontières* currently offers London (Gatwick) to Paris (Charles de Gaulle) daily from around £65 ($100) round trip—or a **Superapex/Late Saver** scheduled ticket (on *British Airways* or *Air France*). These latter must be reserved two

CROSS-CHANNEL FERRY DETAILS

Routes and prices

	Operator	Crossing time	Frequency	One-way fares Car, 2 adults, 2 kids	Foot passenger
Portsmouth–St-Malo	Brittany Ferries	9hr	Mar–Dec 1–2 daily	£107–163	£31–36
Plymouth–Roscoff	Brittany Ferries	7hr 30min	3–12 weekly	£104–160	£31–36
Southampton–Cherbourg	Sealink Stena	6–8 hr	1–2 daily	£91–159	£25–28
Portsmouth–Cherbourg	P&O	4hr 45min	1–3 daily	£90–158	£25–28
Poole–Cherbourg	Brittany Ferries	4hr 15min	May–Sept 1–4 daily	£90–139	£22–26
Portsmouth–Caen	Brittany Ferries	5hr 45min	8–20 weekly	£95–151	£25–29
Portsmouth–Le Havre	P&O	5hr 45min	2–3 daily	£90–158	£25–28
Newhaven–Dieppe	Dieppe Ferries	4hr	3–4 daily	£88–138	£23
Newhaven–Dieppe	Sealink Stena	4hr	2–4 daily	£95–156	£23–25
Folkestone–Boulogne	Sealink Stena	1hr 50min	6–8 daily all year	£70–137	£21
Dover–Boulogne	P&O	1hr 40min	5–6 daily	£69–138	£21
Dover–Calais	Sealink Stena	1hr 30min	6–18 daily	£70–137	£21
Dover–Calais	P&O	1hr 15min	15 daily	£69–138	£21
Dover–Boulogne/Calais	Hoverspeed	35–40min	6–20 daily	£69–138	£23
Ramsgate–Dunkerque	Sally Line	2hr 30min	5 daily all year	£53–104	£13–14.50

The exchange rate at the time of going to press was £1 = $1.63

FERRY COMPANIES, AIRLINES, AND AGENCIES

Air France, 158 New Bond St., London W1 (☎071/499 9511).

British Airways, 156 Regent St., London W1 (Heathrow reservations only ☎081/897 4000).

British Rail, International Rail Centre, Victoria Station, SW1 (☎071/834 2345). The main *British Rail* center for international reservations.

Britannia Airways, 25 Tavistock Place, London WC1 (☎071/388 2881).

Brittany Ferries, Wharf Rd., Portsmouth PO2 8RU (☎0705/827701); Millbay Docks, Plymouth PL1 3EW (☎0752/221321); Poole (☎0202/666466).

Campus Travel, 52 Grosvenor Gardens, London SW1 (☎071/730 3402). Student travel specialists, with regional branches throughout Britain.

Council Travel, 28a Poland St., London W1V 3DB (☎071/437 7767).

Euro-Express, 227 Shepherd's Bush Rd., London W6 7AS (☎081/748 2607).

Eurotrain/London Student Travel, 52 Grosvenor Gardens, SW1 (☎071/730 8111 or ☎071/823 6131). Rail specialists.

Hoverspeed, Maybrook House, Queen's Gardens, Dover CT17 9UQ (☎0304/240101); also London (☎081/554 7061).

Nouvelles Frontières, 11 Blenheim St., London W1Y 5LE (☎071/629 7772). French agency; worth inquiring about *Air-Inter* packages.

P&O, Channel House, Channel View Rd., Dover CT17 9TJ (☎0304/203388); Continental Ferry Port, Mile End, Portsmouth PO2 8QW (☎0705/827677); also London (☎081/575 8555).

Quo Vadis, 243 Euston Rd., London NW1 (☎071/387 6122).

Sally Line, Argyle Centre, York St., Ramsgate, Kent CT11 9DS (☎0843/595522); also at 81 Piccadilly, London W1V 9HF (☎081/858 1127).

SealinkStena Line, Reservations: Charter House, Park St., Ashford, Kent TN24 8EX (☎0233/647047). 24-hour information service for Dover ☎0304/240028; Folkestone ☎0303/42964; Southampton ☎0703/233973; Newhaven ☎0273/512266.

STA Travel, 86 Old Brompton Rd., London SW7 and 117 Euston Rd., London NW1 (☎071/937 9921). Regional branches throughout Britain.

weeks in advance and your stay has to include one Saturday night. Your return date must be fixed when purchasing and no subsequent changes are allowed. Current cost is £102 ($166) round trip. Superpex tickets at £124 ($202) round trip may be booked at any time, but you must stay one Saturday night. *Airtour France* (☎071/706 3737) prices start at £59 ($96) round trip.

For a minimum of hassle, flights from **London City Airport** with *Brymon* (☎071/476 5000) are reliable and convenient. Riverbuses along the Thames from stops by Charing Cross or London Bridge *British Rail* stations leave for the airport every hour, check-in time has been cut to a minimum and tickets (£102/$166 Apex round trip) can be collected at the check-in desk.

LONDON–PARIS BY RAIL

Until such time as the Channel Tunnel finally opens (which is scheduled to be in 1993), the only rail route to Paris is to catch one of the many trains from London's **Victoria** station that connect with cross-Channel ferries or hovercraft, and with onward services on the other side.

On the shortest and most economical Channel crossings the choice is between **train and hovercraft**, for which the total journey time from London to Paris is six hours, or **train and ferry**, taking eight or nine hours. Fare options include special deals on *Eurotrain* (for anyone under 26) and senior citizen reductions for those over 65.

The **hovercraft** crossing links Dover with Boulogne. Services are frequent (up to twenty a day in peak season) and tie in well with the trains. By **train and ordinary ferry**, the cheapest crossing is currently Newhaven–Dieppe; best deals are on the conveniently scheduled (though slightly slower) night trains. Students and anyone under 26 can buy heavily discounted *BIJ* tickets from student travel agents; currently priced at £57.80 ($94) round-trip, £66 ($108) with *Hoverspeed* (1hr 30min faster). *Paris Explorer* on which you can travel to and from your destination

via different routes (with optional stopovers) is £68 ($111) via Dieppe; £73 ($119) via Calais or Boulogne. *British Rail*'s cheapest five-day round-trip fare is £54.50 ($89) via Dieppe, cheapest two-month return is £70.50 ($115) via Dieppe.

LONDON–PARIS BY BUS

Again, for the shortest Channel crossing, the choice is between bus and hovercraft, and bus and ordinary ferry. Prices are very much lower than for trains, especially by hovercraft.

The coach for the **Hoverspeed City Sprint** service leaves in the morning from London's Victoria Coach Station, catches the hovercraft from Dover to Calais or Boulogne, and arrives in Paris eight or nine hours after setting out. There are two coaches per day in winter, four in summer. The regular adult round-trip fare is £47 ($77), and there's a minimal student discount of £1. For details call *Hoverspeed* at ☎081/554 7061.

The main company for the **bus/ferry** combination is *Euroline*, 52 Grosvenor Gardens, Victoria, London SW1 (☎071/730 8235). It runs overnight as well as daytime buses, both taking roughly nine hours, at an adult round-trip fare of £47 ($77).

THE FERRIES

The cheapest and quickest cross-Channel options for drivers are the **ferries** or **hovercraft** between **Dover** and Calais or Boulogne, **Folkestone** and Boulogne, and **Ramsgate** and Dunkerque. If your starting point is farther west than London, it may be worth catching a ferry direct to Normandy or Brittany—**Newhaven** to Dieppe, **Portsmouth**, **Weymouth**, or **Poole** to Le Havre, Caen, Cherbourg, and St-Malo, and **Plymouth** to Roscoff. Ferry prices vary according to the time of year and the size of your car; details of routes, companies, and fares are given on p.7. You can either contact the companies direct to reserve space in advance (which is essential at peak season if you intend to drive), or any travel agent in the UK or France can do it for you.

TRAVEL AGENCIES IN PARIS

Access Voyages, 6 rue Pierre-Lescot, 1er (☎40.13.02.02).

Council Travel, 31 rue St-Augustine, 2^{e} (☎42.66.20.87); 49 rue Pierre-Charron, 8e (☎43.59.09.69); 51 rue Dauphine, 6e (☎43.25.09.86); 16 rue de Vaugirard, 6e (☎46.34.02.90).

Forum Voyages, 55 av Franklin Roosevelt, 8e (☎42.89.07.07).

Go Voyages, 98bis bd Latour-Maubourg, 7e (☎47.53.05.05); 22 rue de l'Arcade, 8e (☎42.66.18.18).

Nouvelles Frontières, branches throughout the city (☎42.73.10.64).

RED TAPE AND VISAS

American and Canadian citizens—like those of all European Community member nations—who visit France as tourists for ninety days or less do not require visas. Anyone planning a longer stay, as well as visiting exchange students, people on official government business, and working journalists, will need a visa, and must apply before leaving the United States.

Obtaining a visa from your nearest French consulate (addresses are given in the box on p.9) is fairly automatic, but check their hours before turning up, and leave plenty of time, since there are often lines.

If you **stay longer than three months** you are officially supposed to apply for a *Carte de Séjour*, for which you'll have to show proof of income at least equal to the minimum wage. However, it's usually much simpler to cross the border, into Belgium or Germany for example, and re-enter for another ninety days legitimately.

FRENCH EMBASSIES AND CONSULATES

USA

Embassy:

4101 Reservoir Rd. NW, **Washington** DC 20007 (☎202/944-6000).

Consulates:

20 Park Plaza, **Boston** MA02116 (☎617/482-2864).

737 N. Michigan Ave., #2020, **Chicago** IL 60611 (☎312/787-5359).

American General Tower, Suite 867, 2727 Allen Parkway, **Houston** TX 77019 (☎713/528-2182).

10990 Wilshire Blvd., #300, **Los Angeles** CA 90024 (☎213/653-3120).

1 Biscayne Tower, **Miami** FL 33131 (☎305/372-9798).

3305 St. Charles Ave., **New Orleans** LA 70115 (☎504/897-6381).

934 Fifth Ave., **New York** NY 10021 (☎212/606-3600).

540 Bush St., **San Francisco** CA 94108 (☎415/397-4893).

IRELAND

36 Ailesbury Road, **Dublin** 4 (☎694 777).

CANADA

Embassy

42 Promenade Sussex, **Ottawa**, Ontario K1M 2C9 (☎613/512-1715).

Consulates

#300 Highfield Place, 10010/106th St., **Edmonton**, Alberta T5J 3LA (☎403/428-0232).

2 Elysée Place Bonaventure, BP202, **Montréal** PQ H5A 1B1 (☎514/878-4381).

1110 Ave. des Laurentides, **Québec** PQ G1S 3C3 (☎418/688-4030).

130 Bloor St. West, **Toronto**, Ontario M5S 1N5 (☎416/925-8041).

736 Granville St., Suite 1201, **Vancouver** BC V6Z 1H9 (☎604/681-2301).

GREAT BRITAIN

French Consulate General (Visas Section), 6a Cromwell Place, South Kensington, **London** SW7 (☎071/823 9555).

7–11 Randolph Crescent, **Edinburgh** (☎031/225 7954).

523/535 Cunard Building, Pier Head, **Liverpool** (☎051/236 8685).

COSTS, MONEY, AND BANKS

The French franc, abbreviated as F or some-times FF, is divided into 100 centimes and comes in notes of 500, 100, 50, and 20F, and coins of 10, 5, 2, or 1F, and 50, 20, and 10 centimes. At the time of writing, one US dollar could be exchanged for something in the region of 6F.

Because of the relatively low cost of accom-modation and eating out, at least by capital city standards, Paris is not an outrageously expensive place to visit. For a reasonably comfortable exis-tence, including a hotel room and restaurant or café stops, you need to allow about 400–500F a day per person. But by watching the pennies, staying at a hostel (between 90 and 160F for bed and breakfast), and being strong-willed about denying yourself cups of coffee and culture, you could manage on 250–300F, including a cheap restaurant meal—considerably less if you limit eating to street snacks or market food.

For two or more people **hotel accommoda-tion** can be almost as cheap as the hostels, though a sensible average estimate for a double room would be around 250F. As for **food**, you can spend as much or as little as you like. There are large numbers of good **restaurants** with three- or four-course menus for between 65 and 100F. **Picnic fare**, obviously, is much less costly, espe-cially when you buy in the markets and cheap supermarket chains. More sophisticated meals— **takeout** salads and ready-to-(re)heat dishes— can be put together for reasonable prices if you shop at *charcuteries* (delis) and the equivalent counters of many supermarkets.

Transport within the city is inexpensive. The Carte Orange, for example, with a 51F weekly (*hebdomadaire*) ticket gives you a week's unlim-ited travel on buses and métro.

Museums and monuments are likely to prove one of the biggest invisible wallet-eroders. *ISIC* (International Student Identity Card) is effec-tively a waste of time, as museums have reduced admission for under-26s, not students. Buying a museum card (details on p.144), if you're going to a lot of museums, is a much better option.

Most importantly, budget-watchers need to be wary of **nightlife and café-lounging**, a major expense being beers in showy pubs and bars.

Travelers' checks are one of the safest ways of **carrying your money.** They're available from almost any major bank (whether you're an account-holder or not), usually for a service charge of one percent on the amount purchased. Some banks take 1.25 or even 1.5 percent, and your own bank may offer checks free of charge provided you meet certain conditions—ask first, as you can easily save $15 to $25. *Visa* and *American Express* are the most widely recognized brands. Obtaining **French franc travelers' checks** can be worthwhile: they can often be used as cash, and French banks are obliged by law to give you the face value of the checks when you change them, so commission is only paid on purchase.

Credit cards are widely accepted; just watch for the window stickers. *Visa*—known as the *Carte Bleue* in France—is almost universally recognized; *Mastercard*—sometimes called *Eurocard*—and *American Express* rank considera-bly lower. To report **lost or stolen credit cards** phone one of the following hotlines: *Carte Bleue* (VISA) ☎42.77.11.90; *American Express* ☎47.77.72.00. Also worth considering are post office **International Giro Cheques**, which work in a similar way to ordinary bank checks except that you can cash them through post offices, more common and with longer opening hours than banks.

Standard **banking hours** are 9:30am to 5 or 6pm; closed Saturday and Sunday. At 66 av des Champs-Elysées, the 24-hour automatic exchange machine of the *Banque Régionale d'Escompte et de Dépôts* accepts dollars, pounds, marks, and lire, while at no. 103 the *Crédit Commercial de*

France stays open Mon–Sat 9am–8pm. The **money-exchange counter** in the Gare du Nord is open until 10pm on weekdays; those at other stations until 8pm. Roissy and Orly airports both have exchange counters open daily 7am–11pm. **Rates of exchange** and **commissions** vary from bank to bank; the *Banque Nationale de Paris* usually offers the best rates and takes the least commission.

Despite the ease of changing money at airports, it remains a sensible precaution to buy some French francs before you leave home.

HEALTH AND INSURANCE

Under the French Social Security system every hospital visit, doctor's consultation, and prescribed medicine is charged (though in an emergency not upfront). Although all employed French people are entitled to a refund of between seventy-five and eighty percent of their medical expenses, this can still leave a hefty shortfall, especially after a stay in hospital (accident victims have to pay even for the ambulance that takes them there).

For details of how to obtain **emergency medical help** in Paris, see the box on p.12. To find a **doctor**, stop at any *pharmacie* and ask for an address, or look under *Médecins Qualifiés* in the Yellow Pages. Consultation fees for a visit should be between 75 and 85F and in any case you'll be given a *Feuille de Soins* (Statement of Treatment) for later documentation of insurance claims. Prescriptions should be taken to a *pharmacie*, which is also equipped—and obliged—to give first aid (for a fee). The medicines you buy will have little stickers (*vignettes*) attached to them, which you must remove and stick to your *Feuille de Soins*, together with the prescription itself.

For minor illnesses, pharmacists will dispense free advice and a wide range of medication (some not normally sold over the counter in North America).

Centre Médical Europe, 44 rue Amsterdam, 9e; Mº Liège (☎42.81.93.33; Mon–Fri 8am–7pm, Sat 8am–6pm), has a variety of different practitioners charging low consultation fees.

INSURANCE

Travel insurance can buy you peace of mind as well as save you money. Before you purchase any insurance, however, check what you have already, whether as part of a family or student policy. You may find yourself covered for medical expenses and loss, and possibly loss of or damage to valuables, while abroad.

For example, **Canadians** are usually covered for medical expenses by their provincial health plans (but may only be reimbursed after the fact). Holders of **ISIC** cards are entitled to $2000 worth of accident coverage and sixty days ($100 per diem) of hospital in-patient benefits for the period during which the card is valid. University **students** will often find that their student health coverage extends for one term beyond the date of last enrollment.

Bank and charge **accounts** (particularly *American Express*) often have certain levels of medical or other insurance included. **Home-owners' or renters'** insurance may cover theft or loss of documents, money, and valuables while overseas, though exact conditions and maximum amounts vary from company to company.

SPECIALIST INSURANCE

Only after exhausting the possibilities above might you want to contact a **specialist travel insurance** company; your travel agent can usually recommend one—*Travelguard* and *The Travelers* are good policies.

EMERGENCY MEDICAL HELP

All **pharmacies** are equipped, and obliged, to give first aid on request—though they will charge. *Dhéry*, 84 av des Champs-Élysées, 8ᵉ (Mº Charles-de-Gaulle-Étoile ☎45.62.02.41) is **open 24 hours**. *Carigliogi*, 10 bd Sébastopol, 4ᵉ (Mº Châtelet; ☎42.72.03.23) is open Mon–Sat 9am–midnight; *Caillaud*, 6 bd des Capucines, 9ᵉ (Mº Opéra; ☎42.65.88.29) is open Mon–Sat 8am–1am, Sun 8pm–1am; and *La Nation*, 13 place de la Nation, 11ᵉ (Mº Nation; ☎43.73.24.03) is open Mon–Sat 8am–midnight, Sun 8pm–midnight. *Swann Pharmacie*, 6 rue Castiglione, 1ᵉʳ (Mº Tuileries; ☎42.60.72.96; Mon–Sat 9am–7:30pm) will translate prescriptions written in English and make up an equivalent medicine.

To trace someone who has been hospitalized, the number to call is ☎42.77.11.22, 8:30am–5:30pm.

Immediate assistance

Police/Rescue service ☎17

Ambulances ☎18 or ☎45.67.50.50 (*SAMU*)

Nursing *SOS Infirmiers* ☎48.87.77.77

Doctors
SOS Médecins 24-hr ☎47.07.77.77
SOS 92 24-hr ☎46.03.77.44
Association pour les Urgences Médicales de Paris 24-hr ☎48.28.40.04

Specific problems

AIDS/HIV
Center Médico-Social, 218 rue de Belleville, 20ᵉ; Mº Télégraphe (☎47.97.40.49).
Center SIDAG, 3 rue de Ridder, 14ᵉ; Mº Plaisance (☎45.43.83.78).
Service de Médecine Interne du Docteur Collin, Hôpital Lariboisière, 2 rue Ambroise-Paré, 10ᵉ; Mº Barbès-Rochechouart (☎49.95.65.65).
Service de Médecine Interne du Docteur Emerit, Hôpital Pitié- Salpétrière, 47 bd de l'Hôpital, 13ᵉ; Mº St-Marcel, Chevaleret (☎45.70.21.72).

Burns (adults)
Hôpital Saint-Antoine, 184 rue du Fbg-St-Antoine, 12ᵉ; Mº Faidherbe-Chaligny (☎43.44.33.33).
Hôpital Cochin, 27 rue du Fbg-St Jacques, 14ᵉ; Mº Port-Royal (☎42.34.12.12).

Burns (children)
Hôpital Trousseau, av du Dr-Arnold-Netter, 12ᵉ; Mº Porte-de-Vincennes (☎43.46.13.90).

Dental treatment
SOS Dentistes ☎43.37.51.00.
Urgences Dentaires, 9 bd St-Marcel, 13ᵉ; Mº St-Marcel (☎47.07.44.44).

Dog bites
Institut Pasteur 213 rue de Vaugirard, 15ᵉ; Mº Pasteur, Volontaires (☎45.67.35.09).

Drugs
Hôpital Marmottan, 19 rue d'Armaillé, 17ᵉ; Mº Argentine (☎45.74.00.04).

Eyes
Hôtel-Dieu, 1 place du Parvis-Notre Dame, 4ᵉ; Mº Cité (24-hr, Mon–Sat; ☎43.29.12.79).
Hôpital des Quinze-Vingts, 28 rue de Charenton, 12ᵉ; Mº Bastille (24-hr every day; ☎43.46.15.20).

Hands
Hôpital Boucicaut, 78 rue de la Convention, 15ᵉ; Mº Boucicaut (Mon–Fri 8am–1pm & 2–4pm; closed hols; ☎45.54.92.92).

Poisoning
Hôpital Femand-Widal, 200 rue du Fbg-St-Denis, 10ᵉ; Mº Gare-du-Nord (☎42.05.63.29).

Sexually transmitted diseases
Syphilis and gonorrhea are treated free by law.
Croix Rouge, 43 rue de Valois, 1ᵉʳ; Mº Palais-Royal (☎42.61.30.04) and 35 rue Claude-Terrasse, 16ᵉ; Mº Porte-de-St-Cloud (☎42.88.33.42).
Dispensaire A-Tournier, 2 rue Dareau, 14ᵉ; Mº St-Jacques (☎43.37.95 40).
Institut Prophylactique, 36 rue d'Assas, 6ᵉ; Mº St-Placide (☎45.44.38.94).
Institut Vernes, 36 rue d'Assas, 6ᵉ; Mº St-Placide (☎45.44.38.94).

Alternative medicine

Association Française d'Acuponcture, 1bis Cité des Fleurs,17ᵉ; Mº Brochant (9am–6pm Mon–Fri ☎42.29.63.63).

Center d'Homéopathie de Paris, 81 rue de Lille, 7ᵉ; Mº Bac (☎45.55.12.15).

Travel insurance offerings are quite comprehensive, anticipating everything from charter companies going bankrupt to delayed (as well as lost) baggage, by way of sundry illnesses and accidents. **Premiums** vary widely—from the very reasonable ones offered primarily through student/youth agencies (though available to anyone), to those so expensive that the cost for two or three months of coverage will probably equal the cost of the worst possible combination of disasters.

A most important thing to keep in mind—and one which is often a source of major disappointment to would-be claimants—is that *none* of the currently available policies insures against **theft** of anything while overseas. North American travel policies apply only to items lost from, or damaged in, the custody of an identifiable, responsible third party, i.e. hotel porter, airline, luggage consignment, etc. Even in these cases, you will still have to contact the local police to make out a complete report in order for your insurer to process the claim.

BRITISH POLICIES

If you are **transiting through Britain**, policies there cost considerably less (under £20/$32 for a month) and include routine cover for theft. You can take out a British policy at almost any travel agency or major bank. ISIS, a "student" policy but open to everyone, is reliable and fairly good value; it is operated by a company called *Endsleigh*, and is available through any student/youth travel agency.

REIMBURSEMENT

All insurance policies—American or Canadian—work by **reimbursing you** once you return home, so be sure to keep all your receipts from doctors and pharmacists. Any thefts should immediately be reported to the nearest police station and a police report obtained; no report, no refund.

If you have had to undergo serious medical treatment, with major hospital bills, contact your consulate. They can normally arrange for an insurance company, or possibly relatives, to cover the fees, pending a claim.

INFORMATION AND MAPS

The French Government Tourist Office gives away large quantities of maps and glossy brochures for every region of France, including lists of hotels and campgrounds. For Paris, these include some useful fold-out leaflets detailing sites to see, markets, shops, museums, ideas for excursions, useful phone numbers, and opening hours, as well as maps and more esoteric information like lists of Paris gardens and squares.

In **Paris**, the **main tourist office** is at 127 av des Champs-Élysées, 8e (☎47.23.61.72; Mon–Sat 9am–8/10pm, Sun 9am–6/8pm), where the efficient but overworked staff will answer questions from the predictable to the bizarre. There are branch offices at the four main railroad stations: Austerlitz, Est, Lyon, and Nord. For **tourist information in English** phone ☎47.20.88.89. Alternative sources of information are the **Hôtel de Ville** cultural service (☎42.74.22.20 and ☎42.76.40.40; Mon–Sat 9am–6:30pm) and electronic billboards in the streets.

For the clearest picture of the layout of the city the best map you can get is *Michelin no. 10,* the 1:10,000 *Plan de Paris.* More convenient is the pocket-sized *Falkplan*, which folds out only as you need it, or, if you're staying any length of time, *Paris-Eclair*, a detailed map book with street index, bus route diagrams, useful addresses, parking lots, and one-way streets—all a great deal more useful than the tourist office free hand-outs.

FRENCH GOVERNMENT TOURIST OFFICES

USA

9454 Wilshire Blvd., **Los Angeles** CA 90212 (☎213/271-6665).

645 N. Michigan Ave., **Chicago** IL 60611 (☎312/337-6301).

2305 Cedar Springs Rd. #205, **Dallas** TX 75201 (☎214/742-7011).

610 Fifth Ave., **New York** NY 10020 (☎212/757-1125).

CANADA

1981 McGill College, Montréal, Québec H3A 2W9 (☎514/288-4262).

1 Dundas St. W. #2405 Box 8, Toronto, Ontario M5G 1Z3 (☎416/593-4723).

UK

178 Piccadilly, London W1 (☎ 071/491 7622).

Paris-Eclair also includes a pull-out environs of Paris map, though you will get more detail as well as a larger area from *Michelin no. 196, Environs de Paris*.

Bookstores stocking European maps include *The Complete Traveller* (199 Madison Ave; ☎212/685-9007) and *Rand McNally Mapstore* (150 East 52nd St; ☎212/758-7488) in **New York**, and *Maplink* (25 East Mason St., Santa Barbara; ☎805/965-4402) in **California**.

THE *ARRONDISSEMENTS*

The number after Paris addresses—3^e, 11^e, etc—indicates the postal district or *arrondissement*. There are twenty of them altogether, the first (written 1er) centered on the Louvre with the rest unfurling in a clockwise spiral from there. Their boundaries are clearly marked on all maps—you'll find them on p.39 of this book—and are an important aid to locating places.

FOOD AND DRINK

French food is as good a reason for a visit to Paris as any other. Cooking has art status, the top chefs are stars, and dining out is a national pastime, whether it's at the bistro on the corner or at a famed house of *haute cuisine*. Eating out doesn't have to cost much as long as you avoid tourist hotspots and treat the business of choosing a place as an interesting appetizer in itself.

BARS AND CAFÉS

Bars and cafés—there's no difference—commonly advertise *les snacks*, or *un casse-croûte* (a bite), with pictures of omelets, fried eggs, hot dogs, or various sandwiches. And even when they don't, they'll usually make you a half or third of a *baguette* (French bread stick), buttered (*tartine*) or filled with cheese or meat. This, or a croissant, with hot chocolate or coffee, is generally the best way to eat **breakfast**—at a fraction of the cost charged by most hotels. Brasseries—which serve full meals (see below)—are also possibilities for cups of coffee, eggs, or whatever you like on their menu.

If you're standing at the counter, which is cheaper than sitting down, you may see a basket of croissants or some hard-boiled eggs (they're usually gone by 9:30 or 10am). Help yourself—the waiter will keep an eye on how many you've eaten and bill you accordingly.

A LIST OF FOODS AND DISHES

Basics

Pain	Bread	*Poivre*	Pepper	*Verre*	Glass
Beurre	Butter	*Sel*	Salt	*Fourchette*	Fork
Oeufs	Eggs	*Sucre*	Sugar	*Couteau*	Knife
Lait	Milk	*Vinaigre*	Vinegar	*Cuillère*	Spoon
Huile	Oil	*Bouteille*	Bottle	*Table*	Table

Snacks

Crêpe	Pancake (sweet)
au sucre	with sugar
au citron	with lemon
au miel	with honey
à la confiture	with jelly
aux oeufs	with eggs
à la crème de marrons	with chestnut purée
Galette	Buckwheat (savory) pancake
Un sandwich/ une baguette ...	A sandwich ...
jambon	with ham
fromage	with cheese
saucisson	with sausage
à l'ail	with garlic
au poivre	with pepper
pâté (de campagne)	with pâté (country-style)
croque-monsieur	Grilled cheese and ham sandwich
croque-madame	Grilled cheese and bacon, sausage, chicken, or an egg
Oeufs	Eggs
au plat	Fried eggs
à la coque	Boiled eggs
durs	Hard-boiled eggs
brouillés	Scrambled eggs

Omelette ...	Omelette ...
nature	plain
aux fines herbes	with herbs
au fromage	with cheese
Salade de ...	Salad of ...
tomates	tomatoes
betteraves	beetroot
concombres	cucumber
carottes rapées	grated carrots

Other fillings/salads:

Anchois	Anchovy
Andouillette	Tripe sausage
Boudin	Black pudding
Coeurs de palmiers	Palm hearts
Fonds d'artichauts	Artichoke hearts
Hareng	Herring
Langue	Tongue
Poulet	Chicken
Thon	Tuna fish

And some terms:

Chauffé	Heated
Cuit	Cooked
Cru	Raw
Emballé	Wrapped
À emporter	Takeout
Fumé	Smoked
Salé	Salted/spicy
Sucré	Sweet

Soups *(soupes)* and appetizers *(hors d'oeuvres)*

Bisque	Shellfish soup
Bouillabaisse	Marseillais fish soup
Bouillon	Broth or stock
Bourride	Thick fish soup
Consommé	Clear soup
Pistou	Parmesan, basil, and garlic paste added to soup
Potage	Thick vegetable soup
Rouille	Red pepper, garlic, and saffron mayonnaise served with fish soup

Velouté	Thick soup, usually fish or poultry

Appetizers

Assiette anglaise	Plate of cold meats
Crudités	Raw vegetables with dressings
Hors d'oeuvres variés	Combination of the above plus smoked or marinated fish

Fish (poisson), seafood (fruits de mer), and shellfish (crustaces or coquillages)

Anchois	Anchovies	Daurade	Sea bream	Louvine,	Similar to sea
Anguilles	Eels	Eperlan	Smelt or	loubine	bass
Barbue	Brill		whitebait	Maquereau	Mackerel
Bigorneau	Periwinkle	Escargots	Snails	Merlan	Whiting
Brème	Bream	Flétan	Halibut	Moules	Mussels (with
Cabillaud	Cod	Friture	Assorted fried fish	(marinière)	shallots in white
Calmar	Squid	Gambas	King prawns		wine sauce)
Carrelet	Plaice	Hareng	Herring	Oursin	Sea urchin
Claire	Type of oyster	Homard	Lobster	Palourdes	Clams
Colin	Hake	Huîtres	Oysters	Praires	Small clams
Congre	Conger eel	Langouste	Spiny lobster	Raie	Skate
Coques	Cockles	Langoustines	Saltwater crayfish	Rouget	Red mullet
Coquilles St-	Scallops		(scampi)	Saumon	Salmon
Jacques		Limande	Lemon sole	Sole	Sole
Crabe	Crab	Lotte	Burbot	Thon	Tuna
Crevettes grises	Shrimp	Lotte de mer	Monkfish	Truite	Trout
Crevettes roses	Prawns	Loup de mer	Sea bass	Turbot	Turbot

Terms: (Fish)

Aïoli	Garlic mayonnaise served with salt cod and other fish	Fumé	Smoked
		Fumet	Fish stock
Béarnaise	Sauce made with egg yolks, white wine, shallots, and vinegar	Gigot de Mer	Large fish baked whole
		Grillé	Grilled
		Hollandaise	Butter and vinegar sauce
Beignets	Fritters	À la meunière	In a butter, lemon, and parsley sauce
Darne	Fillet or steak		
La douzaine	A dozen	Mousse/	Mousse
Frit	Fried	mousseline	
Friture	Deep fried small fish	Quenelles	Light dumplings

Meat (viande) and poultry (volaille)

Agneau (de pré-salé)	Lamb (grazed on salt marshes)	Langue	Tongue
		Lapin, lapereau	Rabbit, young rabbit
Andouille, andouillette	Tripe sausage	Lard, lardons	Bacon, diced bacon
		Lièvre	Hare
Boeuf	Beef	Merguez	Spicy, red sausage
Bifteck	Steak	Mouton	Mutton
Boudin blanc	Sausage of white meats	Museau de veau	Calf's muzzle
Boudin noir	Black pudding	Oie	Goose
Caille	Quail	Os	Bone
Canard	Duck	Porc	Pork
Caneton	Duckling	Poulet	Chicken
Contrefilet	Sirloin roast	Poussin	Baby chicken
Coquelet	Cockerel	Ris	Sweetbreads
Dinde, dindon	Turkey	Rognons	Kidneys
Entrecôte	Ribsteak	Rognons blancs	Testicles
Faux filet	Sirloin steak	Sanglier	Wild boar
Foie	Liver	Steack	Steak
Foie gras	Fattened (duck/goose) liver	Tête de veau	Calf's head (in jello)
Gigot (d'agneau)	Leg (of lamb)	Tournedos	Thick slices of fillet
Grillade	Grilled meat	Tripes	Tripe
Hâchis	Chopped meat or ground hamburger	Veau	Veal
		Venaison	Venison

Meat and poultry—dishes and terms

Boeuf bourguignon	Beef stew with burgundy, onions, and mushrooms	Au four	Baked
Canard à l'orange	Roast duck with an orange-and-wine sauce	Garni	With vegetables
		Gésier	Gizzard
Cassoulet	A casserole of beans and meat	Grillé	Grilled
		Magret de canard	Duck breast
Coq au vin	Chicken cooked until it falls off the bone with wine, onions, and mushrooms	Marmite	Casserole
		Mijoté	Stewed
		Museau	Muzzle
Steak au poivre (vert/rouge)	Steak in a black (green/red) peppercorn sauce	Rôti	Roast
		Sauté	Lightly cooked in butter
Steak tartare	Raw chopped beef, topped with a raw egg yolk		

For steaks:

Bleu	Almost raw
Saignant	Rare
À point	Medium
Bien cuit	Well done
Très bien cuit	Very well cooked
Brochette	Kebab

Terms:

Blanquette, daube, estouffade, hochepôt, navarin and ragoût	All are types of stews
Aile	Wing
Carré	Best end of neck, chop, or cutlet
Civit	Game stew
Confit	Meat preserve
Côte	Chop, cutlet, or rib
Cou	Neck
Cuisse	Thigh or leg
Epaule	Shoulder
Médaillon	Round piece
Pavé	Thick slice
En croûte	In pastry
Farci	Stuffed
Au feu de bois	Cooked over wood fire

Garnishes and sauces:

Beurre blanc	Sauce of white wine and shallots, with butter
Chasseur	White wine, mushrooms, and shallots
Diable	Strong mustard seasoning
Forestière	With bacon and mushroom
Fricassée	Rich, creamy sauce
Mornay	Cheese sauce
Pays d'Auge	Cream and cider
Piquante	Gherkins or capers, vinegar, and shallots
Provençale	Tomatoes, garlic, olive oil, and herbs

Vegetables *(légumes)*, herbs *(herbes)*, and spices *(épices)*, etc

Ail	Garlic	Endive	Chicory	Piment	Pimento
Algue	Seaweed	Épinards	Spinach	Pois chiche	Chickpeas
Anis	Aniseed	Estragon	Tarragon	Pois mange-tout	Snow peas
Artichaut	Artichoke	Fenouil	Fennel		
Asperges	Asparagus	Flageolet	White beans	Pignons	Pine nuts
Avocat	Avocado	Gingembre	Ginger	Poireau	Leek
Basilic	Basil	Haricots	Beans	Poivron	Sweet pepper
Betterave	Beetroot	Verts	String (French)	(vert, rouge)	(green, red)
Carotte	Carrot	Rouges	Kidney	Pommes (de terre)	Potatoes
Céleri	Celery	Beurres	Butter		
Champignons, cèpes, chanterelles	Mushrooms of various kinds	Laurier	Bay leaf	Primeurs	Spring vegetables
		Lentilles	Lentils		
Chou (rouge)	(Red) cabbage	Maïs	Corn	Radis	Radishes
Choufleur	Cauliflower	Menthe	Mint	Ris	Rice
Ciboulettes	Chives	Moutarde	Mustard	Safran	Saffron
Concombre	Cucumber	Oignon	Onion	Salade verte	Green salad
Cornichon	Gherkin	Pâte	Pasta or pastry	Sarrasin	Buckwheat
Échalotes	Shallots	Persil	Parsley	Tomate	Tomato
		Petits pois	Peas	Truffes	Truffles

Vegetables—dishes and terms

Beignet	Fritter	Parmentier	With potatoes
Farci	Stuffed	Sauté	Lightly fried in butter
Gratiné	Browned with cheese or butter	À la vapeur	Steamed
Jardinière	With mixed diced vegetables	Je suis végétarien(ne).	I'm a vegetarian.
À la parisienne	Sautéed in butter (potatoes); with white wine sauce and shallots	Il y a quelques plats sans viande?	Are there any non-meat dishes?

Fruits (fruits) and nuts (noix)

Abricot	Apricot	Framboises	Raspberries	Pistache	Pistachio
Amandes	Almonds	Fruit de la passion	Passion fruit	Poire	Pear
Ananas	Pineapple			Pomme	Apple
Banane	Banana	Groseilles	Redcurrants and gooseberries	Prune	Plum
Brugnon, nectarine	Nectarine			Pruneau	Prune
		Mangue	Mango	Raisins	Grapes
Cacahouète	Peanut	Marrons	Chestnuts		
Cassis	Blackcurrants	Melon	Melon	**Terms**:	
Cérises	Cherries	Myrtilles	Bilberries	Beignets	Fritter
Citron	Lemon	Noisette	Hazelnut	Compôte de ...	Stewed ...
Citron vert	Lime	Noix	Nuts	Coulis	Sauce
Figues	Figs	Orange	Orange	Flambé	Set aflame in alcohol
Fraises (de bois)	Strawberries (wild)	Pamplemousse	Grapefruit		
		Pêche (blanche)	(White) peach	Frappé	Iced

Desserts (desserts or entremets) and pastries (pâtisserie)

Bombe	A molded ice cream dessert	Parfait	Frozen mousse, sometimes ice cream
Brioche	Sweet, high yeast breakfast roll		
Charlotte	Custard and fruit in lining of almond fingers	Petit Suisse	A smooth mixture of cream and curds
Crème Chantilly	Vanilla-flavored and sweetened whipped cream	Petits fours	Bite-sized cakes/pastries
		Poires Belle Hélène	Pears and ice cream in chocolate sauce
Crème fraîche	Sour cream		
Crème pâtissière	Thick eggy pastry filling	Yaourt, yogourt	Yogurt
Crêpes suzettes	Thin pancakes with orange juice and liqueur	**Terms:**	
Fromage blanc	Cream cheese	Barquette	Small boat-shaped flan
Glace	Ice cream	Bavarois	Refers to the mould, could be a mousse or custard
Île flottante/ oeufs à la neige	Soft meringues floating on custard		
		Coupe	A serving of ice cream
Macarons	Macaroons	Crêpes	Pancakes
Madeleine	Small sponge cake	Galettes	Buckwheat pancakes
Marrons Mont Blanc	Chestnut purée and cream on a rum-soaked sponge cake	Gênoise	Rich sponge cake
		Sablé	Shortbread cookie
Mousse au chocolat	Chocolate mousse	Savarin	A filled, ring-shaped cake
		Tarte	Tart
Palmiers	Caramelized puff pastries	Tartelette	Small tart

Cheese (fromage)

There are over 400 types of French cheese, most of them named after their place of origin. Chèvre is goat's cheese. Le plateau de fromages is the cheeseboard, and bread, but not butter, is served with it.

And one final note: always call the waiter or waitress Monsieur or Madame (Mademoiselle if a young woman), never garçon, no matter what you've been taught in school.

Coffee is invariably espresso and very strong. *Un café* or *un express* is black; *un crème* is with milk; *un grand café* or *un grand crème* is a large cup. In the morning you could also ask for *un café au lait*—espresso in a large cup or bowl filled up with hot milk. *Un déca* is decaf, widely available.

Ordinary **tea** (*thé*) is Lipton's nine times out of ten; to have milk with it, ask for *un peu de lait frais* (some fresh milk).

After overeating, herb teas (*infusions* or *tisanes*), served in every café, can be soothing. The more common ones are *verveine* (verbena), *tilleul* (lime blossom), *menthe* (mint), and *camomile*.

Chocolat chaud—hot chocolate—unlike tea, lives up to the high standards of French food and drink and can be had in any café.

Every bar or café displays the full price list, usually without the fifteen percent service charge added, for drinks at the bar (*au comptoir*), sitting down (*la salle*), or on the terrace (*la terrasse*)—all progressively more expensive. You pay when you leave and you can sit for hours over just one cup of coffee.

At **lunchtime** you may find cafés offering a *plat du jour* (chef's daily special) between 25F and 50F or *formules*, a limited or no-choice menu. *Croque-Monsieurs* or *Madames* (variations on the grilled-cheese sandwich) are on sale at cafés, brasseries, and many street stands, along with *frites, crêpes, galettes* (wholewheat pancakes), *gauffres* (waffles), *glaces* (ice creams), and all kinds of fresh sandwiches. For variety, there are Tunisian snacks like *brik à l'oeuf* (a fried pastry with an egg inside), *merguez* (spicy North African sausage), Greek *souvlaki* (kebabs), Middle Eastern *falafel* (deep-fried chickpea balls with salad), and Japanese tidbits. Wine bars (see below) are good for French regional meats and cheeses, usually served with brown bread (*pain de campagne*).

For picnic and takeout food, there's nothing to beat the charcuterie ready-made dishes—salads, meats, and fully prepared main courses—also available at supermarket *charcuterie* counters. You buy by weight, or you can ask for *une tranche* (a slice), *une barquette* (a carton), or *une part* (a portion).

Alternatively, *salons de thé*, which are open from mid-morning to late evening, serve brunches, salads, quiches, etc, as well as cake and ice cream and a wide selection of teas. They tend to be a good deal more expensive than cafés or brasseries—you're paying for the chic surroundings.

RESTAURANTS AND BRASSERIES

There's no difference between restaurants (or *auberges* or *relais* as they sometimes call themselves) and brasseries in terms of quality or price range. The distinction is that brasseries, which resemble cafés, serve quicker meals at most hours of the day, while restaurants tend to stick to the traditional meal times of noon–2pm and 7–9:30 or 10:30pm. After 9pm or so, restaurants often serve only *à la carte* meals, which invariably work out to be more expensive than eating the set *menu fixe*. For the more upscale places it's wise to make reservations—easily done on the same day. But plenty of establishments stay open late, and a few don't shut at all, so you won't starve. When hunting, avoid places that are half-empty at peak time and treat the business of sizing up different menus as an enjoyable appetizer in itself.

Prices and what you get for them are posted outside. Normally there is a choice between one or more *menus fixes*, where the number of courses has already been determined. The choice is limited and the *carte* (menu) has everything listed. *Service compris* or *s.c.* means the **service** charge is included. *Service non compris*, *s.n.c.*, or *servis en sus* means that it isn't and you need to calculate an additional fifteen percent. Wine (*vin*) or a drink (*boisson*) may be included, though rarely on menus under 60F. When ordering wine, ask for *un quart* (quarter-liter), *un demi-litre* (half-liter), or *une carafe* (a liter). You'll normally be given the house wine unless you specify otherwise; if you're worried about the cost ask for *vin ordinaire*.

In the French sequence of courses, any salad (sometimes vegetables, too) comes separate from the main dish, and cheese precedes a dessert. You will be offered coffee, which is always extra, to finish off the meal.

At the bottom of the price range, *menus fixes* revolve around standard dishes such as steak and fries (*steack frites*), chicken and fries (*poulet frites*), or various concoctions involving innards. Look for the *plat du jour*, which may be a regional dish and more appealing.

Going *à la carte* offers much greater choice and, in the better restaurants, access to the chef's specialties. You pay for it, of course, though a simple and perfectly legitimate ploy is to have just one course instead of the expected three or four. You can share dishes or just have several appetizers—a useful strategy for vegetarians. There's no minimum charge.

The current gourmet trend in French cooking has abandoned rich, creamy sauces and bloating portions, concentrating instead on the intrinsic flavors of foods and on new combinations in which the mix of colors and textures complements the tastes. The courses are no more than a few mouthfuls, presented with oriental artistry and finely judged to leave you at the end well-fed but not weighed down. Known as *nouvelle cuisine*, this at its best can induce gastronomic ecstasy from an ungarnished leek or carrot. What it does to salmon, lobster, or a wild strawberry pastry elevates taste sensation to the power of sound and vision. But alas, since this magical method of cooking requires absolutely prime and fresh ingredients and precision skills in every department, *nouvelle cuisine* meals are usually horrendously expensive.

DRINKING

Where you can eat you can invariably drink and vice versa. **Drinking** is done at a leisurely pace whether it's a prelude to food (*apéritif*), a sequel (*digestif*), or the accompaniment, and **cafés** are the standard places to do it.

Wine—*vin*—is drunk at just about every meal or social occasion. Red is *rouge*, white *blanc*, or there's *rosé*. *Vin de table* or *vin ordinaire*—table wine—is generally drinkable and always cheap.

A.C. (*Appellation d'Origine Contrôlée*) wines are another matter. They can be excellent value at the lower end of the price scale, where favorable French taxes keep prices down to $2 or so a bottle, but move much above it and you're soon paying serious prices for serious bottles.

Restaurant markups of *A.C.* wines can be outrageous. **Popular *A.C.* wines** found on most restaurant lists include *Côtes du Rhône* (from the Rhône valley), *St-Emilion* and *Médoc* (from Bordeaux), *Beaujolais*, and very upmarket Burgundy.

The **basic terms** are *brut*, very dry; *sec*, dry; *demi-sec*, sweet; *doux*, very sweet; *mousseux*, sparkling; *méthode champenoise*, mature and sparkling. There are grape varieties as well but the complexities of the subject take up volumes.

A **glass of wine** is simply *un rouge* or *un blanc*. If it is an *A.C.* wine you may have the choice of *un ballon* (round glass) or a smaller glass (*un verre*). *Un pichet* (a pitcher) is normally half a liter.

The familiar Belgian and German brands account for most of the **beer** you'll find, plus brands home-grown from Alsace. Draft (*à la pression*, usually *Kronenbourg*) is the cheapest drink you can have next to coffee and wine—ask for *un demi* (one third of a liter). For a wider choice of drafts and bottles you need to go to the special beer-drinking establishments, or English-style pubs found in abundance in Paris.

Cocktails are served at most late-night bars, discos, and music places, as well as at upscale hotel bars.

Stronger alcohol is drunk from 5am as a pre-work fortifier, right through the day, though the national reputation for drunkenness has lost some of its truth. **Cognac** or **Armagnac** brandies and the dozens of *eaux de vie* (brandy distilled from fruit) and **liqueurs** are made with the same perfectionism as in the cultivation of vines.

Among less familiar names, try *Poire William* (pear brandy), *Marc* (a spirit distilled from grape pulp), or just point to the bottle with the most attractive color. Measures are generous, but they don't come cheap: the same applies for imported spirits like whiskey, always called *Scotch*. *Pastis*, aniseed drinks such as *Pernod* or *Ricard*, are served diluted with water and ice (*glaçons*)—very refreshing and not expensive. Two drinks designed to stimulate the appetite are *Pineau* (cognac and grape juice) and *Kir* (white wine with a dash of blackcurrant syrup—or champagne for a *Kir Royal*).

On the **soft drink** front, bottled fruit juices include apricot (*jus d'abricot*), blackcurrant (*cassis*), and so on. You can also get freshly squeezed orange and lemon juice (*orange/citron pressé*). Otherwise there's the standard canned lemonade, Coke (*coca*), and so forth. Bottles of **spring water** (*eau minérale*)—either sparkling (*pétillante*) or still (*eau plate*)—abound, from the best-seller *Perrier* to the obscurest spa product. But there's not much wrong with the tap water (*l'eau de robinet*).

COMMUNICATIONS—POST, PHONES, AND MEDIA

The French term for a post office is either PTT or *Bureau de Poste*. The main post office at 52 rue du Louvre, 1ᵉʳ, is the best place to have your mail sent unless you have a particular branch office in mind. It's open 24 hours for *Poste Restante* and telephones.

Letters should be addressed (preferably with the last name underlined and in capitals):

Poste Restante, 52 rue du Louvre, 75001 Paris.

To collect your mail you need a passport or other convincing ID and there'll be a small charge. You should ask for all your names to be checked, as filing systems are not great. Other post offices are generally open 8am–noon and 2:30–7pm, Monday to Saturday morning. For sending mail, remember that you can buy **stamps** (*timbres*) with less lining up from *Tabacs*.

You can make international **phone calls** from any booth (or *cabine*) and can receive calls where there's a blue sign of a ringing bell. A 50F **phone card** (called a *télécarte*) is fairly essential, as coin booths are being phased out. Phone cards are available from tabacs and newsagents as well as PTTs. Use the English-speaking operators on ☎19.00.11, or put the money (50-centime, 1F, 5F, 10F pieces) in first, dial ☎19, wait for a tone, and then dial the country code (☎1 for USA) and the number minus its initial 0. To call from Paris to anywhere else in France, dial ☎16 followed by all eight digits of the number; to call a Paris number from anywhere else in France, start by dialling

To phone Paris **from outside France**, dial ☎010-331 followed by the eight-digit number.

☎16-1. To save fiddling around with coins or phone cards, post offices often have metered booths from which you can make calls connected by a clerk; you pay afterwards. To make a collect call, dial ☎19, wait for the tone, then dial 33 and the country code to speak to the bilingual operator. For directory inquiries, phone ☎12.

Major American newspapers, as well as the European-produced ***International Herald Tribune***, are pretty widely on sale. Of the **French daily papers**, *Le Monde* is the most intellectual and respected, with no concessions to entertainment (such as pictures) but a correctly styled French that is probably the easiest to understand. *Libération* is moderately left-wing, independent, and more colloquial with good, if selective, coverage, while the best criticism of the French government from the left comes from *L'Humanité*, the Communist Party paper. All the other nationals are firmly on the right (as are most regional newspapers, which enjoy much higher circulation than the Paris nationals). Weeklies of the *Newsweek/Time* model include the wide-ranging and socialist-inclined *Nouvel Observateur* and its counterpoint *L'Express*, property of James Goldsmith, who sacked the editor for an anti-Giscard article before the 1982 presidential election. The best investigative journalism is in the weekly satirical paper *Le Canard Enchaîné*, unfortunately unintelligible to non-native speakers. And the worst of the lot is *Minute*, organ of the *Front National* .

"Moral" censorship of the press is rare. As well as pornography of every shade, you'll find on the newsstands covers featuring drugs, sex, blasphemy, and bizarre forms of grossness alongside knitting patterns and do-it-yourself. French comic books, which often indulge these interests, are wonderful. *Charlie-Hebdo* is one with political targets; and *À Suivre*, which wouldn't cause problems at US customs, has amazing graphics.

French TV, in contrast, is prudish and lacking in imagination. If you've got a **radio**, you can tune into English-language news on the BBC World Service on 463m or between 21m and 31m shortwave at intervals throughout the day and night. *Radio Classique 24* (FM 101.1) is a classical music station with a minimum of chat and no commercials. For news in French, there's the state-run *France Inter* (FM 87.8), *Europe 1* (FM 104.7), or round-the-clock news on *France Infos* (FM 105.5).

BUSINESS HOURS AND PUBLIC HOLIDAYS

Most shops, businesses, information services, museums, and banks in Paris stay open all day. The exceptions are the smaller shops and enterprises. Basic hours of business are from 8 or 9am to 6:30 or 7:30pm. Sunday and Monday are standard closing days, though you can always find *boulangeries* **and food shops which stay open—on Sunday normally until noon. The standard banking hours are 9:30am to 5 or 6pm, closed Saturday and Sunday; for more details see p.9.**

Museums open at around 10am and close between 5 and 6pm. Summer times may differ from winter times; if they do, both are indicated in the listings. Summer hours usually extend from mid-May or early June to mid-September, but sometimes they apply only during July and August, occasionally even from Palm Sunday to All Saints' Day. Don't forget closing days—usually Tuesday or Monday, sometimes both. Admission charges can be very off-putting, though most state-owned museums have one or two days of the week when they're free and you

can get a big reduction if you're under 26. Churches and cathedrals are almost always open all day, with charges only for the crypt, treasuries, or cloister, and little fuss is made about how you're dressed.

One other factor can disrupt your plans. There are thirteen national holidays (*jours fériés*), when most shops and businesses, though not museums or restaurants, are closed. They are:

January 1

Easter Sunday

Easter Monday

Ascension Day (forty days after Easter)

Pentecost (seventh Sunday after Easter, plus the Monday)

May 1

May 8 (VE Day)

July 14 (Bastille Day)

August 15 (Assumption of the Virgin Mary)

November 1 (All Saints' Day)

Christmas Day

TROUBLE AND THE POLICE

Petty theft is pretty bad in the crowded hangouts of the capital. Take normal precautions: keep your wallet in a front pocket or your purse under your elbow, and you won't have much to worry about. If you should get attacked, hand over the money and dial the cancelation numbers for your travelers' checks and credit cards.

Drivers face greater problems, most notoriously break-ins. Vehicles are rarely stolen, but tape decks as well as luggage left in cars make tempting targets and foreign number plates are easy to spot. Good insurance is the only answer, but even so, try not to leave any valuables in plain sight. If you have an accident while driving, you have officially to fill out and sign a *constat à l'aimable* (jointly agreed statement); car insurers are supposed to give you this with a policy, though in practice few seem to have heard of it.

For non-criminal **driving violations** such as speeding, the police can impose an on-the-spot fine. Should you be arrested on any charge, you

have the right to contact your consulate (see "Directory" below). Although the police are not always as cooperative as they might be, it *is* their duty to assist you—likewise in the case of losing your passport or all your money.

People caught smuggling or possessing **drugs**, even a few grams of marijuana, are liable to find themselves in jail and consulates will not be sympathetic. This is not to say that hard-drug consumption isn't a visible activity: there are scores of kids dealing in *poudre* (heroin) in the big French cities and the authorities are unable to do much about it. As a rule, people are neither more nor less paranoid about marijuana busts than they are in the US.

THE POLICE

French police (in popular argot, *les flics*) are barely polite at the best of times and can be extremely unpleasant if you get on the wrong side of them. In Paris the city police force has an ugly history of screw-ups, including sporadic shootings of innocent people and brutality against "suspects"—often just ordinary teenagers—whom they are prone to pull off the streets for identity checks. You can in fact be stopped at any time and asked to produce ID. If it happens to you, it's not worth being difficult or facetious.

The two main types of police, the **Police Nationale** and the **Gendarmerie Nationale**, are for all practical purposes indistinguishable. If you need to report a theft, or other incident, you can go to either.

The **CRS** (*Compagnies Républicaines de Sécurité*) are a different proposition entirely; mobile forces of heavies, sporadically dressed in green combats and armed with riot equipment, whose brutality in the May 1968 battles turned public opinion to the side of the students. They continue to make demonstrations dangerous.

FESTIVALS AND EVENTS

With all that's going on in Paris, festivals, in the traditional "popular" sense, are no big deal. But there is an impressive array of arts events and, not to be missed for the politically interested, an inspired internationalist jamboree at the *Fête de l'Humanité*.

POPULAR FESTIVALS AND FÊTES

February—*Foire à la Feraille de Paris*. Antiques and bric-à-brac fair in the 12e (Parc Floral de Paris and the Bois de Vincennes).

Week before Lent—*Mardi Gras*. The *Mardi Gras* are avidly celebrated in the south of France but go almost unnoticed in Paris. A few kids take the opportunity to cover unwary passers-by with flour.

End of March, beginning of April—*Festival International: Films des Femmes*. At Créteil; information from Maison des Arts, place Salvador

Allende, 9400 Créteil (☎49.80.18.88). 1992 will be the fourteenth. Tickets are cheap, you can vote for the awards, and it gets better every year.

April—*Foire du Trône*. A funfair located in the 12e, Pelouse de Reuilly and Bois de Vincennes.

May—*Marathon International de Paris*. Departs from Place de la Concorde, arrives at the Hippodrome de Vincennes 42 kilometers later.

June—*Course des Garçons de Café*. Waiters' race in the streets of Paris with laden trays of alcohol. Departs from and arrives at the Hôtel de Ville, 1er.

June 21 (Summer Solstice)—*Fête de la Musique de Paris*. Midsummer's day usually sees parades, including the Gay Pride march, street theater and amusements, and live bands throughout the city.

June—*Paris Villages*. Local festivities including regional folk dancing in various Paris neighborhoods.

July—*Arrivé du Tour de France Cyclistes*. The *Tour de France* cyclists cross the finishing line, in the avenue des Champs-Élysées, 8e.

July 14—*Bastille Day*. The 1789 surrender of the Bastille is celebrated with official pomp in parades of tanks down the Champs-Élysées, firework displays, and concerts, but fails to enthuse most of the city's population.

Autumn—*Festival d'Automne*. Theater and music, including lots of eastern European companies, as well as American and Japanese; multilingual productions. Lots of avant-garde and multi-media stuff, most of it pretty exciting.

Autumn, usually September—*Fête de l'Humanité*. Sponsored by the French Communist Party, this annual event just north of Paris at La

Courneuve attracts people in their thousands and of every political persuasion. The *fête* is a celebration rather than a Party platform, while illustrating the international aspects of communism.

October—*Fêtes des Vendanges*. A grape harvest in the Montmartre vineyard, at the corner of rue des Saules and rue Saint-Vincent.

October—*Foire International d'Art Contemporain (FIAC)*. International contemporary art show.

October—*Les 6 Heures Motonautiques de Paris*. Six-hour motorboat race on the Seine.

October—*Prix de l'Arc de Triomphe*. Horse racing with high stakes.

November—*Mois de la Photo*. Photographic exhibitions are held in museums throughout the city.

November—*Salon d'Automne*. Art exhibition of new talent at the Grand Palais, av Winston-Churchill.

FEMINISM

During the Socialists' first term, the Women's Ministry, created by the government and led by Yvette Roudy, spent the five years getting long-overdue equal pay and opportunity measures through Parliament. Some funding was given to women's groups but the main emphasis was on legislation, including the significant advance of socialized health coverage for abortion. However, a law against degrading, discriminatory, or violence-inciting images of women in the media was thrown out of the National Assembly, provoking outrage and protest from feminists throughout the country.

Meanwhile, the **MLF *(Mouvement de Libération des Femmes*—**Women's Liberation Movement) had been declared by the media to be dead and buried. There were no more Women's Day marches, no major demonstrations, no direct action. Feminist bookstores and cafés started closing, publications reached their last issue, and polls showed that young women leaving school were only interested in men and babies. As the Socialist policies ran out of steam, cuts in public spending and traditional ideas about the male breadwinner sent more and more women back to their homes and hungry husbands.

Under Chirac and the Gaullists, the *Ministère des Droits des Femmes* (Ministry of Women's Rights) had been renamed as the *Ministère des Droits de l'Homme* (Ministry of the Rights of Man). The full title of the Ministry included "the feminine condition" and "the family" but the irony of the implacably male gender bias of the French language went unremarked in government circles and among people in general. The current Socialist minister is at least a woman, but with few apparent feminist interests; she is, rather, just a faithful follower of Michel Rocard, the Prime Minister. **Yvette Roudy** and **Hugeutte Bouchardeau**, the two representatives in the National Assembly with feminist perspectives, have done all they can to keep the issues prominent but with no support from their colleagues, and little from the movement outside.

Feminist intellectuals—always the most prominent section of the French women's movement—have continued their *seminaires*, erudite publications, and university feminist studies courses, while at the other end of the scale, women's refuges and rape crisis centers are still maintained, with some funding from the Ministry. The *MLF* is occasionally seen on the streets, but disorganized and in much diminished numbers.

More recently a key mobilizing issue has again been abortion because of retrogressive steps in the US and the power of the anti-abortion lobby there which French women fear is influencing European public opinion. When a French company applied for a license for the abortion pill RU486, the French SPUC initially forced them to withdraw it, with threats of violence, even death, to its employees. The male Minister for Health, however, declared RU486 to be "the moral property of women" and it has since been used by over 50,000 women for terminations that are far safer and simpler than those by surgical methods. How much the minister was influenced by the needs of the French pharmaceutical industry rather than the needs of women is a matter for interpretation, but it was a significant victory nevertheless.

Feminists continue to be active in unions and political parties; male bastions in the arts and media have been under attack; in business and local government leading roles have been taken by women. But French culture remains stuck with myths about femininity that disable women to a far greater extent than in the US, Britain, or Holland. For example, every French town hall has the female figure of Marianne—currently modeled on Catherine Deneuve—to symbolize *La France*: the country with the most all-pervasive national chauvinism in Europe. This combination of values, plus Catholicism, plus peasantry, plus the language itself, mitigates against ideological equality at a very fundamental level. A woman president is still unthinkable, and Margaret Thatcher was always explained away by French feminists as a proto-male.

To a visitor to Paris, the blatant pornographic images on métro adverts, on TV, in newspapers and magazines—and the lack of any graffiti to subvert them—are most likely to shock and disturb. Street harassment and male outnumbering in public places is not that much different from American cities—you may even find certain advantages in the French male's supposedly chivalrous attitude to women.

Parisian **lesbians** have a strong network, with a scattering of good addresses, but havens for non-lesbian feminists are few—the *Maison des Femmes*, the Marguerite Durand library, and the hammams (Turkish baths) are about it. On the whole, lesbian organizations fight alongside gays on the general issue of anti-homosexuality while campaigning separately on the far more numerous and varied repressions women are subject to.

CONTACTS AND INFORMATION

Maison des Femmes, 8 Cité Prost, off rue Chanzy, 11ᵉ, Mº Faidherbe-Chaligny; ☎43.48.24.91; erratic opening hours. A women's meeting place run by *Paris Féministe* who produce a fortnightly bulletin and organize a wide range of events and actions. It's also home to the **lesbian group** MIEL (*Mouvement d'Information et d'Expression des Lesbiennes*) (☎43.79.61.91; answering machine ☎43.79.66.07). Anti-racist groups, North African women's groups, and rape crisis/battered women's organizations also meet at the *Maison*. This is by far the best place to come if you want to make contact with the movement. Don't be put off by the back-alley entrance, and though English speakers can't be guaranteed, you can count on a friendly reception. There's a

cafeteria run by *MIEL—Hydromel*—operating for drinks and dinner most Friday evenings, occasional open days with exhibitions and concerts or discos, workshops and self-defense classes, discussions, and film shows.

Centre Audio-Visuel Simone de Beauvoir, Palais de Tokyo, 2 rue de la Manutention, 16ᵉ, Mº Iéna; ☎47.23.67.48). An archive of audiovisual works by or about women, financed by de Beauvoir in her lifetime and maintained by her bequest. There are regular screenings (which you'll find listed in *Lesbia* magazine—see below). Payment of a small fee allows you individual access to this comprehensive and compelling collection.

Agence Femmes Information, 21 rue des Jeûneurs, 2ᵉ. Mº Sentier; ☎42.33.37.47; Mon–Fri 10am–6:30pm. A women's news agency producing a weekly bulletin, as well as providing the local and national press with stories. Their library of cuttings and women's publications is open to consultation for around 45F (reductions for unemployed and students).

ARCL (Archives, Recherches et Cultures Lesbiennes), post box (BP) 662, 75531, Paris Cedex 11; ☎48.05.25.89; Wed 4–8pm, Fri 6–10pm—hours may change. ARCL publishes a yearly directory of lesbian and feminist addresses in France (available at the *Bibliothèque Marguerite Durand*) and a fairly regular bulletin. They also organize meetings.

Bibliothèque Marguerite Durand, 3rd floor, 79 rue Nationale, 13ᵉ, Mº Tolbiac; Tues–Sat 2–6pm. The first official feminist library in France, this carries the widest selection of contemporary and old periodicals, news clippings files, photographs, posters and etchings, documentation on current organizations, as well as books on every aspect of women's lives, past and present. A very pleasant place to sit and read: admission is free; in order to consult publications you need to fill out a form and produce identification—the staff are very helpful.

PUBLICATIONS

There's no single, widely available, feminist magazine in France; instead nearly every group produces its own paper or review. Some are stapled, Xeroxed hand-outs issued at random intervals, others are regular, well-printed serials, many of them linked to particular political parties.

Lesbia, the **monthly magazine**, is the most widely available (most newsagents stock it) and the most comprehensive, with a wide range of articles, listings, reviews, personals, and contacts. Although it's written specifically for lesbians, it's the best general magazine for all feminists.

Paris Féministe (see *Maison des Femmes*, above) carries detailed **listings** for events and groups in Paris.

Suites des Cris is a literary and artistic lesbian revue, available from *ARCL* (see above).

Anima is a black women's glossy magazine.

EMERGENCIES

There's no centralized **rape crisis** organization, but the refuges for battered women try to help all victims of male violence. English-speakers are rare, so they may not be of much use, but if things do get bad you will at least get sympathy and an all-women environment, whereas going to the police may well be a further trauma. It is not possible to give up-to-date addresses of the refuges, but they are available from the *Mairies* (town halls) of each *arrondissement* and from the *Maison des Femmes*.

OTHER ADDRESSES

Feminist, lesbian, or sympathetic commercial enterprises are listed in the relevant sections: **bookshops** in *Shops and Markets;* **cafés** in *Drinking and Eating;* **clubs** in *Music and Nightlife;* **hammams** in *Daytime Amusements.*

Organizations for both gay and lesbian groups are given under *Gay and Lesbian Paris* below.

GAY AND LESBIAN PARIS

Paris is one of Europe's major centers for gay men. New bars, clubs, restaurants, saunas, and shops open all the time and in the central street of the Marais, rue Ste-Croix-de-la-Bretonnerie, every other address is gay.

The annual **Gay Pride** parade and festival (which starts from the Bastille, normally on the Saturday closest to the summer solstice) is a major carnival for both lesbians and gays. For a long time the emphasis has been on providing the requisites for a hedonistic lifestyle—rather than political campaigning. The Socialist government made an effort to show its recognition of homosexual rights, but with the legal age of consent set at 15, and discrimination and harassment non-routine, protest was not a high priority.

Matters have changed, here as elsewhere, since the outbreak of AIDS *(SIDA* in French). The resulting homophobia has not been as extreme as in Britain or America but has nevertheless increased the suffering in the group statistically most at risk. The Pasteur Institute in Paris is at the forefront of research into the virus, although gay patients there have complained of being treated like cattle. A group of gay doctors and the association *AIDES* (see *SOS* below) have however been providing sympathetic counseling and treatment, and the gay press has done a great deal in disseminating the facts about AIDS, encouraging the use of condoms, and providing hope and encouragement.

Being gay is certainly not yet acceptable in establishment circles. In 1990 investigations into the murder of Pasteur Doucé, the director of a gay Christian center (*Centre du Christ Libérateur*—see below), brought to light a dirty tricks department in the French internal intelligence services which was out to discredit certain powerful individuals by implicating them in gay sex rings. Gay, lesbian, and civil rights organizations joined forces to demand an official inquiry and have kept up the pressure despite the state's attempt to have the affair forgotten.

French gay and lesbian groups have long been good internationalists. Their publications have given prominent coverage to the situation in Britain, giving full support to the campaigns against anti-homosexual legislation there.

CONTACTS AND INFORMATION

Gay, lesbian, or sympathetic commercial enterprises are listed in the relevant chapters: **bookshops** in *Shops and Markets;* **bars** in *Drinking and Eating;* **clubs** in *Music and Nightlife.*

As well as those, there is a huge number of gay **organizations** in Paris. Here we've listed the most prominent: for a fuller list, consult *Gai Pied's* **Gai Guide** (see below). Lesbian addresses are listed under "Feminism" (above).

Agora, c/o *David & Jonathan*, 92bis, rue Picpus, 12ᵉ; Mº Daumesnil. A federation of twelve gay organizations including **David & Jonathan** (gay Christians; ☎43.42.09.49) and **Homosexualités et Socialisme** (gays in the Socialist Party; ☎43.57.97.25).

Centre du Christ Libérateur, 3bis rue Clairaut, 17ᵉ; Mº La Fourche (☎46.27.49.36). Pasteur Doucé, a gay Baptist minister who was brutally murdered in 1989, set up this Christian center to give medical, juridical, and pastoral care to all sexual minorities. His work continues.

Gay Pride, 4 rue Pasteur, 11ᵉ; Mº St-Ambroise. Brings together all the organizations and media for the Gay Pride festival.

GAGE, c/o *Les Mots à la Bouche*—see below (☎42.61.40.50). Gay students group which meets every Tuesday from 8:30pm to midnight at the *Duplex* bar (25 rue Michel-le-Comte, 3ᵉ; Mº Rambuteau).

GPL (Gais pour les Libertés), ☎42.02.03.03. Left-wing campaigning group.

MEDIA

Frequence Gaie, 94.4 FM; 24-hr gay and lesbian **radio station** with music, news, chats, information on groups and events, etc.

Gai Pied publishes the annual *Gai Guide* which is the most comprehensive gay guide to France, carrying a good selection of lesbian addresses; and the weekly glossy magazine *Gai Pied Hebdo*, which is more exclusively for men. Both have English sections.

Les Mots à la Bouche, 6 rue St-Croix-de-la-Bretonnerie, 4ᵉ; Mº Hôtel-de-Ville. The main gay and lesbian bookshop with exhibition space and meeting rooms.

Ilia, monthly bulletin of the *Centre du Christ Libérateur*.

SOS

SOS Gais and SOS Lesbia, ☎42.61.00.00; women Saturday afternoons only. Equivalent to Gay Switchboard.

Association des Médecins Gais, 45 rue Sedaine, 11ᵉ; Mº Bréguet-Sabin (☎48.05.81.71; Sat 2–4pm, Wed 6–8pm).

AIDES, ☎42.70.03.00; daily 9am–7pm.

SEXUAL AND RACIAL HARASSMENT

Sexual harassment at the verbal level is commonplace in Paris, a city in which everyone makes a habit of looking you up and down, and more often than not, making comments. Generally it is no worse or more vicious than in the USA but the problems are in judging men without the familiar linguistic and cultural signs. If your French isn't great, how do you tell if he's gabbling at you because you left your purse behind in a shop, or he's inciting you to swear at him in English and be cuffed round the head for the insult? The answer is you can't, but there are some pointers. A *"Bonjour"* or *"Bonsoir"* on the street is the standard pick-up opener. If you so much as return the greeting, you've let yourself in for a stream of tenacious chat and a hard shaking-off task. On the other hand, it's not unusual if you're on your own to be offered a drink in a bar and not to be pestered even if you accept. This is rarer in Paris than elsewhere in the country, but don't assume that any contact by a Frenchman is a trap.

Last métros of the night are not as unnerving as some late-night subways in New York simply because of greater passenger numbers. And unlike New York or London people are more inclined to intervene when nasty scenes develop. Hitchhiking out of Paris is a risk—as it is anywhere—and few French women do it. If you need help, go to one of the women's organizations (see above) or to your embassy (see p.28) rather than the police.

You may, as a woman, be warned against *"Les Arabes."* This is simply **French racism**. If you are Arab or look as if you might be, your chances of avoiding unpleasantness are very low. Hotels claim to be booked up, police demand your papers, and abuse from ordinary people is horribly frequent. In addition, being black, of whatever ethnic origin, can make entering the country difficult. Recent changes in passport regulations have put an end to outright refusal to let some British vacationers in, but customs and immigration officers can still, like their transatlantic counterparts, be obstructive and malicious.

The main anti-racist organization is **SOS Racisme** (☎48.06.40.00), which puts on a rally and concert in Paris every June. Its principal figures played a key role in the antiwar demonstrations of January 1991, for which they were strongly criticized on the grounds that the issue was not part of *SOS Racisme*'s brief. To its credit, the organization stuck to the antiwar coalition, making it clear that the war would increase paranoid racism toward people of Arab origin in France. Though it doesn't represent the majority of immigrants and their descendants in France (for rioting kids in the Paris suburbs it's a middle-class outfit of no use to them), *SOS Racisme* has done a great deal over the last few years to raise the consciousness of young white French people.

WORK AND STUDY

Most Americans who manage to survive in Paris do it on luck, brazenness, and willingness to live in pretty grotty conditions. An exhausting combination of bar and club work, freelance translating, data processing, typing, street-performing, providing novel services like home-delivery pizzas, teaching English, or programming, dance or wind-surfing, modeling, and whatever else are the ways people scrape by. Great if you're into self-promotion and living hand-to-mouth, but if you're not, it might be wise to think twice.

Much the simplest way of finding a job in a **French language school** is to apply from America. Check the ads in specialty papers listing overseas jobs (available in some libraries). Late summer is usually the best time. You don't need fluent French to get a post, but a TOEFL (Test of English as a Foreign Language) qualification is a distinct advantage.

If you apply from home, most schools will fix up the necessary papers for you. American citizens will need a work permit—have the school arrange this before you leave home. It's quite feasible to find a teaching job once you're already **in France**, but you will have to accept unofficial status and no job security. For the addresses of schools, look under *Écoles de Langues* in the *Professions* directory of the local phone book.

Offering **private language lessons** (via university noticeboards or classified ads), you'll have lots of competition, and it's hard to reach the people who can afford it, but it's always worth a try.

For **temporary work**, there's no substitute for checking the papers, pounding the streets, and keeping an eye on the noticeboards at the American (65 quai d'Orsay, 7e) and British (St George's English Church, 7 rue Vacquerie, 16e) churches. You could try the noticeboards located in the offices of *CIDJ* at 102 quai Branly, 15e, and *CROUS*, 39 av Georges Bernanos, 5e, both youth information agencies which advertise a number of temporary jobs for foreigners. The British Council Library (9–11 rue de Constantine, 7e; ☎45.55.95.95) has a similar noticeboard, and you may also pick up information here by word of mouth. Other good sources of job advertisements include the *Offres d'Emploi* in the newspapers *Le Monde*, *Le Figaro*, and the *International Herald Tribune*.

Although working as an **au pair** is easily set up through any number of agencies (lists are available from the closest French embassy or consulate), this sort of work is really a last resort, even if you're just using it to learn the language. Conditions, pay, and treatment by your employers are likely to be the next worst thing to slavery. If you're determined to try, it's better to apply once in France, where you can at least meet the family first and check things out.

Another possibility, perhaps more remote, and definitely to be arranged before you leave, is to get a job as a **travel courier.** You'll need good French (German would also help) and should write to as many tour operators as you can, preferably in early spring.

Finally, it's worth noting that if you're a full-time student in France (see below), you can get a **work permit** for the following summer so long as your visa is still valid.

STUDYING

It's relatively easy to be a **student** in France. Foreigners pay no more than French nationals (around 550F a year) to enroll in a course, and of course there's the cost of supporting yourself. You'll be eligible for subsidized accommodation, meals, and all the student reductions. Few people want to do undergraduate degrees abroad, but for higher degrees or other diplomas, the range of options is enormous. Strict entry requirements, including an exam in French, apply only for undergraduate degrees. Generally, French universities are much less formal than American ones and many people perfect their fluency in the language while studying. For **full details and prospectuses**, go to the Cultural Service of any French embassy or consulate (see p.9 for the addresses).

DIRECTORY

AIRLINES *Air France*, 119 av des Champs-Élysées, 8e (☎45:35.61.61); *Air Inter*, 12 rue Castiglione, 1er (☎42.60.36.46); *British Airways*, 91 av des Champs-Élysées, 8e (☎47.78.14.14); *Pan Am*, 1 rue Scribe, 9e (☎42.66:45:45).

AIDS HOTLINE (*SIDA AP*) ☎45.82.93.39, Mon–Fri 9am–5pm.

ALARM ☎3688 for a morning call.

BIKE HIRE See details on p.175.

CONSULATES US—2 av Gabriel, 8e (☎42.96.12.02); Canadian—35 av Montaigne, 8e (☎47.23.01.01); Australian—4 rue Jean-Rey, 15e (☎40.59.33.00); British—16 rue d'Anjou, 8e (M° Madeleine; (☎42.96.87.19); Irish—12 av Foch, 16e (enter from 4 rue Rude; ☎45.00.89.43); New Zealand—7 rue Léonardo-de-Vinci, 16e (M° 45.00. 24.11); Dutch—7–9 rue Eblé, 7e (M° St-François-Xavier; ☎43.06.61.88); Swedish—17 rue Barbet-de-Jouy, 7e (M° Varenne; ☎45.55.92.15).

CONTRACEPTIVES Condoms (*préservatifs*) have always been available at pharmacies, though contraception was only legalized in 1967. You can also get spermicidal cream and jelly (*dose contraceptive*), plus the suppositories (*ovules, suppositoires*) and (with a prescription) the Pill (*la pillule*), a diaphragm, or IUD (*le sterilet*).

CUSTOMS If you bring in more than 5000F worth of foreign cash, you need to sign a declaration at customs. There are also restrictions on taking francs out of the country, but the amounts are beyond the concern of most people. Tobacco and alcohol import limits are 400 cigarettes and two liters respectively.

DISABLED TRAVELERS You'll find details of the various forms of help offered for disabled travelers on Paris' public transit on p.35. Otherwise, the city has no special reputation for ease of access and facilities, but at least information is available. **For detailed information**

about access to museums, banks, pharmacies, markets, churches, theaters, etc, contact the *Comité National pour la Réadaptation des Handicapés*, 30–32 quai de la Loire, 75019 Paris (☎45.48.90.13) and ask for the booklet *Touristes Quand Même*. This also covers accommodation, transport, and particular aids such as buzzer signals on pedestrian crossings. The *ATH* hotel reservation service (☎48.74.88.51) has details of wheelchair access for three- and four-star hotels. The *Access Guide* to Paris is available in English from the *Pauline Hephaistos Survey Project*, 39 Bradley Gdns, London W13, England.

ELECTRICITY 200V out of double, round-pin wall sockets. Most North American appliances will require both a transgormer and plug adaptor. Electricity and gas are supplied by EDF–GDF (Electricité de France–Gaz de France, ☎43.87.59.99 Mon–Fri 8:30am–4pm), who should be contacted concerning bills, gas problems, or blackouts in an apartment building. For problems in individual apartments, contact one of the emergency repair numbers listed below.

EMERGENCY REPAIRS General agencies dealing with gas, electricity, plumbing, car repairs, etc are *Allo Assistance Dépannage* (☎42.55.59.59); *All Dépannage Express* (☎42.50.91.91); *All Dépann 24* (free phone ☎05.13.68.18), and *SOS Dépannage* (☎47.07.99.99).

GAS 24-hour filling stations are *Garage St-Honoré*, 58 pl du Marché, St-Honoré, 1er; *Shell*, 109 rue de Rennes, 6e; 1 bd de la Chapelle, 10e, (☎42.03.49.85); 4 av Foch, 16e; *Total*, 95 av des Champs-Élysées, 8e.

KIDS/BABIES pose few travel problems. They're allowed in all bars and restaurants, most of whom will cook simpler food if you ask. Hotels charge by the room—there's a small supplement for an additional bed or cot. You'll have no difficulty finding disposable diapers, baby foods, and milk powders. The *SNCF* charges half-fare on trains and buses for kids aged 4–12, nothing for under-4s. See *Chapter Three* for full listings of activities.

LAUNDRY Laundromats have multiplied in Paris over the last few years and you'll probably find one close to where you're staying.

LIBRARIES Foreign Cultural Institutes (US: 10 rue du Général- Camou, 7e; British: 9 rue de Constantine, 7e) have free access libraries, with daily newspapers. Interesting French collections include the BPI at Beaubourg (vast, including all the foreign press), Forney (books being a good excuse if you want to visit the medieval bishop's palace at 1 rue Figuiler in the 4e), and the Historique de la Ville de Paris, a sixteenth-century mansion housing centuries of texts and picture books on the city (24 rue Pavée, 4e).

LOST BAGGAGE Orly: ☎46.75.40.38; M° Roissy/Charles de Gaulle: ☎48.62.12.12.

LOST PROPERTY Bureau des Objets Trouvés, 36 rue des Morillons, 15e (M° Convention; Mon–Fri 8:30am–5pm; ☎45.31.14.80).

LUGGAGE STORAGE There are lockers at all train stations and *consigne* for bigger items or longer periods.

SWIMMING POOLS *Butte aux Cailles*, 5 place Paul-Verlaine, 13e—cheap municipal baths in bizarre brick building; *Pontoise*, 19 rue de Pontoise, 5e—reserved for schoolchildren most of the time, but nude swimming two evenings a week, check *Pariscope* etc; *Déligny*, opposite 25 quai d'Anatole France, 7e—open-air, crowded, and an amusing, if expensive, spectacle.

TALKING CLOCK ☎3699.

TELEGRAMS by phone. Internal, ☎3655; English-language, ☎42.33.21.11; Other languages, ☎42.33.44.11.

TIME France is always six hours ahead of EST, and nine hours ahead of PST, except between the end of September and the end of October, when it's five hours ahead.

TOILETS are usually to be found downstairs in bars, along with the phone, but they're often hole-in-the-ground squats and paper is rare.

TRAFFIC/ROAD CONDITIONS *Inter Service Route* (24-hr): ☎48.58.33.33.

WORLD SERVICE English-language BBC radio broadcasts can be found on 463m MW or on frequencies between 21m and 31m shortwave at intervals throughout the day and night. For more details, see p.21.

PART TWO

THE

GUIDE

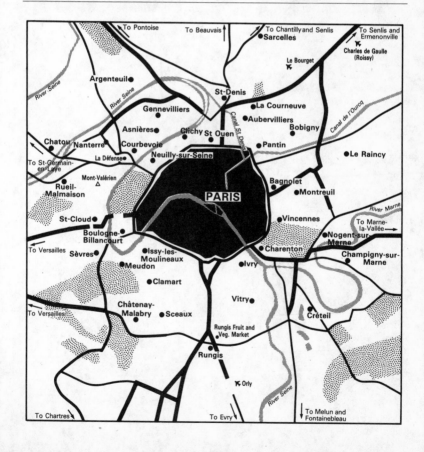

To Pontoise · To Beauvais↑ · To Chantilly and Senlis · To Senlis and Ermenonville

● Sarcelles

Le Bourget ✈

✈ Charles de Gaulle (Roissy)

River Seine

● Argenteuil

River Seine

● St-Denis

● La Courneuve

● Gennevilliers

Canal St-Denis

● Aubervilliers

Canal de l'Ourcq

● Bobigny

● Asnières

● Clichy St Ouen

● Chatou · Nanterre · ● Courbevoie

● Pantin

La Défense

● Neuilly-sur-Seine

● Le Raincy

To St-Germain-en-Laye →

Mont-Valérien △

● Bagnolet

● Rueil-Malmaison

PARIS

● Montreuil

River Marne

● St-Cloud

● Vincennes

To Marne-la-Vallée →

● Boulogne-Billancourt

● Nogent-sur-Marne

To Versailles ← · Sèvres

● Issy-les-Moulineaux

● Charenton

● Champigny-sur-Marne

● Meudon

● Ivry

● Clamart

● Vitry

To Versailles ←

● Châtenay-Malabry · ● Sceaux

● Créteil

Rungis Fruit and Veg. Market

● Rungis

✈ Orly

River Seine

To Chartres ↙

To Evry ↓

To Melun and Fontainebleau ↓

POINTS OF ARRIVAL

BY AIR

The two main Paris **airports** dealing with international flights are **Roissy-Charles de Gaulle** (*TWA, Pan Am, British Airways, Air France*, etc); 24-hr; ☎48.62.22.80) and **Orly Sud/Orly Ouest** (daily 6am–11:30pm; ☎48.84.52.52). Both of these have information desks that can provide maps and accommodation listings.

ROISSY-CHARLES DE GAULLE
Roissy, to the northeast of the city, is connected with the center by the following methods:

Roissy-Rail. A combination of airport bus and RER *ligne B* train to the Gare du Nord (every 15min from 5am to 11:15pm), where you can transfer to the ordinary métro. Taking about 35 minutes, this is the cheapest and quickest route.

Air France **bus**. This costs 35F, and departs from door 6 every 15min from 5:45am to 11pm, terminating at the Porte Maillot (métro) on av MacManon, on the northwest edge of the city, a hundred meters from the Arc de Triomphe.

Taxis into central Paris cost from 150 to 200F, plus a small luggage supplement, and should take between 45 minutes and one hour.

Buses #350 to Gare du Nord and Gare de l'Est, and #351 to place de la Nation.

ORLY
Orly, south of Paris, also has a bus–rail link. *Orly-Rail*, RER *ligne C* **trains** leave every fifteen minutes from 5:30am to 11:30pm for the Gare d'Austerlitz and other Left Bank stops which connect with the métro. Alternatively there are *Air France* **coaches** to the Gare des Invalides in the 7e or *Orlybus* to Denfert-Rochereau métro in the 14e. Both leave every ten or fifteen minutes from 6am to 11pm. Journey time is about 35 minutes. A **taxi** will take about the same time, costing around 100F.

OTHER AIRPORTS
Paris's third airport, **Le Bourget**, handles internal flights only. However, a number of **charter** companies also operate services to **Beauvais**. This is a seventy-kilometer bus journey from Paris, but all air tickets should include the price of the bus trip into place Stalingrad in the center.

BY TRAIN

Paris's six mainline stations are all equipped with cafés, restaurants, *tabacs*, banks, *bureaux de change* (long waits in season) and connected with the métro system.

The **Gare du Nord** (trains from Boulogne, Calais, the UK, Belgium, Holland, and Scandinavia; ☎42.80.03.03 for information, ☎42.06.49.38 for reservations) and **Gare de l'Est** (serving eastern France, Germany, Switzerland, and Austria; ☎42.08.49.90 for information, ☎42.06.49.38 for reservations) are side by side in the northeast of the city, with the **Gare St-Lazare** (serving the UK, Dieppe, and the Normandy coast; ☎43.38.52.29 for information, ☎43.87.91.70 reservations) a little to the west of them.

Still on the Right Bank but toward the southwest corner is the **Gare de Lyon**, for trains from the Alps, the South, Italy, and Greece (☎43.45.92.22 information; ☎43.45.93.33 reservations), while **Gare Montparnasse** is the terminal for Versailles, Chartres, Brittany, and the Atlantic Coast (☎45.38.52.29).

A central number for all *SNCF* information is ☎45.82.50.50.

BY BUS

Almost all the buses coming into Paris—whether international or domestic—use the main *gare routière* at Porte de la Villette; there's a métro station here to get into the center. *Citysprint* buses arrive at and depart from rue St-Quentin, around the corner from the Gare du Nord. Check-in takes place at 135 rue Lafayette (☎42.85.44.55).

BY CAR

If you're driving in yourself, don't try to go straight across the city to your destination. Use the beltway—the *boulevard périphépherique*—to get around to the nearest Porte: it's much quicker, except at rush hour, and easier to find your way.

Once ensconced wherever you're staying, you'd be well advised to garage the car and use public transit. Parking is a big problem in the center.

GETTING AROUND THE CITY

Finding your way around is remarkably easy, because Paris proper, without its suburbs, is compact and relatively small, with a public transit system that is cheap, fast, and meticulously signposted.

To help you get your bearings above ground, think of the **Louvre** as the center. The Seine flows east to west, cutting the city in two. The **Eiffel Tower** is west, the white pimples of the **Sacré-Coeur** on top of the hill of Montmartre north. These are the landmarks you most often catch glimpses of as you move about. The area north of the river is known as the **Right Bank** or *rive droite*; to the south is the **Left Bank** or *rive gauche*. Roughly speaking, west is smart and east is scruffy.

PUBLIC TRANSIT

The **métro** is the simplest way of moving around. Trains run from 5:30am to 12:30am. Stations (abbreviated: M° Concorde, etc) are far more frequent than on the London Underground. **Free maps** are available at most stations. In addition every station has a big plan of the network outside the entrance and several inside. The lines are color-coded and numbered, although they are signposted within the system with the names of the stations at the ends of the lines. For instance, if you're traveling from Gare-du-Nord to Odéon, you follow the sign *Direction Porte-d'Orléans*; from Gare d'Austerlitz to Grenelle you follow *Direction Pont-de-St-Cloud*. The numerous junctions *(correspondances)* make it possible to travel all over the city in a more or less straight line. For

the latest in subway technology, use the express stations' computerized routefinders: at a touch of the button they'll give you four alternative routes to your selected destination, on foot or by public transit.

Don't however use the métro to the exclusion of the **buses**. They are not difficult and of course you see much more. There are **free route maps** available at métro stations, bus terminals, and the tourist office. Every bus stop displays the numbers of the buses which stop there, a map showing all the stops on the route, and the times of the first and last buses. If that is not enough, each bus has a map of its own route inside and some have a recorded announcement for each approaching stop. Generally speaking, they start around 6:30am and begin their last run around 9pm.

Night buses (*Noctambus*) run on ten routes from place du Châtelet near the Hôtel de Ville every half-hour between 1:30am and 5:30am. There is a reduced service on Sunday. Further information is on the *RATP* transport board (53ter quai des Grands-Augustins, 6e; ☎43.46.14.14). They also run numerous excursions, including some to quite far-flung places, much cheaper than the commercial operators; their brochure is available at all railroad and some métro stations.

The **same tickets** are valid for bus, métro and, within the city limits, the RER **express rail lines**, which also extend far out into the suburbs. Long bus journeys can cost two tickets; ask the driver, if in doubt.

The most economical **ticket**, if you are staying more than a day or two, is the *Carte Orange*, obtainable at all métro stations and *tabacs* (you need a passport photo), with a weekly (*hebdomadaire* or *coupon jaune*; valid Monday morning to Sunday evening; currently 51F for zones 1 and 2, ie within the city proper) or monthly (*mensuel*) coupon. Alternatively there is a one-day coupon at 21F and a 3- or 5-day visitor's coupon (*Paris Visites*) at 75F and 120F respectively, available only for first-class travel. The only advantage of the latter is that, unlike the *hebdomadaire* whose validity runs unalterably from Monday to Sunday, they can begin on any day. All entitle you to unlimited travel on bus or métro. On the métro you put the coupon through the turnstile slot, but make sure to return it to its plastic folder; it is reusable throughout the period of its validity. On a bus you show the whole *Carte* to the driver as you board—don't put it into the punching machine.

For a short stay in the city, **single tickets** can be bought in *carnets* of ten from any station or *tabac*—currently 32.80F, as opposed to around 5F for an individual ticket. Don't buy from the touts who hang round the main stations; you'll pay more than you should, quite often for a used ticket. There's a flat rate across the city: you need one ticket per journey. Be sure to keep your ticket until the end of the journey; you'll be fined on the spot if you can't produce one. All tickets are available as first- or second-class, although class distinctions are only in force 9am–5pm.

If it's late at night or you feel like treating yourself, don't hesitate to use the **taxis**. Their charges are very reasonable. To avoid being ripped off, check the meter shows the appropriate fare rate. Even before you get into the taxi you can check by seeing which of the three small indicator lights on its roof is switched on. *A* (passenger side) indicates the daytime rate for Paris and the *boulevard périphérique*; *B* is the rate for Paris at night, on Sunday, and on public holidays, and for the suburbs during the day; *C* is the driver's side) is the night rate for the suburbs. There is a 10F pick-up charge, a supplement of around 5F at the mainline railroad stations, and about the same amount per item of luggage. Tipping is not mandatory, but ten percent will be expected. Some **numbers to call** are: ☎45.85.85.85; ☎42.70.41.41; ☎42.02.42.02.

DISABLED TRAVELERS

If you are **handicapped**, taxis are obliged by law to carry you and to help you into the vehicle—also to carry your guide dog if you are blind. Specially adapted taxis are available on ☎48.37.85.85 or ☎47.08.93.50, but they need to be notified the day before. For **travel on the métro or RER**, the *RATP* offers accompanied journeys for disabled people not in wheelchairs—*Voyage accompagné*—which operates (free) from 8am to 8pm. You have to reserve your minder on ☎46.70.88.74 a day in advance. For wheelchair users there is an RER access guide obtainable from *RATP* at the address given above, and for blind people a Braille métro map, obtainable from *L'Association Valentin Haüy*, 5 rue Duroc, 7e (☎47.34.07.90).

DRIVING

Traveling around by car, in the daytime at least, is hardly worth it because of the difficulty of finding parking space, although the *Service du*

Stationnement de la Ville de Paris (☎43.46.98.30; Mon–Fri 9am–noon & 1:30–5pm) will provide information about parking lots and prices. Whatever you do, don't park in a bus lane or the *Axe Rouge* express routes (marked with a red square). Should you be towed away—and it's extremely expensive—you'll find your car in the pound belonging to that particular *arrondissement*. You'll have to phone the local town hall or *mairie* to get the address.

In the event of a **breakdown** you can call *Aleveque Daniel* (116 rue de la Convention, 15e; ☎48.28.12.00) or *Aligre Dépannage* (92 bd de Charonne, 20e; ☎49.78.87.50) for round-the-clock assistance. Alternatively, ask the police.

For **car rental**, in addition to the big international companies like *Avis*, *Hertz* etc (details from the tourist office), some good local firms are: *Acar* (77 rue Lagny, 20e; Mo Porte-de-Vincennes; ☎43.79.76.48; Mon–Sat 8am–12:30pm & 2–7pm), *Dergi et Cie* (60 bd St-Marcel, 5e; Mo Goberlins; ☎45.87.27.04; Mon–Sat 8am–7pm), *Locabest* (9 rue Abel, 12e; Mo Gare-de-Lyon; ☎43.46.05.05; Mon–Sat 7:30am–7pm), and *Rent a Car* (79 rue de Bercy, 12e; Mo Bercy; ☎45.45.15.15; Mon–Sat 8:30am–7pm).

> **Remember** that you have to be eighteen years of age to drive in France, regardless of whether you hold a license.

CYCLING

If you are reckless enough to want to **cycle** and don't have your own machine, you can rent from *Paris-Vélo*, 2 rue du Fer-à-Moulin, 5e; Mo Censier-Daubenton (☎43.37.59.22; Mon–Sat 10am–12:30pm & 2–7pm; closed public holidays) or *La Maison Du Vélo*, 8 rue de Belzunce (☎42.81.24.72). Take care!

BY BOAT

There remains one final mode of transport—by *Batobus* along the Seine. At the moment there are only five stops, though more are planned, and the service operates from April to September. The stops are: port de la Bourdonnais (Eiffel Tower), port de Solférino (musée d'Orsay), quai Malaquais (musée du Louvre), quai de Montebello (Notre-Dame), and quai de l'Hôtel de Ville. Boats run every 36 minutes from 10am to 7pm; total journey time is 21 minutes and the price 20F, or 10F per individual stop.

THE METRO

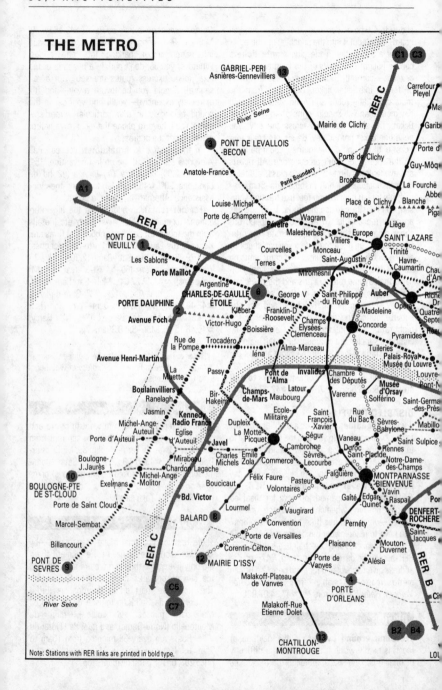

Note: Stations with RER links are printed in bold type.

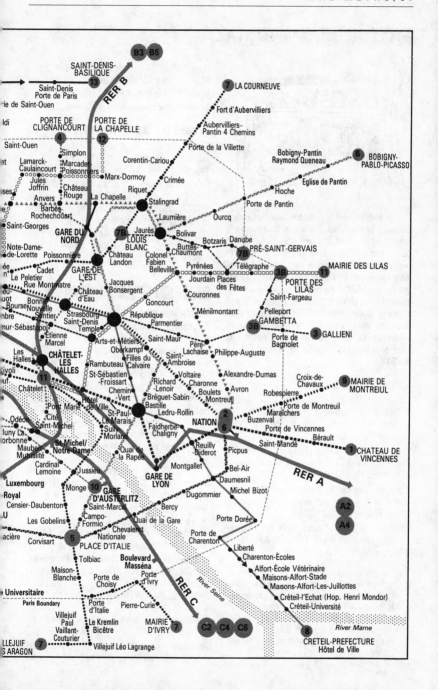

FINDING A PLACE TO STAY

Paris hotels and youth hostels are often heavily booked, so it's wise to reserve a place well ahead of time, if you can. If not, there are two agencies you can turn to for help: the tourist board's *Bureaux d'Accueil* and the youth-oriented *Accueil des Jeunes en France* (*AJF*). The former charges a small commission (from 17F); its function is to bail you out of last-minute difficulty rather than find the most economical deal. The *AJF*, however, actually guarantees "decent and low-cost lodging" (currently around 85F for B&B).

BUREAUX D'ACCUEIL

Office du Tourisme, 127 av des Champs-Élysées, 8e (Mon–Sat 9am–9pm throughout the year; summer Sun 9am–8pm, off season Sun 9am–6pm; ☎47.23.61.72).

Gare d'Austerlitz, bd de l'Hôpital, 13e (summer Mon–Sat 8am–10pm; off season Mon–Sat 8am–3pm; ☎45.84.91.70).

Gare de l'Est, bd de Strasbourg, 10e (summer Mon–Sat 8am–10pm; off season Mon–Sat 8am–1pm & 5–8pm; ☎ 46.07.17.73).

Gare de Lyon, 20 bd Diderot, 12e (summer Mon–Sat 8am–10pm; off season Mon–Sat 8am–1pm & 5–8pm; ☎43.43.33.24).

> The Paris hoteliers' organization publishes an annual list of the most **heavily booked periods** based on the dates of the *salons* or trade fairs (obtainable from FGTO offices). September is invariably the worst month. Otherwise dates vary slightly from year to year. It is worth checking them out when planning a trip.

Gare du Nord, 18 rue de Dunkerque, 10e (summer Mon–Sat 8am–10pm, Sun 8am–8pm; off season Mon–Sat 8am–8pm; ☎45.26.94.82).

24-hour information in English: ☎47.20.88.98.

ACCUEIL DES JEUNES EN FRANCE

Gare du Nord suburban station (June–Oct 8am–10pm; ☎42.85.86.19).

Beaubourg, 119 rue St-Martin, 4e—opposite Centre Beaubourg (M⁰ Châtelet-Les Halles; all year round Mon–Sat 9:30am–7pm; ☎42.77.87.80—this office can also be used as a forwarding address for mail).

Quartier Latin, 139 bd St-Michel, 5e (M⁰ Port-Royal; March–Oct Mon–Fri 9:30am–6:30pm; ☎43.54.95.86).

HOSTELS, FOYERS, AND CAMPSITES

YOUTH HOSTELS

The cheapest **youth accommodation** is to be found in the hostels run by the French **Youth Hostel Association** and those connected with the *AJF* and *UCRIF* (*Union des Centres de Rencontres Internationaux de France*). For the former you need International YHA membership, for which there is no age limit. Current costs for bed and breakfast are: youth hostels 90–115F, *AJF* hostels 85F, and *UCRIF* between 85F and 160F. The determining factor is whether you have an individual or shared room. There is no effective age limit at either.

There are only two **youth hostels** in Paris proper and it's advisable to reserve ahead in summer (send a check or postal order to cover the cost of the first night):

Jules Ferry, 8 bd Jules-Ferry, 11e. M⁰ République. ☎43.57.55.60. In the lively and colorful area at the foot of the Belleville hill.

D'Artagnan, 80 rue Vitruve, 20e. M⁰ Porte-de-Bagnolet. ☎43.61.08.75. There's also an annex at *Hôtel Ste-Marguerite*, 10 rue Trousseau, 11e (☎47.00.62.00) in the Faubourg St-Antoine.

Suburban hostels—all rather inconveniently located—are at:

Auberge Butte Rouge, 3 chemin du Loup-Pendu, Châtenay-Malabry. ☎46.32.17.43. Take

ARRONDISSEMENTS

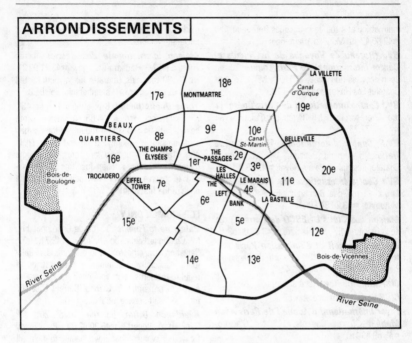

RER *ligne B2* to Robinson, then bus 198A to Cyrano-de-Bergerac.

3 rue Marcel-Duhamel, Arpajon. ☎64.90.28.85; RER *C4* to Arpajon.

125 av Villeneuve-Saint-Georges, Choisy-le-Roi. ☎48.90.92.30. Take RER *ligne C* from St-Michel to Choisy-le-Roi, where you cross the Seine, turn right, and follow the signs—20min.

4 rue des Marguerites, Rueil-Malmaison. ☎47.49. 43.97. 15min by train from Gare St-Lazare to Suresnes plus 15min walk.

FOYERS

The AJF's *foyers*, which cannot be booked in advance and where the maximum length of stay is five days, are:

Résidence Bastille, 151 av Ledru-Rollin, 11ᵉ. Mᵒ Ledru-Rollin/Bastille/Voltaire. ☎43.79.53.86.

Le Fourcy, 6 rue de Fourcy, 4ᵉ. Mᵒ St-Paul. ☎42.74.23.45.

Le Fauconnier, 11 rue du Fauconnier, 4ᵉ. Mᵒ St-Paul/Pont-Marie. ☎42.74.23.45.

Maubuisson, 12 rue des Barres, 4ᵉ. Mᵒ Pont-Marie/Hôtel-de-Ville. ☎42.72.72.09.

François Miron, 6 rue François-Miron, 4ᵉ. Mᵒ Hôtel-de-Ville. Annex of above.

The latter four are superbly and very centrally situated, occupying historic buildings in the Marais.

In addition, the AJF has access to rooms in:

Centre International de Séjour de Paris (CISP) Kellermann, 17 bd Kellermann, 13ᵉ. Mᵒ Porte-d'Italie. ☎45.80.70.76.

Centre International de Séjour de Paris (CISP) Maurice Ravel, 6 av Maurice-Ravel, 12ᵉ. Mᵒ Porte-de-Vincennes. ☎43.43.19.01.

Résidence Coubertin, 53 rue Lhomond, 5ᵉ. Mᵒ Censier-Daubenton. ☎43.36.18.12. July & Aug only.

Résidence Luxembourg, 270 rue St-Jacques, 5ᵉ. Mᵒ Luxembourg/Port-Royal. ☎43.25.06.20. July–Sept only.

Résidence Arts et Métiers, 27 bd Jourdan, 14ᵉ. Mᵒ Cité Universitaire. July–Sept only.

UCRIF has at its disposal eleven hostels in or close to Paris, for which there is no advance booking. *UCRIF* advises you either to phone direct to the hostels on arrival in Paris or go to their main office at 4 rue Jean-Jacques-Rousseau, 1er. ☎42.60.42.40. Mon–Fri 10am–6pm.

BVJ (Bureau de Voyages de la Jeunesse) Centre International de Paris/Louvre, 20 rue Jean-Jacques-Rousseau, 1er. Mº Louvre/ Châtelet-Les Halles. ☎42.36.88.18.

BVJ Centre International de Paris/Opéra, 11 rue Thérèse, 1er. Mº Pyramides/Palais-Royal. ☎42.60.77.23.

BVJ Centre International de Paris/Les Halles, 5 rue du Pélican, 1er. Mº Louvre/ Châtelet-Les Halles/Palais-Royal. ☎40.26.92.45.

BVJ Centre International de Paris/Quartier Latin, 44 rue des Bernadins, 5e. Mº Maubert-Mutualité. ☎43.29.34.80.

Maison des Clubs UNESCO de Paris, 43 rue de la Glacière, 13e. Mº Glacière. ☎43.36.00.63.

Centre d'Accueil et d'Animation Paris 20e, 46 rue Louis-Lumière, 20e. Mº Porte-de-Bagnolet/ Porte-de-Montreuil. ☎43.61.24.51.

CISP Maurice Ravel (see above).

CISP Kellermann (see above).

Foyer International d'Accueil de Paris Jean Monnet, 30 rue Cabanis, 14e. Mº Glacière. ☎45.89.89.15.

Foyer International d'Accueil de Paris La Défense, 19 rue Salvador-Allende, 92000 Nanterre. Mº Nanterre-Préfecture. ☎47.25.91.34. **Special arrangements for families** in July and August, including meals and baby-sitting, if you stay at least one week.

Centre International de Séjour Léo Lagrange, 107 rue Martre, Clichy. Mº Mairie-de-Clichy. ☎42.70.03.22.

All the above provide canteen meals for around 50F.

Further possibilities include more hostel-type accommodation, notably:

Association des étudiants protestants de Paris (Protestant student association), 46 rue de Vaugirard, 6e. Mº Luxembourg. ☎43.54.31.49. Open to people aged 18–25 of all nationalities and creeds. No advance booking; turn up or phone on the day—early. Maximum stay five weeks. Current cost is 10F membership (valid for subsequent visits) and 63–82F for bed and breakfast.

CROUS, Académie de Paris, 39 av Georges-Bernanos, 5e. Mº Port-Royal. ☎40.51.36.00. This is the organization which controls student accom-

modation in Paris and rents free space during university vacations.

Maison Internationale des Jeunes, 4 rue Titon, 11e. Mº Faidherb-Chaligny. ☎43.71.99.21. For 18–30-year-olds. Operates like a youth hostel, but does not require YH membership. 85F B&B.

Three Ducks Hostel, 6 pl Etienne-Pernet, 15e. Mº Emile-Zola. ☎48.42.04.05. A private youth hostel, with no age limit—though as the warden says himself, it's mainly young and noisy. Lock-out 11am–5pm, curfew at 1am. 75F—some rooms for couples. Kitchen facilities. It's necessary to reserve between May and Oct: send the price of the first night.

FOR WOMEN ONLY

Palais de la Femme, 94 rue de Charonne, 11e. Mº Charonne/Faidherbe-Chaligny. ☎43.71.11.27. Salvation Army hostel, where there is usually room, especially in summer, in the absence of regular residents, but you need to reserve in advance, preferably in writing. Current cost 70F for a bed; self-service meal about 40F.

Résidence Orfila, 65 rue Orfila, 20e. Mº Gambetta/Pelleport. ☎46.36.82.80. Particularly for young women, but have begun to take all ages. May to September are the best months for finding vacancies. Current cost is 70–90F for bed and breakfast. There are cooking facilities and the possibility of an evening meal. Nice "villagey" location not far from Père Lachaise cemetery.

For sundry other addresses try the ***CIDJ*** office's information files at 101 quai Branly, 15e. Mº Bir-Hakeim.

CAMPING

There is a **campground**, which is usually booked out in summer and in theory reserved for French camping club members, by the Seine in the Bois de Boulogne (allée du Bord-de-l'Eau, 16e; Mº Porte-Maillot. ☎45.06.14.98). Three more are farther out to the east of the city:

Camping du Tremblay, quai de Polangis, Champigny-sur-Marne. RER Champigny. ☎42.83.38.24.

Camping du Camp des Cicognes, bord-de-Marne, Créteil. RER Créteil-l'Echat. ☎42.07.06.75.

Camping de Paris-Est, bd des Alliés, Champigny-sur-Marne. Mº Joinville-le-Pont. ☎42.83.38.24.

BED AND BREAKFAST

Finally, there remains the possibility of **bed and breakfast**. The best organization to contact is *Bed and Breakfast* (73 rue Notre-Dame-des-Champs, 6ᵉ. Mº Vavin. ☎43.25.43.97; Mon–Fri 9am–1pm & 2–6pm; Jan & Feb 10am–1pm and 2–4pm). Their aim is to match guests and hosts with compatible interests etc and so to provide a real experience of French life. The minimum stay is two days and charges range from 210 to 350F (with breakfast) per day for a single room and from 260 to 450F for a double. Book by phone or letter.

HOTELS

For independence and choice of location there's obviously more scope in **booking a hotel yourself**. There are a great many in all price categories and Paris scores heavily, especially in relation to New York or London, in the still considerable, if dwindling, number of small family-run hotels with rooms under $35 for two, and certainly under $50.

The **hotels listed below** have been divided into three broad **price categories**: under 200F, up to 350F, and up to 500F; and arranged alphabetically by *arrondissement*. Many hotels in the higher categories have some much cheaper rooms. Most of the cheapest-category hotels are perfectly adequate. That means the sheets are clean, you can wash decently, and there isn't a brothel on the floor below. There won't be much luxury, however. Price seems to be chiefly a function of location, the relative newness of the paintwork, the glitziness of the reception area, and the presence or absence of an elevator. Most small Paris hotels are in converted old buildings, so the stairs are often dark and the rooms cramped, with a view onto an internal courtyard, and the decor hardly spanking new. We've assumed that most visitors come to Paris to see the city and will treat their hotel simply as a convenient and inexpensive place to spend a few of the night hours. Where we think conditions are at the limit of what most people will accept, we say "basic."

If you're seriously interested in a **long stay on a low budget**, then it would be worth checking out the various basic and star-less hotels you'll see as you go about the streets, especially in less central districts. Many only rent rooms by the month, often catering to immigrant workers, at very low prices.

All hotel **room prices** have to be displayed somewhere prominent, in the entrance or by the reception desk usually. Certain **standard terms** recur. *Eau courante* (EC) means a room with washbasin only, *cabinet de toilette* (CT) means basin and bidet. In both cases there will be communal toilets on the landing and probably a shower as well. *Douche/WC* and *Bain/WC* mean that you have a shower or bath as well as toilet in the room. A room with a *grand lit* (double bed) is invariably cheaper than one with *deux lits* (two separate beds).

Breakfast (*petit déjeuner* or PD) is sometimes included (*compris*) in the room price, sometimes extra (*en sus*). The amount varies between about 25F and 35F per person. It isn't supposed to be obligatory, though some hotels make a sour face when you decline it. Always make it clear whether you want breakfast or not when you take the room. It's usually a fairly indifferent continental breakfast, and you'll get a fresher, cheaper one at the local café.

1ᵉʳ

UNDER 200F

Hôtel Henri IV, 25 place Dauphine, 1ᵉʳ. Mº Pont-Neuf/Cité. ☎43.54.44.53. An ancient and well-known cheapie in the beautiful place Dauphine at the sharp end of the Île de la Cité. Nothing more luxurious than *cabinet de toilette* and now somewhat run down. Essential to book.

Hôtel Lion d'Or, 5 rue de la Sourdière, 1ᵉʳ. Mº Tuileries. ☎42.60.79.04. Spartan, but clean, friendly, and very central.

Hôtel de l'Ouest, 144 rue St-Honoré, 1ᵉʳ. Mº Louvre/Palais-Royal. ☎42.60.29.89. Rooms rather small and dilapidated. Very close to Louvre and consequently popular. Book two weeks ahead.

UP TO 350F

Hôtel du Centre, 20 rue du Roule, 1ᵉʳ. Mº Louvre/Pont-Neuf. ☎42.33.05.18. Good price for the area.

Hôtel St-Honoré, 85 rue St-Honoré, 1ᵉʳ. Mº Châtelet-les-Halles/Louvre. ☎42.36.20.38. Conveniently close to the heart of things—some cheaper rooms.

Hôtel Richelieu-Mazarin, 51 rue de Richelieu, 1ᵉʳ. Mº Palais-Royal. ☎42.97.46.20. Very good for the price, with a laundry. Some much cheaper rooms.

Hôtel Washington Opéra, 50 rue de Richelieu, 1er. Mº Palais-Royal. ☎42.96.68.06. Pleasant and comfortable.

UP TO 500F

Ducs d'Anjou, 1 rue Ste-Opportune, 1er. Mº Châtelet. ☎42.36.92.24. A carefully renovated old building overlooking the endlessly crowded place Ste-Opportune in the middle of Les Halles nightlife district. A bit fancier than our average.

2e

UNDER 200F

Hôtel Tiquetonne, 6 rue Tiquetonne, 2e. Mº Etienne-Marcel. ☎42.36.94.58. Bargain price in an attractive small street.

Grand Hôtel de Besançon, 56 rue de Montorgueil, 2e. Mº Les Halles/Etienne-Marcel. ☎42.36.41.08. Only a little over 200F at the top end. A great location in a lively market street.

3e

UNDER 200F

Béranger Hôtel, 23 rue Béranger, 3e. Mº République. ☎42.78.55.24. A very decent cheapie.

4e

UNDER 200F

Hôtel Moderne, 3 rue Caron, 4e. Mº St-Paul. ☎48.87.97.05. Much better than the first impression of the staircase would suggest, and the price is amazing for this area.

Le Palais de Fes, 41 rue du Roi-de-Sicile, 4e. Mº St-Paul/Hôtel-de-Ville. ☎42.72.03.68. Very cheap for the area: basic accommodation above a restaurant.

UP TO 350F

Castex Hôtel, 5 rue Castex, 4e. Mº Bastille/Sully-Morland. ☎42.72.31.52. Recently renovated building in a quiet street on the edge of the Marais. Good value.

Grand Hôtel Jeanne d'Arc, 3 rue de Jarente, 4e. Mº St-Paul. ☎48.87.62.11. Clean, quiet, and attractive, though—at such a reasonable price— the Marais location means you have to reserve.

Hôtel du Grand Turenne, 6 rue de Turenne, 4e. Mº St-Paul. ☎42.78.43.25. A few rooms under 200F, otherwise around 300F.

Hôtel Pratic, 9 rue d'Ormesson, 4e. Mº St-Paul/Bastille. ☎48.87.80.47. Doubles go up to 320F, but there are some under 200F.

Sully Hotel, 48 rue St-Antoine, 4e. Mº St-Paul/Bastille. ☎42.78.49.32. A clean and adequate place to lay your head.

UP TO 500F

Hôtel des Célestins, 1 rue Charles-V, 4e. Mº Sully-Morland. ☎48.87.87.04. A very comfortable sleep in a restored seventeenth-century mansion.

L'Hôtel du Septième Art, 20 rue St-Paul, 4e. Mº St-Paul/Pont-Marie. ☎42.77.04.03. A supposedly cinema-like ambience. The beige-brown rooms are disappointing, but the bathrooms live up to the black-and-white-movie style.

5e

UNDER 200F

Hôtel des Alliés, 20 rue Berthollet, 5e. Mº Censier-Daubenton. ☎43.31.47.52. Simple and clean, and bargain prices.

Hôtel des Carmes, 5 rue des Carmes, 5e. Mº Maubert-Mutualité. ☎43.29.78.40. A well-established tourist hotel with singles under 120F and some doubles not much more, though the best go up to 350F.

Hôtel le Central, 6 rue Descartes, 5e. Mº Maubert-Mutualité/Cardinal-Lemoine. ☎46.33.57.93. Clean and decent accommodation in a typically Parisian old house on top of the Montagne Ste-Geneviève, overlooking the gates of the former École Polytechnique. One of a dying breed.

Hôtel du Commerce, 14 rue de la Montagne-Ste-Geneviève, 5e. Mº Maubert-Mutualité. ☎43.54.89.69. Another renowned if somewhat gloomy cheapie (nothing over 120F) in the heart of the Latin Quarter, run by a charming old lady. Communal washing and toilets. No reservations, lots of competition. Turn up early in the morning.

Hôtel Gay-Lussac, 29 rue Gay-Lussac, 5e. Mº Luxembourg. ☎43.54.23.96. Singles under 150F, and all but a few doubles under 200F. Need to reserve at least a week in advance.

Hôtel Marignan, 13 rue du Sommerard, 5e. Mº Maubert-Mutualité. ☎43.54.63.81. One of the best bargains in town—and totally sympathetic to the needs of knapsack-toting foreigners. Free laundry and ironing facilities, plus a room to eat your own food in—plates provided. Even the maid speaks English. Reserve a month ahead in summer, five days in winter, when the prices are lower—though they do hold a few rooms back for people who turn up without booking. Rooms for two, three, and four people. A three will take you close to 300F.

UP TO 350F

Royal Cardinal Hôtel, 1 rue des Écoles, 5ᵉ. Mᵒ Jussieu/Cardinal-Lemoine. ☎43.26.83.64. A comfortable and unexciting two-star, used to foreigners.

Grand Hôtel Oriental, 2 rue d'Arras, 5ᵉ. Mᵒ Jussieu/Cardinal-Lemoine, Maubert-Mutualité. ☎43.54.38.12. Recently refurbished like so many of the old cheapies, but still a pretty good bargain for this locality—and nice people.

UP TO 500F

Hôtel California, 32 rue des Écoles, 5ᵉ. Mᵒ Jussieu/Cardinal-Lemoine. ☎46.34.12.90. This is another comfortable Latin Quarter tourist hotel.

Hôtel Esmeralda, 4 rue St-Julien-le-Pauvre, 5ᵉ. Mᵒ St-Michel/Maubert-Mutualité. ☎43.54.19.20. A discreet and ancient house on square Viviani with a superb view of Notre-Dame, with several much cheaper rooms.

Hôtel des Grandes Écoles, 75 rue du Cardinal-Lemoine, 5ᵉ. Mᵒ Cardinal-Lemoine. ☎43.26.79.23. Refurbished, and comfortable, in a great location with a view over the garden.

Hôtel Mont-Blanc, 28 rue de la Huchette, 5ᵉ. Mᵒ St-Michel. ☎43.54.49.44. Another face-lift and higher prices, but a great if noisy location a stone's throw from Notre-Dame.

Hôtel de la Sorbonne, 6 rue Victor-Cousin, 5ᵉ. Mᵒ Luxembourg. ☎43.54.58.08. An attractive old building, quiet, comfortable, and close to the Luxembourg gardens. Average price around 380 F.

6ᵉ

UNDER 200F

Le Petit Trianon, 2 rue de l'Ancienne-Comédie, 6ᵉ. Mᵒ Odéon. ☎43.54.94.64. Cheap, basic, and right in the heart of things.

UP TO 350F

Hôtel Alsace-Lorraine, 14 rue des Canettes, 6ᵉ. Mᵒ St-Germain/St-Sulpice. ☎43.25.10.14. An old and dingy building in a picturesque lane off place St-Sulpice, in the heart of St-Germain. Rooms clean, quiet and spacious.

Hôtel du Dragon, 36 rue du Dragon, 6ᵉ. Mᵒ St-Germain-des-Prés/Sèvres-Babylone. ☎45.48.51.05. Great location and nice people.

Hôtel St-Michel, 17 rue Gît-le-Coeur, 6ᵉ. Mᵒ St-Michel. ☎43.26.98.70. Simple and okay. Great location in a very attractive old street close to the river. Some rooms under 200F.

Hôtel Michelet Odéon, 6 place de l'Odéon, 6ᵉ. Mᵒ Odéon/Luxembourg. ☎46.34.27.80. Another fantastic location, but prices at the top of this range.

Hôtel St-André-des-Arts, 66 rue St-André-des-Arts, 6ᵉ. Mᵒ Odéon. ☎43.26.96.16. Reasonable and very central. Some cheaper rooms under 150F but no reservations on these.

Hôtel St-Placide, 6 rue St-Placide, 6ᵉ. Mᵒ Rennes/St-Placide. ☎45.48.80.08. Clean and adequate accommodation, right between Montparnasse and St-Germain.

UP TO 500F

Hôtel Récamier, 3bis place St-Sulpice, 6ᵉ. Mᵒ St-Sulpice/St-Germain. ☎43.26.04.89. Comfortable, superbly sited, with one or two cheaper rooms.

Hôtel des Marronniers, 21 rue Jacob, 6ᵉ. Mᵒ St-Germain-des-Prés. ☎43.25.30.60. This is a three-star and a little over the top of our price range, but it is a delightful place with a dining-room overlooking a secret garden. A place for a special occasion, perhaps.

7ᵉ

UP TO 350F

Hôtel du Centre, 24bis rue Cler, 7ᵉ. Mᵒ École-Militaire. ☎47.05.52.53. An old-fashioned, no-frills establishment in a chic and attractive neighborhood. Some cheaper rooms.

Hôtel du Champs-de-Mars, 7 rue du Champs-de-Mars, 7ᵉ. Mᵒ École-Militaire. ☎45.51.52.30. Good comfortable accommodation in a quiet street off av Bosquet.

La Résidence du Champs-de-Mars, 19 rue du Champs-de-Mars, 7ᵉ. Mᵒ École-Militaire. ☎47.05.25.45. Clean and adequate, with some cheaper rooms.

Grand Hôtel Lévêque, 29 rue Cler, 7ᵉ. Mᵒ École-Militaire/Latour-Maubourg. ☎47.05.49.15. Clean and decent; nice people, who speak some English. Good location smack in the middle of the rue Cler market. Book one month ahead.

Hôtel Malar, 29 rue Malar, 7ᵉ. Mᵒ Latour-Maubourg/Invalides. ☎45.51.38.46. Small, with slightly cramped rooms, but in a very attractive street close to the river.

Hôtel du Palais Bourbon, 49 rue de Bourgogne, 7ᵉ. Mᵒ Varenne. ☎45.51.63.32. A handsome old building in a sunny street by the Musée Rodin. Rooms are spacious and light, and some are still under 200F.

Royal Phare Hôtel, 40 av de la Motte-Picquet, 7ᵉ. Mᵒ École-Militaire. ☎47.05.57.30. A bit impersonal, but very convenient and has some good views. Also, close to rue Cler and its sumptuous market.

Splendid Hôtel, 29 av de Tourville, 7ᵉ. Mᵒ École-Militaire. ☎45.51.24.77. Some singles under 200F. A little noisy, but a great area with views, from the top floor, of the Eiffel Tower and Invalides.

UP TO 500F

Le Pavillon, 54 rue St-Dominique, 7ᵉ. Mᵒ Invalides/Latour-Maubourg. ☎45.51.42.87. A tiny former convent set back from the tempting shops of the rue St-Dominique in a leafy courtyard. A lovely setting, but the rooms are a little cramped for the price.

Hôtel de la Tulipe, 33 rue Malar, 7ᵉ. Mᵒ Latour-Maubourg. ☎45.51.67.21. Patio for summer breakfast and drinks. Beamy and cottagey. But as with all hotels in this area you are paying for the location rather than great luxury.

Hôtel de Turenne, 20 av de Tourville, 7ᵉ. Mᵒ École-Militaire. ☎47.05.99 92. Another comfortable bourgeois hotel.

8ᵉ

UP TO 350F

Hôtel d'Artois, 94 rue la Boétie, 8ᵉ. Mᵒ St-Philippe-du-Roule. ☎43.59.84.12. At less than 300F, very cheap for this elegant part of town.

9ᵉ

UP TO 350F

Hôtel des Arts, 7 Cité Bergère, 9ᵉ. Mᵒ Montmartre. ☎42.46.73.30. An agreeable and friendly hotel.

Hôtel de Beauharnais, 51 rue de la Victoire, 9ᵉ. Mᵒ Le Peletier/Havre-Caumartin. ☎48.74.71.13. Louis Quinze, First Empire . . . every room decorated in a different period style.

Hôtel Central, 46 Cité Bergère, 9ᵉ. Mᵒ Montmartre. ☎47.70.52.98. Well-used and agreeable tourist hotel, close to the *Folies Bergère* and so on.

Hôtel Chopin, 46 passage Jouffroy, 9ᵉ. Mᵒ Montmartre. ☎47.70.58.10. Entrance on bd Montmartre, near corner with rue du Faubourg-Montmartre. A splendid period building right in the old *passage*.

Hôtel Clauzel, 33 rue des Martyrs, 9ᵉ. Mᵒ St-Georges. ☎87.81.12.24. Adequate, though not very friendly. Maximum 250F.

Hôtel Comprador, 2 Cité Rougemont, 9ᵉ. Mᵒ Montmartre. ☎47.70.44.42. Entrance by 19 rue Bergère. One of the cheaper hotels hereabouts.

Hôtel d'Espagne, 9–11 Cité Bergère, 9ᵉ. Mᵒ Montmartre. ☎47.70.13.94. Somewhat institutional, but the cheapest in the Cité Bergère. Some rooms under 200F.

Hôtel Lorette, 36 rue Notre-Dame-de-Lorette, 9ᵉ. Mᵒ St-Georges. ☎42.85.18.81. No character, but adequate for sleeping.

Mondial Hôtel, 21 rue Notre-Dame-de-Lorette, 9ᵉ. Mᵒ St-Georges. ☎48.78.60.47. Acceptable, if uninspired; has some cheaper rooms.

Parrotel Paris-Montholon, 11bis rue Pierre-Sémard, 9ᵉ. Mᵒ Poissonnière. ☎48.78.28.94. Not bad at all, though the rooms are a little small and dark.

Victoria Hôtel, 2bis Cité Bergère, 9ᵉ. Mᵒ Montmartre. ☎47.70.18.83. Situated in quiet, pleasant courtyard opposite *Chartier's* restaurant, along with several other slightly overpriced touristy hotels.

10ᵉ

UNDER 200F

Hôtel du Centre Est, 4 rue Sibour, 10ᵉ. Mᵒ Gare de l'Est. ☎46.07.20.74. An excellent value cheapie, but you'll generally need to book. Some rooms a little over 200F.

Hôtel des Familles, 216 rue du Faubourg-St-Denis, 10ᵉ. Mᵒ Gare-du-Nord/Chapelle. ☎46.07.76.56. A rather large and gloomy place, but cheap, and close to the Nord and Est stations.

Hôtel du Jura, 6 rue de Jarry, 10ᵉ. Mᵒ Gare-de-l'Est, Château-d'Eau. ☎47.70.06.66. Primitive, but friendly and decent.

Hôtel Pierre Dupont, 1 rue Pierre-Dupont, 10ᵉ. Mᵒ Château-Landon/Gare-de-l'Est. ☎42.06.93.66.

Primitive but okay, in a quiet working-class street by the canal. Some slightly more expensive rooms.

Hôtel Savoy, 9 rue Jarry, 10ᵉ. Mº Gare-de-l'Est, Château-d'Eau,. ☎47.70.03.72. Cramped and basic and still under 120F.

UP TO 350F

Adix Hôtel, 30 rue Lucien-Sampaix, 10ᵉ. Mº Bonsergent. ☎42.08.19.74. In a pleasant street close to the St-Martin canal and surprisingly elegant for the area.

City Hôtel Gare de l'Est, 5 rue St-Laurent, 10ᵉ. Mº Gare-de-l'Est. ☎42.09.83.50. Recently modernized: comfortable enough anchorage close to the stations. Some fine views from the top floor.

Grand Hôtel de Famille, 46 rue Lucien-Sampaix, 10ᵉ. Mº Gare-de-l'Est. ☎46.07.23.87. A rather gloomy old-fashioned barrack, but good value—located on the St-Martin canal bank.

National Hôtel, 224 rue du Faubourg-St-Denis, 10ᵉ. Mº Gare-du-Nord/La Chapelle. ☎42.06.99.56. Unfriendly but convenient shelter near the Nord and Est stations.

11ᵉ

UNDER 200F

Hôtel Central Bastille, 16 rue de la Roquette, 11ᵉ. Mº Bastille. ☎47.00.31.51. Basic: adequate.

Hôtel de l'Europe, 74 rue Sedaine, 11ᵉ. Mº Voltaire. ☎47.00.54.38. Basic.

Luna Park Hôtel, 1 rue Jacquard, 11ᵉ. Mº Parmentier. ☎48.05.65.50. Good enough for sleeping. The street is quiet, the location interesting. Rooms range from 95F to 280F.

Hôtel Rhetia, 3 rue du Général-Blaise, 11ᵉ. Mº St-Ambroise. ☎47.00.47.18. Basic—on a pleasant square.

Hôtel de Vienne, 43 rue de Malte, 11ᵉ. Mº Oberkampf. ☎48.05.44.42. A pleasant good-value cheapie.

UP TO 350F

Hôtel Baudin, 113 av Ledru-Rollin, 11ᵉ. Mº Ledru-Rollin. ☎47.00.18.91. Clean and pleasant. Traffic noise could be bothersome. Some cheaper rooms.

Hôtel Beaumarchais, 3 rue Oberkampf, 11ᵉ. Mº Filles-du-Calvaire. ☎43.38.16.16. Clean and modern, in a good area.

Cosmo's Hotel, 35 rue Jean-Pierre Timbaud, 11ᵉ. Mº Parmentier. ☎43.57.25.88. Clean and nice, and near some good restaurants.

Garden Hôtel, 1 rue du Général-Blaise, 11ᵉ. Mº St-Ambroise. ☎47.00.57.93. Comfortable but a little overpriced. On the pleasant Square Parmentier.

Hôtel Parmentier, 91 rue Oberkampf, 11ᵉ. Mº Parmentier. ☎43.57.02.09. Clean and friendly and scarcely more than 200F. Better to get a room on the *cour* if you can; the street side is a little noisy.

Plessis-Hôtel, 25 rue du Grand-Prieuré, 11ᵉ. Mº République/Oberkampf. ☎47.00.13.38. A friendly, good-value hotel.

Hôtel St-Martin, 12 rue Léon-Frot, 11ᵉ. Mº Boulets-Montreuil. ☎43.71.09.14. Rather boring neighborhood, but the hotel is nice enough—friendly and newly renovated.

12ᵉ

UNDER 200F

Hôtel du Centre, 112 rue de Charenton, 12ᵉ. Mº Gare-de-Lyon. ☎43.43.02.94. A little gloomy, but not bad—with some rooms over 200F.

Mistral Hôtel, 3 rue Chaligny, 12ᵉ. Mº Faidherbe-Chaligny. ☎46.28.10.20. Cheap and basic.

UP TO 350F

Grand Hôtel du Bel-Air, 102 bd de Picpus, 12ᵉ. Mº Nation. ☎43.45.30.51. Perfectly adequate, if charmless. Some singles under 200F.

Grand Hôtel de Cognac, 8 cours de Vincennes, 12ᵉ. Mº Nation. ☎43.45.13.53. Slightly more expensive, but with a great deal more charm than the others in this group.

Hôtel des Pyrénées, 204 rue du Faubourg-St-Antoine, 12ᵉ. Mº Faidherbe-Chaligny. ☎43.72.07.46. Comfortable and quiet behind its fancy reception area.

13ᵉ

UNDER 200F

Victoria Hôtel, 47 rue Bobillot, 13ᵉ. Mº Place-d'Italie. ☎45.80.59.88. Basic.

Hôtel de la Place des Alpes, 2 place des Alpes, 13ᵉ. Mº Place-d'Italie. ☎45.35.14.14. An agreeable establishment, with some rooms over the 200F mark.

HÔtel de Bourgogne, 15 rue Godefroy, 13ᵉ. Mᵒ Place-d'Italie. ☎45.35.37.92. Friendly and adequate. A few doubles over 200F.

UP TO 350F

Hôtel Verlaine, 51 rue Bobillot, 13ᵉ. Mᵒ Place-d'Italie. ☎45.89.56.14. Comfortable and clean.

14ᵉ
UNDER 200F

Hôtel Clairefontaine, 11 rue Fermat, 14ᵉ. Mᵒ Denfert-Rochereau/Gaîté. ☎43.22.05.20. Basic. Just behind Montparnasse cemetery.

UP TO 350F

Le Central-Hôtel, 1bis rue du Maine, 14ᵉ. Mᵒ Montparnasse/Edgar-Quinet. ☎43.20.69.15. On a convenient quiet square behind Montparnasse.

Hôtel du Parc, 6 rue Jolivet, 14ᵉ. Mᵒ Montparnasse/Edgar-Quinet. ☎43.20.95.54. In the same square as above. Clean rooms and a very nice *patron*. Try before the *Central*.

15ᵉ
UNDER 200F

Mondial Hôtel, 136 bd de Grenelle, 15ᵉ. Mᵒ La Motte-Picquet. ☎45.79.73.57. Simple lodgings for workers and commercial travelers. Friendly and decent. Right under the relevated métro.

UP TO 350F

Hôtel Ini, 159 bd Lefebvre, 15ᵉ. Mᵒ Porte-de-Vanves. ☎48.28.18.35. Comfortable rooms, but the location on the *boulevard périphérique* is dull.

Pratic Hôtel, 20 rue de l'Ingénieur-Keller, 15ᵉ. Mᵒ Charles-Michels. ☎45.77.70.58. Very nice: clean and friendly—with several rooms under 200F. Close to the Eiffel Tower.

Hôtel Printania, 142 bd de Grenelle, 15ᵉ. Mᵒ La Motte-Picquet. ☎45.79.23.97. Overlooking the elevated métro. A bit worn and dingy, but not bad.

Tourisme Hôtel, 66 av de la Motte-Picquet 15ᵉ. Mᵒ La Motte-Picquet. ☎47.34.28.01. Unprepossessing barrack-like building on the corner of bd de Grenelle, but the rooms are fine.

17ᵉ
UNDER 200F

Hôtel Avenir-Jonquière, 23 rue de la Jonquière, 17ᵉ. Mᵒ Guy-Môquet. ☎46.27.83.41. Clean, friendly establishment. Good bargain.

Batignolles Hôtel, 46 rue de la Jonquière, 17ᵉ. Mᵒ Guy-Môquet. ☎46.27.64.67. Basic—nothing over 130F.

Hôtel Bélidor, 5 rue Bélidor, 17ᵉ. Mᵒ Porte-Maillot and RER *ligne A*. ☎45.74.49.91. Clean and cheerful, with some rooms over 200F. Good value and not as far away as it might appear.

Hôtel Gauthey, 5 rue Gauthey, 17ᵉ. Mᵒ Brochant. ☎46.27.15.48. Simple and clean.

UP TO 350F

Hôtel des Batignolles, 26–28 rue des Batignolles, 17ᵉ. Mᵒ Rome/Place-Clichy. ☎43.87.70.40. A quiet and very reasonable establishment in a neighborhood that prides itself on its village character. Some cheaper rooms. Good value.

Lévis-Hôtel, 16 rue Lebouteux, 17ᵉ. Mᵒ Villiers. ☎47.63.86.38. Only ten rooms, but very nice, clean, and quiet, in small side street off the rue de Lévis market. Prices at the top of this category.

Ouest Hôtel, 115 rue de Rome, 17ᵉ. Mᵒ Rome/Villiers. ☎42.27.50.29. A somewhat charmless building, but it has the romance of being alongside the railroad tracks that divide the Beaux Quartiers from the downmarket north of Paris, and is perfectly sound-proofed for undisturbed sleep.

UP TO 500F

Hôtel du Roi René, 72 place Félix-Lobligeois, 17ᵉ. Mᵒ Rome/Villiers. ☎42.26.72.73. Doubles 420F, singles cheaper. Very nice location by a mini-Greek temple and public garden.

18ᵉ
UNDER 200F

Idéal Hôtel, 3 rue des Trois-Frères, 18ᵉ. Mᵒ Abbesses. ☎46.06.63.63. Marvelous location on the slopes of Montmartre. Cheap and clean. A real bargain.

Hôtel Tholozé, 24 rue Tholozé, 18ᵉ. Mᵒ Blanche/Abbesses. ☎46.06.74.83. Another real bargain—clean, friendly, and quiet, in a steep, quiet street below the Moulin de la Galette.

UP TO 350F

Hôtel André Gill, 4 rue André-Gill, 18ᵉ. Mᵒ Pigalle/Abbesses. ☎42.62.48.48. Prices at bottom of range for very adequate rooms in a great location on the slopes of Montmartre. Quiet too, in a dead-end alley off rue des Martyrs.

Hôtel Regyn's, 18 place des Abbesses, 18ᵉ. Mᵒ Abbesses. ☎42.54.45.21. Superb site, and lovely views across the city. Comfortable and relaxed, with doubles just a little over 350F.

UP TO 500F

La Résidence Montmartre, 10 rue Burcq, 18ᵉ. Mᵒ Abbesses. ☎46.06.45.28. Comfortable, quiet, and slightly more upmarket Montmartre hotel.

20ᵉ

UNDER 200F

Ermitage Hôtel, 42bis rue de l'Ermitage, 20ᵉ. Mᵒ Jourdain. ☎46.36.23.44. A clean and proper hotel, close to the leafy, provincial rue des Pyrénées.

Mary's, 118 rue Orfila, 20ᵉ. Mᵒ Pelleport. ☎43.61.51.68. Simple, clean, and friendly. A little far out, at the rue Pelleport end of rue Orfila.

Printana Hôtel, 355 rue des Pyrénées, 20ᵉ. Mᵒ Jourdain. ☎46.36.76.62. Perfectly adequate, if somewhat charmless.

UP TO 350F

Hôtel Nadaud, 8 rue de la Bidassoa, 20ᵉ. Mᵒ Gambetta. ☎46.36.87.79. Closed in August. A very reasonable hotel, close to the Père-Lachaise cemetery.

CHAPTER ONE

MONUMENTAL PARIS

Monumental Paris is the French state in essence, and in fact. It contains the government and parliament, the law courts and police HQ, the Bank of France and stock exchange, the top treasures of the nation, the cathedral, the original opera, and—universal symbol of the city—the Eiffel Tower. And what is more, the buildings that house these make up the very fabric of Paris at its

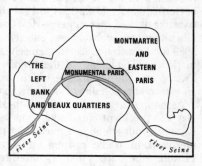

center. It matters not that some are medieval, some are steel, and some are still being built—nothing has scaled down the perspectives or rendered archaic the Neoclassical arrangements of a hundred years ago.

It's the Paris you can't help but see, though it's not all majestic masonry and monolithic streets. Parts of the 2e and 3e *arrondissements* are definitely seedy; the **Île St-Louis and Marais** are cool, quiet, and free of boulevards; the best of food and fashion is to be found near the **Champs-Élysées**; jazz clubs haunt **Les Halles**. Cars and people are on the move 24 hours a day and there's plenty to entertain diverse tastes.

The Champs-Élysées

La Voie Triomphale, or Triumphal Way, stretches ,in a dead straight line from the eastern end of the Louvre to the modern complex of corporate skyscrapers at La Défense, nine kilometers away. It incorporates some of the city's most famous landmarks—the **Champs-Élysées**, the **Arc de Triomphe**, the **Louvre**, and the **Tuileries**. Its monumental constructions have been erected over the centuries by kings and emperors, presidents and corporations, to propagate French power and prestige.

The tradition dies hard. Further self-aggrandisement has recently been given expression in an enormous, marble-clad cubic arch at the head of La Défense, and a **glass pyramid** entrance in the central courtyard of the much-expanded Louvre. This latter project involved moving the Ministry of Finance out of the Louvre into vast new offices in the 12e *arrondissement*, and digging up and rebuilding the foundations of the original medieval Louvre fortress.

The Arc de Triomphe and Place de la Concorde

The best view of this grandiose and simple geometry of kings to capital is from the top of the **Arc de Triomphe**, Napoléon's homage to the armies of France and himself (10am–5pm; 27F, 15F for under-24s, 5F for under-7s; access from stairs on north corner of av des Champs-Élysées). The emperor and his two royal successors spent 10 million francs between them on this edifice, which victorious foreign armies would later use to humiliate the French. After the Prussians' triumphal march in 1871 the Parisians lit bonfires beneath the arch and down the Champs-Élysées to purify the stain of German boots. From 1941 to 1944 Hitler's troops paraded daily around the swastika-decked monument—de Gaulle's arrival at the scene come Liberation was probably less effective than the earlier ashes and flames. In 1989 the French humiliated themselves with their grand parade of nations to mark the bicentennial of the French Revolution. The symbol chosen for France was the locomotive which features in Émile Zola's novel, *La Bête Humaine*, about a railroad worker who murders his wife.

Assuming there are no bizarre theatricals or armies in sight (on Bastille Day the president plus tanks, guns, and flags proceed down the Champs-Élysées), your attention is most likely to be caught not by the view but by the mesmerizing traffic movements directly below you around **place de l'Étoile**—the world's first organized traffic circle. Of the twelve fat avenues making up the star (*étoile*), the one which disgorges and gobbles the most motors is the avenue des Champs-Élysées. Its graceful gradients, like a landing flightpath, finish up eastwards at **place de la Concorde**, where the same crazy vehicles make crossing over to the middle a death-defying task.

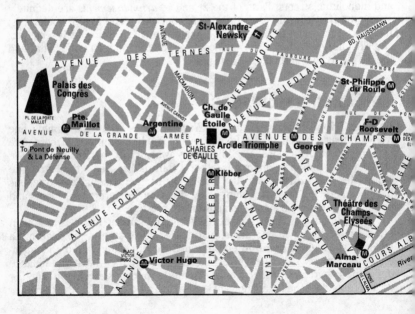

As it happens, some 1300 people did die here between 1793 and 1795, beneath the Revolutionary guillotine: Louis XVI, Marie-Antoinette, Danton, and Robespierre among them. The centerpiece of the *place*, chosen like its name to make no comment on these events, is an **obelisk from the temple of Luxor**, offered as a favor-currying gesture by the viceroy of Egypt in 1829. It serves merely to pivot more geometry: the alignment of the French parliament, the **Assemblée Nationale**, on the far side of the Seine with the church of the Madeleine to the north. Needless to say, it cuts the Voie Triomphale at a precise and predictable right angle. And the symmetry continues beyond the *place* in the formal layout of the **Tuileries Gardens**, disrupted only by the bodies lounging on the grass, kids chasing their boats round the ponds, and gays cruising near the **Orangerie** (see *Museums*) at one end of the western terrace.

Along the Champs-Élysées
Since everything on the Voie Triomphale must maintain the myth of Paris as the world's state-of-the-art capital, plans are afoot for major works on the **Tuileries Gardens**. The Chinese architect of the Pyramid, Ieoh Ming Pei, will be in charge and the as-yet-unveiled scheme is to include a footbridge across the river to the Musée d'Orsay.

The **Jeu de Paume**, empty since its Impressionists moved across the river, is in the process of becoming a gallery for contemporary art. Workers gutting the interior claimed to have found an eighteenth-century tennis ball in the rafters—a wild shot from the building's earliest days as a royal tennis court.

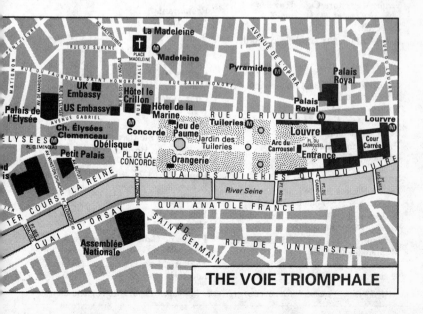

THE VOIE TRIOMPHALE

Back to the west, between Concorde and the Rond-Point traffic circle, whose Lalique glass fountains disappeared during the German occupation, the Champs-Élysées is bordered by chestnut trees and municipal flower beds, pleasant enough to stroll among but not sufficiently dense to muffle the discomforting squeal of accelerating tires. The two massive buildings rising above the greenery to the south are the **Grand and Petit Palais**, with their overloaded Neoclassical exteriors, railroad-station roofs, and exuberantly optimistic flying statuary. On the north side, combat police guard the high walls round the presidential **Élysée palace** and the line of ministries and embassies ending with the US in prime position on the corner of place de la Concorde. On Thursday and at weekends you can see a stranger manifestation of the self-images of states in the **postage stamp market** at the corner of avenues Gabriel and Marigny.

Though the glamour of the Champs-Élysées is not what it was, with airline offices, car showrooms, and brightly lit shopping arcades now dominant, there are still the *Lido* cabaret, *Fouquet's* high-class bar and restaurant, and plenty of movie theaters and outrageously priced cafés to bring the customers in. At Christmas this is where the fairy lights go, and on December 31 it's the equivalent of Times Square with everyone happily jammed, in their cars rather than on foot, hooting in the New Year.

Champs-Élysées: Listings

Cafés

Le Fouquet's, 99 av des Champs-Élysées, 8e. Mº George-V.

Virgin Megastore Café, 52 av des Champs-Élysées, 8e. Mº Franklin-Roosevelt.

Hôtel Crillon, 10 place de la Concorde, 8e. Mº Concorde.

Bars

Ma Bourgogne, 133 bd Haussmann, 8e. Mº Miromesnil.

L'Écluse, rue Mondétour, 1er (Mº Étienne-Marcel) and 64 rue François-1er, 8e (Mº Franklin-Roosevelt).

Pub Winston Churchill, 5 rue Presbourg, 16e. Mº Étoile.

Snacks

La Boutique à Sandwiches, 12 rue du Colisée, 8e. Mº St-Philippe-du-Roule.

Drugstore Elysées, 133 av des Champs-Élysées, 8e. Mº Étoile.

Drugstore Matignon, 1 av Matignon, 8e. Mº Franklin-Roosevelt.

Fauchon, 24 place de la Madeleine, 8e. Mº Madeleine.

Lord Sandwich, 276 rue St-Honoré, 1er, and 134 rue du Faubourg-St-Honoré, 8e. Mº Palais-Royal/St-Philippe-du-Roule.

Restaurants
Under 80F

Bistro de la Gare, 73 av des Champs-Élysées, 8e. Mº Franklin-Roosevelt.

Le Bistro Romain, 122 av des Champs-Élysées, 8e (Mº George-V) and place Victor-Hugo, 16e (Mº Victor-Hugo).

Chez Mélanie, 27 rue du Colisée, 8e. Mº Franklin-Roosevelt.

Under 150F

Le Daru, 19 rue Daru, 8e. Mº Courcelles.

La Fermette Marbeuf, 5 rue Marbeuf, 8e. Mº Franklin-Roosevelt.

Pépita, 21 rue Bayard, 8e. Mº Franklin-Roosevelt.

Over 150F

Fouquet's, 99 av des Champs-Élysées, 8e. Mº George-V.

Prince de Galles, 33 av George V, 8e. Mº George-V.

Yakitori, 24 rue Marbeuf, 8e. Mº Franklin-Roosevelt.

All the establishments listed above are reviewed in Chapter Eight, Drinking and Eating.

La Défense

La Grande Arche has put La Défense high on the list of places to which visitors to Paris must pay homage. It is a beautiful and astounding structure, a 112-meter hollow cube, clad in white marble and angled a few degrees out from the Voie Triumphale. Suspended within the hollow, which could enclose Notre-Dame with ease, are the open lift shafts and a "cloud" panoply. Unlike other new Parisian monuments, La Grande Arche is a pure and graceful example of design wedded to innovative engineering, putting it on a par with the Eiffel Tower. The Danish architect, Johan Otto von Spreckelsen, died before the building was completed—it was originally intended for the 1989 Bicentennial, but squabbles between Chirac and Mitterrand over its use delayed the project. It now houses a government ministry, international businesses, and, in the roof section, the *Arche de la Fraternité* foundation which stages exhibitions and conferences on issues related to human rights.

You can ride up to *le Toit* for 30F (15F for students, senior citizens, and the unemployed; July & Aug Mon & Thurs 9am–7pm, Tues & Wed 9am–5pm, Fri 9am–9pm, Sat 10am–9pm, Sun 10am–7pm; otherwise Mon–Fri 9am–5pm, Sat & Sun 10am–7pm). As well as having access to the *Arche de la Fraternité* exhibitions, you can admire the "Map of the Heavens" marble patios by Jean-Pierre Raynaud, and, on a clear day, scan from the marble path on the *parvis* below you to the Arc de Triomphe and beyond to the Louvre.

Around the Complex

Back on the ground, with La Grande Arche behind you, an extraordinary monument to twentieth-century capitalism stands before and above you. There is no formal pattern to the arrangement of towers. Token apartment blocks, offices of **ELF**, **Esso**, **IBM**, banks, and other businesses compete for size, dazzle of surface, and ability to make you dizzy. Finance made flesh, they are worth the trip out in themselves.

Mercifully, too, **bizarre artworks** transform the nightmare into comic entertainment. **Joan Miro**'s giant wobbly creatures despair at their misfit status beneath the biting edges and curveless heights of the buildings. Opposite, **Alexander Calder**'s red iron offering is a **stabile** rather than a mobile and between them a black marble metronome shape without a beat releases a goal-less line across the *parvis*. **Torricini**'s huge **fat frog** screams to escape to a nice quiet pond. A statue commemorating the **defense of Paris** in 1870 (from which the district takes its name) perches on a concrete plinth in front of a colored plastic waterfall and fountain pool, and nearer the river disembodied people clutch each other around endlessly repeated concrete flowerbeds.

Inside the public buildings, **Art Défense**, alongside Agam's waterworks, displays models and photographs of the artworks and a map for locating them (daily 10am–7pm), as well as temporary art exhibitions (Wed–Mon noon–7pm). The **CNIT building** next to La Grande Arche is also worth wandering into. It's a bit like a covered stadium with businesses instead of seats. The field, all gleaming granite, is softened by slender bamboo trees; all

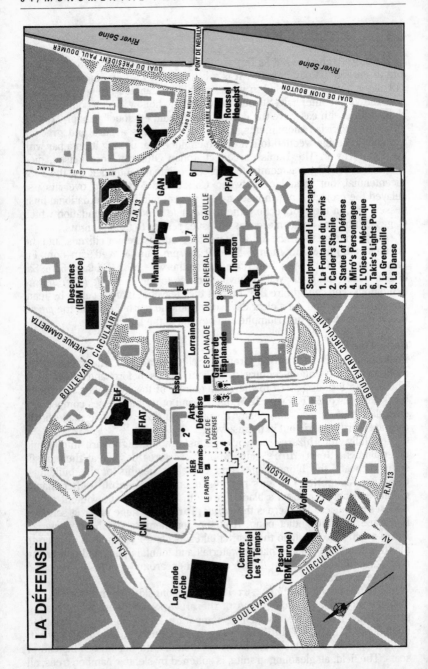

LA DÉFENSE

Sculptures and Landscapes:
1. La Fontaine du Parvis
2. Calder's Stabile
3. Statue of La Défense
4. L'Oiseau Mécanique
5. Miró's Personnages
6. Takis's Lights Pond
7. La Grenouille
8. La Danse

River Seine

River Seine

PONT DE NEUILLY

QUAI DU PRÉSIDENT PAUL DOUMER

QUAI DE DION BOUTON

Assur

Roussel
Hoechst

GAN

PFA

6

Manhattan

7

Thomson

Descartes
(IBM France)

Lorraine

8

Total

5

Esso

ELF

FIAT

Galerie de
l'Esplanade

1

3

Arts
Défense

2

4

RER
Entrance

PLACE DE
LA DÉFENSE

Bull

CNIT

LE PARVIS

WILSON

Voltaire

La Grande
Arche

Centre
Commercial
Les 4 Temps

Pascal
(IBM Europe)

BOULEVARD

CIRCULAIRE

AV.

DU

R.N. 13

ESPLANADE DU GÉNÉRAL DE GAULLE

BOULEVARD CIRCULAIRE

AVENUE GAMBETTA

BOULEVARD CIRCULAIRE

R.N. 13

R.N. 13

R.N. 13

BOULEVARD DE NEUILLY

BOULEVARD PIERRE GAUDIN

RUE LOUIS BLANC

PT. DU

the serious activity takes place beyond the farther goal in the offices of every major computer company. There's one of the big *FNAC* bookstores here, along with overpriced cafés and brasseries. Less damaging to the pocket, though unhealthy for the soul, is the **Quatre-Temps** commercial center, the biggest of its ilk in Europe, across the *parvis*, opposite. To minimize the encounter, enter from the left-hand doors, and you'll find crêperies, pizzerias, and cafés without having to leave ground level.

Access
La Défense lies one **RER** stop beyond Charles-de-Gaulle-Étoile. Follow the exit signs for La Grande Arche, avoiding at all costs the snare of *Quatre-Temps*.

The Passages and Right Bank Commerce

In the narrow streets of the 1er and 2e *arrondissements*, between **the Louvre** and bds **Haussmann**, **Montmartre**, and **Poissonnière**, the grandiose financial, cultural, and political state institutions are surrounded by well-established commerce—the rag trade, newspapers, sex, and well-heeled shopping. A few years ago, the greatest contrast to the hulks of the Bourse, Banque de France, Bibliothèque Nationale, etc, were the crumbling and secretive **Passages**, shopping arcades long predating the concept of pedestrian malls, with glass roofs, tiled floors, and unobtrusive entrances. Almost all have now been rendered chic and immaculate—as they originally were, in the nineteenth century—with mega-premiums on their leases.

The Passages
Foremost among the Passages is the **Galerie Vivienne** (between rue Vivienne and rue des Petits-Champs) with its flamboyant décor of Grecian and marine motifs enticing you to buy Jean-Paul Gaultier or Yuki Torri gear. The neighboring **Galerie Colbert**, gorgeously lit by bunches of bulbous lamps, has become a showcase extension for the Bibliothèque Nationale. But the best stylistically are the dilapidated three-story **passage du Grand-Cerf** (at the bottom of rue St-Denis) and **Galerie Véro-Dodat** (off rue Croix-des-Petits-Champs), named after the two pork butchers who set it up in 1824. This last is the most homogeneous and aristocratic of the Passages, with painted ceilings and paneled storefronts divided by black marble columns. At no. 26, Monsieur Capia keeps a collection of antique dolls in a shop piled high with miscellaneous curios.

North of rue St-Marc the grid of arcades round the **passage des Panoramas** are still a touch dilapidated with no fancy mosaics for your feet. An old brasserie with carved wood paneling has been restored, and new restaurants are moving in, but there are still bric-à-brac shops, bars, stamp dealers, and an upper-crust printshop, with its original 1867 fittings. In **passage Jouffroy** across bd Montmartre, an M. Segas sells walking canes and theatrical antiques opposite a North African and Asian carpet emporium, and Paul Vulin spreads his secondhand books along the passageway.

Crossing rue de la Grange-Batelière, you enter **Passage Verdeau** where the old comic and camera dealers have been replaced by art galleries and a specialist in Tintin paraphernalia. The tiny passage des Princes at the top of rue Richelieu has been stripped and awaits its re-gentrification. Its erstwhile neighbor, the passage de l'Opéra, described in surreal detail by Louis Aragon in *Paris Peasant*, was eaten up by the completion of Haussmann's boulevards.

While in this area you could also take a look at what's up for auction at the Paris equivalent of Christie's and Sotheby's, the **Hôtel Drouot** (9 rue Drouot; Mº Le Pelletier/Richelieu-Drouot). Details of the auctions are announced in the listings magazines, *Pariscope*, etc, under *Ventes aux Enchères*, and in the press. To spare any fear of unintended hand movements landing you in the bankruptcy courts, you can wander around looking at the goods before the action starts: 11am–6pm on the eve of the sale, 11am–noon on the day itself.

Place du Caire: the Rag and Frock Trade

Mass-produced clothes rather than one-off Persian carpets is the business of **place du Caire**, the center of the rag-trade district. The frenetic trading and deliveries of cloth, the food market on rue des Petits-Carreaux, and general toing and froing make a lively change from the office-bound quarters farther west. Beneath an extraordinary pseudo-Egyptian façade of grotesque Pharaonic heads (a celebration of Napoléon's conquest of Egypt), an archway opens on to a series of arcades, the **Passage du Caire**. These, contrary to any visible evidence, are the oldest of all the Passages and entirely monopolized by wholesale clothes shops.

The garment business gets progressively more upmarket westwards from the trade area. The upper end of **rue Étienne-Marcel**, and Louis XIV's **place des Victoires**, adjoined to the north by the appealingly unsymmetrical **place des Petits-Pères**, are the center for new-name designer clothes, displayed to deter all those without the necessary funds. The boutiques on **rue St-Honoré** and its Faubourg extension have the established names, paralleled across the Champs-Élysées by **rue François-1er**, where Dior has at least four blocks on the corner with av Montaigne. The autocratic **place Vendôme**, with Napoléon high on a column clad with recycled Austro-Russian cannons (the felling of which was a major morale boost during the Commune), caters to the same class. Here you have all the fashionable accessories for haute couture—jewelry, perfumes, the original Ritz, a Rothschilds office, and the Law and Order ministry. The need for more underground parking space for the customized BMWs and Citröen Prestiges means that the center of the square is under wraps until July 1992.

The 1er and 2e *Arrondissements*: Sex, Stocks, and Shares

After clothes, bodies are the most evident commodity on sale in the **1er and 2e arrondissements**, on rue St-Denis above all. In the mid-Seventies prostitutes from all over Paris occupied churches and marched down this street demanding, among other things, union recognition. That they got, but the power of the pimps has never been broken and the opiate-glazed eyes of so many of the women indicate the doubly vicious bind in which they're trapped. The pimps get richer toward the Madeleine while around rue Ste-Anne business is less blatant, being gay, transvestite, and under-age. For the kids, reaching the age of 13 or 14 means redundancy. Such are the libertarian delights of Paris streetlife.

In the center of the 2^e stands the **Bourse**—the scene for dealing in stocks and shares, dollars, and gold. The classical order of the façade utterly belies the scene within, like an unruly boys' private school, with creaking floors, tottering pigeonholes, and people scuttling about with bits of paper. There's hardly a computer in sight and the real financial sharks go elsewhere for their deals.

The status of the City of London is the French no. 2 grudge after the dominance of the English language, so plans to modernize the Bourse are always being promised. In the meantime, the efficiency of the antennae-topped building of the French news agency AFP, overshadowing the Bourse from the south, is far more convincing.

Place Madeleine and the Opéra

Another obese Napoleonic structure on the classical temple model is the **church of the Madeleine**, which serves for snob society weddings and for the perspective across place de la Concorde. There's a **flower market** every day except Monday along the east side of the church and a luxurious **Art Nouveau** toilet by the métro at the junction of place and bd Madeleine. But the greatest appeal of the square is for rich or window-gazing gourmets. In the northeast corner are two blocks of the best **food display** in Paris—at *Fauchon's*—and down the west side the smaller *Hédiard's*, plus caviar, truffle, and spirit specialists (see p.200). If you just want a cheap midday meal, try rue des Capucines off bd Madeleine at the point where it becomes bd des Capucines.

It was at 35 bd des Capucines, in Nadar's studio, that the first Impressionist exhibition was shown to an outraged art world. As one critic said of Monet's *Impression: Soleil Levant*, "it was worse than anyone had hitherto dared to paint." That was in 1874, only a year before the most preposterous building in Paris, at the far end of the boulevard, was finally completed—the **Opéra de Paris**. Its architect, Charles Garnier, looks suitably foolish in a golden statue on the rue Auber side of his edifice, that so perfectly suited the by-then defunct court of Napoléon III. Excessively ornate and covering three acres in extent, it provided ample space for aristocratic preening, ceremonial pomp, and the social intercourse of opera-goers, for whom the performance itself was a very secondary matter. These days, with the Bastille opera open, the Opéra Garnier—as this is now called—is used almost exclusively for ballet. By day you can visit the interior (11am–5pm), including the auditorium, where the ceiling is the work of Chagall. The classic horror movie, *The Phantom of the Opera*, was set, though never filmed, here; a real underground stream lends credence to the tale.

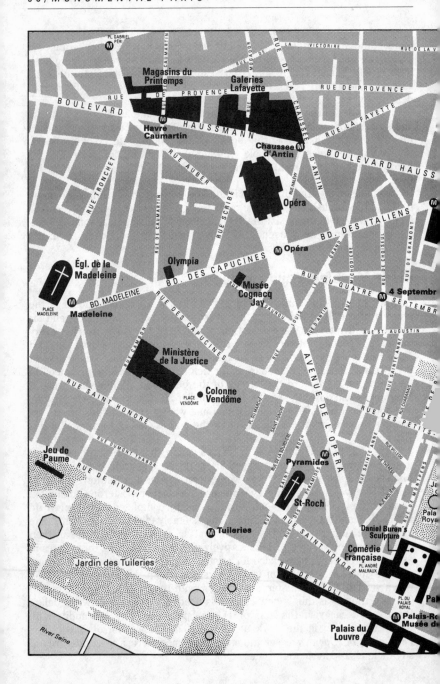

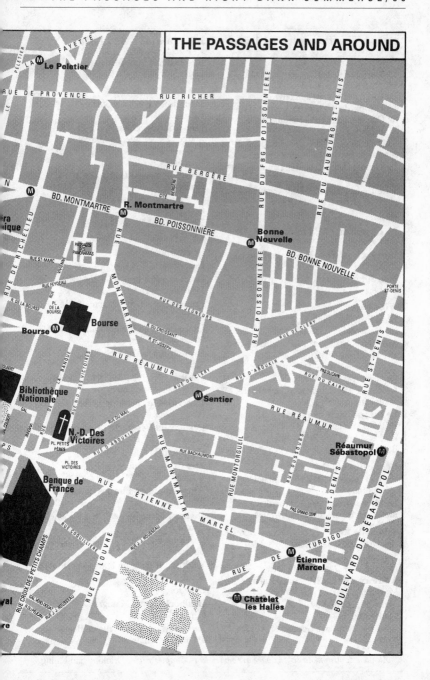

THE PASSAGES AND AROUND

The Passages and Right Bank Commerce: Listings

Cafés

Le Bar de l'Entracte, corner of rue Montpensier and rue Beaujolais, 1er. Mº Palais-Royal/Musée-du-Louvre.

La Chope du Croissant, corner of rue du Croissant and rue Montmartre, 2e. Mº Montmartre.

Café de la Comédie, 153 rue Rivoli, 1er. Mº Palais-Royal/Musée-du-Louvre.

Le Grand Café, 40 bd des Capucines, 9e. Mº Opéra.

Café de la Paix, 12 bd des Capucines/place de l'Opéra, 9e. Mº Opéra.

Bars

La Champsmeslé, 4 rue Chabanais, 2e. Mº Pyramides.

Harry's New York Bar, 5 rue Daunou, 2e. Mº Opéra.

Tigh Johnny, 55 rue Montmartre, 2e. Mº Sentier.

Wine bars

Blue Fox, Cité Berryer, 25 rue Royale, 8e. Mº Madeleine.

Aux Bons Crus, 7 rue des Petits-Champs, 1er. Mº Palais-Royal.

Cave Drouot, 8 rue Drouot, 9e. Mº Richelieu-Drouot.

L'Écluse, 15 place de la Madeleine, 8e. Mº Madeleine.

Le Rubis, 10 rue du Marché-St-Honoré, 1er. Mº Pyramides.

Willi's, 13 rue des Petits-Champs, 1er. Mº Bourse.

Beer cellars/pubs

Kitty O'Shea's, 10 rue des Capucines, 2e. Mº Opéra.

La Micro-Brasserie, 106 rue de Richelieu, 2e. Mº Richelieu-Drouot.

Salons de thé

Angélina, 226 rue de Rivoli, 1er. Mº Tuileries.

Daru, 19 rue Daru, 8e. Mº Ternes.

A Priori Thé, 35–37 galerie Vivienne, 2e. Mº Bourse.

Ladurée, 16 rue Royale, 9e. Mº Madeleine.

Pantera, 2 impasse Gomboust, 1er. Mº Pyramides.

Rose Thé, 91 rue St-Honoré, 1er. Mº Louvre-Rivoli.

Snacks

Jarmolinska, 272 rue St-Honoré, 1er. Mº Palais-Royal.

Lina's Sandwiches, 50 rue Étienne-Marcel, 2e. Mº Étienne-Marcel.

Monoprix, 23 av de l'Opéra, 1er. Mº Pyramides.

Osaka, 1 impasse Gomboust, 1er. Mº Pyramides.

La Patata, 25 bd des Italiens, 2e. Mº Opéra.

Ramen-Tei, 163 rue St-Honoré, 1er. Mº Palais-Royal.

Restaurants

Under 80F

Le Bistro Romain, 9 bd des Italiens, 2e. Mº Richelieu-Drouot.

Country Life, 6 rue Daunou, 2e. Mº Opéra.

La Criée, 31 bd Bonne-Nouvelle, 2e. Mº Strasbourg-St-Denis.

Drouot, 103 rue de Richelieu, 2e. Mº Richelieu-Drouot.

Foujita, 45 rue St-Roch, 1er. Mº Palais-Royal/Musée-du-Louvre.

L'Incroyable, 26 rue de Richelieu, 1er. Mº Palais-Royal.

Restaurant Végétarien Lacour, 3 rue Villedo, 1er. Mº Pyramides.

Under 150F

Aux Crus de Bourgogne, 2 rue Bachaumont, 2e. Mº Sentier.

Hippopotamus, 1 bd des Capucines, 9e. Mº Opéra.

Jhelum, 30 rue St-Marc, 2e. Mº Richelieu-Drouot.

Le Vaudeville, 29 rue Vivienne, 2e. Mº Bourse.

Yakitori, 34 place du Marché-St-Honoré, 2e. Mº Pyramides.

Over 150F

Baalbeck, 16 rue Mazagran, 10e. Mº Bonne-Nouvelle.

Le Grand Véfour, 17 rue de Beaujolais, 1er. Mº Pyramides.

All the establishments listed above are reviewed in Chapter Eight, Drinking and Eating.

Palais Royal

The av de l'Opéra was built at the same time as its namesake—and left deliberately bereft of trees which might mask the vista of the Opéra. It leads down to the **Palais Royal**, originally Richelieu's residence, which now houses various government and constitutional bodies, and the **Comédie Française** where the classics of French theater are performed.

The palace **gardens** to the north were once the gastronomic, gambling, and amusement hot spot of Paris. There was even a *café mécanique* where you sat at a table and sent your order down one of its legs, and were served via the other. The prohibition on public gambling in 1838 put an end to the fun, but the flats above the empty cafés remained desirable lodgings for the likes of Cocteau and Colette.

Folly has returned to the *palais* itself, however, in the form of **black and white pillars** in different sizes standing above flowing water in the main courtyard. The artist responsible, **Daniel Buren**, was commissioned in 1982 by the socialist Minister of Culture. His Chirac-ian successor's decision to let the work go ahead caused paroxysms among self-styled guardians of the city's heritage and set an interesting precedent. After a legal wrangle, the court ruled that artists had the right to complete their creations.

Kids use the monochrome pillars as an adventure playground, the best game being to fish out the coins that people throw into the water. The gardens of the palace remain austere, though new shops have opened in the arcades. It's a useful shortcut from the Louvre to rue des Petits-Champs, and a certain charm lurks about rue de Beaujolais bordering the northern end, with its corner café looking on the Théâtre du Palais Royal and short arcades leading up to the main street. Just to the left, on the other side of rue des Petits-Champs, is the forbidding wall of the **Bibliothèque Nationale**, the French equivalent of the Library of Congress. They have a public display of coins and ancient treasures (1–5pm), so you can at least enter the building should you feel so inclined. And if the great French playwright Molière inspires you, you can bow before his statue on the corner of rues Richelieu and Molière.

Les Halles to Beaubourg

In 1969 the main **Les Halles** market was moved out to the suburbs after more than 800 years in the heart of the city. There was widespread opposition to the destruction of Victor Baltard's nineteenth-century pavilions, and considerable disquiet at what renovation of the area would mean. The authorities' excuse was the RER and métro interchange they had to have below. Digging began in 1971 and the hole was only finally filled at the end of the 1980s. Hardly any trace remains of the working-class quarter, with its night bars and bistros to serve the market traders. Rents now rival the 16e, and the all-night places serve and profit from salaried and speed-popping types. Les Halles is constantly promoted as the in-spot of Paris where the cool and famous congregate. In fact, anyone with any sense and money hangs out in the traditional bourgeois *quartiers* to the west.

Around the Forum des Halles

From Châtelet-Les Halles RER, you surface only after ascending levels -4 to 0 of the **Forum des Halles center**, which stretches underground from the Bourse du Commerce rotunda to rue Pierre-Lescot. The overground section comprises aquarium-like arcades of shops enclosed by glass buttocks with white steel creases sliding down to an imprisoned patio. To cover up for all this commerce, poetry, arts and crafts pavilions top two sides in a simple construction—save for the mirrors—that just manages to be out of sync with the curves and hollows below.

From the terrace you admire the tightly controlled gardens in which shrubs and hedges are caged in wire nets. On the north side a giant head and hand suggest the dislocation of this place, though, to be fair, it does provide much-needed open space and greenery in the center of the city. And beneath the garden, amidst the uninspiring shops, there's scope for serious and appealing diversions such as journeying through a simulated underwater world, swimming, watching games of billiards, discovering Paris through videos, wandering through a tropical garden, and recording a song (see *Daytime Amusements* chapter). Touch-screen computers, with French and English "menus," are on hand to guide you around.

After a spate of multi-levels, air conditioning, and artificial light, however, it's a relief to enter the high Gothic space of **St-Eustache**. A woman "preached" the abolition of marriage from the pulpit during the Commune and the more recent history of the area is depicted in a naive fresco in the chapelle St-Joseph, entitled *Le départ des fruits et légumes du coeur de Paris, le 28 février 1969.*

The alternative antidote to steel and glass troglodytism is to join the throng around the **Fontaine des Innocents**, and watch and listen to water cascading down its perfect Renaissance proportions (skateboarders and ghetto-blasters permitting).

There are always hundreds of people around the Forum, filling in time, hustling, or just loafing about. Pickpocketing and sexual harassment are pretty routine; the law plus canine arm are often in evidence, and at night it can be quite tense. The supposedly trendy streets on the eastern side have about as much appeal as the now-tacky parts of Greenwich Village. The area southwards to **place du Châtelet**, however, teems with jazz bars, nightclubs, and restaurants (see Chapters Five and Six) and is far more crowded at 2am than 2pm.

North of the Forum—and Samaritaine

Old food businesses survive north of the Forum along **rues Montmartre**, **Montorgueuil**, and **Turbigo**. Strictly not for vegetarians, the shops and stalls feature wild boar, deer, and feathered friends, alongside *pâté de foie gras* and caviar. Professional chefs' equipment is for sale as well (see p.199).

Retreating back toward the Louvre, streets like **de l'Arbre-Sec**, **Sauval**, and **du Roule** revive the gentler attractions of sidewalk window-shopping, while on the riverfront the three blocks of the **Samaritaine department store** (Mon, Thurs & Sat 9:30am–7pm; Tues & Fri 9:30am–8:30pm; Wed 9:30am–10:30pm) recall the days when art, not marketing psychology, determined the decoration of a store. It was built in 1903 in pure Art Nouveau style. The gold, green, and glass exteriors, and, inside, the brightly painted wrought-iron staircases and balconies against huge backdrops of ceramic floral patterns have all been recently restored. Best of all is the view from the roof (take the elevator to floor nine in *Magasin 2* and then walk up two flights)—the most central high location in the city.

Beaubourg

In the daytime the main flow of feet is to and from Les Halles and **Beaubourg**, the **Georges Pompidou national art and culture center**.

This famous building by Renzo Piano and Richard Rogers is showing signs of wear and tear, and is easily upstaged by more recent additions to the capital's panoply of dramatic modern architecture. It's so small in comparison with La Grande Arche or the Cité des Sciences, and the idea of a transparent building with all its infrastructure visible no longer seems so shocking. (In fact, there's a much earlier example of a featured metal frame at 124 rue Réaumur, built in 1903.) The architectural jokes of Beaubourg—such as the fact that the colors match the codes traditionally used on plans to distinguish different pipes, ducts, and cables—are mostly lost on the center's public. But it remains one of the most popular Parisian buildings, though perhaps more for the plaza's shifting spectacle by street musicians of mime, magic, music, and fire, than for the more mainstream cultural activities inside.

The Center
The center is open, free (with admission charges for the exhibitions and art museum), every weekday except Tuesday from noon to 10pm, and at weekends from 10am to 10pm. For museum, cinema, and kids activities see pp.145, 185, and 249. On the ground floor the postcard selection and art bookshop betters anything on the streets outside, and there are usually some scattered artworks that you don't have to pay to see. Books, tapes, videos, and international newspapers can be consulted for free at the **Bibliothèque Publique d'Information (B.P.I.)** on the second floor. There are four more libraries: literature at ground level and on the second floor; plastic arts on the fourth floor; and documentation on the current main exhibition on the fifth.

The **escalator** is usually one long line, but you should ride up this glass intestine once. As the circles of spectators on the plaza recede, a horizontal skyline appears: the Sacré-Coeur, St-Eustache, the Eiffel Tower, Notre-Dame, the Panthéon, the Tour St-Jacques with its solitary gargoyle, and La Défense menacing in the distance. From the platform at the top you can look down on the château-style chimneys of the Hôtel de Ville with their flowerpot offspring sprouting all over the lower rooftops.

Back on the ground, **visual entertainments** around Beaubourg don't appeal to every taste. There's the clanking gold *Défenseur du Temps* clock in the Quartier de l'Horloge, courtesy of Jacques Chirac; a *trompe-l'oeil* as you look along rue Aubry-le-Boucher from Beaubourg; a mural of a monkey eating yogurt on rue Renard just south of the center; and sculptures and fountains by Tinguely and Nicky de St-Phalle in the pool in front of Église St-Merri. This waterwork pays homage to Stravinsky and shows scant respect for passers-by, and is the ceiling for IRCAM, the center for contemporary music (see p.244). A new, overground extension to IRCAM has appeared squeezed beside the old public baths on rue St-Merri. It's a Renzo Piano creation with a façade of stark terracotta marked like graph paper.

Quartier Beaubourg and the Hôtel de Ville
Where the *quartier Beaubourg* excels is in its choice of small **commercial art galleries**, in which you can browse to your heart's content for free. **Rue Quincampoix** is particularly full of promise, with photographic greats at *Zabriskie* (no. 37); multi-media installations at *Alain Oudin* (no. 47); the

Support-Surface French movement of the Seventies at *Jean Fournier* (no. 44); and international stars at *Crousel-Robelin-Bama* (no. 40). *Galerie Beaubourg*, for important contemporary works, and *Galerie Néotu*, for avant-garde furniture design (23 and 25 rue du Renard) are both well worth a look.

Rue Renard, the continuation of rue Beaubourg, runs down to **place de l'Hôtel de Ville**, where the oppressively vertical, gleaming, and gargantuan mansion is the seat of the city's local government. An illustrated history of the edifice, always a prime target in riots and revolutions, is displayed along the platform of the Châtelet métro on the Neuilly-Vincennes line.

The opponents to the establishments of kings and emperors created their alternative municipal governments at this building in 1789, 1848, and 1870—the last occasion seeing Gambetta proclaim the third French republic to the crowd from a high window ledge. With the defeat of the Commune, the bourgeoisie, back in control, concluded that the Parisian municipal authority had to go if order, property, morality, and the suppression of the working class were to be maintained. So for 100 years Paris was ruled directly by the government.

The next head of an independent municipality after the leaders of the Commune was Jacques Chirac, who became mayor in 1977. Although he hardly poses the same threat to the establishment, Chirac has nonetheless been a source of constant irritation to President Mitterrand, and has run Paris as his own fiefdom with scant regard for other councillors. He even retained the mayorship while he was prime minister—a power base unequalled in French politics.

Les Halles to Beaubourg: Listings

Cafés

Le Comptoir, 14 rue Vauvilliers, 1ᵉʳ. Mᵒ Les Halles/Louvre-Rivoli.

Café Costes, 4 rue Berger, 1ᵉʳ. Mᵒ Châtelet/Les Halles.

Le Petit Marcel, 63 rue Rambuteau, 3ᵉ. Mᵒ Rambuteau.

La Pointe St-Eustache, 1 rue Montorgueil, 1ᵉʳ. Mᵒ Les Halles.

Bars

Broad Café, 13 rue de la Ferronnerie, 1ᵉʳ. Mᵒ Châtelet.

Conways, 73 rue St-Denis, 10ᵉ. Mᵒ Châtelet.

The James Joyce, 5 rue du Jour, 1ᵉʳ. Mᵒ Châtelet/Les Halles.

Beer cellars/pubs

Gambrinus, 62 rue des Lombards, 1ᵉʳ. Mᵒ Châtelet.

Guinness Tavern, 31 rue des Lombards, 1ᵉʳ. Mᵒ Châtelet.

Le Sous-Bock, 49 rue St-Honoré, 1ᵉʳ. Mᵒ Châtelet/Les Halles.

Au Trappiste, 4 rue St-Denis, 1ᵉʳ. Mᵒ Châtelet.

Snacks

Self-Service de la Samaritaine, 2 quai du Louvre, 1ᵉʳ. Mᵒ Pont-Neuf.

Restaurants

Under 80F

Bistro de la Gare, 30 rue St-Denis, 1ᵉʳ. Mᵒ Châtelet.

Aux Deux Saules, 91 rue St-Denis, 1ᵉʳ. Mᵒ Les Halles.

Le Petit Ramoneur, 74 rue St-Denis, 1ᵉʳ. Mᵒ Les Halles.

Over 150F

Au Pied de Cochon, 6 rue Coquillière, 1ᵉʳ. Mᵒ Les Halles.

All the establishments listed above are reviewed in Chapter Eight, Drinking and Eating.

The Marais and the Île St-Louis

Jack Kerouac translates **rue des Francs-Bourgeois** as "street of the outspoken middle classes." The original owners of the mansions lining its length would not have taken kindly to such a slight on their blue-bloodedness. The name's origin is medieval and it was not until the sixteenth and seventeenth centuries that the **Marais**, as the area between Beaubourg and the Bastille is known, became a fashionable aristocratic district. After the Revolution it was abandoned to the masses who, up until some twenty years ago, were living ten to a room on unserviced, squalid streets. Since then, gentrification has proceeded apace and the middle classes are finally ensconced—mostly media, arty, or gay, and definitely outspoken.

The renovated mansions, their grandeur concealed by the narrow streets, have become museums, libraries, offices, and chic apartments flanked by shops selling designer clothes, house and garden accoutrements, works of art, and one-of-a-kind trinkets. Though cornered by Haussmann's boulevards, the Marais itself was spared the Baron's heavy touch and very little has been pulled down in the recent process of going upmarket. It is Paris at its most seductive—old, secluded, as unthreatening by night as it is by day, and with as many alluring shops, bars, and places to eat as you could wish for.

Marais Hôtels and the Place des Vosges

Rue des Francs-Bourgeois begins with the eighteenth-century magnificence of the **Palais Soubise**, which houses the *Archives de France*. On the other side of the street, at the back of a driveway for the *Crédit Municipal* bank, you can see a pepperpot tower which was part of the city walls when the original fortress of the Louvre was built early in the thirteenth century. Further along, past several more imposing façades and the peculiarly public *lycée* classrooms at no. 28, you can enter the courtyard of the Hôtel d'Albret (no. 29bis). This eighteenth-century mansion is home to the cultural department of the mayor of Paris. Tellingly, the dignified façade is blocked by a revolting sculptural column, a 1989 Bicentennial work by Bernard Pagès, resembling thorns and red and blue sticky tape. So much for progress.

Two of the grandest Marais **hôtels**, Carnavalet and Lamoignon, are the next landmarks on this street, housing respectively the *Musée Carnavalet* (see p.164) and the *Bibliothèque Historique de la Ville de Paris*. Finally you reach the masterpiece of aristocratic urban planning, the **place des Vosges**. This vast square of stone and brick symmetry was built for the majesty of Henri IV and Louis XIII, whose statue is hidden by trees in the middle of the grass and gravel gardens. Expensive high heels tap through the arcades pausing at art, antique, and fashion shops, while toddlers and octogenarians, lunch-break workers and schoolchildren sit or play in the garden, the only green space of any size in the locality.

From the southwest corner of the *place*, a door leads through to the formal château garden, orangerie, and exquisite Renaissance façade of the **Hôtel de Sully**. You can visit the temporary exhibitions mounted by the *Caisse Nationale des Monuments Historiques et des Sites* here or just pass through, nodding at the sphinxes on the stairs, to rue St-Antoine.

The Jewish Quarter: rue des Rosiers

The area around **rue des Rosiers** is the main Jewish quarter of the city. Though the *hammam* has gone, and trendy clothes shops are creeping in, the smells and sounds and the people on the streets are still predominantly Jewish and un-bourgeois. For a long time local apartments were kept empty, not for property speculation, but to try to stem the middle-class invasion, and there are still pockets of low-rent accommodation. If you sense a certain suspicion in this area, the reason is the bomb attacks in recent years on synagogues here and on *Goldenburg's* deli/restaurant. People have died in these assaults, and FN spray cans periodically eject their obscenities on walls and storefronts.

Wandering northwards through the 3e *arrondissement* you're likely to end up at the grimly barren **place de la République**, one of the largest traffic circles in Paris. Dominated on the north side by army barracks, and joining seven major streets all penetrating through the then-surrounding areas of rebellious dissent, this is the most blatant example of Napoléon III's political town planning. In order to build it Haussmann destroyed a number of popular theaters, including the *Funambules* of *Les Enfants du Paradis* fame, and Daguerre's unique diorama.

Just below République is the **quartier du Temple**, a good nightlife area (see p.236–40) which is lively by day as well, with streets of wholesale clothes shops and the Carreau-du-Temple clothes market.

South: the Pavillon de l'Arsenal

In the southern section of the Marais, **below rue de Rivoli/St-Antoine**, the crooked steps and lanterns of rue Cloche-Perce, the tottering timbered houses of rue François-Miron, the medieval *Acceuil de France* buildings behind St-Gervais-et-Protais, and the smell of flowers and incense on rue des Barres are all good indulgence in Paris picturesque. But shift eastwards to the next tangle of streets and you'll find the modern, chi-chi flats of the "Village St-Paul," with expensive clusters of antique shops in the courtyards off rue St-Paul.

This part of the Marais suffered a postwar hatchet job, and though seventeenth- and eighteenth-century magnificence is still in evidence, it lacks the architectural cohesion of the Marais to the north. The **fifteenth-century Hôtel de Sens** on the rue de Figuier (now a public library) looks bizarre in its isolation.

On rue du Petit-Musc there is an entertaining combination of Thirties modernism and florid nineteenth-century additions in the Hôtel Fieubert (now a school). Diagonally opposite, at 21 bd Morland, is an excellent addition to the city's art of self-promotion, the **Pavillon de l'Arsenal**, signaled by a sculpture of Rimbaud, entitled "The man with his souls in front." The aim of the Pavillon (Tues–Sat 10:30am–6:30pm, Sun 11am–7pm; free) is to present the city's current architectural projects to the public and show how past and present developments have evolved as part and parcel of Parisian history. To this end they have a permanent exhibition of photographs, plans, and models, including a model of the whole city with a laser spotlight to highlight a touch-screen choice of 30,000 images. The temporary exhibitions are equally

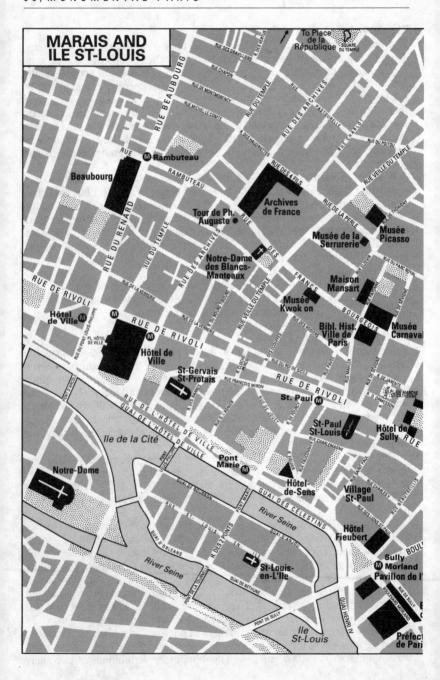

MARAIS AND ILE ST-LOUIS

RUE DES GRAVILLIERS

To Place de la République

SQUARE DU TEMPLE

RUE DE BEAUBOURG

RUE CHAPON

RUE DE MONTMORENCY

RUE DU TEMPLE

RUE DES ARCHIVES

PASTOURELLE

RUE MICHEL LE COMTE

RUE CHARLOT

RUE DU POITOU

RUE

Ⓜ **Rambuteau**

RAMBUTEAU

RUE DES 4 FILS

RUE VIEILLE DU TEMPLE

Beaubourg

R. DES HAUDRIETTES

RUE DE LA PERLE

RUE DU PARC ROYAL

Tour de Ph. Auguste ●

RUE DU RENARD

RUE DU TEMPLE

RUE DES ARCHIVES

Archives de France

DES

Musée de la Serrurerie

Musée Picasso

RUE DE LA VERRERIE

RUE DE RIVOLI

Notre-Dame des Blancs-Manteaux

FRANCS

Maison Mansart

RUE DE LA VERRERIE

RUE DU BOURG TIBOURG

Hôtel de Ville Ⓜ

PL. DU PONT LOUIS PHILIPPE

RUE DE RIVOLI

Ⓜ HÔTEL DE VILLE

Musée Kwok on

BOURGEOIS

Bibl. Hist. Ville de Paris

Musée Carnaval

RUE DES ROSIERS

RUE MALHER

Ⓜ

Hôtel de Ville

St-Gervais St-Protais

RUE FRANÇOIS MIRON

RUE DE RIVOLI

RUE DU ROI DE SICILE

St. Paul Ⓜ

RUE DE L'HÔTEL DE VILLE

QUAI DE L'HÔTEL DE VILLE

St-Paul St-Louis

Hôtel de Sully RUE

Ile de la Cité

PONT MARIE

RUE CHARLEMAGNE

Notre-Dame

Pont Marie Ⓜ

Hôtel-de-Sens

Village St-Paul

RUE CHARLES V

QUAI DE BOURBON

QUAI DES CELESTINS

River Seine

Hôtel Fieubert

QUAI D'ANJOU

RUE ST. LOUIS EN L'ILE

QUAI D'ORLEANS

River Seine

✚ **St-Louis-en-L'Ile**

QUAI DE BÉTHUNE

Ⓜ **Sully Morland**

Pavillon de l'

PONT DE LA TOURNELLE

PONT DE SULLY

Ile St-Louis

QUAI HENRI IV

Préfecture de Paris

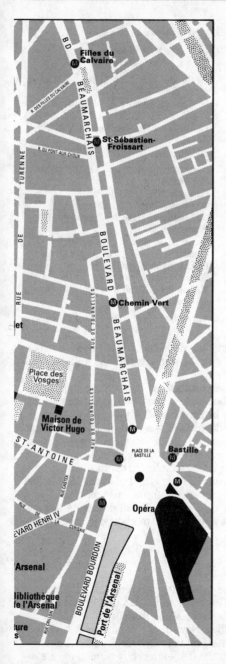

The Marais and the Île St-Louis: Listings

Snacks

La Crêpe St-Louis, 86 rue St-Louis-en-l'Île, 4ᵉ. Mᵒ Pont-Marie.

Sacha Finkelsztajn and **Florence Finkelsztajn**, 27 rue des Rosiers and 24 rue des Écouffes, 4ᵉ. Mᵒ St-Paul.

Fous du Sandwich, 27 rue St-Louis-en-l'Île, 4ᵉ. Mᵒ Pont-Marie/Sully-Morland.

Fleur de Lotus, 2 rue du Roi-de-Sicile, 4ᵉ. Mᵒ St-Paul.

Restaurant du Musée Picasso, Hôtel Salé, 5 rue de Thorigny, 3ᵉ. Mᵒ St-Sébastien.

L'Oiseau Bariolé, 16 rue Ste-Croix-de-la-Bretonnerie, 4ᵉ. Mᵒ Hôtel-de-Ville.

Le Roi Falafel, 34 rue des Rosiers, 4ᵉ. Mᵒ St-Paul.

Yahalom, 22–24 rue des Rosiers, 4ᵉ. Mᵒ St-Paul.

Restaurants

Under 80F

Aquarius, 54 rue Ste-Croix-de-la-Bretonnerie, 4ᵉ. Mᵒ St-Paul/Rambuteau.

Bistro du Marais, 15 rue Ste-Croix-de-la-Bretonnerie, 3ᵉ. Mᵒ St-Paul.

Piccolo Teatro, 6 rue des Écouffes, 4ᵉ. Mᵒ St-Paul.

Le St-Regis, 92 rue St-Louis-en-l'Île, 4ᵉ. Mᵒ Pont-Marie.

Tripti-Kulai, 2 place du Marché Ste-Cathérine, 4ᵉ. Mᵒ St-Paul.

Under 150F

Goldenburg's, 7 rue des Rosiers, 4ᵉ. Mᵒ St-Paul.

Le Gourmet de l'Île, 42 rue St-Louis-en-l'Île, 4ᵉ. Mᵒ Pont-Marie.

Auberge de Jarente, 7 rue Jarente, 4ᵉ. Mᵒ St-Paul.

Le Ravaillac, 10 rue du Roi-de-Sicile, 4ᵉ. Mᵒ St-Paul.

Over 150F

Anahi, 49 rue Volta, 3ᵉ. Mᵒ Arts-et-Métiers.

Au Franc Pinot, 1 quai de Bourbon, 4ᵉ. Mᵒ Pont-Marie.

La Petite Chaumière, 41 rue des Blancs-Manteaux, 4ᵉ. Mᵒ Rambuteau.

CAFÉS and **BARS** *are listed overleaf*

The Marais and the Île St-Louis: Listings

SNACKS and RESTAURANTS are listed on the previous page

Cafés

Ma Bourgogne, 19 place des Vosges, 3ᵉ. Mº St-Paul.

L'Oiseau Bariolé, 16 rue Ste-Croix-de-la-Bretonnerie, 4ᵉ. Mº Hôtel-de-Ville.

Au Petit Fer à Cheval, 30 rue Vieille-du-Temple, 4ᵉ. Mº St-Paul.

Le Taxi Jaune, 13 rue Chapon, 3ᵉ. Mº Arts-et-Métiers.

Le Temps des Cérises, 31 rue de la Cerisaie, 4ᵉ. Mº Bastille.

Bars

Bar Hôtel Central, 33 rue Vieille-du-Temple, 4ᵉ. Mº St-Paul.

Le Duplex, 25 rue Michel-le-Comte, 3ᵉ. Mº Rambuteau.

La Perla, 23 rue du Pont-Louis-Philippe, 4ᵉ. Mº St-Paul.

Le Swing, 42 rue Vieille-du-Temple, 4ᵉ. Mº Hôtel-de-Ville.

Wine bars

Le Coude-Fou, 12 rue du Bourg-Tibourg, 4ᵉ. Mº Hôtel-de-Ville.

Le Rouge Gorge, 8 rue St-Paul, 4ᵉ. Mº St-Paul.

La Tartine, 24 rue de Rivoli, 4ᵉ. Mº St-Paul.

Salons de thé

Berthillon, 31 rue St-Louis-en-l'Île, 4ᵉ. Mº Pont-Marie.

Dattes et Noix, 4 rue du Parc-Royal, 3ᵉ. Mº Chemin-Vert.

L'Ébouillanté, 6 rue des Barres, 4ᵉ. Mº Hôtel-de-Ville.

Eurydice, 10 place des Vosges, 4ᵉ. Mº Chemin-Vert.

Le Loir dans la Théière, rue des Rosiers, 4ᵉ. Mº St-Paul.

Marais Plus, 20 rue des Francs-Bourgeois, 3ᵉ. Mº St-Paul.

All the establishments listed above are reviewed in Chapter Eight, Drinking and Eating.

---

impressive, and the best thing about the whole display is to see schools, industrial units, and hospitals treated with the same respect as La Villette and La Grande Arche.

The southeast corner of the **4ᵉ arrondissement**, jutting out into the Seine, has a separate character. It's been taken up since the last century by the Céléstine barracks and previously by the Arsenal, which used to overlook a third island in the Seine. Boulevard Morland was built in 1843, covering over the arm of the river which formed the Île de Louviers. The mad poet Gérard de Nerval escaped here as a boy and lived for days in a log cabin he made with wood scavenged from the island's timberyards. In the 1830s his more extrovert contemporaries—Victor Hugo, Liszt, Delacroix, Alexandre Dumas, and co.—were using the library of the former residence of Louis XIV's artillery chief as a meeting place. While the literati discussed turning art to a revolutionary form, the locals were on the streets giving the authorities reason to build more barracks.

The Île St-Louis

Another Bohemian hang-out a decade or so later was the **Hôtel Lauzun** at 17 quai d'Anjou on the Île St-Louis. The Hashashins club met here monthly, and Baudelaire lived for a while in the attic, which it was said he had decorated with stuffed snakes and crocodiles. Nowadays you have your home on the island if you're the Aga Khan, the Pretender to the French throne, or equivalent. Unlike its larger neighbor, the Île St-Louis has no monuments or museums, just high houses on single-lane streets, a school, church, restaurants, and cafés, and the best sorbets in the world chez *M. Berthillon*.

You can seek even greater seclusion on the **southern quais**, tightly clutching a triple-sorbet cornet as you descend the various steps or climb over the low gate on the right of the garden across bd Henri-IV to reach the best sunbathing spot in Paris. Nothing can rival the taste of iced passion or kiwi fruit, guava, melon, or whichever flavor—a sensation of which ripe, fresh-picked fruit is but a shadow. And even when Berthillon and his six concessionaries are closed, the island and its *quais* have their own very distinct charm.

Île de la Cité

The **Île de la Cité** is where Paris began. The earliest settlements were sited here, as was the small Gallic town of Lutetia, overrun by Julius Caesar's troops in 52 BC. A natural defensive site commanding a major east–west river trade route, it was an obvious candidate for a bright future. The Romans garrisoned it and laid out one of their standard military town plans, overlapping onto the Left Bank. While it never achieved any great political importance, they endowed it with an administrative center which became the palace of the Merovingian kings in 508, then of the counts of Paris, who in 987 became kings of France. So from the very beginning the Île has been close to the administrative heart of France.

Today the lure of the island lies in its tail-end—the **square du Vert-Galant**, the **quais, place Dauphine**, and the **cathedral of Notre-Dame** itself. Haussmann demolished the central section in the nineteenth century, displacing some 25,000 people and virtually breaking the island's back with four vast edifices in bland Baronial-Bureaucratick, largely given over to housing the law. He also perpetrated the litter-blown space in front of the cathedral, though that at least has the virtue of allowing a full-frontal view.

Pont-Neuf and the Quais

If you arrive on the island by the **Pont Neuf**, the city's oldest bridge (temporarily gift-wrapped a few years ago in 44,000 square meters of straw-colored nylon by the Bulgarian artist Christo), you see a statue of **Henri IV**, the king who commissioned it. He was a Protestant country boy from the Pyrenees, who renounced his faith for the throne; "Paris is worth a Mass," as he put it. It was he who guaranteed the civil rights of the sizable Protestant minority in 1598. When Louis XIV abrogated those guarantees nearly 100 years later, the Protestants scattered across the world from Holland to the New World. As many of them were highly skilled artisans, their departure was a blow to the economy—as was the death and exile of so many *Communards* 200 years later, who were also largely the working-class elite.

Behind his statue, a flight of steps goes down to the **quais** and the **square du Vert-Galant**, a small tree-lined green enclosed within the triangular stern of the island. The prime spot to occupy is the extreme point beneath a weeping willow—haunt of lovers, sparrows, and sunbathers. On the north quay is the dock for the tourist river boats, *Bateaux-Vedettes du Pont-Neuf* (see p.35).

Sainte-Chapelle and the Conciergerie

On the other side of the bridge, across the street from the king, seventeenth-century houses flank the entrance to the sanded, chestnut-shaded **place Dauphine**, one of the city's most secluded and exclusive squares, where Simone Signoret lived, next to the *salon de thé Fanny Tea*, until her death in 1985. The farther end of the square is blocked by the dull mass of the **Palais de Justice**, which swallowed up the palace that was home to the French kings until Étienne Marcel's bloody revolt in 1358 frightened them off to the greater security of the Louvre. In earlier times it had been the Roman governors' residence, too.

The only part of the older complex that remains in its entirety is Louis IX's **Sainte-Chapelle**, built to house a collection of holy relics he had bought at extortionate rates from the bankrupt empire of Byzantium. It stands in a courtyard to the left of the main entrance (bd du Palais), looking somewhat squeezed by the proximity of the nineteenth-century law courts, which, incidentally, anyone is free to sit in on. Though much restored, the chapel remains one of the finest achievements of French Gothic (consecrated in 1248). Very tall in relation to its length, it looks like a cathedral choir lopped

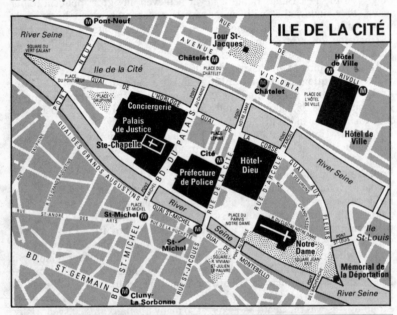

Île de la Cité: Listings

Wine bar
Taverne Henri IV, 13 place du Pont-Neuf, 1er. Mº Pont-Neuf.

Salon de thé
Fanny Tea, 20 place Dauphine, 1er. Mº Pont-Neuf.

Both these establishments are reviewed in Chapter Eight, Drinking and Eating.

off and transformed into an independent building. Its most radical feature is its fragility: the reduction of structural masonry to a minimum to make way for a huge expanse of stunning **stained glass**. The impression inside is of being enclosed within the wings of myriad butterflies—the predominant colors blue and red, and, in the later rose window, grass-green and blue.

It pays to get to Sainte-Chapelle as early as possible (April–Sept 9:30am–6pm, Oct–March 10am–4:30pm; half price Sun & hols). It attracts hordes of tourists, as does the **Conciergerie** (April–Sept 9:30am–6:30pm; Oct–March 10am–5pm), Paris's oldest prison, where Marie-Antoinette and, in their turn, the leading figures of the Revolution were incarcerated before execution. The chief interest of the Conciergerie is the enormous late Gothic *Salle des Gens d'Arme*, canteen and recreation room of the royal household staff. You are missing little in not seeing Marie-Antoinette's cell and various other macabre mementoes of the guillotine's victims.

For the loveliest view of what the whole ensemble once looked like, you need to get hold of the postcard of the June illustration from the fifteenth-century Book of Hours known as *Les Très Riches Heures du Duc de Berry* (see Musée Condé, p.262), the most mouthwatering of all medieval illuminated manuscripts. It shows the palace with towers and chimneys and trellised rose garden and the Sainte-Chapelle touching the sky in the right-hand corner. The Seine laps the curtain wall where now the quai des Orfèvres (gold-smiths) runs. In the foreground pollarded willows line the Left Bank, while barefoot peasant girls rake hay in shocks and their menfolk scythe light green swathes up the rue Dauphine. No sign of the square du Vert-Galant: it was just a swampy islet then, not to be joined to the rest of the Cité for another hundred years and more.

Place Lépine, Pont d'Arcole and Peter Abélard . . .

If you keep along the north side of the island from the Conciergerie you come to **place Lépine**, named for the police boss who gave Paris's coppers their white truncheons and whistles. There is an exuberant **flower market** here six days a week, with **birds and pets**—cruelly caged—on Sunday.

Next bridge but one is the **Pont d'Arcole**, named for a young revolution-ary killed in an attack on the Hôtel de Ville in the 1830 rising (see p.286), and beyond that the only bit of the Cité that survived Haussmann's attentions. In the streets hereabouts once flourished the cathedral school of Notre-Dame, forerunner of the Sorbonne.

Around the year 1200 one of the teachers here was **Peter Abélard**, of Héloïse fame. A philosophical whiz kid and completely irreverent at the estab-lishment intellectuals of his time, he was very popular with his students and not at all with the authorities, who thought they caught a distinct whiff of heresy. Forced to leave the cathedral school, he set up shop on the Left Bank with his disciples and, in effect, founded the university of Paris. His love life was less successful, though much better known. While living near the rue Chanoinesse, behind the cathedral, he fell violently in love with his landlord's niece, Héloïse, and she with him. She had a baby. Uncle had him castrated and the story ended in convents, lifelong separation, and lengthy correspon-dence. Today their tomb lies in the cemetery of Père Lachaise (see p.132).

Notre-Dame

Close by, the **Cathédrale de Notre-Dame** itself (8am–7pm) is so much photographed that even seeing it for the first time the edge of your response is somewhat dulled by familiarity. Yet it is truly impressive, that great H-shaped west front, with its strong vertical divisions counterbalanced by the horizontal emphasis of gallery and frieze, all centered by the rose window. It demands to be seen as a whole, though that can scarcely have been possible when the medieval houses clustered close about it. It is a solid, no-nonsense design, confessing its Romanesque ancestry. For the more fantastical kind of Gothic, look rather at the **north transept façade** with its crocketed gables and huge fretted window-space.

Notre-Dame was begun in 1160 under the auspices of Bishop de Sully and completed around 1245. In the nineteenth century, Viollet-le-Duc carried out extensive renovation work, including remaking most of the statuary—the entire frieze of Old Testament kings, for instance (the originals are in the Musée de Cluny, see p.155)—and adding the steeple and baleful-looking gargoyles, which you can see close-up if you brave the ascent of the towers (April–Sept 10am–5:30pm; Oct–March 10am–4:30pm). Ravaged by weather and pollution, its beauty will be at least partially masked once again for the next few years, as the scaffolding goes up for further restoration work.

Inside, the immediately striking feature, if you can ignore the noise and movement, is the dramatic contrast between the darkness of the nave and the light falling on the first great clustered pillars of the choir, emphasizing the special nature of the sanctuary. It is the end walls of the transepts which admit all this light, nearly two-thirds glass, including two magnificent **rose windows** colored in imperial purple. These, the vaulting, the soaring shafts reaching to the springs of the vaults, are all definite Gothic elements, yet, inside as out, there remains a strong sense of Romanesque in the stout round pillars of the nave and the general sense of foursquareness.

Before you leave, walk around to the public garden at the east end for a view of the **flying buttresses** supporting the choir, and then along the riverside under the south transept, where you can sit in springtime with the cherry blossom drifting down. And say a prayer of gratitude that the city fathers had the sense to throw out President "Paris-must-adapt-itself-to-the-automobile" Pompidou's scheme for extending the quayside expressway along here.

Out in front of the cathedral, in the plaza separating it from Haussmann's police HQ, is what appears to be and smells like the entrance to an underground toilet. It is, in fact, a very well displayed and interesting museum, the **crypte archéologique** (10am–6pm), in which are revealed the remains of the original cathedral, as well as streets and houses of the Cité back as far as the Roman era.

Kilomètre Zéro and Le Mémorial de la Déportation

On the sidewalk by the cathedral west door is a spot known as **kilomètre zéro**, from which all main road distances in France are calculated. For the Île de la Cité is the symbolic heart of the country, or at least of the France that in the textbooks fights wars, undergoes revolutions, and launches space rockets. So it is fitting that the island should also be the symbolic tomb of the

200,000 French men and women who died in the Nazi concentration camps during World War II—Resistance fighters, Jews, forced laborers.

Their moving memorial, **Le Mémorial de la Déportation**, is a kind of bunker-crypt, scarcely visible above ground, at the extreme eastern tip of the island. Stairs scarcely shoulder-wide descend into a space like a prison yard. A single aperture overlooks the brown waters of the Seine, barred by a grill whose spiky ends evoke the torments of the torture chamber. Above, nothing is visible but the sky and, dead center, the spire of Notre-Dame. Inside, the crypt is a tunnel-like chamber, its sides studded with thousands of points of light representing the dead. Floor and ceiling are black and it ends in a black raw hole, with a single naked bulb hanging in the middle. Either side are empty barred cells. "They went to the other ends of the Earth and they have not returned. 200,000 French men and women swallowed up, exterminated, in the mists and darkness of the Nazi camps." Above the exit, the words "Forgive. Do not forget . . ."

Trocadéro, Eiffel Tower, and Les Invalides

The vistas are splendid, from the terrace of the **Palais de Chaillot** (place du Trocadéro) across the river to the Tour Eiffel and École Militaire, from the ornate 1900 Pont Alexandre III along the grassy Esplanade to the Hôtel des Invalides. But once you have said to yourself, "How splendid!," there is little reason to get any closer. This is town planning on the despotic scale, an assertion of power that takes no account of the small-scale interests and details of everyday lives.

The Palais de Chaillot, like a latterday Pharaoh's mausoleum (1937), is, however, home to several interesting museums (see pp.160, 163 & 165) and a theater used for diverse but often radical productions. And across the river—take the Passerelle Debilly footbridge opposite the Palais de Tokyo—the **Tour Eiffel**, though no conventional beauty, is nonetheless an amazing structure.

The Eiffel Tower

When completed in 1889, the **Tour Eiffel** was the tallest building in the world at 300m. Its 7000 tons of steel, in terms of pressure, sit as lightly on the ground as a child in a chair. Reactions to it were violent:

> *"(We) protest with all our force, with all our indignation, in the name of unappreciated French taste, in the name of menaced French art and history, against the erection, in the very heart of our capital, of the useless and monstrous Eiffel Tower . . . . Is Paris going to be associated with the grotesque, mercantile imaginings of a constructor of machines?"*

Eiffel himself thought it was beautiful. "The first principle of architectural aesthetics," he said, "prescribes that the basic lines of a structure must correspond precisely to its specified use . . . . To a certain extent the tower was formed by the wind itself." Needless to say, it stole the show at the 1889 Exposition, for which it had been constructed.

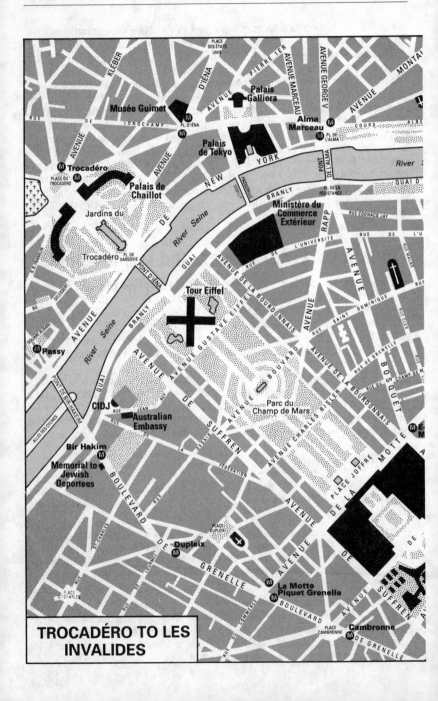

TROCADÉRO TO LES INVALIDES

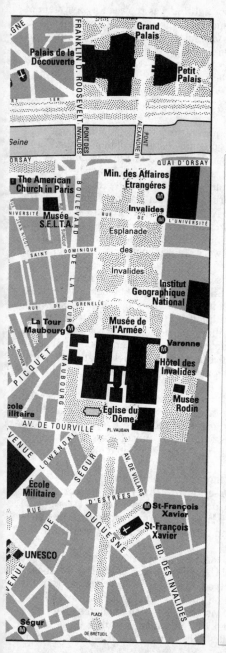

Trocadéro, Eiffel Tower and Les Invalides: Listings

Cafés

Au Bon Accueil, 15 rue Babylone, 7e. Mᵒ Sèvres-Babylone.

Kléber, place du Trocadéro, 16e. Mᵒ Trocadéro.

Salon de thé

La Pagode, 57bis rue de Babylone, 7e. Mᵒ St-François-Xavier/Sèvres-Babylone.

Snacks

Palais de Tokyo, 13 av du Président-Wilson, 16e. Mᵒ Iéna/Alma-Marceau.

Restaurants

Under 80F

Au Babylone, 13 rue de Babylone, 7e. Mᵒ Sèvres-Babylone.

Germaine, 30 rue Pierre-Leroux, 7e. Mᵒ Vaneau.

Over 150F

L'Ami Jean, 27 rue Malar, 7e. Mᵒ Latour-Maubourg.

Aux Délices de Széchuen, 40 av Duquesne, 7e. Mᵒ St-François-Xavier.

Escale de Saigon, 24 rue Bosquet, 7e. Mᵒ École-Militaire.

Au Pied de Fouet, 45 rue de Babylone, 7e. Mᵒ Sèvres-Babylone.

Thoumieux, 79 rue St-Dominique, 7e. Mᵒ Latour-Maubourg.

All the establishments listed above are reviewed in Chapter Eight,
Drinking and Eating.

In 1986 the external night-time **floodlighting** was replaced by a system of illumination from within the tower's superstructure, so that it now looks at its magical best after dark, as light and fanciful as a filigree minaret. **Going to the top** (10am–11pm for stage 1 and 2; 10am–10pm for stage 3) costs 49F (17F and 32F respectively for the first two stages)—so that it is only really worth the expense on an absolutely clear day.

Around the École Militaire

Stretching back from the legs of the tower, the long rectangular gardens of the **Champs de Mars** lead to the eighteenth-century buildings of the **École Militaire**, now the Staff College, originally founded in 1751 by Louis XV for the training of aristocratic army officers. No prizes for guessing who the most famous graduate was. A less illustrious but better-loved French soldier has his name remembered in a neighboring street and square: Cambronne. He commanded the last surviving unit of Napoléon's Imperial Guard at Waterloo. Called on to surrender by the English, although surrounded and reduced to a bare handful of men, he shouted back into the darkness one word: *"Merde"* – Shit!—the commonest French swear word, known euphemistically ever since as *le mot de Cambronne.*

The surrounding *quartier* is expensive and sought after as an address, but uninteresting to look at, like the **UNESCO building** at the back of the École Militaire. Controversial at the time of its construction in 1958, it looks somewhat pedestrian, and badly weathered, today. It can be visited; some of the internal spaces are interesting and there are a number of art works, both inside and in the garden, the most noticeable being an enormous mobile by Alexander Calder. The most attractive feature is a quiet Japanese garden, where you can repair on a summer's day to read a paper bought from the well-stocked kiosk in the foyer.

Most unexpected, therefore, in this rather austere *quartier*, to discover the wedge of **early nineteenth-century streets between av Bosquet and the Invalides**. Chief among them is the market street, **rue Cler**, with its cross streets, rue de Grenelle and rue St-Dominique, full of classy little shops, including a couple of *boulangeries* with their original painted glass panels.

Down on the Quai: the American Church and the Sewers

Out on the riverbank at quai d'Orsay is the **American church**, which, together with the American College in nearby av Bosquet (no. 31), is a nodal point in the well-organized life of the large American community. The notice board is plastered with job offers and demands. The people are friendly and helpful in all kinds of ways.

The other quayside attraction is the **sewers**, *les égouts* (entrance at the corner of Pont de l'Alma and Quai d'Orsay; Mon, Wed & the last Sat of each month, 2–5pm). Your nose will tell you, if not the cadaverous pallor of the superannuated sewermen who wait on you. The guidebooks always bill this as an outing for kids; I doubt it. The visit consists of an unilluminating film, a small museum, and a very brief look at some tunnels with a lot of smelly water swirling about. Cloacal appetites will get much more satisfaction from

Victor Hugo's description in *Les Misérables:* twenty pages on the value of human excrement as manure (25 million francs' worth down the plughole in the 1860s) and the history, ancient and modern, including the sewage flood of 1802 and the first perilous survey of the system in 1805 and what it found—a piece of Marat's winding sheet and the skeleton of an orangutan, among other things.

The **film show** is a laugh for its evasive gentility. It opens with misty sunrises, portraits of monarchs, and a breathless voice saying, "Paris, do you remember when you were little?" before relating how three million *baguettes*, 1000 tons of fruit, 100 tons of fish, and so on make their daily progress through the guts of the city and end up here. As for the **museum**, serious students of urban planning could find some interesting items, if they were only allowed the time to look. In fact, I'd say, stay in the museum and skip the tour. Among other things there is an appropriate memorial to Louis Napoléon: an inscription beginning, "In the reign of His Majesty Napoléon III, Emperor of the French, the sewer of the rue de Rivoli . . ."

Les Invalides

The **Esplanade des Invalides**, striking due south from **Pont Alexandre III**, is a more attractive and uncluttered vista than Chaillot-École Militaire. The wide façade of the **Hôtel des Invalides**, overtopped by its distinctive dome, resplendent with new gilding to celebrate the bicentenary of the Revolution, fills the whole of the farther end of the Esplanade. It was built as a home for invalided soldiers on the orders of Louis XIV. Under the dome are two churches, one for the soldiers, the other intended as a mausoleum for the king but now containing the mortal remains of Napoléon. The Hôtel (*son et lumière* in English, April–Sept) houses the vast **Musée de l'Armée** (see p.163).

Both churches are cold and dreary inside. The **Église du Dôme**, in particular, is a supreme example of architectural pomposity. Corinthian columns and pilasters abound. The dome—pleasing enough from outside—is covered with paintings and flanked by four round chapels displaying the tombs of various luminaries. Napoléon himself lies in a hole in the floor in a cold smooth sarcophagus of red porphyry, enclosed within a gallery decorated with friezes of execrable taste and groveling piety, captioned with quotations of awesome conceit from the great man: "Cooperate with the plans I have laid for the welfare of peoples"; "By its simplicity my code of law has done more good in France than all the laws which have preceded me"; "Wherever the shadow of my rule has fallen, it has left lasting traces of its value."

Immediately east of the Invalides is the **Musée Rodin** (see p.159), on the corner of rue de Varenne, housed in a beautiful eighteenth-century mansion which the sculptor leased from the state in return for the gift of all his work at his death. The garden, planted with sculptures, is quite as pretty as the house, with a pond and flowering shrubs and a superb view of the Invalides dome rising above the trees. The rest of the street, and the parallel rue de Grenelle, is full of aristocratic mansions, including the **Hôtel Matignon**, the prime minister's residence. At the farther end, the **rue du Bac** leads right into rue de Sèvres, cutting across **rue de Babylone**, another of the *quartier*'s livelier streets, with a couple of very agreeable and reasonable restaurants, *Au Babylone* and the tiny *Au Pied de Fouet*, and the crazy folly of the rich. **La Pagode**, down on the left beyond the barracks (see p.248).

CHAPTER TWO

THE LEFT BANK AND BEAUX QUARTIERS

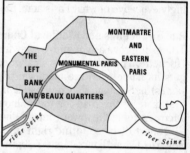

The term **Left Bank** (*rive gauche*) connotes Bohemian, dissident, intellectual—the radical student type, whether eighteen years of age or eighty. As a topographical term it refers particularly to their traditional haunts, the warren of medieval lanes around the **boulevards St-Michel** and **St-Germain**, known as the **Quartier Latin** because that was the language of the university sited there right up until 1789. In modern times its reputation for turbulence and innovation has been renewed by the activities of painters and writers like Picasso, Apollinaire, Breton, Henry Miller, Anaïs Nin, and Hemingway after the First World War, Camus, Sartre, Juliette Greco, and the Existentialists after the Second, and the political turmoil of 1968 which escalated from student demonstrations and barricades to factory occupations, massive strikes, and the near-overthrow of de Gaulle's presidency. This is not to say that the whole of Paris south of the Seine is the exclusive territory of revolutionaries and avant-gardists. It does, however, have a different and distinctive feel and appearance, noticeable as soon as you cross the river. And it's here, too, that the city's mythmakers principally gather: the writers, painters, philosophers, politicians, journalists, designers—the people who tell Paris what it is.

Across the Seine, there's not much to see in the **Right Bank** fashionable residential streets of the **Beaux Quartiers**, though they shelter three first-rate museums in the Marmottan, Arts et Traditions Populaires, and the Palais de Tokyo. The population here signals a distinct shift in social and economic power: this is the land of Hermès scarves, Lacoste sports shirts, and weekend *rallyes* or meets, where the children of the upper classes gather—the BCBGs (bon chic, bon genre), as they're known, France's Preppie equivalents. The old villages of **Auteuil** and **Passy**, however, make for some rewarding walks, as does the **Bois de Boulogne** and the seedy eastern half of the 17e *arrondissement* out toward Montmartre.

Quartier Latin

The pivotal point of the Quartier Latin is **place St-Michel**, where the tree-lined **boulevard St-Michel** begins. It has lost its radical penniless chic now, preferring harder commercial values. The cafés and shops are jammed with people, mainly young and in summer largely foreign. All the world's bobby-soxers unload here—just a canon's throw from Notre-Dame. The fountain in the *place* is a favorite meeting, not to say pick-up, spot. **Rue de la Huchette**, the Mecca of beats and bums in the post-World War II years, with its theater still showing Ionesco's *Cantatrice Chauve* nearly forty years on, is now given over to Greek restaurants of indifferent quality and inflated price, as is the adjoining rue Xavier-Privas, with the odd *couscous* joint thrown in. Connecting it to the riverside is the city's narrowest street, the Chat-qui-Pêche, alarmingly evocative of what Paris at its medieval worst must have looked like.

Rue St-Jacques and Medieval Churches

Things improve as you move away from the boulevard. At the end of rue de la Huchette, **rue St-Jacques** is aligned on the main street of Roman Paris. It gets its name from the medieval pilgrimage to the shrine of St-Jacques (St James) at Santiago de Compostela in northern Spain. This bit of hill was the first taste of the road for the millions who set out from the **church of St-Jacques** (only the tower remains) just across the river.

A short distance to the right, the mainly fifteenth-century **church of St-Séverin** (Mon–Thurs 11am–7:30pm, Fri & Sat 9am–10:30pm, Sun 9am–8pm) is one of the city's most elegant. Built in the Flamboyant Gothic style, it boasts some splendidly virtuoso chiselwork in the pillars of the choir, as well as stained glass by the modern French painter Jean Bazaine.

Back toward the river, **square Viviani** with its welcome patch of grass and trees provides the most flattering of all views of Notre-Dame. The ancient listing tree propped on a concrete pillar by the church wall is reputed to be Paris's oldest, brought over from Guyana in 1680. The church itself, mutilated and disfigured, is **St-Julien-le-Pauvre**. The same age as Notre-Dame, it used to be the venue for university assemblies until some rambunctious students tore it apart in the 1500s. It's a quiet and intimate place, ideal for a moment's soulful reflection. For the last hundred years it has belonged to a Greek Catholic sect, whence the unexpected iconostasis screening the sanctuary. The hefty slabs of stone by the well at the entrance are all that remains of the Roman thoroughfare now overlain by the rue St-Jacques.

The Riverbank and Institut du Monde Arabe

Round to the left on rue de la Bûcherie, the English bookshop **Shakespeare and Co** is haunted by the shades of James Joyce and other great expatriate literati, though only by proxy, as Sylvia Beach, publisher of Joyce's *Ulysses*, had her original shop on rue de l'Odéon.

More books, postcards, prints, sheet music, records, and assorted goods are on sale from the **bouquinistes**, who display their wares in green padlocked boxes hooked onto the parapet of the **riverside quais**—which, in spite of their romantic reputation, are not much fun to walk hereabouts, because of the traffic. There, continuing upstream as far as the tip of the Île St-Louis, you come to the **Pont de Sully** with a dramatic view of the apse and steeple of Notre-Dame and the beginning of a riverside garden dotted with pieces of modern sculpture, known as the **Musée de Sculpture en Plein Air**.

At the end of the Pont de Sully, in the angle between quai St-Bernard and rue des Fossés-St-Bernard, shaming the hideous factory of the university Paris-VI next door, is the **Institut du Monde Arabe** designed by Jean Nouvel. Its elegant glass and aluminum mass is cleft in two, with the river-front half bowed and tapering to a knife-like prow, while the broad southern façade, comprising thousands of tiny light-sensitive shutters which open and close according to the brightness of the day, mimics with hi-tech ingenuity the *moucharaby*—the traditional Arab lattice-work balcony.

The building and its exhibition space are open daily except Monday, from 1 to 8pm (40F). As yet, the building remains more interesting than any of the displays, though the permanent exhibition includes glass, rugs, ceramics, illuminated manuscripts, wood carving, metalwork, and scientific instruments from the Islamic world, much of it acquired from existing collections in the Louvre and the Musée des Arts Décoratifs. Plans for expansion involve the creation of a substantial social archaeology section, covering popular arts and crafts, agricultural implements, clothing, and so forth, as well as loans from the major museums of the Arab world. On the first floor, contemporary Arab paintings and sculptures are exhibited—usually a fascinating mix of styles plus strong political statements.

In the basement *Espace Image et Son* (open 1–7pm) you can watch TV programs from around the Arab world, and consult a large library of audiovisual material. When you need a rest, take the fastest elevators in Paris up to the ninth floor, where you can eat a good, if expensive and entirely un-Arab, meal, or have a mint tea, with a brilliant view over the Seine.

Place Maubert and the Sorbonne

Walking back along bd St-Germain toward bd St-Michel, past rue de Pontoise with its Art Déco swimming pool and primary school, you come to **place Maubert** (good **market** Tues, Thurs, and Sat morning) at the foot of the **Montagne Ste-Geneviève**, the hill on which the Panthéon stands and the best strolling area this side of bd St-Michel. The best way in is either from the *place* or from the crossroads of boulevards St-Michel and St-Germain, where the walls of the third-century **Roman baths** are visible in the garden of the **Hôtel de Cluny**. A sixteenth-century mansion resembling an Oxford or Cambridge college, the *hôtel* was built by the abbots of the powerful Cluny monastery as their Paris pied-à-terre. It now houses a very beautiful museum of medieval art (see p.155). There is no charge for entry to the quiet shady courtyard.

The grim-looking buildings on the other side of rue des Écoles are the **Sorbonne**, **Collège de France**, and **Lycée Louis-le-Grand**, which numbers Molière, Robespierre, Pompidou, and Victor Hugo among its graduates and Sartre among its teachers. All these institutions are major constituents of the

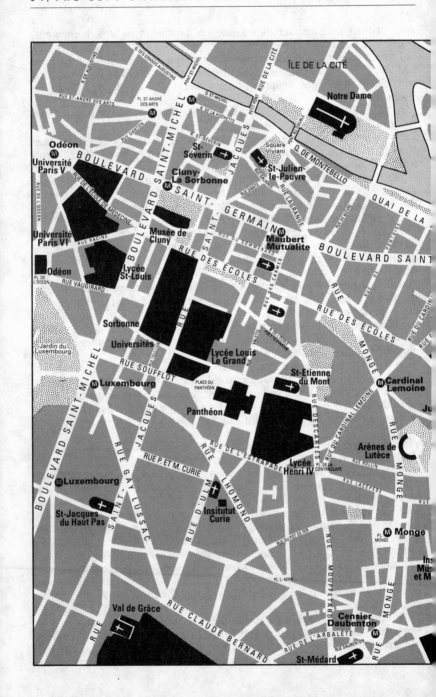

ÎLE DE LA CITÉ

Q. DES GRANDS AUGUSTINS

R. DE NESLE

R. GIT LE COEUR

PONT ST-MICHEL

Q. ST-MICHEL

RUE DE LA CITÉ

Notre Dame

RUE ST-ANDRÉ DES ARTS

PL. ST-ANDRÉ DES ARTS Ⓜ

PETIT PONT

R. DE LA HUCHETTE

Odéon Ⓜ

Université Paris V

BOULEVARD

RUE DE DANTON

RUE DE L'ÉCOLE DE MÉDECINE

SAINT-MICHEL

R. ST-SÉVERIN

St-Séverin

Cluny-La Sorbonne Ⓜ

JACQUES

Square Viviani

St-Julien-le-Pauvre

Q. DE MONTEBELLO

QUAI DE LA

SAINT-GERMAIN

RUE DANTE

RUE GALANDE

RUE LAGRANGE

R. ST-JACQUES

Université Paris VI

RUE RACINE

Musée de Cluny

RUE SAINT-

RUE DU SOMMERARD

Maubert Mutualité Ⓜ

BOULEVARD SAINT

RUE DE BIÈVRE

R. DE PONTOISE

Odéon

PL. DE L'ODÉON

RUE VAUGIRARD

Lycée St-Louis

RUE DES ÉCOLES

RUE DES CARMES

RUE DES ÉCOLES

RUE DU CARDINAL

RUE DE

Jardin du Luxembourg

Sorbonne

Universités

RUE SOUFFLOT

RUE SAINT-JACQUES

R. DE LA MONTAGNE STE GENEVIÈVE

RUE VALETTE

PORTE FOIN

Lycée Louis Le Grand

St-Etienne du Mont

RUE DES ÉCOLES

RUE MONGE

Cardinal Lemoine Ⓜ

Luxembourg Ⓜ

BOULEVARD SAINT-MICHEL

PLACE DU PANTHÉON

Panthéon

RUE DE L'ESTRAPADE

RUE DESCARTES

RUE DU CARDINAL LEMOINE

Ju

Arènes de Lutèce

RUE MONGE

Luxembourg Ⓜ

RUE P. ET M. CURIE

RUE GAY-LUSSAC

RUE SAINT-JACQUES

RUE D'ULM

RUE LHOMOND

Lycée Henri IV

PL. DE LA CONTRESCARPE

RUE ROLLIN

RUE LACEPÈDE

RUE

St-Jacques du Haut Pas

Institut Curie

RUE DU POT DE FER

RUE MOUFFETARD

PL. MONGE

Monge Ⓜ

Ins Mus et M

PL. L. KERN

Val de Grâce

RUE

RUE CLAUDE BERNARD

RUE DE L'ARBALÈTE

RUE DAUBENTON

RUE MONGE

Censier Daubenton Ⓜ

St-Médard

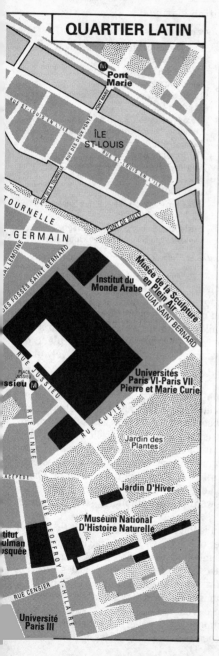

QUARTIER LATIN

Quartier Latin: Listings

Cafés

Café de Cluny, corner of bd St-Michel and bd St-Germain, 5e. Mº St-Michel.

La Chope, place de la Contrescarpe, 5e. Mº Monge.

Café Notre-Dame, corner of quai St-Michel and rue St-Jacques, 5e. Mº St-Michel.

La Périgourdine, corner of quai des Grands-Augustins and place St-Michel, 5e. Mº St-Michel.

Polly Magoo, 11 rue St-Jacques, 5e. Mº St-Michel/Maubert-Mutualité.

Bars

Le Crocodile, 6 rue Royer-Collard, 5e. Mº Luxembourg.

Le Piano Vache, 8 rue Laplace, 5e. Mº Cardinal-Lemoine.

Wine bars

L'Écluse, 15 quai des Grands-Augustins, 6e. Mº St-Michel.

Café de la Nouvelle Mairie, 19 rue des Fossés-St-Jacques, 5e. Mº Luxembourg.

Beer cellars and pubs

Académie de la Bière, 88bis bd Port-Royal, 5e. Mº Port-Royal.

La Gueuze, 19 rue Soufflot, 5e. Mº Luxembourg.

Mayflower Pub, 49 rue Descartes, 5e. Mº Cardinal-Lemoine.

Le Violon Dingue, 46 rue de la Montagne-Ste-Geneviève, 5e. Mº Maubert-Mutualité.

Salons de thé

Café de la Mosquée, 39 rue Geoffroy-St-Hilaire, 5e. Mº Monge.

La Fourmi Ailée, 8 rue du Fouarre, 5e. Mº Maubert-Mutualité.

La Passion du Fruit, 71 quai de la Tournelle, 5e. Mº Maubert-Mutualité.

RESTAURANTS are listed overleaf

Quartier Latin: Listings

CAFÉS and BARS are listed on the previous page

Restaurants

Under 80F

Le Baptiste, 11 rue des Boulangers, 5e. Mo Jussieu.

La Criée, 15 rue Lagrange, 5e. Mo Maubert-Mutualité.

Aux Savoyards, 14 rue des Boulangers, 5e. Mo Jussieu.

Bistro de la Sorbonne, 4 rue Toullier, 5e. Mo Luxembourg.

Tashi Delek, 4 rue des Fossés-St-Jacques, 5e. Mo Luxembourg.

La Vallée des Bambous, 35 rue Gay-Lussac, 5e. Mo Luxembourg.

Under 150F

Le Jardin des Pâtes, 4 rue Lacépède, 5e. Mo Monge.

Le Liban à la Mouff, 18 rue Mouffetard, 5e. Mo Monge.

Perraudin, 157 rue St-Jacques, 5e. Mo Luxembourg.

Le Petit Prince, 12 rue Lanneau, 5e. Mo Maubert-Mutualité.

Pizzeria Roma, 79 rue du Cardinal-Lemoine, 5e. Mo Cardinal-Lemoine.

Restaurant A, 5 rue de Poissy, 5e. Mo Cardinal-Lemoine.

Yakitori, 10 rue Boutebrie, 5e. Mo St-Michel.

Over 150F

Brasserie Balzar, 49 rue des Écoles, 5e. Mo Maubert-Mutualité.

Sud-Ouest, 40 rue de la Montagne-Ste-Geneviève, 5e. Mo Maubert-Mutualité.

All the establishments listed above are reviewed in Chapter Eight, Drinking and Eating.

---

brilliant and mandarin world of French intellectual activity. You can put your nose in the Sorbonne courtyard without anyone objecting. The **Richelieu chapel**, dominating the uphill end and containing the tomb of the great cardinal, was the first Roman-influenced building in seventeenth-century Paris and set the trend for subsequent developments. Nearby, the traffic-free **place de la Sorbonne** with its lime trees, cafés, and student habitués is a lovely place to sit.

The Panthéon and St-Étienne-du-Mont

Further up the hill, the broad rue Soufflot provides an appropriately grand perspective on the domed and porticoed **Panthéon**, Louis XIV's thank you to Sainte Geneviève, patron saint of Paris, for curing him of illness. Imposing enough at a distance, it is cold and uninteresting close up—not a friendly detail for the eye to rest on. The Revolution transformed it into a mausoleum for the great. It is deadly inside (April–Sept 10am–6pm; Oct–March 10am– noon & 2–5pm; closed Tues & public hols). There are, however, several cafés to warm the heart's cockles down toward the Luxembourg gardens, including the beer specialist, *La Gueuze*.

More interesting than the Panthéon is the mainly sixteenth-century church of **St-Étienne-du-Mont** on the corner of rue Clovis, with a façade combining Gothic, Renaissance, and Baroque elements. The interior, if not exactly beautiful, is highly unexpected. The space is divided into three aisles by free-standing pillars connected by a narrow catwalk, and flooded with light by an exceptionally tall clerestory. Again, unusually—for they mainly fell victim to the destructive anti-clericalism of the Revolution—the church still possesses its rood screen, a broad low arch supporting a gallery reached by twining spiral stairs. There is some good seventeenth-century glass in the cloister.

Further down rue Clovis, a huge piece of Philippe Auguste's twelfth-century city walls emerges from among the houses.

Just a step **south from the place du Panthéon**, in the quiet rue des Fossés-St-Jacques, the curbside tables of the *Café de la Nouvelle Mairie* wine bar make an excellent lunch stop, while at the end of the street on rue St-Jacques there are several cheap restaurants, mainly Chinese. There is not much point in going farther south on rue St-Jacques. The area is dull and lifeless once you are over the Gay-Lussac intersection, though Baroque enthusiasts might like to take a look at the seventeenth-century church of **Val-de-Grâce**, with its pedimented front and ornate cupola copied from St Peter's in Rome, while around the corner on **bd de Port-Royal** is another big market and several brasseries, including the *Académie de la Bière* (see p.215).

East of the Panthéon

More enticing wandering is to be had in the villagey streets east of the Panthéon. **Rue de la Montagne-Ste-Geneviève** climbs up from place Maubert across rue des Écoles to the gates of what used to be the **École Polytechnique**, one of the prestigious academies for entry to the top echelons of state power. The school has decamped to the suburbs, leaving its buildings to become the Ministry of Research and Technology. A trip down memory lane for many of its staff, no doubt. There's a sunny little café outside the gate and several restaurants in rue de l'École-Polytechnique facing the new ministry.

From here, rue Descartes runs into the tiny and attractive **place de la Contrescarpe**. Once an arty hangout, where Hemingway wrote—in the café *La Chope*—and Georges Brassens sang, it is now a rendezvous for the down and out. The medieval **rue Mouffetard** begins here, a cobbled lane winding downhill to the church of **St-Médard**, once a country parish beside the now-covered river Bièvre. On the façade of no. 12 is a curious painted glass sign from the Golliwog era, depicting a Negro in striped trousers waiting on his mistress, with the unconvincing legend, "*Au Nègre Joyeux.*" At no. 64 is a shoe shop run by Georges the Armenian, selling genuine Basque espadrilles and the last of the French wooden clogs or *sabots*. But most of the upper half of the street is given over to eating places, mainly Greek and little better than those of rue de la Huchette. Like any place wholly devoted to the entertainment of tourists, it has lost its soul. The bottom half, however, with its sumptuous produce stalls, still maintains an authentic neighborhood air.

The Paris Mosque and Jardin des Plantes

A little **farther east**, across rue Monge, however, are some of the city's most agreeable surprises. Down rue Daubenton, past a delightful Arab shop selling sweets, spices, and gaudy tea-glasses, you come to the crenellated walls of the Paris **mosque**, overtopped by greenery and a great square minaret. You can walk in the sunken garden and patios with their polychrome tiles and carved ceilings, but not the prayer room (9am–noon & 2–6pm; closed Fri & Muslim hols). There is a **tea room** too, open to all, and a **hammam** (see p.174).

Opposite the mosque is an entrance to the **Jardin des Plantes** (gates open summer 7:30am–7:45pm; winter 7:30am–5:45pm), with a small, cramped, expensive zoo (Mon–Sat summer 9am–6pm, winter 9am–5pm, Sun 9am–6:30pm all year), botanical gardens, hothouses, and museums of palae-ontology and mineralogy—a pretty space of greenery to while away the middle of a day. By the rue Cuvier exit is a fine Cedar of Lebanon planted in 1734, raised from seed sent over from Oxford Botanical Gardens, and a slice of an American sequoia more than 2000 years old with Christ's birth and other historical events its life has encompassed marked on its rings. In the nearby physics labs Henri Becquerel discovered radioactivity in 1896, and two years later the Curies discovered radium—unwitting ancestors of the *force de frappe* (the French nuclear deterrent). Pierre ended his days under the wheels of a brewer's dray on rue Dauphine.

A short distance away, with an entrance in rue de Navarre and another through a passage on rue Monge, is Paris's other Roman remain, the **Arènes de Lutèce**, an unexpected and peaceful backwater hidden from the street. It is a partly restored amphitheater, with a *boules* pitch in the center, benches, gardens, and a kids' playground behind.

St-Germain

The northern half of the 6e *arrondissement*, unsymmetrically centered on **place St-Germain-des-Prés**, is the most physically attractive, lively, and stimulating square kilometer in the entire city. It's got the money, elegance, and sophistication, but with it, also, an easygoing tolerance and simplicity that comes from a long association with the mold-breakers and trend-setters in the arts, philosophy, politics, and the sciences. The aspiring and expiring are equally at home.

Across Pont des Arts

The most dramatic approach is to cross the river from the Louvre by the **Pont des Arts**, with the classic upstream view of the Île de la Cité, with barges moored at the quai de Conti, and the Tour St-Jacques and Hôtel de Ville breaking the skyline of the Right Bank.

The dome and pediment at the end of the bridge belong to the **Institut de France**, seat of the Académie Française, an august body of writers and schol-ars whose mission is to safeguard the purity of the French language, and who are currently engaged in a bitter controversy over the reform of French spelling, involving the abolition of such cherished institutions as the circum-flex accent.

This is the grandiose bit of the Left Bank riverfront. To the left is the **Hôtel des Monnaies**, redesigned as the Mint in the late eighteenth century. To the right is the **Beaux-Arts**, the school of Fine Art, whose students throng the *quais* on sunny days, sketchpads on knee. Further down is the ornate erstwhile railroad station now transformed into the **Musée d'Orsay** (see p.152).

The Riverside

The **riverside** part of the quarter is cut lengthwise by **rue St-André-des-Arts** and **rue Jacob**. It is full of bookshops, commercial art galleries, antique shops, cafés, and restaurants. Poke your nose into courtyards and side streets. The houses are four to six stories high, seventeenth- and eighteenth-century, some noble, some stiff, some bulging and skew, all painted in gradations of gray, pearl and off-white. As a rule, the farther west the more sophisticated.

Historical associations are legion. Picasso painted *Guernica* in rue des Grands-Augustins. Molière started his career in rue Mazarine. Robespierre and co split ideological hairs at the *Café Procope*, now an expensive restaurant, in rue de l'Ancienne-Comédie. In rue Visconti, Racine died, Delacroix painted, and Balzac's printing business went bust. In the parallel rue des Beaux-Arts, Oscar Wilde died, Corot and Ampère, father of amps, lived, and the crazy poet Gérard de Nerval went walking with a lobster on a leash.

If you're looking for lunch, **place** and **rue St-André-des-Arts** offer a tempting concentration of places, from Tunisian sandwich joints to seafood extravagance, and a brilliant food market in rue Buci up toward bd St-Germain. Before you get to Buci, there is an intriguing little passage on the left, **Cour du Commerce**, between a *crêperie* and the café, *Le Mazet*, haunt of street musicians and committed drinkers. Marat had his printing press in the passage, while Dr Guillotin perfected his notorious machine by lopping off sheep's heads in the loft next door. A couple of smaller courtyards open off it, revealing another stretch of Philippe Auguste's wall.

An alternative corner for midday food or quiet is around rue de l'Abbaye and place Furstemberg, a tiny square where **Delacroix's old studio** overlooking a secret garden has been converted into a museum (at no. 6; see p.160). This is also the beginning of some very upmarket **shopping territory**, in **rue Jacob, rue de Seine**, and **rue Bonaparte** in particular. On the wall of no. 56 rue Jacob a plaque commemorates the signature of the Treaty of Independence between Britain and the US on September 23, 1783, by Benjamin Franklin, David Hartley, and others. There are also cheap eating places at this end of the street, serving the university medical school by the intersection with rue des Saints-Pères.

Place St-Germain-des-Prés

Place St-Germain-des-Prés, the hub of the *quartier*, is only a stone's throw away, with the *Deux Magots* café on the corner and *Flore* just down the street. Both are renowned for the number of philosophico-politico-poetico-literary backsides that have shined their seats, like the snootier *Brasserie Lipp* across the boulevard, longtime haunt of the more successful practitioners of these trades, admission to whose hallowed portals has become somewhat easier since the decease of the crotchety old proprietor. All these establishments are extremely crowded in summer, expensive, and far from peaceful. And what's more, a place on the *terrasse* in summer will inevitably involve you in the unwanted attentions of second-rate street musicians and street performers.

The tower opposite the *Deux Magots* belongs to the **church of St-Germain**, all that remains of an enormous Benedictine monastery. There has been a

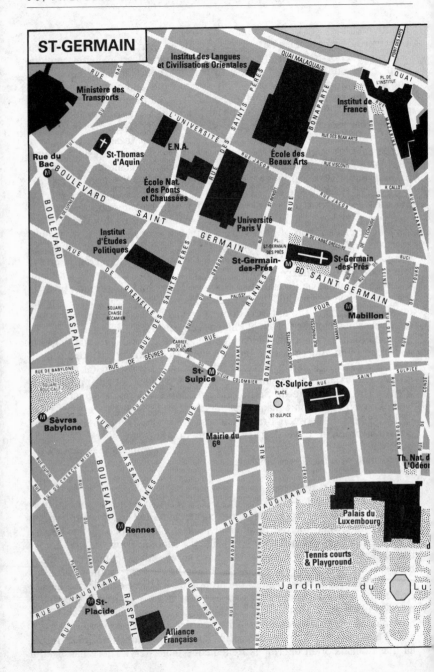

ST-GERMAIN

Institut des Langues et Civilisations Orientales

Ministère des Transports

Rue du Bac

St-Thomas d'Aquin

E.N.A.

École Nat. des Ponts et Chaussées

Institut d'Études Politiques

Université Paris V

St-Germain-des-Prés

St-Germain-des-Prés

École des Beaux Arts

Institut de France

Mabillon

SQUARE CHAISE RECAMIER

CARREF. DE LA CROIX ROUGE

St-Sulpice

Sèvres Babylone

St-Sulpice

PLACE ST-SULPICE

Mairie du 6e

Th. Nat. d L'Odéor

Palais du Luxembourg

Rennes

Tennis courts & Playground

St-Placide

Alliance Française

Jardin du Lu

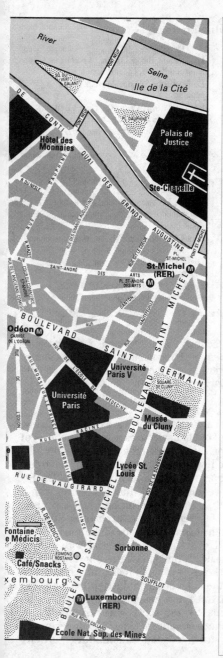

St-Germain: Listings

Cafés

Le Bonaparte, corner rue Bonaparte and place St-Germain. Mº St-Germain-des-Prés.

Café de la Mairie, place St-Sulpice, 6ᵉ. Mº St-Sulpice.

Les Deux Magots, 170 bd St-Germain, 6ᵉ. Mº St-Germain-des-Prés.

Le Flore, 172 bd St-Germain, 6ᵉ. Mº St-Germain-des-Prés.

Le Mandarin, 148 bd St-Germain, 6ᵉ. Mº Mabillon.

Le Mazet, 6 rue St-André-des-Arts, 6ᵉ. Mº Odéon.

Au Petit Suisse, place Claudel, 6ᵉ. Mº Luxembourg.

Sam Kearney's, rue Princesse, 6ᵉ. Mº Mabillon.

Wine bars

Chez Georges, 11 rue des Canettes, 6ᵉ. Mº Mabillon.

Le Petit Bacchus, 13 rue du Cherche-Midi, 6ᵉ. Mº Sèvres-Babylone.

Au Sauvignon, 80 rue des Sts-Pères, 6ᵉ. Mº Sèvres-Babylone.

Beer cellars

Bedford Arms, 17 rue Princesse, 6ᵉ. Mº Mabillon.

London Tavern, 3 rue du Sabot, 6ᵉ. Mº St-Sulpice.

La Pinte, 13 carrefour de l'Odéon, 6ᵉ. Mº Odéon.

Pub Saint-Germain, 17 rue de l'Ancienne-Comédie, 6ᵉ. Mº Odéon.

La Taverne de Nesle, 32 rue Dauphine, 6ᵉ. Mº Odéon.

Twickenham, 70 rue des Sts-Pères, 6ᵉ. Mº Sèvres-Babylone.

Salon de thé

À la Cour de Rohan, 59–61 rue St-André-des-Arts, 6ᵉ. Mº Odéon.

Snacks

Drugstore Saint-Germain, 149 bd St-Germain, 6ᵉ. Mº St-Germain-des-Prés.

La Table d'Italie, 69 rue de Seine, 6ᵉ. Mº Mabillon/St-Germain-des-Prés.

RESTAURANTS are listed overleaf

St-Germain: Listings

CAFÉS and BARS are listed on the previous page

Restaurants

Under 80F

Restaurant des Arts, 73 rue de Seine, 6e. Mº St-Germain-des-Prés.

Restaurant des Beaux-Arts, 11 rue Bonaparte, 6e. Mº St-Germain-des-Prés.

Le Bistro de la Gare, 1 rue du Four, 6e. Mº Mabillon.

La Macrobiothèque, 17 rue de Savoie, 6e. Mº St-Michel.

Orestias, 4 rue Grégoire-de-Tours, 6e. Mº Odéon.

Le Petit Mabillon, 6 rue Mabillon, 6e. Mº Mabillon.

Le Petit Vatel, 5 rue Lobineau, 6e. Mº Mabillon.

Under 150F

L'Alsace à Paris, 9 place St-André-des-Arts, 6e. Mº St-Michel.

La Maison de la Lozère, 4 rue Hautefeuille, 6e. Mº St-Michel.

Le Muniche, 27 rue de Buci, 6e. Mº Mabillon.

Le Petit Saint-Benoît, 4 rue St-Benoît, 6e. Mº St-Germain-des-Prés.

Le Petit Zinc, 25 rue de Buci, 6e. Mº Mabillon.

Polidor, 41 rue Monsieur-le-Prince, 6e. Mº Odéon.

Le Katyouschka, 9 rue de l'Éperon, 6e. Mº Odéon.

Village Bulgare, 8 rue de Nevers, 6e. Mº Odéon/Pont-Neuf.

Over 150F

Aux Charpentiers, 10 rue Mabillon, 6e. Mº Mabillon.

Drugstore Saint-Germain, 149 bd St-Germain, 6e.

Lipp, 151 bd St-Germain, 6e. Mº St-Germain-des-Prés.

All the establishments listed above are reviewed in Chapter Eight, Drinking and Eating.

---

church on the site since the sixth century. The interior is best, its pure Romanesque lines still clear under the deforming paint of nineteenth-century frescoes. In the corner of the churchyard by the rue Bonaparte there is a little Picasso head of a woman dedicated to the memory of the poet Apollinaire.

St-Sulpice and the Luxembourg Gardens

South of bd St-Germain the streets around St-Sulpice are calm and classy. **Rue Mabillon** is pretty, with a row of old houses set back below the level of the modern street. There are two or three restaurants, including the old-fashioned *Aux Charpentiers,* decorated with models of rafters and roof-trees; it is the property of the Guild of Carpenters. On the left are the **halles St-Germain,** on the site of a fifteenth-century market. Rue St-Sulpice, with a delicious *pâtisserie* and a shop called *L'Estrelle* specializing in teas, coffees, and jams, leads through to the front of the enormous **church of St-Sulpice,** with the popular *Café de la Mairie* on the sunny north side of the square.

The church, erected either side of 1700, is austerely classical, with a Doric colonnade surmounted by an Ionic, and Corinthian pilasters in the towers, only one of which is finished, where kestrels come to make their nests. The interior (some Delacroix frescoes in the first chapel on the right) is not to my taste. But softened by the chestnut trees and fountain of the square, the ensemble is peaceful and harmonious. To the south, rue Férou, where a gentleman called Pottier composed the *Internationale* in 1776, connects with **rue de Vaugirard**, Paris's longest street, and the **Luxembourg gardens** (see below).

The main attraction of **place St-Sulpice** is **Yves Saint Laurent Rive Gauche**, the most elegant fashion boutique on the Left Bank. That's on the corner of the ancient **rue des Canettes**. Further along the same side of the *place* there's Saint Laurent for men, and then it's Consume, Consume all the way, with your triple-gilt uranium-plated credit card, down rues Bonaparte, Madame, de Sèvres, de Grenelle, du Four, des Saints-Pères . . . Hard to believe now, but smack in the middle of all this at the Carrefour de la Croix Rouge, there was a major barricade in 1871, fiercely defended by Eugène Varlin, one of the Commune's leading lights, later betrayed by a priest, half-beaten to death, and shot by government troops on Montmartre hill.

But it will be price-shock not shell-shock you'll be suffering from. You may feel safer in rue Princesse at the small, friendly, and well-stocked American bookshop, *The Village Voice*, where you can browse through the latest poetry.

The least elegant bit of the *quartier* is the eastern edge, where the university is firmly implanted, along bd St-Michel, with attendant scientific and medical bookshops, skeletons, and instruments of torture as well as a couple of weird and wonderful shops in rue Racine. But there is really no escape from elegance round here, as you'll see in rue Tournon and rue de l'Odéon, which leads to the Doric portico of the **Théâtre de l'Odéon** and back to the Luxembourg gardens by the rue de Médicis.

It was Marie de Médicis, Henri IV's widow, who had the **Jardin** and **Palais du Luxembourg** built to remind her of the Palazzo Pitti and Giardino di Boboli of her native Florence. The palace forms yet another of those familiar Parisian backdrops that no one pays much attention to, though there would be outrage if they were to disappear. The gardens are the chief lung and recreation ground of the Left Bank, with tennis courts, pony rides, children's playground, *boules* pitch, yachts to rent on the pond, and, in the wilder southeast corner, a miniature orchard of elaborately espaliered pear trees. With its strollers and mooners and garish parterres it has a distinctly Mediterranean air on summer days, when the most contested spot is the shady **Fontaine de Médicis** in the northeast corner. The palace itself is the seat of the French Senate. Opposite the gates, scarcely noticeable on the end wall of the colonnade of 36 rue de Vaugirard, is a meter rule, set up in the Revolution to guide the people in the introduction of the new metric system.

Montparnasse to the Cité Universitaire

Like other Left Bank *quartiers* Montparnasse still trades on its association with the wild characters of the interwar artistic and literary boom. Many were habitués of the cafés *Select, Coupole, Dôme, Rotonde*, and *Closerie des Lilas*, all still going strong on **bd du Montparnasse**, and the clientèle still belongs, at least partly, to the world of the arts and politics—fatter wallets than the old days, though.

Another major sub-community in the *quartier* in the early years of the century consisted of outlawed Russian revolutionaries. They were so many that the Tsarist police ran a special Paris section to keep tabs on them. **Lenin and Trotsky** both lodged in the area. Trotsky lived in **rue de la Gaîté** near the cemetery, now a seedy street of sex shops, questionable lingerie and movie theaters showing titles that are both disgusting and laughable.

Tour du Montparnasse

Most of the life of the quarter is concentrated around the station end of bd du Montparnasse, where the colossal **Tour du Montparnasse** has become one of the city's principal landmarks—at its best at night when the red staple-shaped corner lights give it a certain elegance. At 56 stories it held the record as Europe's tallest office building until it was overtaken by London dockland's Canary Wharf. You can go up on a tour for less than the Eiffel Tower (summer 9:30am–11pm; winter 10am–10pm), though it makes more sense to spend the money on a drink at the **top-floor bar**—the lift up is free—where you get a tremendous view westward over the city, especially at sunset.

The tower is much reviled as a building, not because it is particularly ugly—it's in the bland tombstone style—but because it should not be there at all, totally out of scale with its surroundings. Worse, it has bred a rash of workers' barracks in the area behind it. But no one is too bothered about that: it's the other side of the tracks . . . In front of it, on **place du 18 juin 1940**, is an enormous, largely subterranean shopping complex, with a Galeries Lafayette, C & A, boutiques galore, snack bars, sports center, and what-have-you. Very convenient, if you like shopping underground.

On the front of the complex a plaque records the fact that here General Leclerc of the Free French forces received the surrender of von Choltitz, the German general commanding Paris, on August 25, 1944. Under orders from Hitler to destroy the city before abandoning it, he luckily decided to disobey. And the name of the *place* is also significant in French wartime history. It commemorates the date, June 18, 1940, when de Gaulle broadcast from London, calling on the people of France to continue the struggle in spite of the armistice signed with the Germans by Marshal Pétain.

The animated part of bd du Montparnasse ends at **bd Raspail**, where Rodin's *Balzac* broods over the traffic, though literary curiosity might take you down as far as the *Closerie des Lilas*, on the corner of the tree-lined avenue connecting the Observatory and Luxembourg gardens. Hemingway used to come here to write, and Marshal Ney, one of Napoléon's most glamorous generals, was killed by royalist firing squad on the sidewalk outside in 1815. He's still there, waving his sword, idealized in stone. Hard by, dwarfed by apartment buildings at 100bis rue d'Assas, is the house and garden of the Russian sculptor, **Ossip Zadkine**, now a museum of his work (see p.161) and one of the most delightful oases in the city.

From Montparnasse Cemetery to the Cité Universitaire

Boulevard du Montparnasse marks the boundary between the **6ᵉ and 14ᵉ arrondissements** and is still a class divide. On the north side the streets are sedate and well-heeled, to the south they are working-class and increasingly prey to the developers, especially between av du Maine and the railroad tracks, which in years gone by sucked thousands of émigré Bretons into the city.

Montparnasse Cemetery and the Catacombs

The change is clear as you soon come to the **market in bd Edgar-Quinet**, where the cafés are full of stall-holders. Just off to one side is the main entrance to the **Montparnasse cemetery**, a gloomy city of the dead, with ranks of miniature temples, dreary and bizarre, and plenty of illustrious names for spotters, from Baudelaire to Sartre and André Citroën to Saint-Saens. In the southwest corner is an old windmill, one of the seventeenth-century taverns frequented by the carousing, versifying students who gave the district its name of Parnassus.

If you are determined to spend your time among the dear departed, you can also get down into the **catacombs** (Tues–Fri 2–4pm, Sat & Sun 9–11am & 2–4pm) in nearby **place Denfert-Rochereau** (no. 2), formerly place d'Enfer—Hell Square. These are abandoned quarries stacked with millions of bones cleared from the old charnel houses in 1785, claustrophobic in the extreme, and cold. Some years ago punks and art students developed a taste for this as a party location, but the authorities, alas, soon put an end to that.

The Observatoire and Around

Having surfaced, you will find yourself on rue Rémy-Dumoncel. From here you can stroll back over av du Général-Leclerc to the quiet little streets of clothes and crafts shops and cheap apartments bordered by the cemetery and av du Maine (with a food market on rue Daguerre as well).

Or you can follow rue de la Tombe-Issoire to the **Observatoire de Paris**, where there's a garden open on summer afternoons in which to sit and admire the dome. From the 1660s, when the observatory was constructed, to 1884, all French maps had the zero meridian running through the middle of this building. After that date, they reluctantly agreed that 0° longitude should pass through a village in Normandy that happens to be due south of Greenwich. Visiting the Observatoire is a complicated procedure and all you'll see are old maps and instruments.

If you head south, you'll pass Ste-Anne's psychiatric hospital where the political philosopher, Louis Althusser, died after being committed for murdering his wife. One block farther on, at the bottom of av Réné-Coty, is the **Parc Montsouris**, with a marker of the old meridian on the far side near bd Jourdan. It looks a tempting place to collapse but you'll be up against the city's obsessively whistling park police the moment you touch the grass. A beautiful reproduction of the Bardo palace in Tunis, built for the 1867 *exposition universelle*, is finally being restored. Lenin used to take strolls here when he was living nearby, as, no doubt, did Dali, Lurgat, Miller, Durrell, and other artists who found homes in the tiny cobbled street of **Villa Seurat**, off rue de la Tombe-Issoire just across the reservoirs from the park.

The Cité Universitaire

On the other side of bd Jourdan, several thousand students from over 100 different countries live in the curious array of buildings of the **Cité Universitaire**. The central *Maison Internationale* resembles the Marlin-spike of Tintin books. The others reflect in their mixture of styles the diversity of the nations and peoples willing to subsidize foreign study. Armenia,

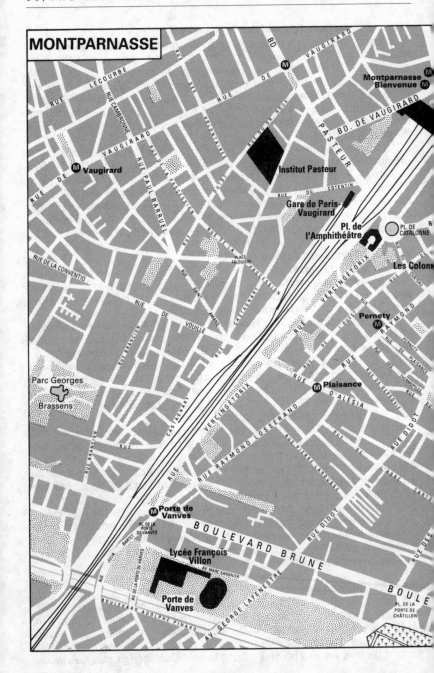

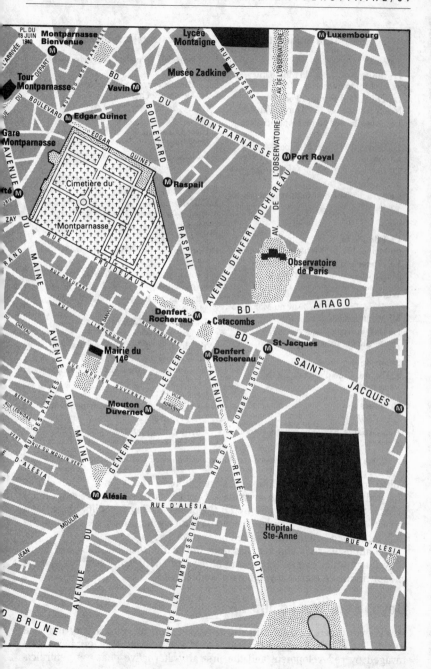

Montparnasse to the Cité Universitaire: Listings

Cafés

Le Boulevard, 73 bd du Montparnasse, 6e. Mº Montparnasse.

Le Chien Qui Fume, 19 bd du Montparnasse, 14e. Mº Duroc/Falguière.

La Coupole, 102 bd de Montparnasse, 14e. Mº Montparnasse.

Le Dôme, 108 bd du Montparnasse, 6e. Mº Vavin.

La Rotonde, 105 bd du Montparnasse, 6e. Mº Vavin.

Le Select, 99 bd du Montparnasse, 6e. Mº Vavin.

Bars

Ciel de Paris, Tour Montparnasse, 33 av du Maine, 15e. Mº Montparnasse.

La Closerie des Lilas, 171 bd du Montparnasse, 6e. Mº Port-Royal.

Wine bars

Au Père Tranquille, 30 av du Maine, 15e. Mº Montparnasse.

Le Rallye, 6 rue Daguerre, 14e. Mº Denfert-Rochereau.

Salon de thé

JeThéMe, 4 rue d'Alleray, 15e. Mº Vaugirard.

Restaurants

Under 80F

Aux Artistes, 63 rue Falguière, 15e. Mº Pasteur.

Le Berbère, 50 rue de Gergovie, 14e. Mº Pernety.

Le Biniou, 3 av du Général-Leclerc, 14e. Mº Denfert-Rochereau.

Bistro de la Gare, 59 bd du Montparnasse, 6e. Mº Montparnasse.

Bistro Romain, 103 bd du Montparnasse, 6e. Mº Vavin.

La Criée, 54 bd Montparnasse, 15e. Mº Montparnasse.

Au Rendez-vous des Camioneurs, 34 rue des Plantes, 14e. Mº Alésia.

Café-Restaurant à l'Observatoire, 63 av Denfert-Rochereau, 14e. Mº Denfert-Rochereau.

Under 150F

Bergamote, 1 rue Niepce, 14e. Mº Pernety.

Hippopotamus, 12 av du Maine, 15e. Mº Falguière.

Chez Maria, 16 rue du Maine, 14e. Mº Montparnasse.

La Route du Château, 123 rue du Château, 14e. Mº Pernety.

Yakitori, 64 rue du Montparnasse, 14e. Mº Edgar-Quinet.

N' Zadette M'Foua, 152 rue du Château, 14e. Mº Pernety.

Over 150F

La Coupole, 102 bd du Montparnasse, 14e. Mº Vavin.

Pavillon Montsouris, 20 rue Gazan, 14e. RER Cité-Universitaire.

All the establishments listed above are reviewed in Chapter Eight, Drinking and Eating.

Cuba, Indo-China, and Monaco are neighbors at one end; Cambodia is guarded by startling stone creatures; Spain was closed by an extradition debate; Switzerland (designed by Le Corbusier during his stilts phase) and the US are the most popular for their relatively luxurious rooms; and the Collège Franco-Britannique is a red-brick monster.

The atmosphere is still very far from internationalist, but there are films, shows, and other events (check the *Maison Internationale)* and you can eat cheaply in the cafeterias if you have a student card.

Beyond the Tracks: the 14e

Once over avenue du Maine to the west, you are into a very different world. The old working-class districts of **Plaisance** and **Pernety** have been ravaged by redevelopment and the first arty-alternative phase of gentrification. While the latter at least has the virtue of preserving the physical, if not the social, texture of the area—the 14e had the highest Green vote in the 1988 local elections—redevelopment has already completely transformed the western sector of the *quartier*. From the windy, impersonal business sector behind the Montparnasse station to the bd Périphérique at Porte de Vanves stretches a nightmare acreage of towers and barracks, from which all street-level life has disappeared. The long **rue de Vercingétorix** has to all intents and purposes ceased to exist.

But local protest has perhaps borne some fruit, for the most recent development—a futuristic complex by the Catalan architect **Ricardo Bofill**, around the intersection of rue de Vercingétorix and rue du Château—at least has some aesthetic interest. A huge new square, **place de Catalogne**— reminiscent of Mansart's classical place des Victoires in the 1er *arrondissement* and place de la Libération in Dijon—has been created, with an enormous tilted disk of cobbles in the center across which water slides to form a fountain. Traffic hurtles around it, overlooked by Bofill's Neoclassical façades complete with metopes, triglyphs, and pediments. In one corner a great square arch leads through into a circular, lawn-filled courtyard called the **place de Séoul**, bounded by glass walls punctuated by a colonnade of four-sided reflective glass columns with stone capitals, opening on the farther side on to a vista of high-rise apartments flanked by two massive Doric columns supporting nothing but sky—the whole known as **Les Colonnes**. Pretentious perhaps, but at least it draws the attention.

To catch the flavor of what the *quartier* used to be like, you need to wander up **rue Raymond-Losserand** and **rue Didot** and look into the cross-streets, where offbeat shops, restaurants, and clubs are beginning to proliferate, and into the *villas*, in one of which—impasse Florimont—Georges Brassens lived for many years.

Porte de Vanves and the Parc Georges Brassens

Rue Raymond-Losserand cuts through the *quartier* to hit the exterior boulevard at place de la Porte de Vanves, where the city fortifications used to run until the 1920s when, despite talk of a green belt, most of the space gained by their demolition was given over to speculative building. Behind the workers' apartments along bd Brune, on the sidewalks of av Marc-Sangnier and av Georges-Lafenestre, one of the city's best **junk markets** takes place on Saturday and Sunday, starting at daybreak (see p.202).

Book-lovers can take a short stroll along bd Lefebvre and down rue Brancion to the old Vaugirard abattoir, transformed in the 1980s into the very successful **Parc Georges-Brassens**. Here, in the sheds of the old horse market, every Saturday and Sunday morning, **dozens of book dealers** set out their genuinely interesting stock.

The park itself is a delight, especially for children. Two bronze bulls flank the main entrance on rue des Morillons. A pond surrounds the old abattoir clock tower. There is a garden of scented herbs and shrubs for the blind, houses and rocks and merry-go-rounds for the kids, a mountain stream with pine and birch trees, beehives, and a tiny terraced vineyard facing the sun behind the towering apartment buildings.

Just the other side of the park, in **passage Dantzig** off rue Dantzig, in a secluded garden, stands an unusual polygonal building known as **La Rûche**, the Beehive. It was designed by Eiffel as the wine pavilion for the 1900 trade fair and transported here from its original site in the Champs de Mars. It has been used ever since as artists' studios, rented by some of the biggest names in twentieth-century art, starting with Chagall, Modigliani, and Léger.

Commerce and Convention: the 15^e

Between the Montparnasse railroad tracks and the river lies the big, unfashionable 15e *arrondissement*, home of the city's least visible inhabitants. It was in the **rue du Commerce** here that George Orwell worked as a dishwasher in a White Russian restaurant in the late Twenties, described in his *Down and Out in Paris and London*.

A Walk from the École Militaire

If you start walking, say, in **av de la Motte-Picquet** by the École Militaire, you'll get the full flavor of the *quartier*. That's the staid end, with the brasseries full of officers from the École and the rather dreary **Village Suisse** with its 150 expensive antique shops (open Thurs–Mon)—all Louis Quinze and Second Empire. The nature of the *quartier* changes at **bd de Grenelle** where the métro runs on iron piers above the street. Seedy hotels rent rooms by the month and the corner cafés offer cheap *plats du jour*. **Rue du Commerce** begins here, a lively, old-fashioned main street full of small shops and peeling, shuttered houses. Scale and architecture give it a sunny, friendly atmosphere. There are cheap eating places in rues Tiphaine and Letellier. The best-known establishment is *Le Commerce* at no. 51 (see p.228).

Toward the end of the street, **place du Commerce**, with a Belle Époque butcher's on the corner and a bandstand in the middle, is a model of old-fashioned petty-bourgeois respectability. It might be a frozen frame from a 1930s movie.

If you carry on south, rue de la Croix-Nivert brings you to the **Porte de Versailles** where, at an informer's signal, government troops first entered the city in their final assault on the Commune on May 21, 1871. Today it is the site of several large **exhibition halls** where the *Foires* are held—Agricultural Show, Ideal Home Exhibition, and the like. Behind it, a few minutes' walk away past the headquarters of the French air force, is the **Aquaboulevard**, the city's largest leisure center, where the principal attraction is an artificial tropical lagoon complete with beaches and exotic plants and giant helter-skelter-type water chutes (see p.173).

The Riverbank Section: Allée des Cygnes

The western edge of the *arrondissement* fronts the Seine from the **Port de Javel** to the Eiffel Tower. Most of the riverbank is marred by a sort of mini-Défense development of half-cocked futuristic towers with pretentious galactic names like Castor and Pollux, Vega and Orion, rising out of a litter-blown pedestrian platform some ten meters above street level.

Out in midstream a narrow island, the **Allée des Cygnes**, a pleasant place to walk, joins the Pont de Grenelle and the double-decker road and rail bridge, Pont de Bir-Hakeim. A scaled-down version of the **Statue of Liberty** stands at the downstream end, while just off Pont de Bir-Hakeim in the beginning of bd de Grenelle, in a rather undignified enclosure sandwiched by highrise buildings, a plaque commemorates the notorious **rafle du Vel d'Hiv**: the Nazi and French-aided roundup of 13,152 Parisian Jews in July 1942. Nine thousand of them, including four thousand children, were interned here at the now vanished cycle track for a week before being carted off to Auschwitz. Thirty adults were the only survivors.

A couple of hundred meters farther along the river, at 101 quai Branly, is the useful information and advice bureau for young people, the **CIDJ** or *Center d'Information et de Documentation Jeunesse* (see p.40). Opposite is the Australian embassy, and on the exposed end wall of a neighboring house an enormous mural portrait of 477 people who have made the twentieth century—"*Ils ont fait le XXe siècle.*"

A map of the **15ᵉ arrondissement**, together with listings, is on pages 102–103.
A map of **Auteuil** and **Passy** is on p.105.

The Beaux Quartiers, Auteuil, and Passy

The **Beaux Quartiers** are essentially the 16ᵉ and 17ᵉ *arrondissements*. The 16ᵉ is aristocratic and rich; the 17ᵉ, or at least the southern part of it, bourgeois and rich, embodying the staid, cautious values of the nineteenth-century manufacturing and trading classes. The northern half of the 16ᵉ, toward place Victor-Hugo and place de l'Étoile, is leafy and distinctly metropolitan in feel. The southern part, around the old villages of **Auteuil** and **Passy**, has an almost provincial air, and is full of pleasant surprises for the walker. A good peg on which to hang a walk is a visit to the **Musée Marmottan** (see p.157) in av Raphael, with its marvelous collection of late Monets. There are also several interesting pieces of **twentieth-century architecture** scattered through the district, especially by Hector Guimard (designer of the swirly green Art Nouveau métro stations) and by Le Corbusier and Mallet-Stevens, architects of the first "cubist" buildings.

Auteuil

A good place to start an architectural exploration is the **Église d'Auteuil** métro station. Around this area are several of Hector Guimard's **Art Nouveau** buildings: at 34 rue Boileau; 8 av de la Villa-de-la-Réunion; 41 rue Lagache-Chardon; 192 av de Versailles; and 39 bd Exelmans. For more of the life of the quarter follow the old village main street, **rue d'Auteuil**, from the métro exit to **place Lorrain**, which hosts a Saturday market. More Guimard houses are to be found at the farther end of rue La Fontaine, which begins here; no. 60 is perhaps the best in the city. In rue Poussin, just off the *place*,

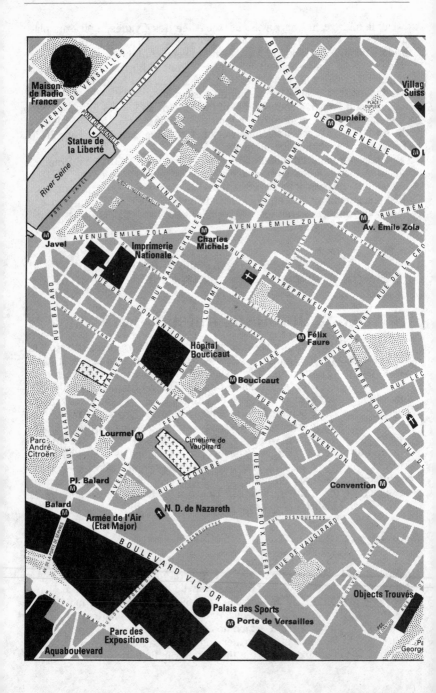

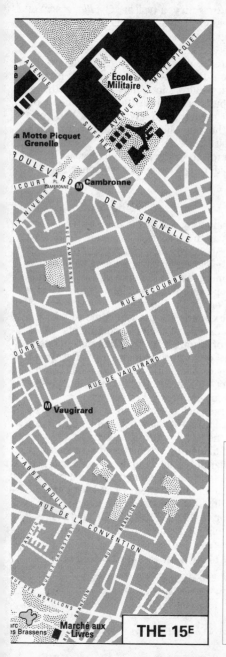

THE 15E

The 15e: Listings

Salon de thé

La Passion du Fruit, 31 av de Suffren, 7e. Mº Bir-Hakeim.

Restaurants

Under 80F

Le Commerce, 51 rue du Commerce, 15e. Mº Émile-Zola.

Sampieru Corsu, 12 rue de l'Amiral-Roussin, 15e. Mº Cambronne.

All these establishments are reviewed in Chapter Eight, Drinking and Eating.

carriage gates open on to **Villa Montmorency**, a typical 16e *villa*, a sort of private village of leafy lanes and English-style gardens. Gide and the Goncourt brothers of Prix fame lived in this one.

Behind it is rue du Dr-Blanche (see below) where, in a cul-de-sac on the right, are **Le Corbusier's first private houses** (1923), one of them now the *Fondation Le Corbusier* (Mon–Fri 10am–1pm & 2–6pm; closed Aug). Built in strictly cubistic style, very plain, with windows in bands, the only extravagance is the raising of one wing on piers and a curved frontage. They look commonplace enough now, but what a contrast to anything that had gone before. Further along Dr-Blanche, the tiny rue Mallet-Stevens was built entirely by Mallet-Stevens also in "cubist" style.

To continue on to the **Musée Marmottan** (see p.157), an underpass under the now disused *Petite Ceinture* railroad brings you out by av Raphael.

Passy

Passy too offers scope for a good meandering walk, from place du Trocadéro to Balzac's house and up rue de Passy to the spectacles museum. If you start in rue Franklin, take a left after place de Costa-Rica and go down the steps into square Alboni, a patch of garden enclosed by tall apartment buildings as solid as banks. Here the métro line emerges from the once vine-covered hillside beneath your feet at the Passy stop—more like a country station—before rumbling out across the river by the Pont de Bir-Hakeim.

Below the station, in **rue des Eaux**, Parisians used to come to take the Passy waters. It too is enclosed by a canyon of capitalist apartments, which dwarf the eighteenth-century houses of **square Charles-Dickens**. In one of them, burrowing back into the cellars of a vanished monastery, the **Musée du Vin** puts on a disappointing display of viticultural odds and bobs (*dégustation*, if you need it). Its vaults connect with the ancient quarry tunnels—not visitable—from which the stone for Notre-Dame was hewn.

If you keep along the foot of the Passy hill, down the back of the ministry of *urbanisme* and *logement*, whose appearance does not bode well for the aesthetics of its works, you arrive in the cobbled **rue d'Ankara** at the gates of an eighteenth-century château half-hidden by greenery and screened by a high wall. It's a brave soul who will march resolutely up to the gate and peer in with the confident air of the connoisseur. And you'd better make it convincing, for all the time your nose is pressed between the bars, at least four CRS are watching the small of your back intently, fingers on the trigger. This is the Turkish embassy. Not a parked car, nothing to obstruct the field of fire. It was once a clinic where the pioneering Dr Blanche tried to treat the mad

---

The Beaux Quartiers, Auteuil, and Passy: Listings

Salon de thé	**Restaurant**
Le Coquelin Aîné, 67 rue de Passy, 16e.	*Over 150F*
M^o Muette.	**Le Mouton Blanc**, 40 rue d'Auteuil, 16e.
	M^o Église d'Auteuil.

Both these establishments are reviewed in Chapter Eight, Drinking and Eating.

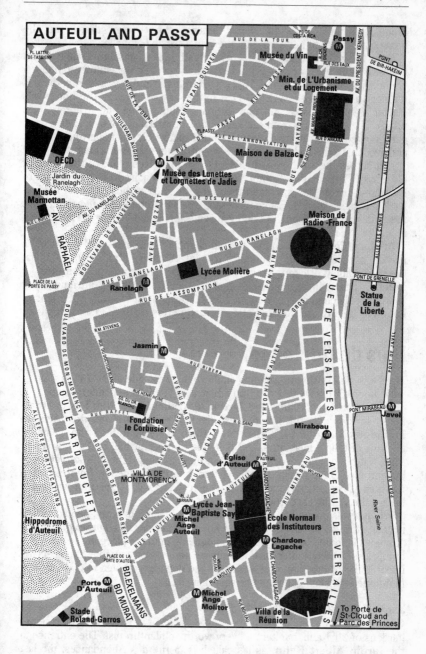

Maupassant and Gérard de Nerval, among others; before that it was the home of Marie-Antoinette's friend, the Princesse de Lamballe.

From the gates **rue Berton**, a cobbled path with its gas lights still in place, follows around the ivy-covered garden wall. By an old green-shuttered house a boundary stone bears the date 1731. Apart from the embassy security, there is nothing to say that it is not still 1731 in this tiny backwater. The house was **Balzac's** in the 1840s, and now contains memorabilia and a library (see p.165). The entrance is from rue Raynouard, down a flight of steps into a dank garden overshadowed by a singularly unattractive block of apartments built, and lived in, by the architect Auguste Perret, father of French concrete.

Just across the road, **rue de l'Annonciation** gives more of the flavor of old Passy. You may not want your Bechstein repaired or your furniture lacquered, but as you approach the end of the street there'll be no holding back the saliva glands. Sacks of herbs, wheels of cheese, coffees and teas, figs, dates and nuts, pheasant and venison, salmon and lobster . . . and health foods, for the morning after.

At **place de Passy**, you join the old shopping strip, **rue de Passy**, and a parade of eye-catching boutiques: Daniel Hechter, Fikipsy, Manoukian, Caroll Wembley, Kickers for kids, Guérlain etc, stretching up to **métro La Muette**. There, in an opticians' shop at 2 av Mozart, is an intriguing and beautiful collection of specs, lorgnettes, binoculars, and sundry other lenses, known as the **Musée des Lunettes et Lorgnettes de Jadis** (see p.162).

Bois de Boulogne

The **Bois de Boulogne**, running all down the west side of the 16e, is supposedly modeled on Hyde Park, though it is a very French interpretation. It offers all sorts of facilities: the **Jardin d'Acclimatation** with lots of attractions for kids (see p.180); the excellent **Musée National des Arts et Traditions Populaires** (p.163); the **Parc de Bagatelle**, with beautiful displays of tulips, hyacinths, and daffodils in the first half of April, irises in May, waterlilies and roses at the end of June; a riding school; **bike rental** at the entrance to the Jardin d'Acclimatation; **boating** on the Lac Inférieur; **race courses** at Longchamp and Auteuil. The best, and wildest, part for walking is toward the southwest corner.

When it was opened to the public in the eighteenth century, people said of it, "*Les mariages du bois de Boulogne ne se font pas devant Monsieur le Curé*"– "Unions cemented in the Bois de Boulogne do not take place in the presence of a priest." Today's after-dark unions are no less disreputable, the specialty in particular of Brazilian transvestites—and don't be tempted to go in for any nighttime sightseeing: it could be very dangerous.

Jardin Albert Kahn and Île de la Jatte

Chaster and more tender encounters take place not too far away in the secret gardens of Mr Kahn, banker and very worthy philanthropist. The entrance to the **Jardin Albert Kahn**, as it's called, is in rue des Abondances, the last

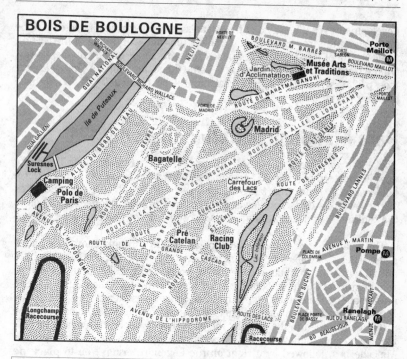

BOIS DE BOULOGNE

Bois de Boulogne: Listings

Restaurants

Over 150F

Café de la Jatte, 67 bd de Levallois, Île de la Jatte. Mº Pont-de-Levallois.

La Guinguette de Neuilly, 12 bd de Levallois, Île de la Jatte. Mº Pont-de-Levallois.

Both these establishments are reviewed in Chapter Eight, Drinking and Eating.

---

turning on the right as you approach the Pont de St-Cloud from Porte de St-Cloud (last two weeks of March & Oct to mid-Nov 9:30am–12:30pm & 2–6pm; April–Sept 9:30am–12:30pm & 2–7pm; Mº Pont-de-St-Cloud; bus #72 to Rhin-et-Danube stop). Maybe you wouldn't make it a special expedition, but it is an enchanting place, with gaudy rhododendrons under blue cedars, palm house and rose garden, forest and hillock, and a Japanese garden complete with pagoda, tea house, streams, and maples.

North of here, downstream from the Bois, the **Île de la Jatte** floats in the Seine off the shore of rich and leafy Neuilly. It too is good for a romantic riverside walk, as well as some gastronomic indulgence. From the Pont de Levallois, close to the métro of the same name, a flight of steps descends to the tip of the island. Formerly an industrial site, it is now part public garden (Mon–Fri 8:30am–6pm, Sat & Sun 10am–8pm), part stylish new housing development. What remains of the island's erstwhile rustic character is to be found along the tree-lined bd de Levallois (on the Neuilly side of the island), where a line of Rube Goldberg houses and workshops quietly molders away. On the right, a former manège has become the smart people's *Café de la Jatte* (see p.228), while by the bridge at no. 12 the *Guinguette de Neuilly* (see p.229) still flourishes.

Parc Monceau to Batignolles: the 17^e

The 17e *arrondissement* is most interesting in its eastern half. The more upscale western end is cold and soulless, cut by too many wide and uniform boulevards. A route that takes in the best of it would be from **place des Ternes** with its cafés and flower market through **parc Monceau** and on to the **"village" of Batignolles** on the wrong side of the St-Lazare railroad tracks.

The nearest *parc* entrance is from av Hoche through enormous gilded gates. There's a roller-skating rink and kids' play facilities, but basically it's a formal garden with antique colonnades, grots, and the like. Half the people who command the heights of the French economy spent their infancy there, promenaded in prams by proper nannies. In av Velasquez on the far side the **Musée Cernuschi** houses a small collection of ancient Chinese art (see p.160) bequeathed to the state by the banker, Cernuschi, who nearly lost his life for giving money to the Commune. From there a left turn on bd Malesherbes, followed by a right on rue Legendre brings you to **place de Lévis**, already much more interesting than the sedate streets you have left behind.

Rue de Lévis and Batignolles

Between the *place* and bd de Courcelles, the **rue de Lévis** has one of the city's most strident, colorful, and appetizing **food and clothes markets**, every day of the week except Monday. From here rue Legendre and rue des Dames lead across the railroad line to **rue des Batignolles**, the heart of Batignolles "village," now sufficiently conscious of its uniqueness to have formed an association for the preservation of its *caractère villageois*. At the northern end of the street the attractive semicircular **place Félix-Lobligeois** frames the colonnaded church of **Ste-Marie-des-Batignolles**, modeled on the Madeleine, behind which the tired and trampled greenery of **square Batignolles** stretches back to the big marshaling yards. On the corner of the *place*, the modern bar *L'Endroit* attracts the bourgeois kids of the neighborhood until 2am.

To the northeast the long **rue des Moines** leads toward Guy-Môquet, with a covered market on the corner of rue Lemercier. This is the working-class Paris of the movies, all small, animated, friendly shops, four- to five-story houses in shades of peeling gray, brown-stained bars where men drink standing at the "zinc." Across the avenue de Clichy round **rue de La Jonquière**, the quiet streets are redolent of petty-bourgeois North African respectability, interspersed with decidedly upper-crust enclaves as in the film-set perfection of the **Cité des Fleurs**, a residential lane of magnificent private houses and gardens.

From Guy-Môquet it's a short walk back along av de St-Ouen to rue du Capitaine-Madon, a cobbled alley with washing strung at the windows, leading to the wall of the Montmartre cemetery, where the ancient *Hôtel Beau-Lieu* still survives. Ramshackle and peeling, on a tiny courtyard full of plants, it epitomizes the kind-hearted, no-nonsense, instinctively arty, sepia Paris that every romantic visitor secretly cherishes. Most of the guests have been there fifteen years or more.

On the north side of the cemetery, with its entrance on rue Carpeaux, the **Hôpital Bretonneau**—a curious assembly of brick and iron-frame pavilions condemned to demolition for subsidence—has been given a temporary reprieve by being loaned to an organization called *Usines Ephémères*, whose raison d'être is to recuperate old buildings for use as studios and performance spaces by young artists and musicians, both French and foreign. Its lease will run out in 1992, but in the meantime there are many free shows and exhibitions. The base office for this and other spaces is La Base, 6bis rue Vergniaud, 92300 Levallois-Perret (☎47.58.49.58; Mº Louise-Michel; Mon–Fri 10am–7pm).

Cemeteries: Human and Canine

Tucked down below street level in the hollow of an old quarry, the **Montmartre cemetery** (Mon–Fri 8am–5:30pm, Sat 8am–8:30pm, Sun 8am–9pm) has its entrance on av Rachel under rue Caulaincourt, with an antique cast-iron poor box—*Tronc pour les Pauvres*—by the gate. A tangle of trees and funerary pomposity, it holds the graves of Zola, Stendhal, Berlioz, Degas, Feydeau, Offenbach, Dalida, and François Truffaut among others, with a large Jewish section under the east wall.

Not far away, up av de Clichy near the Porte-de-Clichy métro, there are more literary graves in the **Cimetière des Batignolles**—André Breton, Verlaine, and Blaise Cendrars.

Quirkier and more lugubrious, and accessible on the same métro line, about fifteen minutes' walk from Mº Mairie-de-Clichy along bd Jaurès and just to the left at the far end of Pont de Clichy, lies the privately owned **Cimetière des Chiens** (Dog Cemetery; mid-March to mid-Oct 10–12am & 3–7pm, mid-Oct to mid-March 10–12am & 2–5pm; closed Tues & hols).

Thousands of tiny graves decked with plastic flowers line a tree-shaded ridgelet—once an island—beside the Seine. Most of them, going back to 1900, belong to dogs and cats, many with epigraphs of the kind: "To Fifi, the only consolation of my wretched existence." There is a surprising preponderance of Anglo-Saxon names—Boy, Pussy, Dick, Jack: a tribute perhaps to the peculiarly English sentimentality about animals. Among the more exotic cadavers are a Muscovite bear, a wolf, a lioness, the 1920 Grand National winner, and the French Rintintin, vintage 1933.

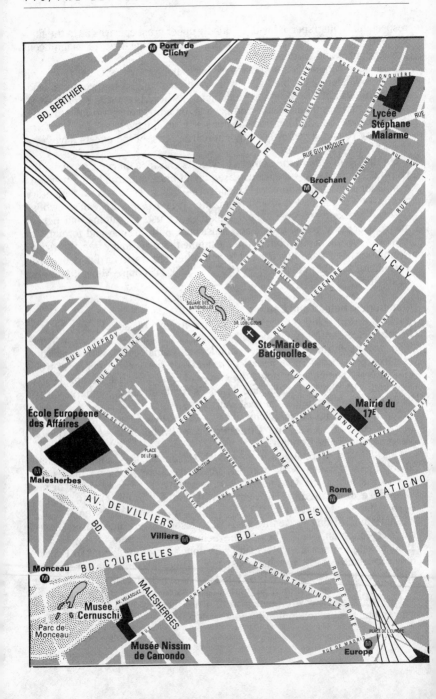

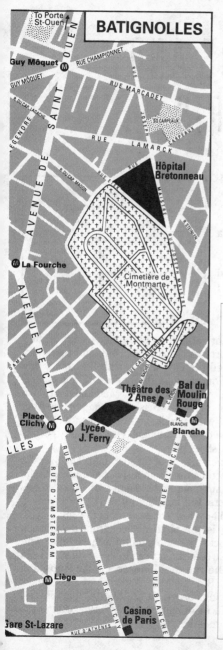

Parc Monceau to Batignolles: Listings

Bar
L'Endroit, 67 place Félix-Lobligeois, 17ᵉ. Mᵒ Batignolles/Brochant.

Beer cellar
Bar Belge, 75 av de St-Ouen, 17ᵉ. Mᵒ Guy-Môquet.

Restaurants
Under 80F
Le Bistro Romain, 9 av des Ternes, 17ᵉ. Mᵒ Ternes.

Natacha, 35, rue Guersant, 17ᵉ. Mᵒ Porte-Maillot.

Port de Pidjiguiti, 28 rue Etex, 18ᵉ. Mᵒ Guy-Môquet.

Sangria, 13 bis rue Vernier, 17ᵉ. Mᵒ Porte-de-Champerret.

Under 150F
L'Entrecôte, 271 bd Péreire, 17ᵉ. Mᵒ Porte-Maillot.

All the establishments listed above are reviewed in Chapter Eight,
Drinking and Eating.

MONTMARTRE AND EASTERN PARIS

F or all the bulldozing and gentrification, the areas from **Pigalle** and **Montmartre** in the **north**, **eastwards** down to the 13e *arrondissement*, are still home to a significant working-class population, both immigrant and French. It may not be for long, if the developers and planning authorities have their way; the steady flight from the city's unaffordable rents shows no sign of letting up.

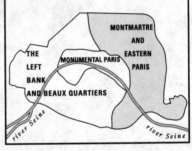

It was in these streets that the **great rebellions** of the nineteenth century were fomented and fought: the insurrections of 1830, 1848, and the short-lived **Commune** of 1871, that divided the city in two, with the center and west battling to preserve the status quo against the oppressed and radical east. Even in the 1789 revolution, when Belleville, Ménilmontant, and Montmartre were still just villages, the most progressive demands came from the artisans of Faubourg-St-Antoine. By the middle of the nineteenth century, **Baron Haussmann** had incorporated all of militant Paris within the city boundaries and his own authoritarian street plan.

Today, precious little stands in remembrance of these events. The *Mur des Fédérés* in Père Lachaise cemetery records the death of 147 *Communards*; the Bastille column and its inscription commemorate 1830 and 1848; a few streets bear the names of the people's leaders. But nothing in the 11e, for instance, suggests its history as the most fought-over *arrondissement* in the city.

What is also slowly disappearing is the physical backdrop: demolished sites get filled with shelving unit blocks, with no attempt to harmonize with what's on either side. True, narrow streets and artisan houses still survive in **Belleville**, **Ménilmontant**, around **the rue de Flandres** and the **Butte aux Cailles**, and off **Canal St-Martin**. But the old character of these most Parisian areas of Paris is gradually being effaced. At **La Villette**, abattoirs and factories have become high-tech palaces of culture, totally transforming the old meat trading center and barge port of the city.

The hill of **Montmartre**—the *Butte*—with its literary and artistic links, its **Sacré-Coeur**, and open, airy feel, provides the main tourist focus. **Père Lachaise**, too, over in the east, draws its devotees, though the charms of the higher *quartiers* beyond are less often explored. Out on the edge, the **Bois de Vincennes** is more or less a mirror image of the Bois de Boulogne, without the high society history; it is a good place to take children, not least for its zoo. So too, for casual wandering, is the hilly **Parc des Buttes-Chaumont**.

Montmartre and the 9ᵉ

Montmartre lies in the middle of the largely petty-bourgeois and working-class 18ᵉ *arrondissement*, respectable round the slopes of the *Butte*, distinctly less so toward the **Gare du Nord** and **Gare de l'Est**, where depressing slums crowd along the railroad tracks. On its northern edge lies the extensive St-Ouen flea market.

The Butte itself has a relaxed, sunny, countrified air. Pigalle at its foot is the land of sleaze. You won't find the golden-hearted whores and Bohemian artists of popular tradition. It's all sex shops and peep shows, the women tired and bored in the doorways. Like any red-light district, the tourists have to be shown it, or so their masters of ceremonies think. To the south, all the way down to the Grands Boulevards, stretches the uneventful but in places attractive 9ᵉ *arrondissement*.

The Butte and Sacré-Coeur

In spite of being one of the city's chief tourist attractions, the **Butte Montmartre** still manages to retain the quiet, almost secretive, air of its rural origins. Only incorporated into the city in the mid-nineteenth century, it received its first major influx of population from the poor displaced by Haussmann's rebuilding program. Its **heyday** was from the last years of the century to World War I, when its rustic charms and low rents attracted crowds of artists. Although that traditional population of workers and artists has been largely supplanted by a more chic and prosperous class of bohemian, the *quartier*'s physical appearance has changed little, thanks largely to the warren of plaster-of-Paris quarries that perforate its bowels and render the ground too unstable for new building.

The **most popular access** route is via the rue de Steinkerque and the steps below the Sacré-Coeur (the funicular railroad from place Suzanne-Valadon is covered by the *Carte Orange*). But for **a quieter approach** you can go up via place des Abbesses or rue Lepic and still have the streets to yourself.

Place des Abbesses to the Butte
Place des Abbesses is postcard-pretty, with one of the few complete surviving **Guimard métro entrances** (transferred from the Hôtel de Ville): the glass porch as well as the railings and the slightly obscene orange-tongued lanterns. The bizarre-looking **church of St-Jean-l'Évangéliste** on the down-

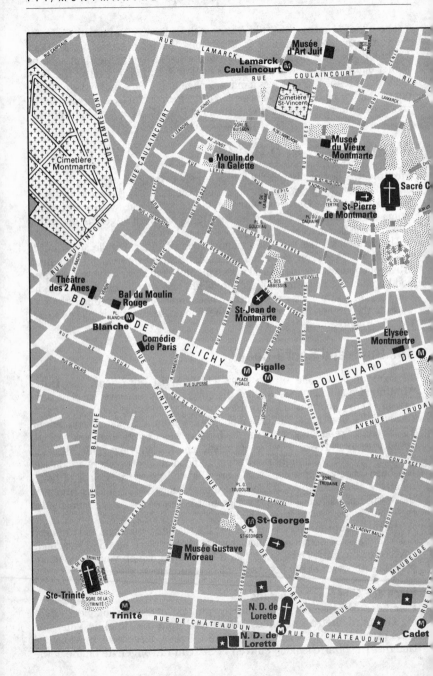

Cimetière
Montmartre

Théâtre
des 2 Anes

Bal du Moulin
Rouge

Blanche

Comédie
de Paris

Musée
d'Art Juif

Lamarck
Caulaincourt

Cimetière
St-Vincent

Moulin de
la Galette

Musée
du Vieux
Montmartre

Sacré C

St-Pierre
de Montmartre

St-Jean de
Montmartre

CLICHY

Pigalle

BOULEVARD DE

Élysée
Montmartre

AVENUE TRUDAI

St-Georges

Musée Gustave
Moreau

Ste-Trinité

Trinité

N. D. de
Lorette

N. D. de
Lorette

Cadet

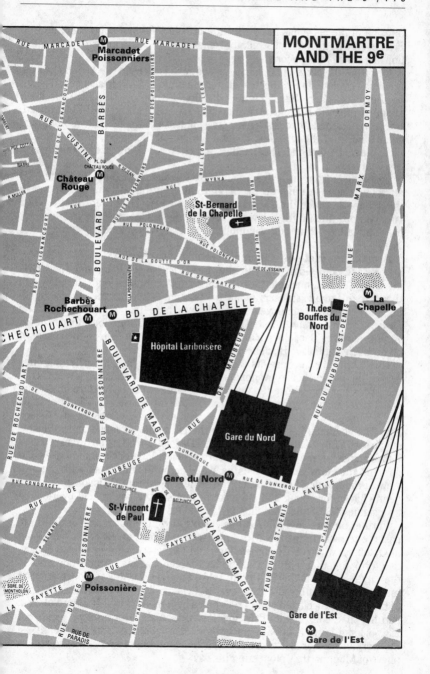

MONTMARTRE AND THE 9ᵉ

RUE MARCADET

Marcadet Poissonniers Ⓜ

RUE MARCADET

RUE DE CLIGNANCOURT

RUE DES POISSONNIERS

BARBÈS

RUE LÉON

DORMOY

PGE MOSSIN

PL. DU CHÂTEAU ROUGE

R. D'JEAN

Château Rouge Ⓜ

R. MULLER

RUE CUSTINE

MYRHA

RUE DES POISSONNIERS

RUE MYRHA

MARX

BOULEVARD

RUE DE LA GOUTTE D'OR

St-Bernard de la Chapelle ✝

RUE AFFRE

VILLA POISSONNIÈRE

RUE DE CLIGNANCOURT

RUE POLONCEAU

RUE POLONCEAU

RUE AFFRE

RUE DE JESSAINT

RUE DE CHARTES

Barbès Rochechouart Ⓜ

BD. DE LA CHAPELLE

CHECHOUART Ⓜ

Th.des Bouffes du Nord

Ⓜ **La Chapelle**

RUE DU FAUBOURG ST-DENIS

RUE DE ROCHECHOUART

DE

RUE DU FG POISSONNIÈRE

Hôpital Lariboisière

RUE DE MAUBEUGE

DUNKERQUE

RUE DE DUNKERQUE

BOULEVARD DE MAGENTA

RUE DE DUNKERQUE

Gare du Nord

RUE CONDORCET

MAUBEUGE

DE

RUE DE BELZUNCE

Gare du Nord Ⓜ

RUE DE DUNKERQUE

RUE DE

BELZUNCE

RUE DE

St-Vincent de Paul ✝

LA

FAYETTE

RUE P. BERNARD

RUE DU FG POISSONNIÈRE

FAYETTE

BOULEVARD DE MAGENTA

RUE DU FAUBOURG ST-DENIS

RUE D'ALSACE

SORE DE MONTHOLON

LA

FAYETTE

Ⓜ **Poissonière**

RUE DE

RUE D'HAUTEVILLE

Gare de l'Est

RUE DE PARADIS

Ⓜ **Gare de l'Est**

hill side of the *place* has the distinction of being the first concrete church in France (1904), its internal structure remarkably pleasing in spite of the questionable taste of the decoration.

East from the *place*, at the Chapelle des Auxiliatrices in rue Yvonne-Le-Tac, Ignatius Loyola founded the **Jesuit** movement in 1534. It is also supposed to be the place where **Saint Denis**, the first Bishop of Paris, had his head chopped off by the Romans around 250 AD, carrying it until he dropped, where the cathedral of St-Denis now stands, in a traditionally Communist suburb north of the city. Just beyond the end of the street, in the beautiful little **place Dullin**, the Théâtre de l'Atelier is still going strong after nearly two centuries.

To continue from place des Abbesses to the top of the Butte, two quiet and attractive routes are up **rue de la Vieuville** and the stairs in rue Drevet to the minuscule **place du Calvaire** with a lovely view back over the city, or up **rue Tholozé**, then right below the **Moulin de la Galette**—the last survivor of Montmartre's forty odd windmills, immortalized by Renoir—into rue des Norvins.

Artistic associations abound hereabouts. Zola, Berlioz, Turgenev, Seurat, Degas, and Van Gogh lived in the area. Picasso, Braque, and Juan Gris invented Cubism in an old piano factory in place Emile-Goudeau, known as the **Bateau-Lavoir**, still serving as artists' studios, though the original building burned down some years ago. It was here that Picasso painted *les Demoiselles d'Avignon*. And Toulouse Lautrec's inspiration, the **Moulin Rouge**, survives also, albeit a mere shadow of its former self, on the corner of bd de Clichy and place Blanche.

Rue Lepic begins here, its winding contours recalling the lane that once served the plaster quarry wagons. A busy market occupies the lower part of the street, but once above rue des Abbesses it reverts to a mixture of tranquil and furtive elegance. Around the corner above rue Tourlaque a flight of steps and a muddy path sneak between gardens to **av Junot**, where the still delectable Anouk Aimée has her home. To the left is the secluded and exclusive cul-de-sac, **Villa Léandre**. To the right, Dadaist poet Tristan Tzara's cubist house stands on the corner of another exclusive little enclave of houses and gardens, the **Hameau des Artistes**, while higher up the street, with the best view of the Moulin de la Galette, the **square Suzanne-Buisson** provides a gentle haven for young and old alike, with a sunken *boules* field overlooked by a statue of St Denis clutching his head to his breast.

Further on, **rue des Saules** tips steeply down the north side of the Butte past the terraces of the tiny **Montmartre vineyard** (harvest at the beginning of October), with rue Cortot leading right to the water tower whose distinctive form, together with that of the Sacré-Coeur, is one of the landmarks of the city's skyline. No. 12, a pretty old house with a grassy courtyard and magnificent view from the back over the vineyard and the northern reaches of the city, was occupied at different times by Renoir, Dufy, Suzanne Valadon, and her mad son, Utrillo. It is now the **Musée de Montmartre** (Mon–Sat 2:30–5:30pm, Sun 11am–5:30pm), whose disappointing exhibits (nearly all the works by major artists are reproductions) attempt to recreate the atmosphere of Montmartre's pioneering heyday.

Montmartre and the 9ᵉ: Listings

Café
Le Pigalle, 22 bd de Clichy, 9ᵉ. Mᵒ Pigalle.

Bar
Le Dépanneur, 27 rue Fontaine, 9ᵉ. Mᵒ Pigalle.

Wine bar
Aux Négociants, 27 rue Lambert, 18ᵉ. Mᵒ Château-Rouge.

Beer cellar
Au Général La Fayette, 52 rue La Fayette, 9ᵉ. Mᵒ Le Peletier.

Restaurants
Under 80F
Casa Miguel, 48 rue St-Georges, 9ᵉ. Mᵒ St-Georges.

Chartier, 7 rue du Faubourg-Montmartre, 9ᵉ. Mᵒ Montmartre.

Fouta Toro, 3 rue du Nord, 18ᵉ. MᵒMarcadet-Poissonniers.

Au Grain de Folie, 24 rue de la Vieuville, 18ᵉ. Mᵒ Abbesses.

Under 150F
Chez Ginette, 101 rue Caulaincourt, 18ᵉ. Mᵒ Lamarck-Caulaincourt.

Le Maquis, 69 rue Caulaincourt, 18ᵉ. Mᵒ Lamarck-Caulaincourt.

Over 150F
À la Pomponnette, 42 rue Lepic, 18ᵉ. Mᵒ Blanche.

Les Chants du Piano, 10 rue Lambert, 18ᵉ. Mᵒ Château-Rouge.

Flo, 7 cours des Petites-Écuries, 10ᵉ. Mᵒ Château-d'Eau.

Julien, 16 rue du Faubourg-St-Denis, 10ᵉ. Mᵒ Strasbourg-St-Denis.

Au Petit Riche, 25 rue Le Peletier, 9ᵉ. Mᵒ Richelieu-Drouot.

Terminus Nord, 23 rue de Dunkerque, 10ᵉ. Mᵒ Gare-du-Nord.

All the establishments listed above are reviewed in Chapter Eight, Drinking and Eating.

Place du Tertre to Sacré-Coeur

Hence to the heart of Montmartre, the **place du Tertre**, photogenic but totally bogus, jammed with tourists, overpriced restaurants, and "artists" doing quick portraits while you wait. Its trees, until recently under threat of destruction for safety reasons by overzealous officialdom, have been saved by the well-orchestrated protests of its influential residents.

Between place du Tertre and the Sacré-Coeur, the old church of **St-Pierre** is all that remains of the Benedictine convent which occupied the Butte Montmartre from the twelfth century on. Though much altered, it still retains its Romanesque and early Gothic feel. In it are four ancient columns, two by the door, two in the choir, leftovers from a Roman shrine that stood on the hill—*mons mercurii*, Mercury's Hill, the Romans called it.

As for the **Sacré-Coeur** itself, graceless and vulgar pastiche though it is, its white pimply domes are an essential part of the Paris skyline. Construction was started in the 1870s on the initiative of the Catholic church to atone for the "crimes" of the Commune. The thwarted opposition, which included Clemenceau, eventually got its revenge by naming the space at the foot of the monumental staircase **square Willette**, after the local artist who turned out on inauguration day to shout, "Long live the devil!"

The best thing about it is the **view from the top** (summer 9am–7pm; winter 9am–6pm). It costs 15F, is almost as high as the Eiffel Tower, and you

THE PARIS COMMUNE

In the **place du Tertre**, on March 18, 1871, Montmartre's most illustrious mayor and future prime minister of France, Georges Clemenceau, flapped about trying to prevent the bloodshed that started that terrible and long-divisive civil war between the Commune and Thiers' Third Republic.

Having provoked a disastrous war with Bismarck's Germany, Napoléon III was captured and Paris surrounded. The Germans refused to accept surrender from any but a properly elected government. A cautious and reactionary government was duly elected and promptly capitulated, handing over Alsace and Lorraine. Frightened of Paris in arms, they tried to get hold of the artillery still in the hands of the National Guard at Montmartre. However, when government troops were sent to fetch the guns, the people, fearing another restoration of empire or monarchy such as had happened after the 1848 revolution, persuaded them to take no action. Two of their generals were seized and shot against the wall in rue du Chevalier-de-la-Barre behind the Sacré-Coeur, and the terrified government fled to Versailles, leaving the Commune in control of the city until they could pluck up courage to attack.

Divided among themselves and isolated from the rest of France, the *Communards* only finally succumbed to government assault after a week's bloody street-fighting between May 21 and 28. No one knows how many of them died; certainly no fewer than 20,000, with another 10,000 executed or deported. A working-class revolt, as the particulars of those involved clearly demonstrate, but it hardly had time to be as socialist as subsequent mythologizing would have it. The terrible cost of repression had long-term effects on the French working-class movement, both in terms of numbers lost and psychologically. And after it, not to be revolutionary could only appear a betrayal of the dead.

can see the layout of the whole city, how it lies in a wide flat basin ringed by low hills, with the stands of high-rise apartments in the southeastern corner, on the heights of Belleville, and at La Défense in the west, and the tall flat faces of the suburban workers' barracks like slabs of tombstone in the hazy beyond.

North and East of the Butte

On the north side of the Butte the long **rue du Mont-Cenis**, where Berlioz lived with his English wife, descends across the quiet and agreeable rue Caulaincourt, past the *mairie* of the 18e, through an increasingly immigrant *quartier*, to bd Ornano and the **Porte de Clignancourt**, where the main **flea market, the puces de St-Ouen**, is located under the *boulevard périphérique* (see below).

To the east the stepped rue Utrillo and rue Ronsard drop steeply down through a reposeful public garden to the recently renovated *halles*-like structure of the **Marché Saint-Pierre**, where African, Arab, and French women jostle in colorful quest of some of the best fabric and textile bargains in town. Outside in rue Ronsard, masked by a fringe of overhanging greenery, are the now-sealed entrances to the quarries where plaster of Paris was extracted.

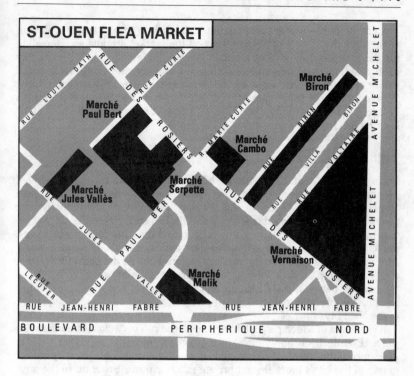

The Flea Market: les Puces de St-Ouen

Officially open 7:30am to 7pm—unofficially, from 5am—the **puces de St-Ouen** claim to be the largest flea market in the world, the name "flea" deriving from the state of the secondhand mattresses, clothes, and other junk sold here when the market first operated in the free-fire zone outside the city walls. Nowadays it is predominantly a proper—and very expensive—antique market (mainly furniture, but including old café bar counters, telephones, traffic lights, posters, juke boxes, and gas pumps), with what is left of the rag-and-bone element confined to the farther reaches of **rue Fabre and rue Lécuyer**

First impressions as you arrive from the métro are that there is nothing for sale but jeans and leather jackets. There are, however, seven official markets within the complex: Marché **Biron**, with serious and expensive antique furniture; Marché **Cambo**, next to Biron, also with expensive furniture; Marché **Vernaison**—the oldest—with the most diverse collection of old and new furniture and knick-knacks; Marché **Paul-Bert**, with modern furniture, china etc; Marché **Malik**, with mostly clothes, some high-class couturier stuff, and a lot of uninteresting new items; Marché **Serpette**, specializing in 1900–30; and Marché **Jules-Vallès**, which is the cheapest, most junk-like, and most likely to throw up something affordable.

It can be fun to wander around, but it's foolish to expect any bargains. In some ways the streets of St-Ouen beyond the market are just as interesting for the glimpse they give of a tempo of living long vanished from the city itself. Should hunger overtake you, there is a touristy *restaurant-buvette* in the center of Marché Vernaison, *Chez Lisette*, where the great gypsy jazz guitarist Django Reinhardt sometimes played. But for safer and cheaper **eating** it's best to go to one of the brasseries on av Michelet just outside the market, or back on bd Ornano.

Pigalle

From place Clichy in the west to Barbès-Rochechouart in the east, the hill of Montmartre is underlined by the sleazy **boulevards of Clichy and Rochechouart**, the center of the roadway often occupied by bumper-car pistes and other funfair sideshows. At the Barbès end, where the métro clatters by on iron trestles, the crowds teem round the *Tati* department stores, the city's cheapest, while the sidewalks are lined with West and North African street vendors offering watches and trinkets. At the place Clichy end, tour buses from all over Europe feed their contents into massive hotels. In the middle, between place Blanche and place Pigalle, sex shows, sex shops, and prostitutes, both male and female, keep alive the tawdry, tarnished image of the Naughty Nineties.

It is an area in which respectability and sleaze rub very close shoulders. On **place Pigalle** itself huge anatomical blow-ups (unveiled only after dark in deference to the residents' sensibilities) assail the senses on the very corner of one of the city's most elegant private *villas*, **avenue Frochot**. In the adjacent streets—rues Douai, Victor-Massé, Houdon—specialist music shops (this is *the* area for instruments and sound systems) and gray bourgeois homes are interspersed with tiny bars where hostesses lurk in complicated tackle.

The Rest of the 9ᵉ

The rest of the 9ᵉ is rather dull, with the exception of some blocks of streets **around place St-Georges**, where Thiers, president of the Third Republic, lived, in a house which is now a library (rebuilt after being burned by the Commune). In the center of the *place* stands a statue of the nineteenth-century cartoonist, Gavarni, who made a specialty of lampooning the mistresses that were almost *de rigueur* for bourgeois males of the time. This was their *quartier*—they were known as *lorettes* after the nearby church of Notre-Dame-de-Lorette.

Place Toudouze, **rue Clauzel**, **rue Milton**, and **rue Rodier** are also worth a look, and rue St-Lazare, between the station and the hideous church of Ste-Trinité, is a welcome swathe of activity amid the residential calm. Close by is the bizarre and little-visited museum dedicated to the works of the Symbolist painter, **Gustave Moreau** (see p.161), opposite rue de la Tour-des-Dames, where two or three gracious mansions and gardens recall the days when this was the very edge of the city.

CABARETS AND SEX: AROUND PIGALLE

For many foreigners, Paris is still synonymous with a use of the stage perpetuated by those mythical names, the *Moulin Rouge*, *Folies Bergères*, and *Lido*. These **cabarets**, which flash their presence in the 9ᵉ and 18ᵉ, from bd de Clichy to bd Montmartre, predate the film industry, though it appears as if the glittering Hollywood musicals of the 1930s are their inspiration rather than their offspring. They define an area of pornography that would have trouble titillating a prudish Anglo-Saxon and though the audience is mainly male, the whole event is to live sex shows what glossy fashion reviews are to "girlie" mags. Apart from seeing a lot of bare breasts, your average bused-in tourist may well feel he has not got what he paid, rather excessively, for. All the more easy prey for the pimps of Pigalle.

The *Lido*, for example, takes breaks from multicolored plumage and illuminated distant flesh to bring on a conjurer to play tricks with the clothes and possessions of the audience. Then back come the computer-choreographed "Bluebell Girls," in a technical tour-de-force of light show, music, and a moving stage transporting the thighs and breasts to more far away exotica—the sea, a volcano, ice, or Pacific island. The scale is far too spectacular for the dirty raincoat crowd.

The oldest cabaret, unique in attracting a local audience, is similar but makes no attempt, even in the production, to be modern. What turned the customers on at the *Folies Bergères* in the 1860s keeps them happy today—the cancan, some *ancien régime* waltzing, flouncing, frilly and extravagant costumes, songs, and standard cabaret routines. If you're curious, this is the one to waste least money on (see *Pariscope* etc, for details). The cancan, they say, is nothing now to the days when Toulouse Lautrec painted the *Moulin Rouge*. The singers, acrobats, and comedians provide the dubious talent to the show that is advertised as "women, women, women."

At the *Crazy Horse* the theatrical experience convinces the very bourgeois audience that they are watching art and the prettiest girls in Paris. In the ranks of defenses for using images of female bits to promote, sell, lure, and exploit, Frenchmen are particular in putting "art and beauty" in the front line. In upholding the body gartered and pouting, weak and whimpering, usually nude and always immaculate, they claim to protect the femininity, beauty, and desirability of the Frenchwoman as she would wish it herself.

Moving from the glamour cabarets to the **"Life Sex"** and **"Ultra-hard Life Sex"** venues (never "Live Sex" for some reason) is to leave the world of elegant gloss and exportable Frenchness for a world of sealed-cover porn that knows no cultural borders.

The Goutte d'Or and the Northern Stations

Along the north side of bd de la Chapelle, between bd Barbès and the Gare du Nord railroad lines, stretches the poetically named and picturesque-squalid quarter of the **Goutte d'Or**—the Drop of Gold: a name that derives from the medieval vineyard that occupied this site. Since World War I, when large numbers of North Africans were first imported to replenish the ranks of Frenchmen dying in the trenches, it has gradually become an immigrant ghetto. In the late 1950s and early 1960s, during the Algerian war, its reputation struck terror in respectable middle-class hearts, as much for the clandestine political activity and settling of scores as its low dives, brothels, and drugs.

Though less ferocious now that the political tension has gone, its buildings remain in a lamentable state of decay, prostitutes linger in evil-smelling court-yards, and there's a good chance you'll be offered dope if you appear aimless and irresolute on the street—offers best ignored as the quality is notoriously poor and there's almost certainly a plain-clothes *flic* keeping watch nearby.

With artists, writers, and others moving in, attracted by the only affordable property left in the city, and the municipal authorities, directed by mayor Chirac, going ahead with a program of closing down, pulling down, and clean-ing up, the character of the area is clearly set to change over the next decade. For the moment, however, the daytime appearance of rue de la Goutte-d'Or and its tributary lanes (especially to the north: **rue Myrha**, **rue Léon**, the **Marché Dejean**, **rue Polonceau** with its basement mosque at no. 55 and the cobbled alley and gardens of **villa Poissonnière**) remains distinctly **North African**. The textile shops are hung with *djellabas* and gaudy fabrics. The windows of the *pâtisseries* are stacked with trays of equally gaudy cakes and pastries. Sheep's heads grin from the slabs of the Hallal butchers, the grocers shovel their wares from barrels and sacks, and the plangent, evoca-tive sounds of Arab music blare forth from the record shops. But despite these exotic elements there is a sense of watching and waiting in the atmos-phere which makes most outsiders reluctant to linger, and the cafés certainly give the impression you would not be welcome. It's a neighborhood to be treated with caution and sensitivity.

The Stations and Faubourgs

On the **south side of bd de la Chapelle** lie the big northern stations, the **Gare du Nord** (serving the Channel ports and places north) and **Gare de l'Est** (serving northeastern and eastern France and eastern Europe), with the major traffic thoroughfares, bd de Magenta and bd de Strasbourg, both bustling, noisy, and not in themselves of much interest. From here to the river the ground was all marsh in Roman times; the first bit of land to be built on was the site now occupied by the unattractive church of St-Laurent.

The liveliest part of the quarter is the **rue du Faubourg-St-Denis**, full, especially toward the lower end, of *charcuteries*, butchers, greengrocers, and foreign delicatessens, as well as a number of restaurants, including the *Brasserie Julien* and *Brasserie Flo* (see p.230), the latter in an old-world stable-yard, the cour des Petites-Écuries. Spanning the end of the street is the **Porte St-Denis**, a triumphal arch built in 1672 on the Roman model to cele-brate the victories of Louis XIV. Feeling secure behind Vauban's extensive frontier fortifications, Louis demolished Charles V's city walls and created a swathe of leafy promenades, where the Grands Boulevards now run. In place of the city gates he planned a series of triumphal arches on the Roman model, of which this and the neighboring **Porte St-Martin**, at the end of rue du Faubourg-St-Martin, were the first.

The whole area between the two faubourgs through to the provincial **rue du Faubourg-Poissonnière** is honeycombed with passages and courtyards. China and glass enthusiasts should take a walk along **rue de Paradis** whose shops specialize in such wares, with the Baccarat firm's **Musée du Cristal** at no. 30 (see p.161), tucked away behind the classical façade of Louis XV's *cris-*

tallerie. Close by at no. 18, the magnificent mosaic and tiled façade of Monsieur Boulanger's Choisy-le-Roi tileworks shop is all that remains of the **Musée de la Publicité** (see p.162), now transferred to 107 rue de Rivoli.

Canal St-Martin and La Villette

The **Bassin de la Villette** and the **canals** at the northeastern gate of the city were for generations the center of a densely populated working-class district. The jobs were in the main meat market and abattoirs of Paris or in the many interlinked industries that spread around the waterways. The amusements were skating or swimming, betting on cockfights, or eating at the numerous restaurants famed for their fresh meat. Now La Villette is the wonderworld of laser-guided culture, the pride of politicians, and the recipient of over ten billion francs' worth of public spending.

Canal St-Martin

The **Canal St-Martin** was built as a shortcut to lop off the great western loop of the Seine around Paris. It runs underground at the Bastille to surface again in bd Jules-Ferry by the rue du Faubourg-du-Temple, another key point in the annals of revolutionary street-fighting. Barricaded by the *Communards* in 1871 and the *quarante-huitards* in 1848, it is now a peaceable, populous, run-down street of small shops, cafés, Arab sweatshops, and crummy passages (bargain prices on fruit and veg). Much of it obviously has not changed: the poverty, at least in relative terms, and the physical dilapidation too.

The **southern stretch** of the canal is the most attractive. Plane trees line the cobbled *quais* and elegant high-arched footbridges punctuate the spaces between the locks, where you can still watch the occasional immaculate barge slowly rising or sinking to the next level. The houses are solid bourgeois-looking residences of the mid-nineteenth century. Although small back-street workshops and businesses still exist, gentrification and modernization are well on the way. The idea of canal frontage has clearly put a light in the developers' eyes, although you can at least be thankful it has not been turned into the motorway that president Pompidou envisioned.

Ancient corners do continue to exist. Down the steps to **rue des Vinaigriers**, the shoemakers' union has its HQ, *Fédération Nationale des Artisans de la Chaussure*, behind a Second-Empire shop front. Fluted wooden pilasters flank the door, crowned with capitals of grapes and a gilded Bacchus. A lion ramps above the lintel. Pineapple finials top the railings, while across the street the surely geriatric *Cercle National des Garibaldiens* still has a meeting place. At no. 35, Poursin has been making brass buckles in the same premises since 1830.

Across the lock, in the rustic-sounding **rue de la Grange-aux-Belles**, two café names evoke the canal's more vigorous youth: *Le Pont-Tournant*—the Swing-Bridge—and *L'Ancre de Marine*—The Anchor. Traditionally, the bargees came from the north, whence the name of the **Hôtel du Nord** at 102 quai de Jemappes, made famous by Marcel Carné's film starring Arletty and

Jean Gabin. For a long time there was talk of transforming it into a movie museum, but sadly all that remains of it now is the façade, held up by scaffolding. Just behind it is one of the finest and least visited buildings in Paris, the early seventeenth-century **Hôpital St-Louis**, built in the same style as the place des Vosges. Although it still functions as a hospital, you can walk through into its quiet central courtyard to admire the elegant brick and stone façades and steep-pitched roofs.

The most drastic canalside changes are taking place north of the rue des Recollets, where, on the corner, a curious Turkish-style house just barely maintains its precarious existence at the time of writing. In behind, a major dispute is going on that exactly exemplifies the conflict of interest between the priorities of developers and the values of those who attach importance to the quality of urban life. In 1976 the garden of the old military Hôpital Villemin was opened to the public. In 1986 a stretch along the canal was added to it. In the meantime, the property values in this once completely undesirable *quartier* have skyrocketed. Result: in 1989 Mayor Chirac allows his business cronies to buy the canalside bit for conversion into office space. The residents are physically blocking entrance to the worksite, and there for the moment the matter rests. The owners of the socialist street names that abound hereabouts—Louis Blanc, Eugène Varlin, Colonel Fabien, among others—must be turning in their graves.

Colonel Fabien, who gave his name to the *place* where the French Communist Party has its HQ, was really called Pierre Georges. He committed the first official act of Communist armed resistance against the Nazis after the confusion caused in Party ranks by the Stalin–Hitler pact, on August 21, 1941, by shooting a German sailor on the platform of the Barbès-Rochechouart métro station in revenge for the execution of Samuel Tyszelmann, a Jewish Polish resistance worker who had carried out the first recorded act of sabotage by stealing some dynamite a few days previously.

Toward Place de Stalingrad

From here to La Villette, both banks of the canal have been thoroughly sanitized, and the *petit peuple* driven out for good. The one major improvement has been the restoration of the place de Stalingrad. It has been sanded and grassed and the stone work of the Rotonde de la Villette washed clean. This was one of the toll houses designed by the architect Ledoux as part of Louis XVI's scheme to tax all goods entering the city—a major irritant in the run-up to the 1789 Revolution. It is a clean-cut Roman-inspired building with a Doric portico and pediments surmounted by a rotunda. One of the side effects of the clean-up has been to enhance the elegant aerial stretch of métro, supported on Neoclassical iron and stone pillars, which backs the toll house. Looking back from farther up the Bassin de la Villette it provides a focus for an impressive new monumental vista.

Recobbled, and with its dockside buildings converted into offices for canal boat trips, the Bassin has lost all vestiges of its former status as France's premier port. The shuttered and peeling façade of the *Café Au Rendezvous du Port* echoes sadly this change of life. At the rue de Crimée, where a unique hydraulic bridge (1885) crosses the canal, only one of the facing pair of warehouses, itself now converted into trendy offices, survives. Its twin, which featured in the film *Diva*, burned down. Opposite, even the burrowing slums of the rue de Flandres are succumbing to the bulldozer and crane.

If you keep to the south bank on quai de la Marne, you can cross directly into the Parc de la Villette, where the only reminders of a different past are the Gothic towers of the Grands Moulins de Pantin flour mills rising above the crinkled elephant hide of the *Zenith*.

La Villette

The **Porte de Pantin** entrance faces the largest of La Villette's old market halls—an iron-frame structure designed by Baltard, the engineer of the vanished Les Halles pavilions—now a vast and brilliant exhibition space, the **Grande Salle**.

This is flanked by two contemporaries, the **Pavillon Janvier** housing the Grande Salle offices, and the **Théâtre Paris-Villette**, now hidden behind the new **Cité de la Musique** spread into two blocks on av Jean-Jaurès. The one to the right, due to open in 1992, will have the concert hall, a **Musée de la Musique**, and commercial outlets for everything to do with music-making. Its separate buildings form a cake-slice wedge that makes sense with the place de la Fontaine aux Lions.

The same cannot be said of the **Conservatoire National Supérieur de Musique** (the national music academy) to the left. Designed with the worst indulgence to architectural pseudo-intellectualism, it combines waves and funnels, irregular polygons and nonparallel lines, gangways, greenhouses, and aggressive slit windows. The architect, Christian de Portzamparc, is proud of the confusion of its corridors and passageways: "You search, you discover" and presumably you miss your lesson. The curving roof, he says, is like a Gregorian chant. At least there's one link between the Conservatoire and the rest of La Villette, in the wavy walkway shelter that runs in a straight line right up to the av Corentin-Cariou entrance.

Still on the south side of the canal de l'Ourcq, there are bizarrely land-scaped gardens featuring giant bits of a bicycle half-buried in the ground. Over to the east is the **Zenith** rock venue inflatable, signaled by its sculpted logo of a diving airplane (see p.245). Bright red constructivist "folies" by Bernard Tschumi punctuate the park, providing space for cafés, day-care, first aid, and information centers. Best of the outdoors surprises, just over the canal, is the **dragon slide**, made from recycled cable drums and pipes (and exclusively for children).

Cité des Sciences et de l'Industrie

The major extravagance and *pièce de résistance* of La Villette is the **Science and Industry Museum**, built onto the concrete hulk of the abandoned abat-toirs building on the north side of the canal. Three times the size of Beaubourg, this is by far the most astounding monument to be added to the capital in the last decade. Giant walls of glass hang beneath a dark blue lattice of steel, with white rod walkways accelerating out from the building across an approximation of a fortress moat. See p.153 for details of the collection.

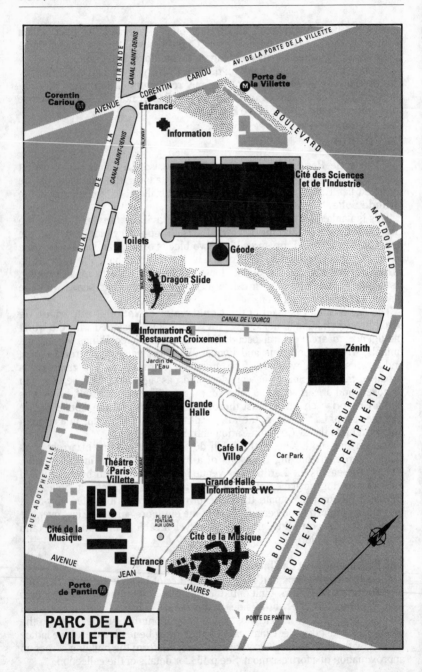

PARC DE LA
VILLETTE

In front of the complex balances the **Géode**, a bubble of reflecting steel dropped from an intergalactic *boules* game into a pool of water that ripples the mirrored image of the Cité and the dragon slide. Within it, half the sphere is a projection screen—the largest currently existing on the planet. It's a stroke of genius that draws you to the Cité, which without it would be too cold, complicated, and threatening in its dimensions to approach.

Access to La Villette

The Parc de la Villette is accessible from Mº Porte-de-la-Villette to the north or Mº Porte-de-Pantin to the south. There are information centers by the northern entrance and by the canal bridge. For opening hours and details of the Cité des Sciences, the Géode, the Musée de la Musique, and kids' activities in the Parc, see pages 153 and 185.

Canal St-Martin and La Villette: Listings

Cafés

Café de la Ville, Parc de la Villette, between the Grande Salle and the Zenith, 19ᵉ. Mº Porte-de-Pantin/Corentin-Cariou.

Bar

L'Opus, 167 quai de Valmy, 10ᵉ. Mº Château-Landon.

Snacks

Le Croixement, Parc de la Villette, by the bridge over the canal, 19e. Mº Porte-de-Pantin/Corentin-Cariou.

Restaurant
OVER 150F
Au Ras du Pavé, 15 rue du Buisson-St-Louis, l0ᵉ. Mº Colonel-Fabien.

All the establishments listed above are reviewed in Chapter Eight, Drinking and Eating.

Belleville, Ménilmontant, and Charonne: the Old Villages of Eastern Paris

At the northern end of the Belleville heights, a short walk from La Villette, is the **parc des Buttes-Chaumont** (Mº Buttes-Chaumont/Botzaris), constructed under Haussmann in the 1860s to camouflage what until then had been a desolate warren of disused quarries, garbage dumps, and miserable shacks. The sculpted, beak-shaped park stays open all night and, equally rarely for Paris, you're not cautioned off the grass.

At its center is a huge rock upholding a delicate Corinthian temple and surrounded by a lake which you cross via a suspension bridge or the shorter *"Pont des Suicides."* This, according to Louis Aragon, the literary grand old man of the French Communist party,

> . . . *before metal grills were erected along its sides, claimed victims even from passers-by who had had no intention whatsoever of killing themselves but were suddenly tempted by the abyss . . . And just see how docile people turn out to be: no one any longer jumps off this easily negotiable parapet.*

> *Le Paysan de Paris*

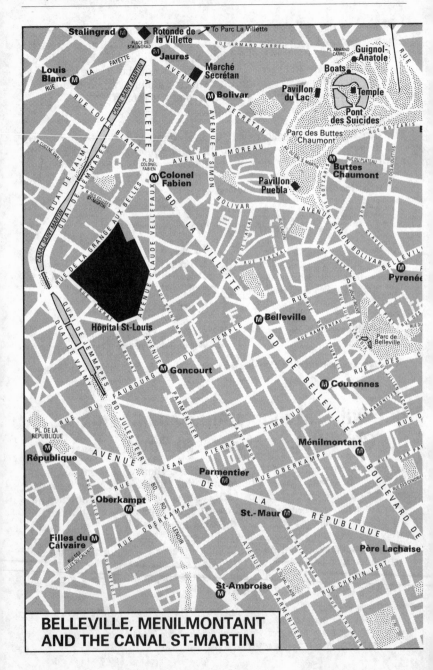

BELLEVILLE, MENILMONTANT
AND THE CANAL ST-MARTIN

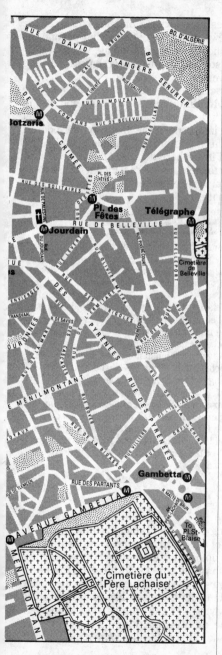

Belleville, Ménilmontant and Charonne: Listings

Bar

La Mouette Rieuse, 66 place de la Réunion, 20ᵉ. Mᵒ Alexandre-Dumas/ Maraîchers.

Wine bars

Le Baratin, 3 rue Jouye-Rouve, 20ᵉ. Mᵒ Pyrénées.

Les Envierges, 11 rue des Envierges, 20ᵉ. Mᵒ Pyrénées.

Snacks

Aux Rendez-vous des Amis, 10 av Père-Lachaise, 20ᵉ. Mᵒ Gambetta.

Le Pavillon du Lac, Parc des Buttes-Chaumont, 19ᵉ. Mᵒ Buttes-Chaumont.

Restaurants

Under 80F

Au Trou Normand, 9 rue Jean-Pierre Timbaud, 11ᵉ. Mᵒ République.

Under 150F

Astier, 44 rue Jean-Pierre Timbaud, 11ᵉ. Mᵒ Parmentier.

Égée, 19 rue de Ménilmontant, 20ᵉ. Mᵒ Ménilmontant.

Chez Justine, 96 rue Oberkampf, 11ᵉ. Mᵒ St-Maur.

Mère-Grand, 20 rue Orfila, 20ᵉ. Mᵒ Gambetta.

L'Occitanie, 96 rue Oberkampf, 11ᵉ. Mᵒ St-Maur.

Le Pacifique, 35 rue de Belleville, 20ᵉ. Mᵒ Belleville.

Chez Roger, 145 rue d'Avron, 20ᵉ. Mᵒ Porte-de-Montreuil.

Le Royal Belleville, 19 rue Louis-Bonnet and **Le Président** (the floor above), 11ᵉ. Mᵒ Belleville.

Aux Tables de la Fontaine, 3 rue des Trois-Bornes, 11ᵉ. Mᵒ Parmentier.

Taverna Restaurant, 50 rue Piat, 20ᵉ. Mᵒ Pyrénées.

Thaï Yen, 5 rue de Belleville, 20ᵉ. Mᵒ Belleville.

Chez Vincent, 60 bd Ménilmontant, 20ᵉ. Mᵒ Père-Lachaise.

Over 150F

Au Pavillon Puebla, Parc des Buttes-Chaumont, 19ᵉ. Mᵒ Buttes-Chaumont.

_All the establishments listed above are reviewed in Chapter Eight,
Drinking and Eating._

Perhaps the attraction for suicides and roving Commie writers is the unlikeliness of this park, with its views of the Sacré-Coeur and beyond, its grotto of stalactites, the fences of concrete molded to imitate wood, and its very existence in this corner of a city so badly deprived of green space. There are enticements for kids and other lovers of life (see p.181).

From Buttes-Chaumont to Père-Lachaise and eastwards is the one-time village of **Belleville** and its hamlet **Ménilmontant**, while south and east of the cemetery **Charonne** was once little more than orchards and market gardens. They were all incorporated into Paris in the 1860s. As the poorest working-class quarters of the city, there was nearly unanimous and active support for the Paris Commune. And it was here that the *Communards* took their last stand, having retreated back to their homes from the merciless counter-revolutionary offensive. For several decades thereafter, building works in Charonne would strike mass graves of the *Fédérés*.

DEVELOPING THE EAST

The eastern *arrondissements* are still among the poorest of the city and opposition to encroaching yuppiedom is visibly expressed in graffiti. Belleville and Ménilmontant have large immigrant populations—Yugoslavs, Greeks, Jews, Portuguese, Chinese, Arabs, and Africans—and, inevitably, a reputation for danger among western Parisians.

Around every corner the narrow streets are blocked by bulldozers and concrete mixers. There is already a massive number of 1960s and 1970s high-rises, and in all probability Belleville will end up looking more like the suburbs than Paris proper. Some of the more recent architectural changes are sympathetic in their scale and colorful style—for example, the block between the junction of rues de la Mare and de Savies, and rue des Cascades, which farther along has abandoned terraced gardens and crumbling apartment buildings where poverty is evident.

Of the old villages there remain **odd little villas** (cul-de-sacs of row houses): **Castel**, rue du Transvaal; **Olivier-Métra**, rue Olivier-Métra; **Ermitage**, rue de l'Ermitage and rue des Pyrénées; **Cité Leroy**, off rue des Pyrénées; several off **rue de Mouzaia**; or streets just wide enough for a tricycle of the sort the roving knife-grinders still use—**passage de la Duée**, 17 rue de la Duée; and roads narrowing to stairways and footbridges—**rue de la Voulze**, and **rue de la Mare**, with the old footbridge over the Petite Ceinture railroad.

Belleville

The first main street you cross coming down from Buttes-Chaumont, **rue de Belleville**, could be the main street of almost any French town, save for the Vietnamese and Chinese restaurants dominating the lower end. *Boulangeries* and *charcuteries* proliferate the length of the street, and there's a market at the distinctly unfestive **place des Fêtes** at the top of the hill, once the village green and now totally unrecognizable under the tower blocks and shopping strips. For a look at the densest surviving concentration of *villas*, take a ten-minute walk north of the *place* to **rue de Mouzaia**, where a dozen or more alleys of row houses and gardens tip downhill in the direction of the Porte de Pantin.

A short way farther down rue de Belleville, a plaque on the wall of no. 72 commemorates **Edith Piaf**: she was abandoned as a baby on the steps. On the corner of rue Julian-Lacroix a gigantic mural illustrates a fictional detective. At the bottom end, just southeast of the crossroads with bd de Belleville, is a small sequence of streets and passages doomed for demolition. Rue Ramponneau was where the last *Communard* on the last barricade held out alone for fifteen minutes.

Ménilmontant

Halfway down to bd de Belleville, on the left, the cobbled **rue Piat**, only partly damaged by redevelopment, climbs past the beautiful wrought-iron gate of the jungly **Villa Otoz** to the newly completed **Parc de Belleville**. From the terrace at the junction with rue des Envierges there is a fantastic view across the city, especially at sunset. At your feet the small park descends in a series of terraces and waterfalls. Continuing straight ahead, a path crosses the head of the park past a minuscule vineyard and turns into steps that drop down to rue des Couronnes. A left and a right take you into **rue Henri-Chevreau**, past the rue de la Mare footbridge, and into the steep **rue de Ménilmontant**, which gives the most spectacular perspective just before it kinks above rue de l'Ermitage. The rooftop of Beaubourg is the infinity meeting point of the sides of the street as it descends into rue Oberkampf.

Opposite rue de l'Ermitage at 25 rue Boyer, the splendid mosaicked and sculpted constructivist façade of **La Bellevilloise**, built for the *PCF* in 1925 to celebrate fifty years of work and science, has been saved from demolition by a preservation order. Just beyond it, a narrow lane of houses and gardens, **rue Laurence-Savart**, climbs up to rue du Retrait, while near the northeast corner of Père-Lachaise, the barely surviving upper reaches of the poetically named **rue des Partants** (street of the departers) offers the most poignantly evocative streetscape in the *quartier*. Lower down, a few odd corners survive with their local cafés and original shop fronts. Only the **street names** echo the long-vanished orchards and agricultural activities: *Amandiers* (almond trees), *Pruniers* (plum trees), *Mûriers* (mulberry trees), *Pressoir* (wine press).

The same village character survives in other isolated corners, in **rue Orfila**, **rue de la Chine**, **rue Villiers-de-l'Isle-Adam**, for example, on the other side of **rue des Pyrénées**, the main cross-route through the *quartier* and itself redolent of the provinces. Just above the intersection with rue de Ménilmontant, at no. 140, is one of the first attempts—in the 1920s—at purpose-built workers' housing, a massive sort of neo-Gothic fortress of brick and stone with slit windows. Almost next door is *Ganachaud*, one of the best bakers in Paris (see p.198).

If you find you're a real aficionado of these old villages, try to get hold of a collection of 1940s and early 1950s photographs of Belleville and Ménilmontant by Willy Ronis. Failing that, the area which comes closest to how they must once have been is below bd de Belleville, around **rue Oberkampf**, **rue St-Maur**, and **rue du Faubourg-du-Temple**, with their passages and courtyards within courtyards, workshops, ethnic cafés and snack bars, and dozens of tiny colorful shops.

Charonne

If you like churches and need a reason to wander around Charonne, **St-Germain-de-Charonne** on place St-Blaise has changed little since it served a village, and the belfry not at all since the thirteenth century. It has its own graveyard—unique in Paris churches, save for St-Pierre in Montmartre. Charnel houses were the norm, with the bones emptied into the catacombs (see p.183) as more space was required. It was not until the nineteenth century that public cemeteries appeared on the scene, the most famous being **Père-Lachaise**, one block away from St-Germain-de-Charonne.

Père-Lachaise Cemetery

The **cimitière Père-Lachaise** is like a miniature city devastated by a neutron bomb: a great number of dead, empty houses and temples of every size and style, and exhausted survivors, some congregating aimlessly, some searching persistently. The first response manifests itself best around **Jim**

JIM MORRISON IN PARIS

The most famous occupant of Père Lachaise's Division Six – **Jim Morrison** (1943–71), lead singer of The Doors – had visited the cemetery only a few weeks before his death. Oscar Wilde's grave made a big impression. Morrison's own burial took place on July 7, in the presence of five mourners; since then his own grave has over-shadowed Oscar's in terms of visitors. Graffitied and a mess, however, it is a very modest memorial to America's finest white rock singer of the 1960s. The reason is that nobody is allowed to touch the grave except for the Morrison Estate—and Jim loathed everything his family stood for. They, it seems, reciprocated.

The singer's last months in Paris, as retold in Oliver Stone's movie *The Doors*, aren't likely to change their assessment. The Paris period was a sad, shambling, and distinctly uncool epilogue to an archetypal rock'n'roll life—Morrison becoming unrecognizably fat and boring from alcohol abuse, adopting heroin, and, by all accounts, abusing women even more than himself. The one high point was the arrival of a copy of *LA Woman*, which The Doors had recorded at the end of 1970 in the USA. There were vague plans for another record, maybe a tour, but The Doors never played with Jim in Paris.

The bare facts of the life and death are these. Morrison arrived in Paris in March 1971, already a confirmed alcoholic, to meet up with an old girlfriend, Pamela Courson. They stayed initially at the five-star *Hotel Georges V*, off the Champs-Élysées, but later moved to an apartment at 17 rue Beautreillis (near place de la Bastille), not far from Père-Lachaise in the eastern Marais. Jim then moved for a while into *L'Hôtel* at 13 rue des Beaux-Arts on the Left Bank (in which Oscar Wilde died). From these bases, he rambled about the city, seeking out the haunts of Baudelaire and Rimbaud, Miller and Hemingway, drinking, and taking smack.

The End came on July 3. It seems that Morrison spent the evening at *Rock' n'Roll Circus* (still going today, as the *Whisky A Gogo*, at 57 rue de la Seine), where someone gave him a line of heroin to snort. It was Chinese and very pure—too pure for Americans according to the chauvinist myth perpetuated by French junkies. By some accounts, Jim died in the club, then was moved—dead—back to his apartment. Officially, he died in the bath.

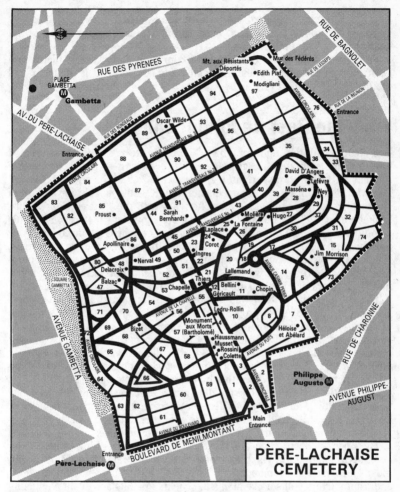

**PÈRE-LACHAISE
CEMETERY**

Morrison's tomb, where a motley assembly of European hippies roll spliffs against a backdrop of Doors' lyrics and declarations of love and drug consumption graffitied in every western language on every stone in sight. The alternative response, the searchers, are everywhere, looking for their favorite famous dead in an arrangement of numbered divisions that is neither entirely haphazard nor strictly systematic.

A safe bet for a high score is to head for the southeastern corner (near the rue de la Réunion entrance). There you will find memorials to concentration camp victims and executed Resistance fighters of the last war, Communist Party general-secretaries, Laura Marx, and the **Mur des Fédérés**, where troops of the Paris Commune were lined up and shot in the last days of the battle. Defeat is everywhere. The oppressed and their oppressors interred with the same ritual. Abélard and Heloïse side by side in prayer, still chastely separate, the relative riches and fame as unequal among the tombs of the dead as in the lives of the living.

The cemetery is open from 7:30am to 6pm every day. Nearest métros are Gambetta, Père-Lachaise, and Alexandre-Dumas. Rue de la Réunion and around place Gambetta are the best places to seek out sustenance.

From the Bastille to Vincennes

The column with the "Spirit of Liberty" on **place de la Bastille** was erected not to commemorate the surrender of **the prison**—whose only visible remains have been transported to square Henri-Galli at the end of bd Henri-IV—with its seven remaining occupants in 1789, but the July Revolution of 1830 which replaced the autocratic Charles X with the "Citizen King" Louis-Philippe (see p.286). When he fled in the more significant 1848 revolution, his throne was burned beside the column and a new inscription added. Four months after the birth of the Second Republic, the workers took to the streets. Eastern Paris was barricaded, with the fiercest fighting on rue du Faubourg-St-Antoine. The rebellion was quelled with the usual massacres and deportation of survivors, and it is still the 1789 Bastille Day that France celebrates.

The Bicentennial in 1989 was marked by the inauguration of the **Opéra-Bastille**, Mitterrand's pet project and subject of the most virulent sequence of disputes and resignations of any of the *grands projets*. Almost filling the entire block between rues de Lyon, Charenton, and Moreau, this bloated building has totally altered place de la Bastille. The column is no longer pivotal; in fact, it's easy to miss it altogether when dazzled by the nighttime glare of lights emanating from this hideous "hippopotamus in a bathtub," as one perceptive critic put it. The building might have been excusable as a new terminal building for Roissy, but here, in the capital's most symbolic square, it's an outrage. Internally, of course, the acoustics and stage vision are unrivaled—to get a seat you need to reserve months in advance.

The opera's construction destroyed no mean amount of low-rent housing and the **quartier de la Bastille** is now trendier than Les Halles. But as with most speculative developments, the pace of change is uneven: old tool shops and ironmongers still survive alongside cocktail haunts and sushi bars; laundromats and cobblers neighbor Filofax outlets. **Place and rue d'Aligre**, where local protest against the opera centered, still has its raucous daily market, with food in the covered *halles* and second-hand clothes and junk on the *place* (for a very congenial snack, try *Le Baron Rouge*, the totally unstuck-up wine bar next door; see p.214).

Faubourg St-Antoine

The mania of traffic around place de la Bastille, of pedestrians as much as cars, has not improved, but there are quiet havens in the courtyards of **rue du Faubourg-St-Antoine**. No. 54, for example, has ivy and roses curtaining three shops, window boxes on every story, and lemon trees in tubs tilted on the cobbles. After Louis XI licensed the establishment of craftsmen in the fifteenth century, the faubourg became the principal working-class *quartier* of Paris, cradle of revolutions and mother of street-fighters. From its beginnings the principal trade associated with it has been **furniture-making**; the classic styles of French furniture—Louis Quatorze, Louis Quinze, Second Empire— were developed here and the maze of interconnecting yards and passages are still full of the workshops of the related trades: marquetry, stainers, polishers, inlayers etc, many of whom are still producing those styles.

Heading east on rue du Faubourg-St-Antoine, just past the evocatively named passage de la Main-d'Or, take a left up the crumbling **rue de la Forge Royale**. Overlooking a patch of cleared ground among the houses stands the rustic-looking **church of Ste-Marguerite**, with a garden beside it dedicated to the memory of Raoul Nordling, the Swedish consul who persuaded the retreating Germans not to blow up Paris in 1944.

The church (Mon–Sat 8am–noon & 3–7:30pm, Sun 8:30am–noon & 5–7:30pm) was built in 1624 to accommodate the growing population of the faubourg, which was about 40,000 in 1710 and 100,000 in 1900. The sculptures on the transept pediments were made by its first full-blown parish priest, who was himself a sculptor. Inside it is wide-bodied, low, and quiet, with a very local and un-urban feel, as if it were still out in the fields. The stained glass windows record **a very local history**: the visit of Pope Pius VII in 1802, in Paris for Napoléon's coronation; the miraculous cure of a Madame Delafosse in the rue de Charonne on May 31, 1725; the fatal wounding of Monseigneur Affre in the faubourg on June 25, 1848 (presumably by a dastardly revolutionary bullet); the murder of sixteen Carmelites at the Barrière du Trône in 1794 (presumably, more revolutionary anti-clericalism); the *quartier*'s dead in World War I . . . In the now disused cemetery, the story goes—though no one has been able to find it—lies the body of Louis XVII, the ten-year-old heir of the guillotined Louis XVI, who died in the Temple prison. The cemetery also received the dead from the Bastille prison.

Rue de Lappe and into the 11ᵉ

On **rue de Lappe** there are remnants of a very Parisian tradition: the *bals musettes*, or music halls of 1930s "gai Paris," frequented between the wars by Piaf, Jean Gabin, and Rita Hayworth. The most famous is *Balajo*, founded by one Jo de France, who introduced glitter and spectacle into what were then seedy gangster dives, and brought Parisians from the other side of the city to the rue de Lappe lowlife.

To the north, and east toward Père-Lachaise, **off rue de la Roquette and rue de Charonne**, there's nothing very special about the passages and ragged streets that make up the 11ᵉ *arrondissement*, except that they are utterly Parisian, with the odd detail of a building, the obscurity of a shop's specialty, the display of veg in a simple greengrocer's, the sunlight on a café table, or the graffiti on a Second-Empire street fountain to charm an aimless wander. And the occasional reminder of the sheer political toughness of French working-class tradition, as in the plaque on some apartment buildings in rue de la Folie-Regnault commemorating the first FTP Resistance group, which used to meet here until it was betrayed and executed in 1941.

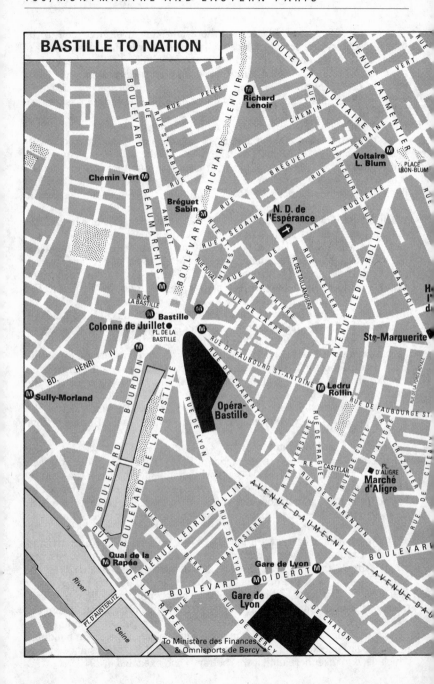

BASTILLE TO NATION

BOULEVARD VOLTAIRE

AVENUE PARMENTIER

BOULEVARD

RUE

RUE PELÉE

RUE ST-SABIN

RUE RICHARD LENOIR

RUE

RUE

CHEMIN

SEDAINE

VERT

RUE

AVENUE

Richard Ⓜ
Lenoir

Voltaire Ⓜ
L. Blum

PLACE
LÉON-BLUM

Chemin Vert Ⓜ

Bréguet
Sabin Ⓜ

BOULEVARD BEAUMARCHIS

RUE AMELOT

RUE ST-SABIN

RUE SEDAINE

RUE DUVAL

RUE DE LAPPE

RUE

BRÉGUET

POPINCOURT

ROQUETTE

DE

LA

N. D. de
l'Espérance

PAS THIÈRE

RUE DESTAILLANDIERS

RUE KELLER

RUE D'ESTAILLANDIERS

R. DESTINÉ

R. RUE LEDRU-ROLLIN

BASFROI

AVENUE

RUE

H-
l'
de

R. DE
LA BASTILLE

Ⓜ

Ⓜ Bastille ●
Colonne de Juillet ●
PL. DE LA
BASTILLE

Ⓜ

Ste-Marguerite ●

RUE DE FAUBOURG ST-ANTOINE

BD. HENRI IV

Ⓜ

BOULEVARD BOURDON

BOULEVARD DE LA BASTILLE

RUE DE LYON

RUE DE CHARENTON

Opéra-
Bastille

Ledru Ⓜ
Rollin

RUE DE FAUBOURGE ST-

Ⓜ Sully-Morland

R. DE LA ROQUETTE

RUE DE COTTE

R. TRAVERSIÈRE

R. DE PRAGUE

CASTELAR

RUE DE CHARENTON

RUE D'ALIGRE

RUE DE CITEAUX

RUE CROZATIER

PL
D'ALIGRE
Marché
d'Aligre

AVENUE DAUMESNIL

BOULEVARD DE

AVENUE LEDRU-ROLLIN

RUE DE LYON

R. TRAVERSIÈRE

BOULEVARD

Quai de la Ⓜ
Rapée

Gare de Lyon Ⓜ

Ⓜ DIDEROT

AVENUE DAU

BOULEVARD

BOURDON

RUE DE BERCY

Gare de
Lyon

RUE DE CHALON

River

PT. D'AUSTERLITZ

Seine

To Ministère des Finances
& Omnisports de Bercy ▲

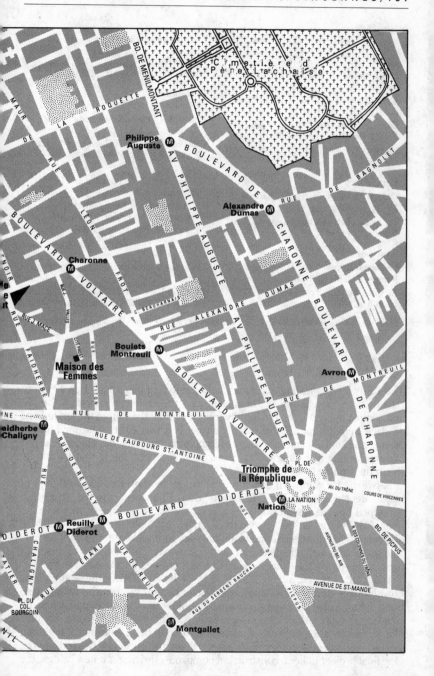

From The Bastille to Vincennes: Listings

Cafés

Le Clown, 114 rue Amelot, 11ᵉ. Mᵒ Filles-du-Calvaire.

Iguana, corner of rue de la Roquette and rue Daval, 11ᵉ. Mᵒ Bastille.

Café de L'Industrie, 16 rue St-Sébastien, 11ᵉ. Mᵒ Bastille/Bréguet-Sabin.

Le Petit Lappe, 20 rue de Lappe, 11ᵉ. Mᵒ Bastille.

Bars

Café de la Plage, 59 rue de Charonne, 11ᵉ. Mᵒ Bastille.

Tapas Nocturnes, rue de Lappe, 11ᵉ. Mᵒ Bastille.

Wine bars

Le Baron Rouge, 1 rue Théophile-Roussel, 12ᵉ. Mᵒ Ledru-Rollin.

Jacques-Mélac, 42 rue Léon-Frot, 11ᵉ. Mᵒ Charonne.

Beer cellar

Shake, 16 rue Daval, 11ᵉ. Mᵒ Bastille.

Restaurants
Under 80F

Palais des Femmes, 94 rue de Charonne, 11ᵉ. Mᵒ Faidherbe-Chaligny.

Chez Robert, 80 bd Richard-Lenoir, 11ᵉ. Mᵒ Richard-Lenoir/St-Ambroise.

Under 150F

Chardenoux, 1 rue Jules-Vallès, 11ᵉ. Mᵒ Charonne.

La Mansouria, 11 rue Faidherbe-Chaligny, 11ᵉ. Mᵒ Faidherbe-Chaligny.

Nini Peau d'Chien, 24 rue des Taillandiers, 11ᵉ. Mᵒ Bastille.

Over 150F

Bofinger, 3–7 rue de la Bastille, 3ᵉ. Mᵒ Bastille.

Le Train Bleu, 1st floor, Gare de Lyon, 20 bd Diderot, 12ᵉ. Mᵒ Gare-de-Lyon.

All the establishments listed above are reviewed in Chapter Eight, Drinking and Eating.

The 12ᵉ

The 12ᵉ is less appealing and much better suited to bus travel. Bus #29 from Bastille takes you down av Daumesnil past the ebullient *mairie* of the 12ᵉ and, almost opposite, the old Reuilly freight station, then on to the smug lions of place Félix-Eboué. The disused railroad line was earmarked for a green promenade and bicycle track from Bastille to the Bois de Vincennes. But other priorities have blocked its passage at so many points that it's hardly worth the trouble to follow.

Between av Daumesnil and the river is yet another area in the throes of major development. The **Ministère des Finances**, evicted from the revamped Louvre, has new quarters, very modest, stretching from above the river (where the higher bureaucrats arrive by boat) to rue de Bercy, a distance of 400 meters. Kafka would have loved it and contemporary Czechs would probably hallucinate the hand of Stalin on it. The best view of it is from the Charles-de-Gaulle–Nation métro line as it crosses the Pont de Bercy.

You can also see, on the other side of bd de Bercy, the **Palais des Omnisports de Bercy**, a major sports and culture venue, with its concrete bunker frame clad with sloping lawns. The old warehouses beyond are being cleared for more pricey executive creations, while back toward the Bastille, along quai de la Rapée, office buildings have long been ensconced, belittling a classic nineteenth-century work behind them, the gorgeous **Gare de Lyon**. One final project to keep construction companies thriving is a new bridge, the

Pont Charles-de-Gaulle, alongside the Pont d'Austerlitz, scheduled for completion in 1993.

Vincennes

From Faubourg St-Antoine, various buses will take you out **toward the Bois de Vincennes**. Bus #86 crosses **place de la Nation**, adorned with the Triumph of the Republic bronze, and, at the start of the Cours de Vincennes, the bizarre ensemble of two medieval monarchs, looking very small and sheepish in pens on the top of two high columns. Bus #46, with the same destination, crosses place Félix-Eboué and passes the **Musée des Arts Africains et Océaniens** (see p.155) with its 1930s colonial façade of jungles, hard-working natives, and the place names of the French Empire representing the "overseas contribution to the capital." The bus's next stop is the **Parc Zoologique**, which was one of the first zoos to replace cages with trenches and give the animals room to exercise themselves. The entrance is at 53 av de St-Maurice (Mº Porte-Dorée; summer 9am–6pm, winter 9am–5:30pm).

In the **Bois de Vincennes** itself, you can spend an afternoon **boating** on Lac Daumesnil (just by the zoo) or rent a bike from the same place and take some stale *baguette* to the ducks on Lac des Minimes on the other side of the wood (or bus #112 from Vincennes métro).

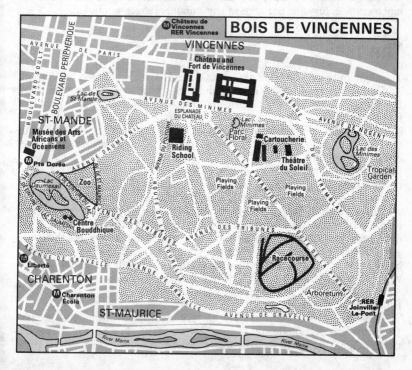

The fenced enclave on the southern side of Lac Daumesnil is a **Buddhist center** with a Tibetan temple, Vietnamese chapel, and international pagoda, all of which are visitable. As far as real woods go, the *bois* opens out and flowers once you're east of av de St-Maurice, but the area is so overrun with roads that countryside sensations don't stand much chance. *Boules* competitions are popular, however—there's usually a straggling collection of devotees between route de la Tourelle and av du Polygone.

To the north, near the château, the **Parc Floral** (Mon–Fri & Sun 9:30am–6:30pm, Sat in summer 9:30am–10pm, in winter 9:30am–6:30pm; bus #112 from Mᵒ Vincennes) testifies to the French lack of flair in landscape gardening. But the flowers are very pleasant with lily ponds and a Four Season Garden for all-year-round displays. In summer there are fun things for kids (see p.180). Despite this being a wood, tree lovers are encouraged to visit the arboretum (Mon, Wed & Fri 1–4:30pm; route de la Pyramide: RER Joinville-le-Pont) where eighty different species of greenery are tended.

To the east of the Parc Floral is the **Cartoucherie de Vincennes**, an old ammunitions factory, now home to four theater companies including the radical *Théâtre du Soleil* (see p.250).

On the northern edge of the *bois*, the **Château de Vincennes**, royal medieval residence, then state prison, porcelain factory, weapons dump, and military training school, is still undergoing restoration work started by Napoléon III. A real behemoth of a building, it's unlikely to be beautified by the removal of the nineteenth-century gun positions or any amount of stone-scrubbing.

The 13ᵉ

The tight-knit community on and around rue Nationale between bd Vincent-Auriol and the inner beltway never had much to hope for in the postwar days. But they made do with their crowded, rat-ridden, ramshackle slums not just for lack of choice but because life at least could be lived on the street—in the shops, the cafés (of which there were 48 on rue Nationale alone), and with the neighbors who all shared the same conditions. Paris was another place, rarely ventured to.

But come the 1950s and 1960s, the city planners, here as elsewhere, came up with their sense-defying solution to the housing problem. Each high-rise apartment is hygienic, secure, and costly to run, and only a couple of cafés remain on rue Nationale. The person next door is no longer a schoolmate and fellow worker but a well-dressed office type from north of the river. It's a depressing part of town, save for the odd untouched *quartiers* like the Butte aux Cailles, the bits and bobs of prewar architecture like Le Corbusier's Salvation Army hostel at 12 rue Cantagrel, and the admirable *Dunois* jazz venue (see p.241).

Bibliothèque Nationale

The 13ᵉ is, however, soon to have its very own mega-monument, the new **Bibliothèque Nationale**, on the site between rue du Chevaleret and the river. Judging from the models, this could be the loveliest of all the city's

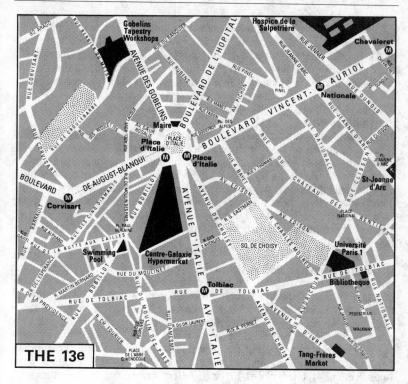

escapades into dreamland architecture. It is to have four transparent L-shaped towers, 100 meters high, at each corner of an open space the size of sixteen soccer fields around a sunken garden. The reading rooms are underground. The architect is a young Frenchman, Dominique Perrault, who was virtually unknown before he won the competition. If all goes well—and the logistics, not to mention costs, are horrendous—the most advanced library in the world will open its doors to anyone and everyone in 1995.

The 13e: Listings

Bar
Le Merle Moqueur, 11 rue des Buttes-aux-Cailles, 13e. Mº Place-d'Italie/Corvisart.

Restaurants
Under 150F
Hawaï, 87 av d'Ivry, 13e. Mº Tolbiac.
L'Oustalou/Gladines, 30 rue des Cinq-Diamants, 13e. Mº Corvisart.

Phuong Hoang, Centre Commercial Mercure, 52 rue du Javelot, 13e. Mº Tolbiac.

Les Temps des Cérises, 18–20 rue de la Butte-aux-Cailles, 13e. Mº Place-d'Italie/Corvisart.

Thuy Huong, Kiosque de Choisy, 15 av de Choisy, 13e. Mº Porte-de-Choisy.

All the establishments listed above are reviewed in Chapter Eight, Drinking and Eating.

Meanwhile, there's a wonderful municipal library at 93 rue de Tolbiac in a steel-frame building illuminated by bright blue spotlights. It houses the feminist Bibliothèque Marguerite Durand (see p.24) and has newspapers and a video auditorium. If you prefer to relax outside, the square de Choisy, on the north side of rue de Tolbiac leading to av de Choisy, has outdoor ping-pong tables with concrete nets, archery targets, and birds and trees.

Paris Chinatown

To the south, the area between rue de Tolbiac, av de Choisy, and bd Masséna is the **Chinatown** of Paris, with no concessions to organic matter unless it's to be eaten. From rue Tolbiac, just west of the library, steps lead up to a concrete *dalle* where the high-rises hide brilliant *Asiatique* restaurants and a covered mall of Chinese shops and businesses—travel agents, video libraries, hairdressers etc—where no transactions are carried out in French. Exiting onto av d'Ivry, you'll find the Tang-Frères supermarket and larger covered market where birds circle above the mind- and stomach-boggling goodies (see p.206).

Nearer to the city center, above bd Vincent-Auriol, the buildings are ornate and bourgeois, dominated by the immense **Hôpital de la Salpêtrière**, built under Louis XIV to dispose of the dispossessed. It later became a psychiatric hospital, fulfilling the same function. Jean Charcot, who believed that susceptibility to hypnosis proved hysteria, staged his theatrical demonstrations here, with Freud one of his greatly interested witnesses. If you ask very nicely in the *Bibliothèque Charcot* (block 6, red route), the librarian may show you a book of photographs of the poor female victims of these experiments. For a more positive statement on women, take a look at the building at 5 rue Jules-Breton, which declares in large letters on its façade, "In humanity, woman has the same duties as man. She must have the same rights in the family and in society."

Butte aux Cailles and the Gobelins Tapestry Workshops

West of av d'Italie, small houses with fancy brickwork or decorative timbers have remained intact: around place de l'Abbé-Henocque, rue Dr-Leray, the Cité Floral between rues Boussingault and Brillat-Savarin, and the villa Daviel. Closer to place d'Italie there's a rare taste of pre-high-rise life in the **Butte aux Cailles** *quartier* around the street of the same name. You'll find on it book and food shops, one of the green Art Nouveau municipal drinking fountains donated by Sir Richard Wallace, a community action center, a workers' cooperative jazz bar *(Le Merle Moqueur* at no. 11), and bars and bistros open until midnight. The *Bar des Sports* (no. 15) occasionally announces crocodile and turtle on the day's menu. And there's a food market nearby on bd Auguste-Blanqui.

Place d'Italie was the scene of one short-lived victory of the Left in the 1848 revolution. A government general and his officers were allowed through the barricade only to be surrounded and dragged off to the police station, where the commander was persuaded to write an order of retreat and a letter promising three million francs for the poor of Paris. Needless to say, neither was honored and the reprisals were heavy. Many of those involved in the uprising were tanners, laundry-workers, or dye-makers, with their workplace the banks of the Bièvre river. This was covered over in 1910 (creating rues Berbier-du-Mets and Croulebarbe) as a health hazard, the main source of pollution being the dyes from the **Gobelins tapestry workshops**, in operation here for some four hundred years. Tapestries are still being made by the same methods on cartoons by contemporary painters—a painfully slow process which you can watch (guided visits Tues, Wed & Thurs 2–3pm; 42 av des Gobelins; Mᵒ Gobelins).

CHAPTER FOUR

THE MUSEUMS

You may find there is sufficient visual stimulation just wandering
around Paris streets without exploring what's to be seen in the city's
galleries and museums. It's certainly questionable whether the
Louvre, for example, can compete in pleasure with the Marais, the
quais, or parts of the Latin quarter. But if established art appeals to you at all,
the Paris collections are not to be missed.

The most popular are the various **museums of modern art**: in the
Beaubourg Pompidou Centre, Palais de Tokyo, and Musée Picasso, and, for
the brilliantly represented opening stages, in the **Musée d'Orsay,
Orangerie**, and **Marmottan**. Since Paris was the well-rocked cradle of
Impressionism, Fauvism, Cubism, Surrealism, and Symbolism, there's both
justice and relevance in such a multitude of works being here. No less breath-
taking, going back to earlier cultural roots, are some of the **medieval works**
in the **Musée Cluny**, including the glorious *La Dame à la Licorne* tapestry.

Among the city's extraordinary number of technical, historical, social, and
applied art museums, pride of place must go to the dazzling **Cité des
Sciences**, radical in both concept and architecture—and fun. Entertaining
too, if more conventional, is the **Musée National des Arts et Traditions
Populaires**, its equivalent for the past. Some of the smaller ones are dedicated to a single person—Balzac, Hugo, Piaf—and others to very particular
subjects—spectacles, counterfeits, tobacco. We've detailed all but a very few
of the smallest and most highly specialized, like the freemasonry and
lawyers' museums, details of which can be obtained from the tourist office. A
few others, like **Le Corbusier**, **Montmartre**, the **Pavillon de l'Arsenal,
the Gobelins**, and the **Bibliothèque Nationale** have been incorporated in
the text in the relevant chapters.

The **Big Four—Louvre, Beaubourg, d'Orsay**, and **Cité des Sciences**—
are described first. The remainder follow under five headings: Art, Fashion
and Fripperies, History, Performance Arts and Literature, and Science and
Industry.

Admission prices vary: some, like the Institut du Monde Arabe, are
expensive at 40F, others, like Kwok-On, are excellent value at only 10F. Most
of the large museums charge around 25F and offer reductions to the under-
25s and over-60s (ID such as passport required). The Louvre and other state-
owned museums **close on Tuesday** and have half-price admission on
Sunday (free days have been abolished); the city-owned museums **close on
Monday**. If you're going to visit a great many museums in a short time, it's
worth buying the *Carte Inter-Musées* **museum pass** (50F 1-day; 100F 3-day;
150F 5-day; available from RER stations and museums) which is valid for 62
museums in and around Paris, and allows you to **bypass the ticket lines**. A

student card, despite claims to the contrary, is no help in getting reductions unless you're under 25.

Lastly, keep an eye out for **temporary exhibitions**, some of which match any of Paris's regular collections. Beaubourg, the Grand Palais, and the Grande Salle at La Villette have the major ones, well advertised by posters and detailed in *Pariscope* and the other listings magazines. Many of the museums and **commercial galleries** host themed exhibitions during the various arts festivals (see pp.22, 190). The commercial galleries (heavily concentrated in the Beaubourg and St-Germain areas and detailed in Chapter Seven) are always good for a look-in, which of course you can do without charge.

Beaubourg: Musée National d'Art Moderne

Centre Beaubourg, rue Beaubourg, 4ᵉ. Mᵒ Rambuteau/Hôtel-de-Ville. Mon & Wed–Fri noon–10pm, Sat & Sun 10am–10pm; Musée National d'Art Moderne 23F/17F; Galeries Contemporaines 16F; day pass 50F/45F; free Sun 10am–2pm.

The Musée National d'Art Moderne on the fourth floor of Beaubourg is second to none. The art is exclusively twentieth-century and constantly expanding. Contemporary movements and works dated the year before last find their place here along with the late-Impressionists, Fauvists, Cubists, Figuratives, Abstractionists, and the rest of this century's First World art trends. The lighting and spacing is superb but only a sixth of the whole collection is hung at any one time. The works rotate and word is going around that the whole lot may move out of Beaubourg—an excuse for yet another new billion-franc mammoth building some time in the future.

One of the earliest paintings is Henri Rousseau's *La Charmeuse de Serpent* (1907), an extraordinary, idiosyncratic beginning. In a different world, Picasso's *Femme Assise* of 1909 brings in the reduced colors and double dimensions of **Cubism**, presented in its fuller development by Braque's *L'Homme à la Guitare* (1914) and, later, in Léger's solid balancing act, *Les Acrobates en Gris* (1942–44).

Among **Abstracts**, there's the sensuous rhythm of color in Sonia Delaunay's *Prismes Electriques* (1914) and a good number of Kandinskys at his most harmonious and playful. Dali disturbs, amuses, or infuriates with *Six apparitions de Lénine sur un piano* (1931), and there are more surrealist images from Magritte and de Chirico.

Moving to the Expressionists, one of the most compulsive pictures—of 1920s female emancipation as viewed by a male contemporary—is the portrait of the journalist Sylvia von Harden by Otto Dix. The gender of the sleeping woman in *Le Rêve* by Matisse has no importance—it is the human body at its most relaxed that the artist has painted.

Jumping forward, to Francis Bacon, you find the tension and the torment of the human body and mind in the portraits, and—no matter that the figure is minute—in *Van Gogh in Landscape* (1957). Squashed-up cars, lines and squares, wrapped-up grand pianos and Warhol's *Electric chair* (1966) are there to be seen, while for a reminder that **contemporary** art can still hold its roots, there's the classic subject of *Le Peintre et son modèle* by Balthus in 1980–81.

MUSEUMS

1. M. National des Arts et Traditions Populaires
2. M. Arménien & M. d'Ennery
3. M. des Contrefaçons
4. M. Marmottan
5. Atelier d'Henri Bouchard
6. M. des Lunettes
7. M. du Vin
8. Maison de Balzac
9. M. de Radio-France
10. Palais Chaillot
    (M. du Cinema, M. des Monuments Français & M. de l'Homme)
11. M. Guimet
12. M. des Costumes
13. Palais de Tokyo
    (M. d'Art Moderne de la Ville de Paris & Centre National de la Photographie)
14. M. Intercoiffure
15. M. Cernuschi
16. M. de S.E.I.T.A.
17. M. de l'Armée
18. M. d'Orsay
19. M. Rodin
20. M. Valentin-Haüy
21. M. Bourdelle
22. M. de la Poste
23. M. Branly
24. M. Ernest-Hébert
25. M. Zadkine
26. Institut Français de l'Architecture
27. M. Delacroix
28. M. Cluny
29. M. de la Préfecture de Police
30. Institut du Monde Arabe
31. M. Assistance Publique
32. Orangerie
33. Jeu de Paume
34. M. Cognacq-Jay
35. M. de la Parfumerie
36. M. Gustave Moreau
37. M. Renan-Scheffer
38. M. Art Juif
39. M. de Montmartre
40. M. Grévin I
41. M. du Cristal
42. M. des Arts de la Mode (Louvre)
43. M. des Arts Décoratifs (Louvre)
44. M. de la Publicité (Louvre)
45. Centre Culturel des Halles
    (M. Grévin II/M. Holographie)
46. M. National Techniques
47. Beaubourg (M. National d'Art Moderne)
48. M. des Instruments de Musique Mécanique
49. M. de la Serrurerie
50. M. Kwok-on
51. M. Picasso
52. M. Carnavalet
53. M. de l'Histoire de France
54. Maison Victor Hugo
55. M. Adam Mickiewicz
56. Pavillon de l'Arsenal
57. M. Arts Africains et Océaniens
58. M. Edith Piaf
59. Cité de la Musique
60. Cité des Sciences
61. Centre International de l'Automobile

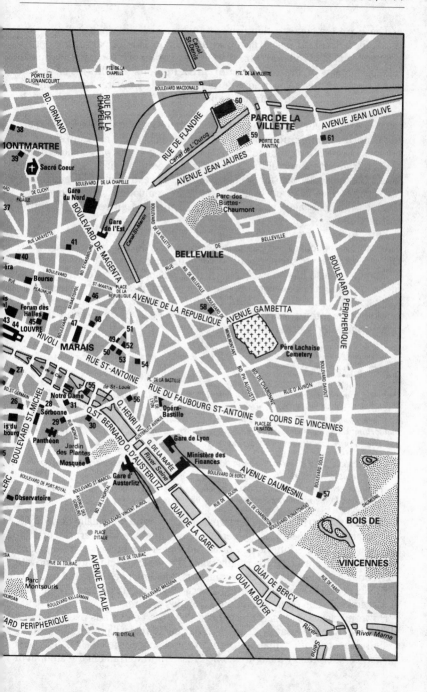

There are temporary exhibitions of photographs, drawings, collages, and prints in the **Salle d'Art Graphique and Salon Photo**, part of the permanent collections of the museum. If your grasp of French is sufficient you can take advantage of the **audiovisual presentations** on the major artistic movements of this century, or the films, projected several times daily, on contemporary art, on current exhibitions, or as experimental art in themselves.

On the mezzanine floor (down the stairs to the right of the plaza doors) are the **Galeries Contemporaines** where the overspill of the museum's contemporary collection gets rotated and young artists get a viewing. The **Grande Galerie** right at the top of the building is where the big-time exhibitions are held. These usually last for several months, are extremely well publicized, and can, occasionally, be brilliant. Yet more temporary shows on equally diverse themes take place in the basement **Centre de Création Industrielle**.

Entry to the Centre is free but the Museum and Galeries Contemporaines have admission charges (except on Sunday) as do the major exhibitions. Given the amount to see it may be worth getting a day pass.

Beaubourg also has an excellent cinema (see p.249), a **reference library** including foreign newspapers open to all, a record library where you can take a music break, a **snack bar and restaurant** (with seating on the roof), a **bookshop, contemporary music center** (see p.244), **dance and theater space**, and **kids' workshop** (see p.185).

The Louvre

Pyramide, Cour Napoléon, Palais du Louvre, 1ᵉʳ. Mᵒ Palais-Royal–Musée du Louvre/Louvre–Rivoli. Mon 9am–9:45pm (certain galleries only), Wed 9am–9:45pm (all galleries), Thurs–Sun 9am–6pm; temporary exhibitions noon–10pm; Histoire du Louvre rooms, medieval Louvre, auditorium, shops, cafés etc, 9am–10pm; free for under-18s, reduced price 18–25s and over-60s; half-price Sun (no reductions); closed Tues.

> "You walked for a quarter of a mile through works of fine art; the very floors echoed the sounds of immortality . . . It was the crowning and consecration of art . . . These works instead of being taken from their respective countries were given to the world and to the mind and heart of man from whence they sprung . . ."

William Hazlitt, writing of the Louvre in 1802, goes on, in equally florid style, to proclaim this museum as the beginning of a new age when artistic masterpieces would be the inheritance of all, no longer the preserve of kings and nobility. Novel the Louvre certainly was. The palace, hung with the private collections of monarchs and their ministers, was first opened to the public in 1793, during the Revolution. Within a decade Napoléon had made it the largest art collection on earth with takings from his empire.

However inspiring it might have been then, the Louvre has been a bit of a nightmare over the last few decades, requiring heroic willpower and stamina to find one work of art that you want to see amongst the 300,000. The new "*Grand Louvre,*" finally inaugurated by President Mitterrand in the autumn of

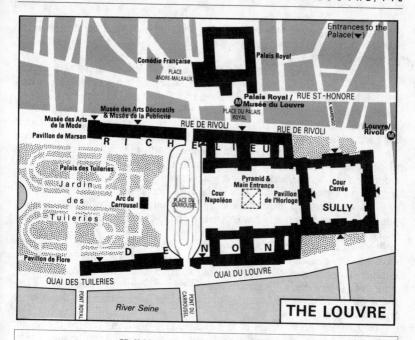

THE LOUVRE

Hall Napoléon (below the pyramid)

Lower level: tickets, cloakroom, café, restaurant, bookshop, post office, bureau de change, temporary exhibitions, auditorium, conference rooms.
Mezzanine: cafeteria, access to Sully, Denon, and Richelieu divisions, to **Histoire du Louvre** permanent exhibition, and to the **Medieval Louvre**.

The Galleries

	Ground Floor (*Blue*)	First Floor (*Red*)	Second Floor (*Yellow*)
SULLY	Antiquities *Venus de Milo* *Kneeling Scribe*	Antiquities Applied Arts	French paintings, 14–17th centuries
DENON	Antiquities **Sculptures:** French, medieval to 19th century; Italian, 11–19th centuries; German and Dutch *Slaves of Michelangelo*	Antiquities Crown Jewels *Winged Victory of Samothrace* **Paintings:** French, 18th & 19th centuries; Italian, 13–18th centuries; Flemish and Dutch, 17th century; Spanish; German, 15th & 17th centuries Beistegui collection *Mona Lisa* *Leonardo cartoons*	**Paintings:** British; German, 18th & 19th centuries Lyon collection deCroy collection Temporary Graphic Arts exhibitions Changing exhibitions of the museum's collection
RICHELIEU	Opening scheduled for 1993		

1988, provoking passionate responses of love and hate for its centerpiece, the 21-meter glass pyramid in the *Cour Napoléon*, has failed to solve the problems.

The pyramid is now the main entrance, a subterranean but day-lit concourse—the *Hall Napoléon*—with elevators and escalators leading into the newly arranged sections of the museum: *Sully* (around the Cour Carrée), *Denon* (the south wing), and *Richelieu* (the north wing, which will not be open until 1993). These are then divided into numbered rooms, color-coded for each of the three floors. For a start, three major divisions for a building this size is not a great deal of help. Second, the trouble with the Louvre has always been horizontal not vertical orientation and distance, so the access up from the *Hall Napoléon* doesn't get you very far. The signing system, including the giant electronic billboards in the *Hall Napoléon*, and the arrangement of the works, remains as mysterious and frustrating as it ever was. And when you need a break, you still have to get back down to the ticket concourse to find a cup of coffee.

A bonus from the building works, however, has been the opportunity to excavate the remains of the medieval Louvre—Philippe Auguste's twelfth-century fortress and Charles V's fourteenth-century palace conversion—under the *Cour Carrée*. These are now on show along with a permanent exhibition on the *Histoire du Louvre* from the Middle Ages right up to the current transformations.

The seven basic divisions of the museum's collections remain the same: three lots of antiquities, sculpture, painting, and applied and graphic arts. **Oriental Antiquities** (*Sully* ground floor 1–5) covers the Sumerian, Babylonian, Assyrian, and Phoenician civilizations, plus the art of ancient Persia. **Egyptian Antiquities** (*Sully* ground floor 5–7 & 1st floor 6–8) contains jewelry, domestic objects, sandals, sarcophagi, and dozens of examples of the delicate naturalism of Egyptian decorative technique, like the wall tiles depicting a piebald calf galloping through fields of papyrus and a duck taking off from a marsh. Some of the major exhibits are: the pink granite *Mastaba Sphinx,* the *Kneeling Scribe* statue (*Sully* ground floor 6), a wooden statue of *chancellor Nakhti,* the *god Amon,* protector of Tutankhamen, a bust of *Amenophis IV, Sethi I,* and the *goddess Hathor.*

The **Greek and Roman Antiquities** (*Denon* ground floor 2–4, first floor 3; *Sully* ground floor 7–8, first floor 8) include the *Winged Victory of Samothrace* (*Denon* first floor 3) and the *Venus de Milo* (*Sully* ground floor 8), biggest crowd-pullers in the museum after the *Mona Lisa. Venus,* striking a classic model's pose, is one of the great sexpots of all time. She dates from the late second century BC. Her antecedents are all on display, too, from the delightful *Dame d'Auxerre* (seventhcentury BC) and the fifth-century BC bronze *Apollo of Piombino,* still looking straight ahead in the archaic manner, to the classical perfection of the *Athlete of Benevento* and the beautiful *Ephebe of Agde.* In the Roman section are some very attractive mosaics from Asia Minor and luminous frescoes from Pompeii and Herculaneum, which already seem to foreshadow the decorative lightness of touch of a Botticelli still 1000 years and more away.

The **Applied Arts** collection (*Sully* first floor 1–6 & 8; *Denon* first floor 8) is heavily weighted on the side of vulgar imperial opulence. Beautifully crafted and extravagantly expensive pieces of furniture arouse no aesthetic response whatever, just an appalled calculation of the cost. The same has to be said of the renowned cabinet-maker Boulle's work (active around 1700), immediately recognizable by the heavy square shapes and lavish use of inlays in copper, bronze, and pewter and such ecologically catastrophic exuberance as entire doors of tortoiseshell. There are also several acres of tapestry—all of the very first quality and artistry, but a chore to look at. Relief has to be sought in the smaller, less public items: Marie-Antoinette's traveling case, for example, fitted up with the intricacy of a jigsaw to take an array of bottles, vials, and other queenly necessaries. Or the carved Parisian ivories of the thirteenth century: angels with rouged cheeks and the Virgin pulling a sharp little tit from her dress to suckle the Babe. Or the Limoges enamels and even earlier Byzantine ivories.

The **Sculpture** section (*Denon* ground floor 5 & 7–10) covers the entire development of the art in France from Romanesque to Rodin and includes Michelangelo's *Slaves* designed for the tomb of Pope Julius II (*Denon* ground floor 10). But once you have seen the Greeks, you are not likely to want to linger over many of the items here.

The largest and most indigestible section by far is the **paintings** (*Sully* second floor 1–4; *Denon* first floor 1, 2 & 4–10, second floor 9): French from the year dot to mid-nineteenth century, with Italians, Dutch, Germans, Flemish, and Spanish represented too. Among them are many paintings so familiar from reproduction in advertisements and on chocolate boxes that it is a surprise to see them on a wall in a frame. And unless you're an art historian, it is hard to make much sense of the parade of mythological scenes, classical ruins, piteous piety, acrobatic saints, and sheer dry academicism. A portrait, a domestic scene, a still life, is a real relief. Walking by with eyes selectively shut is probably the best advice.

The early Italians (*Denon* first floor 5 & 7) are the most interesting part of the collection, at least up to Leonardo and the sixteenth century. Giotto, Fra Angelico, Uccello's *Battle of San Romano*, Mantegna, Botticelli, Filippo Lippi, Raphael . . . all the big names are represented. It is partly their period, but there is still an innate classical restraint which is more appealing to modern taste than the exuberance and grandiloquence of the eighteenth and nineteenth centuries. If you want to get near the *Mona Lisa* (*Denon* first floor 5), go first or last thing in the day. No one, incidentally, pays the slightest bit of attention to the other Leonardos right alongside, including the *Virgin of the Rocks*.

Access to the *Hall Napoléon* and its shops, information services, audiovisual shows, etc, is free. You can reach it through passage Richelieu from rue de Rivoli, from the underground parking lot, or through the Tuileries, taking the spiral staircase down from the base of the pyramid.

The Palais du Louvre houses three other museums—decorative arts, fashion, and publicity—listed under "The Rest of the Art" and "Fashion and Fripperies" below.

Musée d'Orsay

1 rue de Bellechasse/quai Anatole-France (for major exhibitions), 7ᵉ. Mᵒ Solférino, RER Musée d'Orsay. Tues, Wed, Fri & Sat 9/10am–6pm, Thurs 9/10am–9:45pm, Sun 10am–6pm; half-price Sun; free guided tours in English by staff lecturer 11am & 2pm.

The conversion of the disused railroad station, the Gare d'Orsay, into the spanking new *Musée d'Orsay* marked a major advance in the reorganization of the capital's art collections. It houses the painting and sculpture of the immediately pre-modern period, 1848–1914, bridging the gap between the Louvre and the Centre Beaubourg. Its focus is the cobweb-clearing, eye-cleansing collection of **Impressionists** rescued from the cramped corridors of the Jeu de Paume, though not, unavoidably, from the bus tours and gangs of brats. Scarcely less electrifying are the works of the **Post-Impressionists** brought in from the Palais de Tokyo.

The general layout is as follows. On the **ground floor**, the mid-nineteenth-century sculptors, including Barye, caster of super-naturalistic bronze animals, occupy the center gallery. To their right, a few canvases by Ingres and Delacroix (the bulk of whose work is in the Louvre) serve to illustrate the transition from the early nineteenth century. Puvis de Chavannes, Gustave Moreau, the Symbolists, and early Degas follow, while in the galleries to the left Daumier, Corot, Millet, and the Realist school lead on to the first Impressionist works, including Manet's *Déjeuner sur l'Herbe*, which sent the critics into apoplexies of rage and disgust when it appeared in 1863. *Olympia* is here too, equally controversial at the time, for the color contrasts and sensual surfaces, rather than the content, though the black cat was considered peculiar.

To get the chronological continuation you have to go straight up to the top level, where numerous landscapes and outdoor scenes by Renoir, Sisley, Pissarro, and Monet owe much of their brilliance to the novel practice of setting up easels in the open to catch a momentary light. Monet's waterlilies are here in abundance, too, along with five of his Rouen cathedral series, each painted in different light conditions.

Le Berceau (1872), by Morisot, the only woman in the early group of Impressionists, is one of the few to have a complex human emotion as its subject—perfectly synthesized within the classic techniques of the movement. A very different touch, all shimmering light and wide brush strokes, is to be seen in Renoir's depiction of a good time being had by all in *Le Moulin de la Galette*—a favorite Sunday afternoon out on the Butte Montmartre.

Cézanne, a step removed from the preoccupations of the mainstream Impressionists, is also wonderfully represented. One of the canvases most revealing of his art is *Still life with apples and oranges* (1895–1900), in which the background abandons perspective while the fruit has an extraordinary reality.

The rest of this level is given over to the various offspring of Impressionism. Among a number of pointilliste works by Seurat and others is Signac's horrible *Entrée du Port de Marseille*. There's Gauguin, post- and pre-Tahiti, as well as some very attractive derivatives like Georges Lacombe's carved wood panels; several superb Bonnards and Vuillards and lots of

Toulouse-Lautrec at his caricatural night-clubbing best—one large canvas including a rear view of Oscar Wilde at his grossest. Plus all the blinding colors and disturbing rhythms of the Van Goghs.

The **middle level** takes in Rodin and other late nineteenth-century sculptors, three rooms of superb Art Nouveau furniture and *objets*, and, lastly, some Matisses and Klimts to mark the transition to the moderns in the Beaubourg collection.

As if these exhibition riches weren't enough, **the building** is itself a handsome structure, especially the interior, a huge vault of glass and steel, pusillanimously disguised by a façade of bourgeois stone. It was inaugurated in time for the 1900 World Fair and continued to serve the stations of southwest France until 1939. Orson Welles used it as the setting for his film of Kafka's *Trial*, and de Gaulle used it to announce his coup d'état of May 19, 1958, his messianic return to power to save the *patrie* from disintegration over the Algerian liberation war. Notwithstanding this illustrious history, it was only saved from a hotel developer's bulldozer by the colossal wave of public indignation and remorse at the destruction of Les Halles.

Cité des Sciences et de l'Industrie

Parc de la Villette, 19ᵉ. Mᵃ Corentin-Cariou/Porte de la Villette. Tues–Sun 10am–6pm; 35F, reduced charge 25F; planétarium 10:30am, 12:30pm, 2pm, 3:30pm & 5pm—15F extra; Géode Tues–Sun 10am–7pm—45F/35F, combined ticket with Cité 70F/60F (available from Géode only, see p.125).

This is the science museum to end all science museums, and worth visiting for the interior of the building alone: all glass and stainless steel, crow's nests and cantilevered platforms, bridges, and suspended walkways, the different levels linked by elevators and escalators around a huge central space open to the full 40-meter height of the roof. It may be colossal, but you are more likely to lose yourself mentally rather than physically, and come out after several hours reeling with images and ideas, while none the wiser in actual fact about DNA, quasars, bacteria reproduction, rocket launching, or whatever.

The **permanent exhibition**, called *Explora*, takes up the top two floors and is divided into thirty units (pick up a detailed plan from the *Accueil général Explora* on *niveau 1*). These cover different subjects such as microbes, maths, sounds, robots, flying, energy, space, information, language etc. The emphasis, as the name suggests, is on exploring; the means used are interactive computers, videos, holograms, animated models, and games. Most of the explanations and instructions are in English as well as French; one exception, unfortunately, is the *Jeux de lumière*—"light games," a whole series of experiments to do with color, optical illusions, refraction etc. But then you can treat working out what you're supposed to do as an experiment in itself.

In *Mille millards de microbes*, a rabies virus, looking like an evil multi-colored *Dr Who* dalek, is scaled to the equivalent of you being the height of Everest. A classic example of chaos theory introduces the maths section: a wheel of glasses rotating below a stream of water in which the switch between clockwise and anticlockwise motion is entirely unpredictable. In *Expressions et comportements* you can intervene in stories acted out on videos, changing the behavior of the characters to engineer a different outcome. Hydroponic plants grow for real in a green bridge across the central space. You can steer robots through mazes; make music by your own movements; try out a flight simulation; watch computer-guided puppet shows and holograms of different periods' visions of the universe; and stare at two slabs of wall parting company at the rate of 2cm a year—enacting the gradual estrangement of Europe and America.

When all this interrogation and stimulation becomes too much, you can relax at the café within *Explora* (*niveau 2* by the planetarium), where the cheapest sit-down cup of coffee in the city is served and even smoking is allowed. When you want your head to start reeling again, just join the line for the **planetarium**.

Back on the ground floor there's a **cinema** (*Cinéma Louis-Lumière:* main film shown at 2pm & 3:30pm, and additionally at 2:45pm, 4:15pm & 5pm during school holidays; 10F; other programs 10:30am, 2:30pm, 4pm & 5pm during school terms; free); **kids' activity center** (*inventorium*—see Chapter Six); an exhibition of current scientific research (in the *Salles Sciences Actualités*; no admission charge); and a whole program of **temporary exhibitions**. Below ground, on *niveau S1*, there are **libraries** (the *médiathèque*) which you can freely consult, and on *niveau S2*, **restaurants** and an **aquarium**. Outside, by the Géode, is a real 1957 French **submarine**, *L'Argonaute*. The only thing missing is accommodation—then you could be entertained for several days non-stop.

The entire building is accessible by wheelchair; the *médiathèque* has a Braille room; and there are signers (in FSL).

The Rest of the Art

Musée d'Art Moderne de la Ville de Paris

Palais de Tokyo east wing, 11 av du Président-Wilson, 16ᵉ. Mᵒ Iéna/Alma-Marceau. Tues & Thurs–Sun 10am–5:30pm, Wed 10am–8pm; closed holidays.

It is difficult to predict which works will be on display and where, for this gallery suffers from seemingly chronic St Vitus's Dance. But you can rest assured that the museum's schools and trends of twentieth-century art will always be richly represented by artists such as Vlaminck, Zadkine, Picasso, Braque, Juan Gris, Valadon, Matisse, Dufy, Utrillo, both Delaunays, Chagall, Modigliani, Léger, and many others, as well as by sculpture and painting by contemporary artists.

Among the most spectacular works on permanent show are Robert and Sonia Delaunay's huge whirling wheels and cogs of rainbow color (now displayed in the ground floor corridor); the pale leaping figures of Matisse's *La Danse*; and Dufy's enormous mural, *La Fée Electricité* (done for the electricity board), illustrating the story of electricity from Aristotle to the then modern power station, in 250 lyrical, colorful panels filling three entire walls.

The upper floors of the gallery are reserved for all sorts of contemporary and experimental work, including music and photography.

On sale in the bookshop are a number of artists' designs, among them a set of Sonia Delaunay's playing cards, guaranteed to rejuvenate the most jaded cardsharp. Next to it is an excellent and reasonably priced snack bar.

Musée des Arts Africains et Océaniens

293 av Daumesnil, 12ᵉ. Mᵒ Porte-Dorée. Mon & Wed–Fri 9:45am–noon & 1:30–5:20pm, Sat & Sun 12:30–6pm; 23F/13F; half-price Sun.

This strange museum—one of the least crowded in the city—has an African gold brooch of curled-up sleeping crocodiles on one floor and, in the basement, five live crocodiles in a tiny pit surrounded by tanks of tropical fishes. Imperialism is much in evidence in a gathering of culture and creatures from the old French colonies: hardly any of the black African artifacts are dated, as the collection predates European acknowledgement of history on that continent, and the captions are a bit suspicious too. These masks and statues, furniture, adornments, and tools should be exhibited with paintings by Expressionists, Cubists, and Surrealists to see in which direction inspiration went. Picasso and friends certainly came here often. And though the casual tourist might not respond with a bit of painting or sculpture, there is enjoyment enough to be had.

Musée de Cluny

6 place Paul-Painlevé, 5ᵉ (off rue des Écoles). Mᵒ Odéon/St-Michel. Wed–Mon 9:45am–12:30pm & 2–5:15pm; 15F/8F.

If you have always found tapestries boring, this treasure house of medieval art may well provide the flash of enlightenment. The numerous beauties include a marvelous depiction of the grape harvest; a Resurrection embroidered in gold and silver thread, with sleeping guards in medieval armor; and a whole room of sixteenth-century Dutch tapestries, full of flowers and birds, a woman spinning while a cat plays with the end of the thread, a lover making advances, a pretty woman in her bath, overflowing into a duck pond.

But the greatest wonder of all is *La Dame à la Licorne—The Lady with the Unicorn:* six enigmatic scenes featuring a beautiful woman flanked by a lion and a unicorn, late fifteenth-century, perhaps made in Brussels. Quite simply, it is the most stunning piece of art you are likely to see in many a long day. The ground of each panel is a delicate red worked with a thousand tiny flowers, birds, and animals. In the center is a green island, equally flowery, framed by stylized trees, and here the scene is enacted. The young woman plays a portable organ, takes a sweet from a proffered box, makes a necklace of carnations while a pet monkey, perched on the rim of a basket of flowers, holds one to his nose . . .

Unfortunately, the lighting and general atmosphere of this museum is a trifle gloomy, and it doesn't feature on the list for dramatic renovations, but nevertheless it's a treat (and generally uncrowded).

Musée des Arts Décoratifs

107 rue de Rivoli, 1er. Mº Palais-Royale–Musée du Louvre. Wed–Sat 12:30–6pm, Sun 11am–6pm; 20F/15F.

This is an enormous museum, except by the standards of the building housing it—the Louvre—of which it takes up the Tuileries end of the north wing. The contents are the furnishings, fittings, and objects of French interiors: beds, blankets, cupboards, tools, stained glass, and lampshades, in fact almost anything that illustrates the decorative skills from the Middle Ages to the 1990s.

The meager contemporary section has been added to recently—works by French, Italian, and Japanese designers mainly, including, inevitably, Philippe Starck. The rest of the twentieth century (also on the first floor) is fascinating—a bedroom by Guimard, Jeanne Lanvin's Art Deco apartments, and a salon created by Georges Hoentschel for the 1900 Expo Universelle. You can work your way back through the nineteenth century's fascination with the foreign and love of vivid coloring (fourth floor), to the intricate wood-carving of the eighteenth century (third floor), to seventeenth-century marquetry and Renaissance tapestries and ivories (second floor).

A section on the third floor is dedicated to toys throughout the ages, with changing exhibitions. The museum shop, with books, clothes, accessories, playing cards, and other amusements is good, though not cheap.

Musée-Fondation Dapper

50 av Victor-Hugo, 16e. Mº Étoile. Daily 11am–7pm during exhibitions; 15F/7.50F.

The art of pre-colonial Africa is presented in superb temporary exhibitions based around a region, a period, or a particular aspect of culture. Check *Pariscope* etc for details. The library is open to students and researchers.

Grand and Petit Palais

Av W-Churchill, 8e. Mº Champs-Elysées-Clémenceau. Grand Palais Mon & Thurs–Sun 10am–8pm, Wed 10am–10pm; Petit Palais Tues–Sun 10am–5:40pm; closed holidays; 28F/18F.

The **Grand Palais Galeries** hold major temporary art exhibitions, good ones being evident from the lines stretching down av Churchill. *Pariscope* and co will have details, and you'll probably see plenty of posters around.

In the **Petit Palais**, whose entrance hall is a brazenly extravagant painted dome, you'll find the *Beaux Arts* museum, which seems to be a collection of leftovers, from all periods, after the other main galleries had taken their pick. There's a certain interest—you can compare the ugliness of an Art Nouveau dining room with the effete eighteenth-century furniture in the *Salles Tuck*—but this collection shouldn't be at the top of your list. And that despite its considerable section of nineteenth-century French painting.

At the back of the Grand Palais (av F-Roosevelt) is the **Palais de la Découverte** (Tues–Sun 10am–6pm; 50F/40F/30F), which has become a bit of an anachronism now that La Villette is open. Troops of French school children are still taken around this stuffy traditional science museum, shown demonstrations of classic experiments, and given a break in the planetarium. However, it does sometimes have good temporary exhibitions, so check *Pariscope* etc.

Musée Guimet

6 place d'léna, 16ᵉ. Mᵒ léna. 9:45am–5:15pm; closed Tues & holidays; 23F; Sun half-price.

Little visited, this features a huge and beautifully displayed collection of Oriental art, from China, India, Japan, Tibet, and southeast Asia. There is a particularly fine collection of Chinese porcelain on the top floor.

Musée Marmottan

2 rue Louis-Boilly, 16ᵉ (off av Raphael). Mᵒ Muette. Tues–Sun 10am–5:30pm; 25F/10F.

The Marmottan house itself is interesting, with some splendid pieces of First Empire pomposity, chairs with golden sphinxes for armrests, candelabra of complicated headdresses and twining serpents. There is a small and beautiful collection of thirteenth- to sixteenth-century manuscript illuminations, but the star of the show is the collection of **Monet paintings** bequeathed by the artist's son. Among them is the canvas entitled *Impression, Soleil Levant* (*Impression, Sunrise*), an 1872 rendering of a misty sunrise over Le Havre, whose title the critics usurped to give the Impressionist movement its name. There's a dazzling collection of canvases from Monet's last years at Giverny (see p.266). They include several *Nymphéas* (Waterlilies), *Le Pont Japonais, L'Allée des Rosiers, La Saule Pleureur*, where rich colors are laid on in thick, excited whorls and lines. Marks on white canvas: form dissolves. To all intents and purposes, these are abstractions—so much more "advanced" than the work of, say, a Renoir, Monet's exact contemporary.

Impression, Soleil Levant was stolen from the gallery in October 1985, along with four other Monets, two Renoirs, a Berthe Morisot, and a Naruse. After a police operation lasting five years, and going as far afield as Japan, the paintings were discovered in a villa in southern Corsica, and are back on show—with greatly tightened security measures.

The Orangerie

Place de la Concorde, 1ᵉʳ. Mᵒ Concorde. 9:45am–5:15pm; closed Tues; 23F/12F; half-price Sun.

The **Orangerie**, on the south side of the Tuileries terrace overlooking place de la Concorde, reopened in 1985 (after everyone had forgotten what it had inside) to reveal its two oval rooms arranged by **Monet** as panoramas for his largest waterlily paintings. In addition, there are works by no more than a dozen other **Impressionist** artists—Matisse, Cézanne, Utrillo, Modigliani, Renoir, Soutine, and Sisley among them.

This is a private collection, inherited by the state with the stipulation that it should always stay together. Consequently none of the pictures moved to the Musée d'Orsay, and the Orangerie remains one of the top treats of Paris art museums.

Cézanne's southern landscapes, the portraits by Van Dongen, Utrillo, and Derain of Paul Guillaume and Jean Walter, whose taste this collection represents, the massive nudes of Picasso, Monet's *Argenteuil*, and Sisley's *Le Chemin de Montbuisson* are the cherries on the cake of this visual feast. What's more, you don't need marathon endurance to cover the lot and get back to your favorites for a second look. The only black mark is the gilt heaviness of the frames.

Centre National de la Photographie

Palais de Tokyo west wing, 13 av du Président-Wilson, 16ᵉ. Mᵒ Iéna/Alma-Marceau. 9:45am–5pm; closed Tues; 25F/14F.

The small permanent exhibition on the "History of Seeing" is not greatly exciting. Some of the temporary exhibitions here which can call on the vast national archives of photographic images, are, however, well worth seeing. Check *Pariscope* etc for details.

Musée Picasso

5 rue de Thorigny, 3ᵉ. Mᵒ St-Paul/Filles-du-Calvaire. Wed 9:15am–10pm, Mon & Thurs–Sun 9:15am–5:15pm; 28F/16F.

The French are justly proud of this 1980s art museum. The grandiloquent seventeenth-century mansion, the Hôtel Salé, was restored and restructured at a cost to the government of 30–40 million francs. The spacious but undaunting interior is admirably suited to its contents: the largest collection of Picassos anywhere. A large proportion of the works were personally owned by Picasso at the time of his death, and the state had first option on them in lieu of taxes owed. They include all the different media he used, the paintings he bought or was given by his contemporaries, his African masks and sculptures, photographs, letters and other personal memorabilia.

All of which said, it's a bit disappointing. These are not Picasso's most enjoyable works—the museums of the Côte d'Azur and the Picasso gallery in Barcelona are more exciting. But the collection does leave you with a definite sense of the man and his life in conjunction with his production. This is partly because these were the works he wanted to keep. The paintings of his wives, lovers, and families are some of the gentlest and most endearing: the portrait of *Marie-Thérèse and Claude dessinant, Françoise et Paloma*. This one is accompanied by a photo of Picasso drawing with his children Claude and Paloma. Throughout the chronological sequence, the photographs are vital in showing this charismatic (and highly photogenic) man seen at work and at play by friends and family.

The portrait of Dora Maar, like that of Marie-Thérèse, was painted in 1937, during the Spanish Civil War when Picasso was going through his worst personal and political crises. This is the period when emotion and passion play hardest on his paintings and they are by far the best (though *Guernica* is in Madrid, not here). A decade later, Picasso was a member of the Communist Party—his cards are on show along with a drawing entitled *Staline à la Santé* (Here's to Stalin), and his delegate credentials for the 1948

World Congress of Peace. The *Massacre en Corée* (1951) demonstrates the lasting pacifist commitment in his work.

Temporary exhibitions will bring to the Hôtel Salé works from the periods least represented: the Pink Period, Cubism (despite some fine examples here, including a large collection of collages), the immediate postwar period, and the 1950s and 1960s.

The modern museological accoutrements are all provided: audiovisuals and films in a special cinema; biographical and critical details displayed in each room; a library; and a good and not too expensive restaurant/tea room.

Musée Rodin

77 rue de Varenne, 7ᵉ (just to the east of the Invalides). Mᵒ Varenne. Tues–Sun 10am–5/5:45pm; 20F/10F; half-price Sun.

This collection represents the whole of Rodin's work. Major projects like *Les Bourgeois de Calais*, *Le Penseur*, *Balzac*, *La Porte de l'Enfer*, *Ugolini et fils* are exhibited in the garden—the latter forming the centerpiece of the ornamental pond. Indoors (and very crowded) are works in marble like *Le Baiser*, *La Main de Dieu*, *La Cathédrale*—those two perfectly poised, almost sentient, hands. There is something particularly fascinating about the works, like *Romeo and Juliet* and *La Centauresse*, which are only, as it were, half-created, not totally liberated from the raw block of stone.

There is a reasonably priced café in the garden.

Individual artists and smaller museums

Institut Français de l'Architecture
6 rue de Tournon, 6ᵉ. Mᵒ Odéon. Tues–Sat 10:30am–7pm; free.

Temporary exhibitions on individual architects, architectural trends, etc, with plenty of models and photographs as well as plans and architect-speak (a babble to which the French language lends a dangerous seduction).

Musée d'Art Juif
42 rue des Saules, 18ᵉ. Mᵒ Lamarck-Caulaincourt. Sun–Thurs 3–6pm; closed Aug; 15F/10F.

Some contemporary art, models of the great synagogues, and numerous objects to do with worship, supplemented by temporary exhibitions.

Atelier d'Henri Bouchard
25 rue de l'Yvette, 16ᵉ. Mᵒ Jasmin. Wed & Sat only, 2–7pm; 15F/10F.

Another studio of a sculptor (1875–1960), with works in bronze, stone, wood, and marble exhibited.

Musée Bourdelle
16 rue Antoine-Bourdelle, 15ᵉ. Mᵒ Montparnasse/Falguière. Tues–Sun 10am–5:40pm; closed holidays; 18F/12F.

The work of the early twentieth-century sculptor, including casts, drawings, and tools, in the studio and house where he lived.

Musée Cernuschi

7 av Velasquez, 17ᵉ (by east gate of Parc Monceau); Mᵒ Monceau/Villiers. Tues–Sun 10am–5:40pm; closed holidays; 15F.

A small collection of ancient Chinese art with some exquisite pieces, but of fairly specialized interest.

Musée Cognacq-Jay

Hôtel Donon, 8 rue Elzévir, 3ᵉ. Mᵒ St-Paul/Chemin-Vert/Rambuteau. Tues–Sun 10am–5:40pm; closed holidays; 12F.

For lovers of European art of the eighteenth century—Canaletto, Fragonard, Tiepolo—and early Rembrandt. Also porcelain, furniture, and aristocratic trinkets in a matching setting of wood-paneled rooms.

Musée Delacroix

6 rue Furstemburg, 6ᵉ. Mᵒ St-Germain-des-Prés. 9:15am–12:30pm & 2–5:15pm; closed Tues; 1F/6F.

Delacroix lived and worked here from 1857 till his death in 1863. Some attractive watercolors, illustrations from *Hamlet,* and a couple of versions of a lion hunt hang in the painter's old studio, but there's nothing much in the way of major work.

Musée de l'Holographie

15 Grand-Balcon, niveau -1, Forum des Halles, 1ᵉʳ. Mᵒ RER Châtelet-Les Halles. Sun, Mon & holidays 1–7pm, Tues–Sat 10:30am–7pm; 28F/24F.

Like most holography museums to date, this one is less exciting than you expect, the fault lying with the state of the art. But there are a couple of holograms more inspired than women winking as you pass, and works where artists have combined holograms with painting. The most impressive technically are the reproductions of museum treasures; just like the originals, you can't touch them.

Musée Jacquemart-André

158 bd Haussmann, 8ᵉ. Mᵒ Miromesnil/St-Philippe-du-Roule. Wed–Sun noon–6:30pm; 35F/25F.

The ceilings of the staircase and three of the rooms of this museum are decorated with Tiepolo frescoes. His French contemporaries of the eighteenth century hang in the ground-floor rooms as well as his fellow Venetian, Canaletto. The collection contains several Rembrandts and, best of all, fifteenth- and sixteenth-century Italian genius in the works of Botticelli, Donatello, Mantegna, Tintoretto, Titian, and Uccello.

Musée des Monuments Français

Palais de Chaillot, place du Trocadéro, 16ᵉ. Mᵒ Trocadéro. 9am–6pm; closed Tues & holidays; 15F.

In the east wing of the Palais, the Musée des Monuments Français comprises full-scale reproductions of the most important church sculpture from Romanesque to Renaissance. All the major sites are represented. This is the place to come to familiarize yourself with the styles and periods of monumental sculpture in France. Also included are repros of the major frescoes.

Musée Gustave Moreau

14 rue de la Rochefoucauld, 9ᵉ. Mᵃ Trinité. Mon & Thurs–Sun 10am–12:45pm & 2–5:15pm, Wed 11am–5:15pm; closed holidays; 16F; half-price Sun.

An out-of-the-way bizarre, overcrowded collection of cluttered, joyless paintings by the Symbolist Gustave Moreau. If you know you like him, go along. Otherwise, give it a miss.

Espace Photo

4–8 Grande Galerie, niveau -1, Porte Pont-Neuf, Forum des Halles, 1ᵉʳ. Mᵃ RER Châtelet-Les Halles. Tues–Sat 1–6pm; 15F/7F.

A new space for photographic art with changing exhibitions of the greats—Cartier-Bresson, Brandt, Cameron, etc—as well as the lesser known.

Musée Valentin-Haûy

5 rue Duroc, 7ᵉ. Mᵃ Duroc. Tues & Wed only 2:30–5pm; closed July and Aug; free.

Not for the blind but about them—the aids devised over the years as well as art and objects made by blind people.

Musée Zadkine

100bis rue d'Assas, 6ᵉ. Mᵃ Vavin. Tues–Sun 10am–5:40pm; closed holidays; 9F/4.50F.

In Zadkine's own house and garden—a secret, private garden hidden away among tall apartment buildings. His angular Cubist bronzes are sheltered by the trees or emerge from a clump of bamboos. The rustic cottage, like the garden, is full of his sculptures. A place you want to linger in.

Fashion and Fripperies

Musée des Arts de la Mode

109 rue de Rivoli, 1ᵉʳ. Mᵃ Palais-Royal. Wed–Sat 12:30–6pm, Sun 11am–6pm; 25F/18F.

The newer of the two fashion museums of Paris adjoins the *Musée des Arts Décoratifs* in the Louvre. The circular roof windows of the building look out on the Eiffel Tower, the Sacré-Coeur, Beaubourg, and the line of the Louvre disappearing down rue de Rivoli—rather better views than within. Exhibitions, based for example around a couturier, a fabric, or a period, change every two to three months, and tend to take a far too obsequious attitude to the industry.

Musée du Cristal

30bis rue de Paradis, 10ᵉ. Mᵃ Gare de l'Est, Château-d'Eau. Mon–Fri 9am–6pm, Sat 10am–noon & 2–5pm; closed holidays; free.

The most intricate and beautiful examples of crystal glass from the manufacturers Baccarat in a modern building behind a seventeenth-century arcade.

Musée des Lunettes et Lorgnettes de Jadis

2 av Mozart, 16e. Mo La Muette. Tues–Sat 9am–1pm & 2–7pm; closed Aug; free.

Don't look for a museum. This superb collection of focusing aids resides in an ordinary commercial optician's shop, with nothing on the outside to advertise its existence. The exhibits span pretty much the whole history of the subject, from the first medieval corrective lenses to modern times, taking in binoculars, microscopes, and telescopes on the way. Many items are miniature masterpieces: bejewelled, inlaid, enamelled, and embroidered—an intricate art that readily accommodated itself to the gimmickry its rich patrons demanded. There are, for example, lenses set in the hinges of fans and the pommels of gentlemen's canes, and a lorgnette case that pops open to reveal an eighteenth-century dame sitting on a swing above a waterfall. A special collection consists of pieces that have sat upon the bridges of the famous: Audrey Hepburn, the Dalai Lama, Sophia Loren, and ex-President Giscard.

Musée de la Mode et du Costume

Palais Galliera, 10 av Pierre ler-de-Serbie, 16e. Mo Iéna/Alma-Marceau. Tues–Sun 10am–5:40pm; 22F.

Clothes and fashion accessories of the rich and powerful, from the eighteenth century to today, exhibited in temporary thematic exhibitions. They last about six months and during change-overs (usually May–Nov) the museum is closed.

Musée de l'Affiche et de la Publicité

107 rue de Rivoli, 1er. Mo Palais-Royale–Musée du Louvre. Mon & Wed–Sat 12:30–6pm, Sun 11am–6pm; 20F/15F.

This has recently moved from its Art Nouveau surroundings in the 10e to join the decorative arts and fashion museums in the Louvre. Publicity posters, print ads and TV and radio commercials are presented in monthly exhibitions, concentrating either on the art, the product, or the politics.

SEITA

12 rue Surcrouf, 7e; Mo Invalides/Latour-Maubourg. Mon–Sat 11am–6pm; closed holidays; free. Reopening after building works some time in 1991.

The state tobacco company has this small and delightful museum in its offices, presenting the pleasures of smoking, and none of the harm, with pipes and pouches from every continent—early Gauloise packets, painted *tabac* signs, and, best of all, a slide show of tobacco in painting from the seventeenth century to now.

Musée du Vin

Rue des Eaux, 16e. Mo Passy. Tues–Sun noon–6pm.

25F badly spent! The collection of paraphernalia connected with the wine trade—supposedly the museum's *raison d'être*—is thoroughly unconvincing. The setting of cellars and tunnels of an erstwhile monastery and quarry is waxwork-cutesy. What with the restaurant, *dégustation*, and wines for sale, it is clear that profit is the goal, not information. Leave to the bus tours.

History and Social Sciences

Musée de l'Armée

Hôtel des Invalides, 7ᵉ. Mᵒ Invalides/Latour-Maubourg/École-Militaire. Daily 10am–5pm; 25F/13F.

France's national war museum is enormous. The largest part is devoted to the uniforms and weaponry of Napoléon's armies with numerous personal items of Napoléon's, including his campaign tent and bed, and even his dog, stuffed. Later French wars are illustrated, too, through paintings, maps, and engravings. Sections on the two world wars are good, with deportation and resistance covered as well as battles. Some of the oddest exhibits are Secret Service sabotage devices—for instance, a rat and a lump of coal stuffed with explosives.

Musée Arménien and Musée d'Ennery

59 av Foch, 16ᵉ. Mᵒ Porte-Dauphine. Sun & Thurs 2–6pm; closed Aug; free.

On the ground floor artifacts, art, and historical documents of the Armenian people from the Middle Ages to the genocide by the Turks at the start of this century. On the floors above, the personal acquisitions of a nineteenth-century popular novelist: Chinese and Japanese objects including thousands of painted and sculpted buttons.

Musée de l'Homme

Palais de Chaillot, place du Trocadéro, 16 ᵉ. Mᵒ Trocadéro. 9:45am–5pm; closed Tues & holidays.

Jack Lang, the culture minister, is currently waving his multi-million-franc wand over this collection illustrating the way of life, costumes, characteristic occupations, etc of numerous countries in all parts of the world. After a renovation on the scale of the d'Orsay museum, the new *Musée de l'Homme* is bound to be very showy, full of high-tech facilities and still oblivious to the problem of its title to half the world.

Musée National des Arts et Traditions Populaires

6 av du Mahatma Gandhi, Bois de Boulogne, 16ᵉ (beside main entrance to Jardin d'Acclimatation). Mᵒ Les Sablons/Porte-Maillot. 9:45am–5:15pm; closed Tues; 14F/9F.

Those who have any interest in the beautiful and highly specialized skills, techniques, and artifacts which were developed in the long ages that preceded industrialization, standardization, and mass-production, should find this museum fascinating. Boat-building, shepherding, farming, weaving, blacksmithing, pottery, stonecutting, games, clairvoyance . . . all beautifully illustrated and displayed. Downstairs, there is a study section with cases and cases of implements of different kinds, and cubicles where you can call up explanatory slide shows at the touch of a switch.

Musée de l'Assistance Publique

Hôtel de Miramion, 47 quai de la Tournelle, 5ᵉ. Mᵒ Maubert. Wed–Sun 10am–5pm; closed holidays; 10F/5F.

This covers the history of Paris hospitals from the Middle Ages to the present with pictures, pharmaceutical containers, surgical instruments, and decrees relating to public health.

Musée Carnavalet
23 rue de Sévigné, 3e. Mo St-Paul. Tues–Sun 10am–5:40pm; closed holidays; 15F/8.50F.

A Renaissance mansion in the Marais presents the history of Paris as viewed and lived in by royalty, aristocrats, and the bourgeoisie from François I to 1900. The rooms for 1789–95 are full of sacred mementos: models of the Bastille, original *Declarations of the Rights of Man and the Citizen*, tricolors and liberty caps, sculpted allegories of Reason, crockery with revolutionary slogans, glorious models of the guillotine, and execution orders to make you shed a tear for the royalists as well. In the rest of the gilded rooms, the display of paintings, maps, and models of Paris is too exhaustive to give you an overall picture of the city changing. And unless you have the historical details on hand, it's hard to get intrigued by any one period.

Musée Grévin I
10 bd Montmartre, 9e. Mo Montmartre. Daily 1–7pm, during school hols 10am–7pm; no admissions after 6pm; 46F, children 32F.

The main Paris waxworks are not nearly as extensive as London's Madame Tussauds and only worth it if you are desperate to do something with the kids and can afford to throw money around. The ticket includes a ten-minute conjuring act.

Musée Grévin II
Forum des Halles, niveau 1, 1er. Mo RER Châtelet-Les Halles. Mon–Sat 10:30am–7:30pm, Sun & holidays 1–8pm; 38F, children 26F.

One up on the wax statue parade of the parent museum but typically didactic. It shows a series of wax model scenes of French brilliance at the turn of the century, with automatically opening and closing doors around each montage to prevent you from skipping any part of the voice-over and animation.

Musée de l'Histoire de France
Archives Nationales, 60 rue des Francs-Bourgeois, 3e. Mo Rambuteau/St-Paul. 1:30–5:45pm; closed Tues & holidays; 12F/8F.

The **Archives Nationales** have on show some of the authentic bits of paper that fill the vaults: edicts, wills, and papal bulls; a medieval English monarch's challenge to his French counterpart to stake his kingdom on a duel; Henry VIII's RSVP to the Field of the Cloth of Gold invite; fragile cross-Channel treaties; Joan of Arc's trial proceedings with a doodled impression of her in the margin; and more recent legislation and constitutions. The Revolution section includes Marie-Antoinette's book of samples from which she chose her dress each morning and a Republican children's alphabet where J stands for Jean-Jacques Rousseau and L for laborer. It's scholastic stuff (and no English translations), but the early documents are very pretty, dangling seals and penned in a delicate and illegible hand.

Musée de la Marine
Palais de Chaillot, place du Trocadéro, 16ᵉ. Mᵒ Trocadéro. 10am–6pm; closed Tues; 22F/10F.

Dozens of beautiful models of French ships, ancient and modern, warlike and commercial.

Les Martyrs de Paris
Porte du Louvre, Forum des Halles, 1ᵉʳ. Mᵒ RER Châtelet-Les Halles. Daily 10:30am–6:30pm; 40F/26F; no entry for under-12s.

The Town Hall put the age restriction on this new chamber of horrors soon after it opened, after complaints that it had deeply disturbed young visitors. It is a shame they didn't close it down altogether. It is far more realistically staged than the Madame Tussauds equivalent, with almost pitch-dark corridors linking the cells and torture chambers, and echoing with high-fidelity screams of agony. But, aside from the appalling pornography of violence these places represent, the horror is in what is not exhibited—the contemporary methods of torture used by the security services of almost every country in the world—allowing one to believe that all this barbarianism is past history.

Musée de la Préfecture de Police
1bis rue des Carmes, 5ᵉ. Mᵒ Maubert. Mon–Thurs 9am–5pm, Fri 9am–4:30pm; closed holidays; free.

The history of the Paris police force as presented in this collection of uniforms, arms, and papers stops at 1944 and is, as you might expect, all of the legendary criminals variety.

Performance Arts, Literature, and Sport

Maison de Balzac
47 rue Raynouard, 16ᵉ. Mᵒ Passy/La Muette. Tues–Sun 10am–5:40pm; closed holidays; 15F/10F.

Contains several portraits and caricatures of the writer and a library of works by him, his contemporaries, and his critics. Balzac lived here between 1840 and 1847, but literary grandees seem to share the common fate of not leaving ghosts.

Musée du Cinéma Henri Langlois
Palais de Chaillot, place du Trocadéro, 16ᵉ. Mᵒ Trocadéro. Guided tours only at 10am, 11am, 2pm, 3pm, and 4pm; closed Tues & holidays; 20F.

Costumes, sets, cameras, projectors, etc from magic lanterns to the latest Depardieu performance, ending with a showing of a rare movie from the archives. A must for cineastes.

Centre Culturel des Halles
Terrasse du Forum des Halles, 101 rue Rambuteau, 1ᵉʳ. Mᵒ RER Châtelet-Les Halles. Tues–Sun 11:30am–6:30pm; closed holidays.

Temporary exhibitions, events, and workshops of poetry, crafts, and arts take cover beneath the queasy strictured structures above the Forum: in the **Maison de la Poésie**, **Pavillon des Arts**, and **Maison des Ateliers**.

Maison de Victor-Hugo

6 place des Vosges, 4ᵉ. Mᵒ Bastille/Chemin-Vert. Tues–Sun 10am–5:10pm; closed holidays; 15F.

This museum is saved by the fact that Hugo decorated and drew, as well as wrote. Many of his ink drawings are exhibited and there's an extraordinary Japanese dining room he put together for his lover's house. That apart, the usual portraits, manuscripts, and memorabilia shed sparse light on the man and his work.

Musée Instrumental

In the process of moving to the Cité de la Musique in the Parc de la Villette.

Several thousand musical instruments dating from the Renaissance onwards, owned by the Paris Conservatory. Many of them have been played by the classical greats.

Instruments de Musique Mécanique

Impasse Berthaud, 3ᵉ. Mᵒ Rambuteau. Sat, Sun & holidays only, one-hour guided visits 2–7pm; 25F/15F.

Barrel organs, gramophones, and automata with demonstrations.

Musée Kwok-On

41 rue des Francs-Bourgeois, 4ᵉ. Mᵒ St-Paul/Rambuteau. Mon–Fri 10am–5:30pm; 10F/5F.

Changing exhibitions feature the popular arts of southern Asia—the musical instruments, festival decorations, religious objects, and, most of all, the costumes, puppets, masks, and stage models for theater, in eleven different countries stretching from Japan to Turkey. The collection includes such things as figures for the Indonesian and Indian Theaters of Shadows, Peking Opera costumes, and storytellers' scrolls from Bengal. The color is overwhelming and the unfamiliarity shaming—much recommended.

Musée Adam Mickiewicz

6 quai d'Orléans, 4e. Mᵒ Pont-Marie. Tues–Fri 2–6pm, Sat 10am–1pm; closed holidays; free.

A tiny museum dedicated to one of the greatest Polish poets, a Romantic and nationalist who came to France in 1832 unable to bear the partitioned nonexistence of his homeland. A collection of nineteenth- and early twentieth-century paintings by Polish artists who spent some time in France is evidence of the long-lasting Franco-Polish connection.

Musée Edith Piaf

5 rue Créspin-du-Gast, 11ᵉ. Mᵒ Ménilmontant/St-Maur. Admission by appointment only: ☎43.55.52.72. Mon–Thurs 1–6pm; closed July; free.

For the fans of the great cabaret singer: her clothes and letters; posters, photographs, and all the existing recordings.

Musée Renan-Scheffer/La Vie Romantique
16 rue Chaptal, 9e. Mo Pigalle/St-Georges. Tues–Sun 10am–5:40pm; closed holidays; 15F.

The life of intellectuals and literati in the nineteenth century is the subject of changing exhibitions in this museum. The permanent collection has to do with just one thinker, writer, and activist of that century—George Sand. Her jewels and trinkets are on show, rather than her manuscripts, but there are some beautiful drawings by Delacroix, Ingres, and Sand herself.

Musée du Sport Français
Parc des Princes, 24 rue du Commandant-Guilbaud. Mo Porte-de-St-Cloud. Mon, Tues, Thurs, Fri & Sun 9:30am–12:30pm & 2–5pm; closed holidays; 20F/10F.

Books, posters, paintings, and sculptures to do with the history of French sport are exhibited here on a rotating basis, along with trophies and boots, caps, racquets, and gloves worn by the famous, and the vanity case of the greatest French Wimbledon champion, Suzanne Lenglen.

Science and Industry

Centre National de l'Automobile
25 rue d'Estienne-d'Orves, Pantin, (east along av Jean-Lolive and 2nd right) Mo Hoche. Mon & Wed–Sun 10:30am–6:30pm, Tues 10:30am–10pm; 40F, 6–12-year-olds 30F.

Dazzling collection of rare and revolutionary motors—Delahayes, Hispano-Suizas, Lamborghinis, VWs, Mercedes, Minis—with rotating temporary exhibitions illustrating various trends and aspects of automobile manufacture.

Musée Branly
21 rue d'Assas, 6e. Mo St-Placide. Mon–Fri 9am–noon & 2–5pm; closed Aug; free.

In the 1890s Marconi used Branly's invention of an electric wave detector—the first coherer—to set up the startling system of communication which didn't need wires. The coherer in question is exhibited along with other pieces from the physicist's experiments.

Musée de la Contrefaçon
16 rue de la Faisanderie, 16e. Mo Porte-Dauphine. Mon, Wed & Fri 2:30–6pm, Sun 9:30am–noon.

One of the odder ones—examples of imitation products, labels, and brand names trying to pass off as the "genuine article."

Muséum d'Histoire Naturelle
Jardin des Plantes, 57 rue Cuvier, 5e. Mo Austerlitz/Jussieu. Mon & Wed–Fri 10am–5pm, Sat & Sun 11am–6pm.

There are plans for this natural history museum, too, and not before time: paleontology, botany, and mineralogy, represented by bits and pieces on dusty shelves. Fine if fossils in any circumstances fascinate you; if not, give this a miss until renovation happens.

Musée de la Poste

34 bd de Vaugirard, 15e. Mo Montparnasse. Mon–Sat 10am–5pm; closed holidays; 15F, under-18s free.

Not just stamps, though plenty of those. Also the history of sending messages, from the earliest times to the high-tech, inefficient present.

Musée de Radio-France

116 av du Président Kennedy, 16e. Mo Passy/Ranelagh/Mirabeau. Mon–Sat guided visits at 10:30am, 11:30am, 2:30pm, 3:30pm, 4:30pm; closed holidays; 10F/5F.

Models, machines, and documents covering the history of broadcasting in the national TV and radio building.

Musée de la Serrure

1 rue de la Perle, 3e. Mo Chemin-Vert/Rambuteau. Tues–Sat 10am–noon & 2–5pm; closed Aug.

This collection of elaborate and artistic locks throughout the ages includes the Napoleonic fittings for his palace doors (the one for the Tuileries bashed in by revolutionaries), locks that trapped your hand or shot your head off if you tried a false key, and a seventeenth-century masterpiece made by a craftsman under lock and key for four years. The rest of the exhibits are pretty boring, though the setting in a Marais mansion is some compensation.

Musée National des Techniques

292 rue St-Martin, 3e. Mo Réaumur-Sébastopol/Arts-et-Métiers. Tues–Sun 10am–5:30pm; closed holidays; 20F; half-price Sun.

Utterly traditional and stuffy glass-case museum with thousands of technical things from fridges to flutes, clocks, and trains. The only exceptional part is the entrance—an early Gothic church filled with engines, airplanes, cars, and bikes.

A DAY-TRIPPER'S GUIDE TO OUTLYING MUSEUMS

Chapter Eleven, *Out from the City*, includes details of several more museums within a day's excursion from central Paris. Among the more interesting are:

Musée d'Art et d'Histoire at **St-Denis**. Local archaeology and Commune documents; p.259.

Musée de l'Air et de l'Espace, at **Le Bourget**. Planes and spacecraft; p.261.

Musée National de la Renaissance at **Ecouen**. Lush furnishings in a Renaissance château; p.263.

Musée des Antiquités Nationales at **St-Germain-en-Laye**. Evocative archaeological displays, from cave-dwellers onwards; p.266.

Musée National de la Céramique at **Sèvres**. Ceramics from all over the world as well as the local stuff; p.269.

Musée Condé and Musée Vivant du Cheval at **Chantilly**. Live horses and lots of paraphernalia, at the château which also contains the magnificent medieval *Très Riches Heures du Duc de Berry*; pp.262, 263.

Musée Français de la Photographie at **Bièvres**. The (disappointing) national photographic collection; p.270.

Musée de l'Île de France at **Sceaux**. Local history, from kings to artists; p.270.

Musée de la Résistance Nationale at **Champigny-sur-Marne**. Worthy Resistance museum; p.275.

CHAPTER FIVE

AMUSEMENTS AND SPORTS

When it's cold and wet, and you've peered enough at museums, monuments, and the dripping panes of shop fronts and café vistas, don't despair or retreat back to your hotel. There are **Golden Oldie movies** to be seen (see Chapter Ten), **music halls** are playing the tango for anyone to dance to, there are **saunas** to soak in, **ice rinks** to fall on, **bowling alleys**, **billiards**, **swimming pools**, and **gyms**.

You can take advantage of the Parisian love of high technology to call up a choice of **music** and **videos** on CD-Rom, or produce your own tape with a professional studio mix. If you're feeling brave, you could also change your hairstyle and indulge in a total body tonic. And when the weather isn't so bad, you can go for a **ride in a boat**, or even a **helicopter**, after a successful flutter on the horses in the Bois de Boulogne. The two-wheeled and essentially French **trotting races** take place in the Bois de Vincennes and both woods are good places for **cycling**, **jogging**, or just lying about.

Paris's range of both **spectator and participatory amusements** is also outlined below. For additional possibilities check *L'Officiel des Spectacles* (the best of the listings mags for sports facilities) or, for current sporting events, *L'Équipe*, the **daily sports newspaper**.

Boat Trips, Balloon and Heli Rides

Seeing Paris by boat and from the air is one of the city's most enduring tourist pulls—and a lot of fun if the mood grabs you.

Bateaux-Mouches

From the *quais* or the bridges, after the light has fallen, the sudden appearance of a *Bateau-Mouche*, with its blaring multilingual commentaries and dazzling floodlights, can come as a nasty shock to romantic contemplations. One way of avoiding the ugly sight of these hulking hulls is to get on the boat yourself. You can't escape the rote descriptions but the evening rides certainly give the best close-up glamorized gazing at classic Seine-side buildings.

Bateaux-Mouches start from the *Embarcadère du Pont de l'Alma* on the right bank in the 8ᵉ, Mᵒ Alma-Marceau; rides (1hr–1hr 15min) every half-hour from 10am to noon and 2 to 11pm; winter departures at 11am, 2:30, 4, and 9pm only (30F, under-14s 15F). Make sure you avoid the outrageously priced lunch and dinner trips, for which "correct" dress is mandatory. *Bateaux-Mouches'* **competitors** are *Bateaux Parisiens*, *Bateaux-Vedettes de Paris*, and *Bateaux-Vedettes du Pont Neuf*. They're all much of a muchness and detailed in *Pariscope* etc under *Promenades*.

An alternative Seine ride, without commentaries, is the *Batobus*, a river transport system operating from port de la Bourdonnais by the Eiffel Tower to quai de l'Hôtel-de-Ville, via port de Solférino, quai Malaquais, and quai de Montebello (May–Sept 10am–8pm; 10F per stop or 50F for a day pass).

Canal Trips

Less blatantly tourist fodder are the **canal boat trips**. *Canauxrama* (reservations ☎42.39.15.00) chugs up and down between the Port de l'Arsenal (opposite 50 bd de la Bastille 12ᵉ; Mᵒ Bastille) and the Bassin de la Villette (13bis quai de la Loire, 19ᵉ; Mᵒ Jaurès) on the Canal St-Martin. At the Bastille end is a long tunnel from which you don't surface till the 10ᵉ *arrondissement*. The ride lasts three hours—not a bad bargain for 70F (65F weekend afternoons). The company also runs day trips along the Canal de l'Ourcq, west as far as Meaux, returning by bus.

A more stylish vessel for exploring the canal is the catamaran of *Paris-Canal* with trips between the Musée d'Orsay (quai Anatole-France, 7ᵉ; Mᵒ Solférino) and the Parc de la Villette (11 quai de la Loire, 19ᵉ; Mᵒ Porte-de-Pantin), which also last three hours: Musée d'Orsay departures at 9:30am daily, and 2:15pm Saturday and Sunday; Parc de la Villette 2:30pm daily, and 9:45am Saturday and Sunday; 90F; reservations ☎42.40.96.97. When not on deck, you sit in a little green and white house with windowboxes full of geraniums. Space is limited, so booking is essential.

Paris by Helicopter or Balloon

Having seen Paris from the water, the next step up is Paris from the air. A **helicopter** tour above all the city's sights is somewhat prohibitive but if whirligig rides turn you on as much or more than a four-star meal or a stalls seat at the theater, then a quick loop around La Défense is on. The two companies operating are *Héli-France* (9am–7:30pm) and *Hélicap* (8:45am–7:30pm), both at the Héliport de Paris, 4 av de la Porte-de-Sèvres, 15 ᵉ (Mᵒ Balard).

Even classier, and equally extravagant, how about going up in a **balloon**? *Espace Plus* (14 rue de Sèvres, Boulogne-Billancourt; Mᵒ Porte-de-St-Cloud; ☎46.05.91.25) can oblige.

Afternoon Tangos

One pastime to fill the afternoon hours that might not cross your mind is the **bals musette**. These dance halls were the between-the-wars solution in the down-and-out parts of *Gai Paris* to depression, dole, and the demise of the Popular Front—they crossed social scales, too, with film stars and jaded aristocrats coming to indulge in a bit of rough. Three or four generations of owners later, they still attract a mainly working-class clientele, and run both afternoon and evening sessions. Turn up on a weekday afternoon and you'll find people dancing to abandon, cheek-to-cheek, couple squashed against couple. Their clothes aren't elegant, their French isn't academy, men dance with women, and everyone drinks.

Balajo, 9 rue de Lappe, 11e. M° Bastille. Open in the afternoon 3–6:30pm, before reopening at 10pm for the evening session (see p.237). The original venue. Music, all recorded, is a mixture of waltz, tango, java, disco, and rock. Admission price of around 50F includes one drink.

Le Tango, 13 rue au Maire, 3e. M° Arts-et-Metiers. 2:30–6:30pm. Sited in the still downmarket *quartier* north of the Marais, this is one of the oldest dance halls in town with an ancient jumble of décors to prove it. Teenagers, septuagenarians, and every age in between waltz, tango, and cha-cha, none of them chic and no one seriously on the pick-up. Entry is free—just cloakroom and drinks to pay for.

La Java, 105 rue du Faubourg-du-Temple, 10e. M° Belleville. Open Sun & Mon afternoons and Fri & Sat nights. The oldest of the dance halls, similar in feel to *Le Tango*.

Tea dances

Less conducive to participation but potentially entertaining are the **tea dances**, weekdays at *La Coupole* (102 bd Montparnasse, 6e; M° Vavin) and on Sunday afternoons at *Le Bataclan* (50 bd Voltaire, 11e; M° Oberkampf).

Le Palace (8 rue du Faubourg-Montmartre, 9e; M° Rue Montmartre) has a **gay** Sunday afternoon tea dance.

Musical and Visual Discoveries

You want to listen to CDs all day, watch videos, record your own cassette to sell down on the *quais*? Paris has all these possibilities . . .

FNAC, 4 place de la Bastille, 11e. M° Bastille. Tues–Sat am & pm, Mon am only. *FNAC*'s newest **music shop** has touch-screen access to a limited but interesting **selection of CDs**. Once you've donned the headphones, touch the square on the screen reading "*Touchez l'écran*." If you then touch first "*Répérages FNAC*," then "*Variétés Françaises*," then "*Rock*" you'll end up with a list of recent French rock recordings which you can listen to, adjusting the volume or flicking forwards by touching arrows. "*Sommaire*" takes you back to the previous list. Of course you can choose medieval church music, jazz, or Pierre Boulez instead—it's very simple and when the shop isn't crowded you can spend as long as you like for free.

Vidéothèque de Paris, 2 Grande Gallerie, Porte St-Eustache, Forum des Halles, 1er. RER Châtelet-Les Halles. Tues–Sun 12:30–8:30pm. Even more sophisticated than *FNAC*. For 20F you can watch any of the four videos or films screened each day, and, in the *Salle Pierre Emmanuel*, make your own selection from 3500 film clips, newsreel footage, commercials, documentaries, soaps, etc from 1896 to the present day. All the material is connected to Paris in some way, and you can make your choice—on your individual screen and keyboard—via a Paris place-name, an actor, a director, a date, and so on. Don't be put off by the laboratory atmosphere or by the idea that this can't be for just anyone to play with. It is, and there are instructions in English at the desk and a friendly "librarian" to help you out. Once you're in the complex you can go back and forth between the projection rooms, the *Salle Pierre Emmanuel,* and a café, open 12:30–6pm.

Je Chante, 3 Grand Balcon, Niveau-1, Porte Lescot. Mon–Sat 11am–7:30pm. Also in the Forum des Halles, though not for the timid or toneless, *Je Chante* enables anyone to **record your own vocal version** of one of four hundred songs. You're given the word sheet and two practice runs in a private booth, with backing coming over headphones; then into the studio. It costs 170F and you come out with a nicely packaged cassette imprinted with your name and photo. It has launched some on their way to professional contracts, if not stardom, but the people running it are sympathetic to giggling amateurs. There's also a café (50F menu).

The Body Beautiful

The transatlantic craze for twisting, stretching, and straining muscles, while competing in style rather than scores, is, predictably, big with the Parisians. Aerobics, dance workouts, and anti-stress fitness programs are big business, along with the trans-Pacific activities of yoga, tai-chi, and martial arts.

Fitness Venues

Many fitness club activities are organized in courses or involve a minimum month's or year's subscription (the big gym chains *Garden Gym*, *Gymnase Club*, and *Vitatop* are all prohibitive), and even the exceptions are costly enough to excuse you. But if your last meal has left you feeling you need it, here are some options.

Centre de Danse du Marais, 41 rue du Temple, 4^e. M^o Hôtel-de-Ville. 9am–7pm. You can try out rock'n'roll, folkloric dances from the East, tap-dancing, modern dance, physical expression, or flamenco. Expect to pay around 75F per session.

Espace Vit'Halles, 48 rue Rambuteau, 3^e. RER Châtelet-Les Halles. Mon–Fri 9am–10pm, Sat 11am–7pm, Sun 11am–3pm. Back across bd Sebastopol, *Vit'Halles* charges 150F, for which fanatics can spend a day doing every kind of tendon-shattering gyration. It's divided into four "work zones"—the parquet, gym floor, body-building room, and the multi-gym room. *Détente* is also provided for with a sauna, hammam, solarium, and diet bar. For 80F you can have access to these and one floor session.

Centre de Danse de Paris, 252 rue du Faubourg-St-Honoré, 8e. M^o Étoile–Charles-de-Gaulle/Ternes. Mon–Sat 8:45am–8pm. Offers professional classes in contemporary dance and ballet, including some for beginners. Costs are around 70F per session.

Les Jardins de la Forme, 47 rue des Francs-Bourgeois, 4e. M^o St-Paul. For 100F per session this provides workouts on particular parts of the body, low impact, modern jazz, and traditional gymnastics, all in a hall with natural lighting.

Swimming

For straightforward exercise, and for under 20F, you can go swimming in any of the **municipal baths**, but check first in *L'Officiel des Spectacles* for opening times (under *Piscines*) as varying hours are given over to schools and clubs. These are among the best:

Piscine Susanne Berlioux/Les Halles, 10 place de la Rotonde, niveau-3, Porte du Jour, Forum des Halles, 1er. RER Châtelet-Les Halles. A brand new 50m pool with a vaulted concrete ceiling and a glass wall looking through to the tropical garden.

Butte aux Cailles, 5 place Verlaine, 13e. M^o Place d'Italie. Housed in a 1920s brick building with an Art Déco ceiling, recently spruced up. One of the pleasantest swims in the city.

Jean Taris, 16 rue de Thouin, 5e. M^o Cardinal-Lemoine. An unchlorinated pool in the center of the Latin Quarter and a students' favorite.

Henry-de-Montherlant, 32 bd Lannes, 16e. M^o Porte-Dauphine. This has two pools, a terrace for sunbathing, a solarium, and the Bois de Boulogne close by.

Other good municipal addresses include: *Bernard-Lafay* (70 rue de la Jonquière, 17e; M^o Guy-Moquet); *Château-Landon* (31 rue du Château-Landon, 10e; M^o Château-Landon); *Amiraux* (6 rue Hermann-Lachapelle, 18e; M^o Simplon); *Armand-Massard* (66 bd Montparnasse, 15e; M^o Vavin); and *Georges-Vallerey* (148 av Gambetta, 20e; M^o St-Fargeau).

Privately Run Pools

Non-municipal pools are twice as expensive or more, but some have their attractions.

Pontoise, 19 rue de Pontoise, 5e. Mo Maubert-Mutualité. Features nude swimming Monday and Thursday evenings.

Molitor, 2–8 av de la Porte-Molitor. Mo Porte-d'Auteuil. For outside bathing, try this 1930s pool on the edge of the Bois de Boulogne.

Deligny, 25 quai Anatole-France, 7e. Mo Chambre-des-Deputés. Crowded but an amusing, if expensive, spectacle of rich bodies sunning themselves on the vast deck above the Seine.

Roger-Le Gall, 34 bd Carnot, 12e. Mo Porte-de-Vincennes. Most of the extras are reserved for club members but anyone can swim in the pool (covered in winter and open in summer).

Aquaboulevard, 4 rue Louis-Armand, 15e. Mo Balard/RER Boulevard Victor. An American-style multi-sports complex with wave machines and water slides.

Hairdressing Salons

The range is as wide—style-wise and price-wise—as you'd expect in this supremely fashion-conscious city.

Alexandre, for women at 3 av Matignon, 8e Mo Franklin-Roosevelt (☎42.25.57.90). Also for men at 29 rue Marbeuf, 8e (Mo Alma-Marceau;☎42.25.29.41). The long-established *haut-coiffeur* of Paris could be an intimidating experience unless you're wearing Yves St-Laurent or Gaultier. Wash-cut-and-blow-dries for women are not that expensive considering the client-tele—around 420F—but the men's salon, with saunas, massage, manicure, pedicure, etc would cost you your beautified arm and leg.

Jacques Dessange, 37 av Franklin-Roosevelt, 8e. Mo Franklin-Roosevelt. ☎43.59.31.31. And at thirteen other addresses. Less classic, but still very elegant, this is Charlotte Rampling's favorite cutter; around 420F for wash, cut, and blow-dry.

Desfossé, 19 av Matignon, 8e. Mo St-Philippe-du-Roule. ☎43.59.95.13. Men can spend three hours having their hair, hands, feet, and skin attended to at this equally upmarket address—hair 280F, full works 375F.

Jean-Marc Maniatis, 18 rue Marbeuf, 8e. Mo Alma-Marceau. ☎47.23.30.14. Another branch at 35 rue de Sèvres 6e, (Mo Sèvres-Babylone; ☎47.44.16.39). Younger and less established beauties come here for the renowned and meticulous cutting.

Cheaper Cuts—and Schools

The more run-of-the-mill Paris hairdressers may be more appealing. Around **Les Halles**, the **Bastille**, and **St-Germain** many salons go for maximum visibility, so you can watch what's being done and take your pick. It's always a gamble anyway, and it could be fun trying out your French in the intimate trivial chit-chat that all hairdressers insist on. Book a couple of days in advance.

Various **salons or schools** offer free wash-cut-and-blow-dries to those bold enough to act as guinea pigs for new cuts and techniques and for trainees to try their hands on. These include the following:

École Jacques Dessange, 24 rue St-Augustin, 2e. Mo 4-Septembre. ☎47.42.24.73. Mon–Wed, by appointment.

Jardin de Roxiane, 71 rue de Seine, 6e. Mo Odéon. ☎46.33.54.60. Men, women, and kids—by appointment.

Maniatis, phone ☎47.20.00.05 for details of where and when.

L'Oréal, 14 rue Royale, 8e. Mo Opéra. ☎40.20.63.60. Perms and tinting only, for a contribution of 50F.

Hammams

A steam bath and a massage may be as necessary after a trip to the Louvre as after intentional physical exercise. The **hammams**, or Turkish baths, are one of the unexpected delights of Paris. Much more luxurious than the standard Swedish sauna, these are places to linger and chat.

Hammam de la Mosquée, 39 rue Geoffroy-St-Hilaire, 5ᵉ. Mᵒ Censier-Daubenton. You can order mint tea and honey cakes after your baths, around a fountain in a marble and cedarwood-covered courtyard. It's very good value for 60F (massage 50F extra). Hours for women are Mon & Wed 11am–7pm, Thurs 11am–9pm, Sat 10am–7pm; for men, Fri 11am–8pm & Sun 10am–7pm; closed August.

Hammam de St-Paul, 4 rue des Rosiers, 4ᵉ. Mᵒ St-Paul. The all-time favorite is currently gutted with major works going on. Whether this is a renovation, or the end, no one seems to know.

Les Bains d'Odessa, 5 rue d'Odessa, 14ᵉ. Mᵒ Montparnasse. ☎43.20.91.21 for hours; around 75F. The oldest hammam in the city with various beauty treatments as well as saunas and massage.

Plage 50, 50 rue du Faubourg-St-Denis, 10ᵉ. Mᵒ Château-d'Eau. ☎47.70.06.64 for hours; around 90F. Another handy address.

Meditation

If you don't want to do anything physical at all, you can join the meditation session at 5pm on Saturday and Sunday in the Tibetan temple in the **Bois de Vincennes** (40 rte Circulaire du Lac Daumesnil, 12ᵉ; Mᵒ Porte Dorée).

Participatory Sports

Skating, roller-skating, skateboarding, jogging, bowling, billiards, *boules*— it's all here to be played . . .

Ice-skating

If it's your ankles and shock absorbers you want to exercise, get on the ice at the city's only **ice rink**. The *Patinoire des Buttes-Chaumont* (30 rue Edouard-Pailleron, 19ᵉ; Mᵒ Bolivar; ☎46.03.18.00) costs 37F including skate rental, and is popular and fun. *L'Officiel des Spectacles* and other such magazines will have details of its seasonally changing hours and of the other rinks in the suburbs.

Roller-skating and Skateboarding

Roller-skating has a special disco rink at *La Main Jaune* (pl de la Porte-de-Champerret, 17ᵉ; Mᵒ Champerret; Wed, Sat & Sun 2:30–7pm, Fri & Sat also 10pm–dawn). Day sessions cost F40.

The main official outdoor roller-skating and **skateboarding** arena is the concourse of the Palais de Chaillot (Mᵒ Trocadéro). **Les Halles** (around the Fontaine des Innocents) and the **Beaubourg piazza** are equally popular.

Jogging—and the Marathon

The **Paris Marathon** is held in May over a route from place de la Concorde to Vincennes. If you want to join in and need details and equipment, the best place for information is a shop owned by a dedicated marathon runner, *Marathon* (29 rue de Chazelles, 17e; Mº Monceau; ☎42.27.48.18). A shorter race, *Les 20km de Paris*, takes place mid-October and begins and ends at the Eiffel Tower.

If you are compelled **to run or jog** by yourself, take great care with the traffic. The Jardin du Luxembourg, which is popular with Parisian joggers, the Parc Monceau, and even the Tuileries all provide decent, varied runs, and all are more or less flat. If you want to run hills, head for the Parc des Buttes-Chaumont for plenty of suitably punishing gradients. If you have access to them, the Bois de Boulogne and the Bois de Vincennes are the largest open spaces. These are good places to explore for trails, but the Bois de Vincennes, for example, offers fine running around the Lac Daumesnil, and even on and around the islands in the lake.

Cycling

Very few people **cycle** in Paris, with good reason, though in these days of traffic congestion, numbers are increasing. If you've arrived in Paris by bike, and want to keep the muscles in shape, the *Bicyclub* (8 place de la Porte-Champerret, 17e; Mº Porte-Champerret; ☎47.66.55.92; Mon–Fri, and Sat afternoons) arranges outings. You can **rent bicycles** there, or at *Paris-Vélo* (2 rue du Fer-à-Moulin, 5e; Mº Gobelins; Mon–Sat)—from 100 to 160F per day.

Riding

If you want to get on a horse yourself, you need to have come already equipped with a hat, boots and crop. Secondly, you have to buy a license, the *Carte Nationale de Cavalier*—around 90F, before you can mount. This can be obtained from the *Fédération Equestre Française* (164 rue du Faubourg-St-Honoré, 8e) or from the clubs, which may charge a bit more for it.

Centre Bayard UCPA, av du Polygone in the Bois de Vincennes. Mº/RER Vincennes. ☎43.65.46.87. Trail rides and lessons for around 65F, Tues–Sat 9am–noon & 3:30–7:30pm, Sun 9am–noon.

Manège de Neuilly, 19bis rue d'Orléans, Neuilly. Mº Sablons. ☎46.24.06.41. Open 7am–7pm, closed Sun afternoon. On the other side of town and a little bit more expensive; an hour's Sunday-morning canter in the Bois de Boulogne costs around 110F.

Bowling Alleys

There's nothing particularly Parisian about bowling alleys, but they exist and they're popular, should the urge to scuttle skittles take you. Prices vary around 18F a session, double where you have to rent shoes, and more at weekends. In addition to the venues named over the page, you'll find full listings in *L'Officiel des Spectacles*.

Gaîté-Montparnasse, 25 rue Commandant-Mouchotte, 14e. Mo Montparnasse-Bienvenue. Mon–Thurs & Sun 10am–2am, Fri & Sat 10am–4am. A complex with sixteen lanes. Entertainment is complete, with bar, brasserie, pool tables, and video games.

Bowling-Académie de Billard, 66 av d'Ivry, 13e. Mo Tolbiac. Attracts an active and young clientele to roll the balls in Chinatown. 2pm–2am, with bar billiards and pool alongside.

Bowling Mouffetard, Centre-Commercial Mouffetard-Monge, 73 rue Mouffetard, 5e. Mo Monge. The cheapest in town, well favored by students, with bar and billiards.

Bowling de Paris, Jardin d'Acclimatation, Bois de Boulogne. Mo Sablons. Popular with the chic types west of town.

Billiards

Billiards, unlike bowling, is an original, and ancient, French game. Unlike the English or American versions, the table has no pockets. If you want to watch or try your hand (for around 40F per hour), head for one of the following, most of which also cater to **pool** players.

Académie de Clichy-Montmartre, 84 rue de Clichy, 9e. Mo Clichy. 1:30–11:30pm.

Académie de Paris, 47 av de Wagram, 17e. Mo Ternes. Mon–Fri 12:30–11pm, Sat & Sun 2–11pm.

Bowling-Académie de Billard, 66 av d'Ivry, 13e. Mo Tolbiac. 2pm–2am. See above.

Bowling Mouffetard, 73 rue Mouffetard, 5e. Mo Monge. See above.

Salle des Billards des Halles, niveau-2, Porte du Jour, Forum des Halles, 1er. RER Châtelet-Les Halles. Members only, but you can watch experts play; Mon–Fri noon–8pm, Sat noon–7pm.

Boules

The classic French game involving balls, *boules*, or *pétanque*, is best performed (or watched) at the Arènes de Lutece (see p.88) and the Bois de Vincennes. On balmy summer evenings you're likely to see it played in any of the city's parks and gardens.

Other Sports

Tennis, squash, golf, skiing on artificial slopes, **archery, rock-climbing, canoeing, fishing, windsurfing, waterskiing**, and **parachuting**—you name it, you can do it, in or around the city. Whether you'll want to spend the time and money on booking and renting equipment is another matter. If you're determined, you'll find some details in *L'Officiel des Spectacles* etc, or you can ring **Allo Sports** on ☎42.76.54.54 (Mon–Fri 10:30am–5pm) or pay a visit to the **Direction Jeunesse et Sports** (25 bd Bourdon, 4e; Mo Bastille; Mon–Fri 10am–5:30pm). These are both municipal outfits, so the places they have listed will all be subsidized and cheap.

Of the private clubs and complexes, **Aquaboulevard** (4 rue Louis-Armand, 15e; Mo Balard/RER Boulevard Victor) is the newest and biggest, with squash and tennis courts, a brilliant climbing wall, golf tees, aquatic diversions, hammams, dance floors, shops, restaurants, and other money-extracting paraphernalia. Some prices are: swimming pool 68F, under-12s 49F; tennis 196F per hour; squash 42F per half-hour.

Spectator Sports

Paris is currently outflanked by Marseille in soccer glamour, but the capital retains a special status in the rugby, cycling, and tennis worlds—and horse-racing is as serious a pursuit as in the US.

Cycling

The biggest event of the French sporting year is the grand finale of the **Tour de France**, which arrives in the city through the Arc de Triomphe in the third week of July. In theory the last day of the race is a competitive time-trial, but most years this amounts to a triumphal procession, the overall winner of the Tour having been long since determined. Only very rarely does Paris witness memorable scenes such as those of 1989, when American Greg Lemond snatched the coveted *maillot jaune* (the winner's yellow jersey) on the final day.

For details of the current situation, it's only necessary to switch on the TV or open a paper. *Allez Fignon!*

Soccer and Rugby

The *Parc des Princes* (24 rue du Commandant-Guilbaud, 16e; Mº Porte-de-St-Cloud; ☎40.71.91.91/48.74.84.75) is the capital's main stadium for both **rugby union** and **soccer** events, and home ground to the first-division Paris soccer team *Paris-SG* (St-Germain) and the 1990 rugby champions, *Le Racing*.

Tennis

The French equivalent of Wimbledon, *Roland-Garros*, lies between the *Parc des Princes* and the Bois de Boulogne, with the ace address of 2 av Gordon-Bennett, 16e (Mº Porte d'Auteuil; ☎47.43.00.47). The French Tennis Open takes place in the last week of May and first week of June, and tickets need to be reserved before February. A few are sold each day, but only for unseeded matches—unlike Wimbledon, you can't get near the main courts once inside the turnstiles.

Athletics and Other Sports

The *Palais des Omnisports Paris-Bercy* (*POPB*) at 8 bd Bercy, 12e (☎40.02.60.60) hosts all manner of sporting events, including athletics, cycling, handball, dressage and show-jumping, ice hockey, ballroom dancing, judo, and motorcross. If you keep an eye on the sports pages of the newspapers (other than *Le Monde*, which has no sports coverage at all), you might find something on that interests you. The complex holds 17,000 people, so you've a fair chance of getting a ticket at the door, championships excepted.

Horse-racing

Being a spectator at a **horse race** could make a healthy change from looking at art treasures. If you want to fathom the **betting system**, any bar or café with the letters PMU will take your money on a three-horse bet, known as *le tiercé*. The **biggest races** are the *Prix de la République* and the *Grand Prix de L'Arc de Triomphe* on the first and last Sundays in October at Auteuil and Longchamp. The week starting the last Sunday in June sees nine big events, at Auteuil, Longchamp, St-Cloud, and Chantilly (see p.261). **Trotting races**, with the jockeys in chariots, run from August to September on the *Route de la Ferme* in the Bois de Vincennes.

St-Cloud *champ de courses* is in the Parc de St-Cloud off Allée de Chamillard. Auteuil is off the rte d'Auteuil, and Longchamp off the rte des Tribunes, both in the Bois de Boulogne. *L'Humanité* and *Paris-Turf* carry details, and admission charges are around 20F.

CHAPTER SIX

KIDS STUFF

Parisian parents complain that the capital is strictly an adult city, with nothing for energetic 4- to 12-year-olds to do. But when they cross the Channel they find to their horror that in England you can't even have your offspring with you while you drink: people's attitude to children here, by contrast, is usually welcoming, though a certain amount of discipline is expected. And where the Parisian parent may have suggested the same outing a hundred times, the novelty for visiting kids should keep them going for a while at least. On the other hand, it should be said that keeping teenagers amused is as hard in Paris as anywhere.

In this chapter we assess the principal outdoor spaces and indoor attractions Paris can offer your kids as well as shops specializing in items for children, and special events such as theater performances and circuses. From 1992 on, all of these will be eclipsed by the opening of **European Disneyland** (see p.279).

The most useful **sources of information**, for current shows, exhibitions, and events, are the special sections in the listings magazines, *"Pour les jeunes"* in *Pariscope*, *"Enfants"* in *7 Jours à Paris*, and *"Jeunes"* in *L'Officiel des Spectacles*. The best place for **details of organized activities**, whether sports, courses, or local youth clubs, is the *Centre d'Information et de Documentation de la Jeunesse* (*CIDJ*), 101 quai Branly, 15e; Mo Bir-Hakeim (Mon–Fri 9am–7pm, Sat 10am–6pm).

PARIS WITH BABIES

You will have little problem in getting hold of **essentials for babies**. Familiar brands of baby food are available in the supermarkets, as well as disposable diapers (*couches à jeter*) etc. After hours, you can get most goods from late-night pharmacies (see p.11).

Getting around with a stroller poses the same problems as in most big cities. The métro is particularly bad with constant flights of stairs (and few escalators), difficult turnstiles, and very stiff doors. One particular place to avoid is the Louvre: taking a stroller in there is like spelunking with a backpack.

For emergency medical care, see the "Directory," p.11.

BABYSITTERS

The two main **babysitting** agencies are *Ababa* (☎45.49.46.46) and *Allo Maman Poule* (☎47.47.78.78). Both have English speakers; charges are around 25F per hour plus agency fees of around 45F and taxis home after the métro's stopped running. Other possibilities include *Kid Services* (☎47.66.00.52; 28F per hour plus 50F fees) or individuals' notices at the *American Church* (65 quai d'Orsay, 6e; Mo Invalides), the *Alliance Française* (101 bd Raspail, 6e; Mo St-Placide), or *CIDJ* (101 quai Branly, 15e; Mo Bir-Hakeim). If you know someone who has a phone, you could dial up *Babysitting* on *"Elletel"* via their minitel.

Parks, Gardens, and Zoos

The **parks and gardens** within the city cater well to younger kids, though some may find the activities too structured or even cutesy. One of the most standard forms of entertainment is **puppet shows** and *Guignol*, the French equivalent of Punch and Judy. Adventure playgrounds hardly exist, and there aren't, on the whole, open spaces for spontaneous games of soccer or cricket. French **sport** tends to be thoroughly organized (see Chapter Five).

The real star attraction for young children has to be the **Jardin d'Acclimatation**, though you can also let your kids off the leash at the **Jardin des Plantes** (57 rue Cuvier, 5e; Mº Jussieu/Monge; open 7:30 or 8am until dusk) with a small zoo (9am–5:30pm), a playground, hothouses, and plenty of greenery. A better **zoo**—but just as expensive—is in the **Bois de Vincennes** (53 av de St-Maurice, 12e; Mº Porte-Dorée; summer 9am–6pm, winter 9am–5:30pm; 30F/15F; see p.139).

Jardin d'Acclimatation

In the Bois de Boulogne by Porte des Sablons. Mº Sablons/Porte-Maillot. 7.50F, under-16s 3.50F, under-3s free. Daily 10am–6pm, with special attractions Wed, Sat, and Sun and all week during school holidays, including a little train to take you there from Mº Porte-Maillot (behind the L'Orée du Bois *restaurant; every 10min, 1:30–6pm; 4F).*

The garden is a cross between funfair, zoo, and amusement park, with temptations ranging from bumper cars, go-carts, pony and camel rides, to sea lions, birds, bears, and monkeys; a magical mini-canal ride (*la rivière enchantée*), distorting mirrors, scaled-down farm buildings, a puppet theater, and a superb collection of antique dolls at the *Grande Maison des Poupées*. Astérix and friends may be explaining life in their Gaulish village, or Babar the world of the elephants—created by archaeologists in the **Musée en Herbe**. If not, there'll be some other kid-compelling exhibition with game sheets (in English), workshops, and demonstrations of traditional crafts. And if they just want to watch and listen, the **Théâtre du Jardin pour l'Enfance et la Jeunesse** puts on musicals and ballets. In addition to the entrance charge, you have to pay for many of the activities separately, which can add up.

Outside the *jardin*, in the **Bois de Boulogne**, older children can amuse themselves with **mini-golf and bowling**, or **boating** on the *Lac Inférieur*. By the entrance to the *jardin* there's **bike rental** for roaming the wood's cycle trails.

Parc Floral

In the Bois de Vincennes, on rte de la Pyramide. Mº Château-de-Vincennes then bus #112. Summer daily 9:30am–10pm, costing 8F, and 4F for 6- to 9-year-olds; winter daily 9:30am until 5 or 6pm, costing 4F, and 2F for the 6–9s; under-6s always get in free. A little train tours all the gardens (April–Oct Wed–Sun 10:30am–5pm; 4F).

There's always fun and games to be had at the **Parc Floral**, on the other side of the Bois de Vincennes to the zoo. The excellent playground has **slides**, **swings**, **ping-pong**, and **pedal carts**; a few paying extras like **mini-golf**, an **electric car** circuit, and **pony rides** (April–Oct daily 2–6pm); and **clowns**, **puppets**, and **magicians** on summer weekends. Most of the activities are

---

FOOD FOR KIDS

Junk-food addicts no longer have any problems in Paris—*McDonald's, Quick Hamburger,* and their clones are to be found all over the city. The French-style *fast foude* chain, *Hippopotamus,* is slightly healthier. Otherwise, **restaurants** are usually good at providing small portions or allowing children to share dishes. The *Bistro Romain* chain and the drugstores have special children's menus, and drugstores are good for ice creams, too. Keeping away from ice creams rather than finding them is the main problem in Paris. For details of these restaurants, and snacks and ice creams, see Chapter Eight. One thing to remember with steaks, hamburgers, etc is that the French serve them rare unless you ask for them *"bien cuit."*

---

free and in general you'll be far less out of pocket after an afternoon here than at the Jardin d'Acclimatation. Also in the park is a children's theater, the **Théâtre Astral**, which may have mime, clowns, or other none-too-verbal shows.

Jardin des Halles

105 rue Rambuteau. Mº RER Châtelet-Les Halles. 7- to 11-year-olds only; Tues, Thurs & Fri 9am–noon & 2–6pm, Wed & Sat 10am–6pm, Sun 1–6pm; winter closing 4pm; closed in bad weather; 2.20F per hour.

Right in the center of town at Les Halles, and great if you want to lose your charges for the odd hour. A whole series of fantasy landscapes fill this small but cleverly designed space; on Wednesdays animators organize adventure games; and at all times the children are supervised by professional childcarers. You may have to reserve a place an hour or so in advance; on Saturday mornings you can go in and play too.

Other Parks, Squares, and Public Gardens

All of these assorted open spaces can offer play areas, puppets, or at the very least a bit of room to run around in, and are open from 7:30 or 8am till dusk. *Guignol* and puppet shows take place on Wednesdays and weekend afternoons (and more frequently in the summer holidays).

Buttes-Chaumont, 19e Mº Buttes-Chaumont/Botzaris. Donkey-drawn carts, puppets, grassy slopes to roll down.

Champs-de-Mars, 7e. Mº École-Militaire. Puppet shows.

Jardin du Luxembourg, 6e. Mº St-Placide/Notre-Dame-des-Champs, RER Luxembourg. A large playground, pony rides, toy boat rental, bicycle track, roller-skating rink, and puppets.

Jardin du Ranelagh, av Ingres, 16e. Mº Muette. Donkey-carts, *Guignol,* pony-rides, cycle track, roller-skating rink, and playground.

Jardins du Trocadéro, place du Trocadéro, 16e. Mº Trocadéro. Roller-skating, skateboarding, and aquarium.

Parc Georges-Brassens, rue des Morillons, 15e. Mº Convention/Porte-de-Vanves. Climbing rocks, puppets, pony rides, artificial river, playground, and scented herb gardens.

Parc Monceau, bd de Courcelles, 17e. Mº Monceau. Roller-skating rink.

Parc Montsouris, 14e. Mº Glacière, RER Cité-Universitaire. Puppet shows by the lake.

Parc de la Villette, 19e. Mº Corentin-Cariou/Porte-de-la-Villette/Porte-de-Pantin. The Dragon slide is the best in Paris, while there are also curious gardens and sculptures (see p.125).

Funfairs

One last outdoor thrill—**funfairs**—are, alas, few and far between. There's usually a **merry-go-round** at the Forum des Halles and beneath Tour St-Jacques at Châtelet, with ones for smaller children on place de la République and place de la Nation. Very occasionally, rue de Rivoli around Mº St-Paul hosts a mini-fairground.

Fantasy Worlds and Theme Parks

Should your kids by some chance start to find the reality of Paris a little mundane, here are some suggestions which might put their imaginations into gear. A number of high-tech fantasy attractions have recently opened, though the **Parc Océanique Cousteau** in particular is a bit of a disappointment; you'd probably get more out of a proper ride on some real water. (Various river and canal trips are detailed in Chapter Five). **Planète Magique** gives a choice of all sorts of simulated environments, though if **outer space** is the kids' prime interest then bear in mind the two **planetariums**, in the *Palais de la Découverte* (see p.156) and the *Cité des Sciences* (see p.154). If their minds are firmly on more earthly matters, an excursion into the **catacombs** or even the **sewers** might be an idea.

We've also included a couple of **amusement parks**, both of which are situated well outside Paris. **Parc Astérix** is the better of the two, but expensive and not that easy to get to without a car.

Parc Océanique Cousteau

Forum des Halles, niveau -1, Porte du Jour, 1er. Mº RER Châtelet-Les Halles. Tues & Thurs 10am–4pm, Wed & Fri–Sun 10am–5:30pm   75F, students 65F, under 12s 50F.

A simulated underwater exploration which is a bit of a rip-off for the price, given that all you're being shown in the ride are films and models of ocean life, but the passage through the blue whale is quite fun. Don't let the kids be deceived—there's no water and no real fish.

Planète Magique

3bis rue Papin, 3e. Mº Réaumur-Sébastopol. During school holidays the hours are Mon 1–7pm, Tues–Sun 10am–7pm; for the rest of the time Wed, Sat, Sun & holidays 10am–7pm, Thurs & Fri 1–7pm.

Another new American-inspired simulation fantasy, but rather better than the *Parc Océanique*. It's a series of rooms fitted out as different worlds—a space station, an Inca palace, an Arthurian dungeon, a time machine, a Barbie-doll's dressing-room—with video projections and interactive computers for you to work out the riddle, the escape route, the future of the universe, and what Barbie's going to wear tonight. All very unoriginal but the kids will probably love it. Unfortunately, the pricing system is itself a sophisticated toy that will cost you dearly. Each game-world costs between one and three "*gadgets*." You buy a 5 *gadgets* or 10 *gadgets* glossily designed magnetic card costing 50F or 100F, which, with every consuming pressure on the youngsters to demand it, can be recharged for another 50F or 100F.

Going Underground

The ghoulish and horror fanatics should get a really satisfying shudder from the **catacombs** at place Denfert-Rochereau, 14ᵉ (RER Denfert-Rochereau; Mon–Fri 2–4pm, Sat & Sun 9–11am & 2–6pm; closed holidays; 15F/8.50F), but read p.95 first; while the archetypal pre-teen fixation might find fulfillment in the **sewers**—*Les Égouts* at place de la Résistance, on the corner of quai d'Orsay and the Pont de l'Alma (Mº Alma-Marceau; guided tours Mon–Wed, Sat & Sun 11am–5pm; 20F/10F)—see p.78.

Parc Mirapolis

rte de Courdimanche, Cergy-Pontoise. A free shuttle train takes you to the entrance from Cergy-St-Christophe station (RER line A3 terminal). April–Aug daily 10am–6:30pm; Sept Sat & Sun 10am–6:30pm. Admission is 100F, 5–13s 75F, under-5s free, and gives you access to all the rides.

From autoroute 15, thirty kilometers northwest of Paris, you can see the looming head of Gargantua, the gourmand giant created by Rabelais in the sixteenth century, who sets the theme for the park as a whole. A visit through his entrails and a bite of meat from huge roasting spits is about as far as the literary inspiration goes. Otherwise it's huge, wild slides, raft rides, ghost trains, horse rides, and so forth.

Parc Astérix

In Plailly, easiest reached by shuttle bus from Mº Fort-d'Aubervilliers (every half-hour). April–June Mon–Fri 10am–6pm, Sat 10am–8pm, Sun & hols 10am–7pm; July Mon–Fri 10am–7pm, Sat 10am–10pm, Sun & hols 10am–7pm; Aug daily 10am–10pm; Sept & Oct Wed 10am–6pm, Sat 10am–8pm, Sun & hols 9am–7pm; closed Nov–March. Admission is 140F, 3–12s 100F.

This one is really quite a long way out of Paris, 38km north off the A1 autoroute. It gets a lot more mileage than the *Mirapolis* from its much more promising literary source. A *Via Antiqua* shopping street, with buildings from every country in the Roman empire, leads to a Roman town where gladiators play comic battles and bumper chariots line up for races. There's a legionaries' camp where incompetent soldiers attempt to keep watch, and a wave-manipulated lake which you cross on galleys and longships. In the Gaulish village, Getafix mixes his potions, Obelix slavers over boars, Astérix plots farther sorties against the occupiers, and the dreadful bard is exiled up a tree. In another area, street scenes of Paris show the city changing from Roman Lutetia to the present-day capital. All sorts of rides are on offer (with long lines for the best ones); dolphins and sea lions perform tricks for the crowds; there are parades and jugglers; restaurants for every budget; and most of the actors speak English (even if they occasionally get confused with the variations on the names).

Circus, Film, and Theater

Language being less of a barrier for smaller children, the younger your kids, the more likely they are to appreciate Paris's many special **theater shows** and **films**. There's also **mime** and the **circus**, which need no translations.

Circus

Circuses, unlike funfairs, are taken seriously in France. They come under the heading of culture as performance art (and there are no qualms about performing animals). Some have permanent venues, of which the most beautiful in Paris is the nineteenth-century *Cirque d'Hiver Bouglione* (see below). You'll find details of the seasonal ones under "*cirques*" in *Pariscope* etc, and there may well be visiting circuses from Warsaw or Moscow.

Cirque d'Hiver Bouglione, 110 rue Amelot, 11ᵉ. The strolling players and fairy lights beneath the dome welcome circus-goers from October to January (and TV and fashion shows the rest of the year).

Cirque National Alexis Gruss. Performs at various venues between October and mid-February.

Cirque Bormann Diana Moreno. This touring circus crops up at several diferent locations, April–June & Sept–Dec.

Cirque de Paris, on the corner of av Hoche and av de la Commune-de-Paris, Nanterre. RER Nanterre-Ville. ☎47.24.11.70. A dream day out; for 215F+ adults, 175F+ children, you can spend an entire **day at the circus** (Nov–June Wed, Sun & school holidays 10am–5pm). In the morning you are initiated into the arts of juggling, walking the tightrope, clowning, and makeup. You have lunch in the ring with your artist tutors, then join the spectators for the show, after which, if you're lucky, the lion-tamer takes you around to meet his cats. You can, if you prefer, just attend the show at 3pm (60–150F/40–95F), but if so, don't let the kids know what they have missed.

Theater

Several **theaters**, apart from the ones in the *Parc Floral* and the *Jardin d'Acclimatation*, specialize in shows for children: the *Blancs Manteaux* and *Point Virgule* in the Marais, *Au Bec Fin* in the 1ᵉʳ, *Le Dunois* in the 13ᵉ, and the *Bateau Théâtre* moored by the Passerelle des Arts all have excellent reputations, but it's doubtful how much pleasure your children will get unless they're bilingual. Still, it's worth checking in the listings magazines which usually detail magic, mime, dance and music in any show.

One exception is the **English theater**, *Galerie 55* (55 rue de Seine, 6ᵉ; Mᵒ Odéon/Mabillon/St-Germain-des-Près; ☎43.26.63.51). They do a short winter season of matinées, usually classics of the Alice-in-Wonderland Toad-of-Toad-Hall ilk, on Wednesday and Saturday at 3pm (tickets 100F/60F). You'll find full details of Paris theaters in Chapter Ten, *Film, Theater, and Dance*.

Cinema

There are many **movie theaters** showing cartoons and children's films, but if they're foreign they are inevitably dubbed into French. Listings of the main Parisian movie theaters are given in Chapter Ten, *Film, Theater, and Dance*. Watching an Omnimax projection at *La Géode*, however—see the description on p.249—is greatly enhanced by not understanding the commentary. Films at the *Louis-Lumière* cinema (also in the *Cité des Sciences*—see below) may be less accessible, but you can ask at the inquiry desk for advice.

Museums

The best treat for children, of every age from three upwards, is the **Cité des Sciences** in the Parc de la Villette. Its only competitor, from most children's point of view, will be the European Disneyland when that opens in 1992. All the other **museums**, despite entertaining collections and special activities and workshops for children, pale into insignificance. So beware that if you visit the *Cité* on your first day, your offspring may decide that's where they want to stay.

Given kids' particular and sometimes peculiar tastes, the choice of other museums and monuments is best left to them, though the *Musée des Enfants* itself, which boringly purveys sentimental images of childhood, is certainly one to avoid. On the other hand, don't forget the **gargoyles of Notre-Dame**, and the **aquariums** at the Musée des Arts Africains et Océaniens (see p.155) and beneath the Palais de Chaillot (place du Trocadéro, 16e; Mº Trocadéro; daily 10am–5:30pm).

Certain museums have **children's workshops**, giving you the freedom to enjoy the sort of things that bore most children to tears. When they've exhausted **Beaubourg's** free attractions—the performers on the plaza and the building in itself—you can deposit 6- to 14-year-olds in the *Atelier des Enfants* (Wed & Sat 2–3:30pm & 3:45–5pm; free for visitors to the art museum; some English-speaking animators) where they can create their own art and play games. The **Musée d'Art Moderne de la Ville de Paris** has special exhibitions and workshops in its children's section (Wed, Sat & Sun; entrance 14 av de New-York). The **Musée d'Orsay** provides worksheets (English promised) for 8- to 12-year-olds that makes them explore every aspect of the building. Other municipal museums with sessions for kids include the *Musée Carnavalet, Musée de la Mode et du Costume*, and the *Petit Palais*; costs are 25F.

Full details of all the state museums' activities for children—which are all included in the admission charge—are published in *Objectif Musée*, a booklet available from the museums or from the *Direction des Musées de France* (34 quai du Louvre, 1er; closed Tues).

Cité des Sciences et de l'Industrie

Parc de la Villette, 19e. Mº Corentin-Cariou/Porte- de-la-Villette. Opening times and charges are: Tues–Sun 10am–6pm; 35F/25F. **Inventorium** *Mon–Fri 11am, 12:30pm, 2pm & 3:30pm; Sat & Sun noon, 1:30pm, 3pm & 4:30pm; 15F, free for two accompanying adults.* **Cinéma Louis-Lumière** *9am–noon & 2–6pm; 10F extra.* **Planétarium** *10:30am, 12:30pm, 2pm, 3:30pm & 5pm; 15F extra.* **Géode** *Tues–Sun 10am–7pm; 45F/35F, combined ticket with Cité 70F/60F (available from Géode only).*

The **Inventorium**, the Cité's special section for 3- to 6-year-olds and 6- to 12-year-olds, is totally engaging. The kids can touch and smell and feel inside things, play about with water, construct buildings on a miniature construction site complete with cranes, hard hats, and barrows, experiment with sound and light, and carry out genetic tests with computers. It's beautifully organized and managed, and if you haven't got a child it's worth borrowing one to get in here.

The rest of the museum (see p.153) is also pretty good for kids and if you want to wander around the park, or see an exhibition at the Grande Salle without them, there are two "follies" where they can be dumped. *La Petite Folie*, across the canal from the *Cité*, is a game-filled **daycare** for 2- to 5-year-olds (Wed–Sun 1:30–7:30pm; 3hr maximum stay; reservations ☎42:40.15.10; 15F per hour). The *Folie Arts Plastiques* near the Grande Salle is a painting workshop for 7- to 10-year-olds (Sat & Sun 2–5:30pm; reservations ☎40.40.03.22; 50F).

Shops

If your offspring belong to the modern breed of sophisticated consumers, then keeping them away from shops will be your biggest saving. This can be difficult given the Parisian art of enticing window displays, practiced to the full on every other street. Children with an eye for clothes are certain to spy boots or gloves or dresses without which life will be not worth living. Huge cuddly animals, gleaming models, and the height of fashionable sports equipment will beckon them from every turn, not to mention ice creams, waffles, fries, and pancakes. The only goodies you are safe from are high-tech toys which aren't any better than those found back home and have French instructions to detract.

However, the brats may get the better of you, or you may decide to treat them anyway. So here's a small selection of shops—to seek out, to be dragged into, or to avoid at all costs.

Books

Among shops stocking a good selection of English books are the following; but be warned, they're expensive.

Brentano's, 37 av de l'Opéra, 2e. Mº Opéra. Mon–Sat 10am–7pm.

Chantelivre, 13 rue de Sèvres, 6e. Mº Sèvres-Babylone. Mon 1–6:30pm, Tues–Sat 10am–6:30pm; closed Mon in Aug. A huge selection of everything to do with and for children, including good picture books for the younger ones, an English section, a play area, and drawing and mime classes.

Galignani, 224 rue de Rivoli, 1er. Mº Tuileries. Mon–Sat 9am–7pm.

WH Smith, 248 rue de Rivoli, 1er. Mº Concorde. Mon–Sat 9:30am–6:30pm.

Toys and Games

As well as the assortment of shops listed below, ranging from **kites** to **masks**, **puppets** to **train sets**, it's worth bearing in mind that if children have enjoyed a museum they'll probably want what's on offer in the **museum shops**. The boutiques at *Beaubourg* and the *Cité des Sciences* have wonderful books, models, games, scientific instruments, and toys covering a wide price range.

Ali Baba, 29 av de Tourville, 7e. Mº Varenne/St-François-Xavier. Mon–Sat 10am–1pm & 2–7pm. Traditional toy store covering three floors—for all ages.

Art et Joie, 74 rue de Maubeuge, 9e. Mº Poissonnière. Mon–Fri 9:30am–6:30pm, Sat 10am–12:30pm; closed Aug. Everything you need for painting, modeling, graphic design, pottery, and every other art and craft.

Baby Train, 9 rue du Petit-Pont, 5e. Mº St-Michel. Mon 10am–6:30pm, Tues–Sat 10am–9pm. The best collection of electric trains, radio-controlled planes, buggies, and boats.

Boutique D.A.C., 10 rue du Cardinal-Lemoine, 5e. Mº Cardinal-Lemoine. Tues–Sat 10am–7:30pm; closed Aug. Musical boxes, puppets, wooden dolls.

Le Ciel Est à Tout le Monde, 10 rue Gay-Lussac, 5e. Mº Luxembourg. Also at 7 av Trudaine, 9e; Mº Anvers. Mon–Sat 10:30am–7pm; closed Mon in Aug. The best kite shop in Europe also sells frisbees, boomerangs, etc, and books and traditional toys.

Le Comédien, 20 passage Verdeau, 9e. Mº Le Peletier. Mon–Sat 1:30–6:30pm. Models and costumes of fictional characters, starring Tintin and Captain Haddock.

Au Cotillon Moderne, 13, bd Voltaire, 11e. Mº Oberkampf. Mon–Sat 10am–noon & 1:30–6:30pm; closed Aug. Celluloid and supple plastic masks of animals, characters from fiction, politicians, etc, trinkets, festoons, and other party paraphernalia.

Les Cousins d'Alice, 36 rue Daguerre, 14e. Mº Gaîté/Edgar-Quinet. Tues–Sat 10am–1pm & 3–7pm, Sun 11am–1pm; closed Aug. Alice in Wonderland decorations, toys, games, puzzles, and mobiles, plus a general range of books and records.

Deyrolle, 46 rue du Bac, 7e. Mº Bac. Mon–Sat 9am–12:30pm & 2–6:30pm. The best-known taxidermist: insects, butterflies, stuffed animals—from the biggest to the smallest, plus rocks and fossils. Fun to look at.

Magie Moderne, 8 rue des Carmes, 5e. Mº Maubert-Mutualité. Tues–Sat 10am–7pm. A magician's paradise.

La Maison de la Peluche, 74 rue de Seine, 6e. Mº Odéon/St-Germain-des-Près. Mon–Sat 10am–7:30pm. More lovely stuffed animals, of the cuddly type.

Le Monde en Marche, 34 rue Dauphine, 6e. Mº Odéon. Tues–Sat 10:30am–7:30pm; closed Aug. Wooden toys of all sorts, from puzzles to dolls' houses.

Au Nain Bleu, 406–410 rue St-Honoré, 8e. Mº Concorde. Mon–Sat 9:45am–6:30pm; closed Mon in Aug. Huge and all-inclusive.

Puzzles d'Art, 116 rue du Château, 14e. Mº Pernéty. Mon–Fri 8:30am–8pm, Sat 11am–8pm. Exactly what it says; with workshop on the premises.

Pains d'Epices, 29 passage Jouffroy, 9e. Mº Montmartre. Mon 12:30–7pm, Tues–Sat 10am–7pm. Fabulous dolls' house necessities from furniture to wine glasses, and puppets.

Rigodon, 13 rue Racine, 6e. Mº Odéon. Mon–Sat 10:30am–7pm; closed Aug. A weird and wonderful wizard's cave of marionettes, puppets, horror-masks, and other spooks.

Si Tu Veux, 68 galerie Vivienne, 2e. Mº Bourse. Mon–Sat 10:30am–7pm. Well-made traditional toys plus do-it-yourself and ready-made costumes.

Le Train Bleu, 55 rue St-Placide, 6e. Mº St-Placide. Mon 2–7pm, Tues–Sat 10am–7pm. Also at Centre Beaugrenelle, 16 rue Linois, 15e (Mº Charles-Michels; Tues–Sun 10am–7:30pm); and 2 & 6 av Mozart, 16e (Mº Ranelagh; Mon 2–7pm, Tues–Sat 10am–7pm). A fairly expensive chain with the biggest array at St-Placide; good on electric trains, remote control vehicles, and other things you don't want to carry home with you.

Clothes

Besides the specialist shops we list here, most of the big department stores and the discount stores have children's sections (see Chapter Seven, *Shopping*). Of the latter, *Tati* and *Monoprix* are the cheapest places to go for vital clothing purchases.

Agnès B, 2 rue du Jour, 1er. Mº RER Châtelet-Les Halles. Mon–Sat 10:30am–7pm. Very fashionable, desirable, and unaffordable.

Baby Dior, 28 av Montaigne, 8e. Mº Alma-Marceau/F-Roosevelt. Mon–Sat 10am–6:30pm. Even more unaffordable, less desirable but entertaining—the prices, most of all.

Chercheminippes Enfants, 110 rue du Cherche-Midi, 6e. Mº Rennes. Mon–Sat 10:30am–7pm. High quality secondhand clothes for ages 0–10.

Elizabeth de Senneville, 38 place du Marché-St-Honoré, 1er. Mº Pyramides. Mon noon–7pm, Tues–Sat 10am–7pm. Also at 55 rue Bonaparte, 6e (Mº Rennes; Mon 1–7pm, Tues–Sat 10:30am–7pm). Original and up-to-date designs in denim or cotton for babies to 12-year-olds.

Benetton, 59 rue de Rennes, 6e. Mº St-Sulpice. Mon–Sat 10:30am–7:30pm. A greater range than in the US stores.

Gullipy, 66 rue de Babylone, 7e. Mº St-François-Xavier. Mon–Fri 9am–7pm, Sat 11am–1pm. Fun accessories as well as clothes—satchels, bags, wallets, etc.

Jacadi, 46 rue de l'Université, 7e. Mº Bac. Mon–Sat 10am–6:45pm. Also at 23 other addresses. Dependable, hard-wearing, and reasonably priced clothes for up to 14-year-olds.

La Petite Gaminerie, 32 rue du Four, 6e. Mº St-Germain-des-Près. Mon–Sat 10:15am–7pm; closed Mon in Aug. All the top name designers for the kiddies of all the top names. Good stuff, though not cheap.

Pom d'Api, 13 rue du Jour, 1er. Mº RER Châtelet-Les Halles. Mon–Sat 10:30am–7pm. Also at 28 rue du Four, 6e (Mº St-Germain-des-Près; Mon–Sat 10am–7pm) and 6 rue Guichard, 16e (Mº La Muette; Mon–Fri 10am–1pm & 2–7:30pm, Sat 10am–7:30pm). The most colorful, imaginative, and well-made shoes for kids in Paris. Up to size 40 (9).

CHAPTER SEVEN

SHOPS AND MARKETS

F lair for style and design is as evident in shops as it is in other aspects of the city's life. Parisians' fierce attachment to their small local traders, especially when it comes to food, has kept alive a wonderful variety, despite the pressures to concentrate consumption in gargantuan underground and multistory complexes.

Even if you don't plan—or can't afford—to buy, Parisian **shops** are one of the chief delights of the city. Some of the most entertaining and tempting are those small, cluttered affairs which reflect their owners' **particular passions**. You'll find traders in offbeat merchandise in every *quartier*—some are detailed in Chapters One to Three.

Markets, too, are grand spectacle. Mouthwatering arrays of **food** from half the countries of the globe, intoxicating in their color, shape, and smell, assail the senses in even the drabbest parts of town. In Belleville and the Goutte d'Or North Africa predominates; Southeast Asia in the 13e *arrondissement*. Though the food is perhaps the best offering of the Paris markets, there are also street markets dedicated to **secondhand goods** (the *marchés aux puces*), **clothes and textiles, flowers, birds, books, and stamps**.

SHOPS

The most distinctive and unusual **shopping possibilities** are in the nineteenth-century arcades of the *passages* in the 2e and 9e *arrondissements*, almost all now elegantly renovated. On the streets proper, the square kilometer around **place St-Germain-des-Prés** is hard to beat, packed with books, antiques, gorgeous garments, artworks, and playthings. Les Halles is another well-shopped district, with its focus the submarine shopping complex of the *Forum des Halles*, good for everything from records through to designer clothes. The aristocratic **Marais** and the new trendies' *quartier* of the **Bastille** have filled up with dinky little boutiques, arty and specialist shops, and galleries. For window-shopping the really **moneyed** Parisian *haute couture*, your Hermès and suchlike, the two traditional areas are **av Montaigne, rue François 1er**, and **rue du Faubourg-St-Honoré** in the 8e and **av Victor-Hugo** in the 16e. The fashionable newer designers, lead by the Japanese, are to be found around **place des Victoires** in the 1er and 2e.

For **food and essentials**, the cheapest supermarket chains are *Ed Discount* and *Franprix*. Other **last-minute** or **convenience shopping** is probably best at *FNAC* shops (for books and records) and the big department stores (for practically everything else).

LATE-NIGHT SHOPPING

As Eco, 11 rue Brantôme, 3ᵉ. Mᵒ Rambuteau. Supermarket open Mon–Fri 9am–1am, Sat 9am–11pm.

Le Cochon Rose, 44 bd de Clichy, 17ᵉ. Mᵒ Blanche. Groceries, fruit and veg, and *charcuterie*; Fri–Wed 6pm–5am.

La Favourite Bar-Tabac, 3 bd St-Michel, 5ᵉ. Mᵒ St-Michel. *Tabac* open Sun–Thurs 8am–3am, Fri & Sat 24-hr.

Le Terminus Bar Tabac, 10 rue St-Denis, 1ᵉʳ. Mᵒ Châtelet-Les Halles. 24-hr *tabac*.

The three **drugstores** (see p.218–19 for addresses) are open for books, newspapers, tobacco, and all kinds of gift gadgetry until 2am every night.

Toy shops, and shops selling **children's clothes** and **books**, are detailed in Chapter Six, *Kids' Stuff*.

Opening Hours

Shop **opening hours** are variable throughout the city, but most tend to stay open fairly late—until 7 or 8pm as often as not—and to close for up to two hours at lunchtime somewhere between noon and 3pm. Most are closed on Sundays, many on Mondays as well.

Art and Design

For an idea of what is going on in the world of contemporary art, the best thing is to take a look at the **commercial art galleries**. They are concentrated in three main areas: in the 8ᵉ, especially in and around av Matignon; in the Marais; and in Saint-Germain.

There are literally hundreds of galleries, and for an idea of who is being exhibited where, you'll need to consult the booklet *Rive Droite Rive Gauche*, available from the galleries themselves or from more upmarket hotels, or *Pariscope*, which carries details of major exhibitions under *Expositions* and *Galeries*. Entry to the commercial galleries is free to all.

Design

A small selection of places where contemporary and the best of twentieth-century **design** can be seen is listed below. Also worth checking out are the shops of the art and design museums, and the rue St-Paul which has a particularly high concentration of shops specializing in particular periods.

IA (Valorization de l'Innovation dans l'Ameublement), place Ste-Opportune, 1ᵉʳ. Mᵒ Châtelet. Tues–Fri 10:30am–7pm, Sat & Mon 11am–7pm; closed Aug. Intended to promote and assist young designers. The showrooms mount a variety of exhibitions.

Artistes et Modèles, 1 rue Christine, 6ᵉ. Mᵒ Odéon. Bits and pieces by young and established designers.

Collectania, 2 place du Palais-Royal, 1ᵉʳ. Mᵒ Palais-Royal–Musée-du-Louvre. In the middle of the Louvre des Antiquitaires, featuring an assortment of tableware and furniture by big European names.

Écart, 111 rue St-Antoine, 4ᵉ. Mᵒ St-Paul. Reproductions of early twentieth-century furniture designs: beautiful constructivist and Art Déco carpets, Mallet-Stevens chairs, angular desks, etc—mostly 10,000F and over.

En Attendant les Barbares, 50 rue Étienne-Marcel, 2ᵉ. Mᵒ Châtelet-Les Halles. The style known as neo-Barbarian: Baroque gilding on bizarre experimental forms—nothing you'd actually trust your weight to, but fun to look at.

État de Siège, 1 quai de Conti, 6ᵉ. Mᵒ Pont-Neuf. Also at 21 av de Friedland, 8ᵉ (Mᵒ George-V). Closed two weeks in Aug. Chairs, chairs, chairs . . . from Louis XIII to contemporary.

Eugénie Seigneur, 16 rue Charlot, 3ᵉ. Mᵒ République. The place to take your print or original for a highly unique frame.

Galerie Documents, 53 rue de Seine, 6ᵉ. Mᵒ Odéon. Best antique posters.

Les Petits Champs, 50 rue Croix-des-Petits-Champs, 1er. Mᵒ Bourse. Open afternoons only. The real, not repro, 1930s furniture, jewelry, lamps, and oddities like a pair of giant spectacles.

Bookshops

Books are not cheap in France—foreign books least of all. But don't let that stop you browsing. The best areas are the Seine *quais* with their rows of **stalls** perched against the river parapet and the narrow streets of the Quartier Latin, but don't neglect the array of specialist shops listed below.

English-language Books

Abbey Bookshop/La Librairie Canadienne, 29 rue de la Parcheminerie, 5ᵉ. Mᵒ St-Michel. Mon–Thurs 11am–10pm, Fri & Sat 11am–12pm, Sun noon–10pm. A new Canadian bookshop around the corner from *Shakespeare & Co.* Lots of secondhand British and North American fiction; good social and political science sections; knowledgeable and helpful staff . . . and free coffee.

Attica, 34 rue des Écoles, 5ᵉ. Mᵒ Maubert-Mutualité. Mon 2–7pm, Tues–Fri 10am–7pm, Sat 10am–1pm & 2–7pm. Most reasonably priced English-language books in Paris—literature rather than best-sellers.

Brentano's, 37 av de l'Opéra, 2ᵉ. Mᵒ Opéra. Mon–Sat 10am–7pm. English and American books. Good section for kids.

Galignani, 224 rue de Rivoli, 1er. Mᵒ Concorde. Mon–Sat 9:30am–7pm. Good range, including children's books.

Shakespeare & Co, 37 rue de la Bûcherie, 5ᵉ. Mᵒ Maubert-Mutualité. Noon–midnight every day. A cosy, friendly, famous literary haunt, with the biggest selection of secondhand English books in town. Also poetry readings and such.

WH Smith, 248 rue de Rivoli, 1er. Mᵒ Concorde. Mon–Sat 9am–6:30pm. Wide range of books and newspapers. *Salon de thé* upstairs.

Village Voice, 6 rue Princesse, 6ᵉ. Mᵒ Mabillon. Tues–Sat 11am–8pm. Principally poetry and modern literature, both British and American.

Books in French

For **general French titles,** the biggest and most convenient shop has to be the *FNAC* in the Forum des Halles, though it's hardly the most congenial of places. If you fancy a prolonged session of browsing, the other general bookstores overleaf are probably more suitable.

Le Divan, 37 rue Bonaparte, 6e. Mº St-Germain-des-Prés. Mon–Sat 10am–7:30pm.

FNAC, at the Forum des Halles—level-2, Porte Pierre-Lescot. Mº RER Châtelet-Les Halles. Mon 2–7:30pm, Tues–Sat 10am–7:30pm. Also at 136 rue de Rennes, 6e (Mº Montparnasse) and 26 av de Wagram, 8e (Mº Courcelles), both open Mon 2–7pm, Tues–Sat 10am–7pm; and CNIT, 2 place de la Défense (RER La Défense), Mon 2–8pm, Tues–Sat 10am–8pm. Lots of *Bandes Dessinées*, guidebooks, and maps among everything else.

Gallimard, 15 bd Raspail, 7e. Mº Sèvres-Babylone. Sept–July Mon–Sat 10am–7pm; Aug Mon–Fri 10am–7pm.

Gibert Jeune, 5 place St-Michel, 5e, and 27 quai St-Michel, 5e. Mº St-Michel. Mon–Sat 9:30am–7:30pm. With lots of sales, some English books and secondhand, too.

La Hune, 170 bd St-Germain, 6e. Mº St-Germain-des-Prés. Mon 2pm–midnight, Tues–Fri 10am–midnight, Sat 10am–7:30pm. One of the biggest and best.

Secondhand and Antiquarian

In addition to the *quais*, you might try:

Albert Petit Siroux, Galerie Vivienne, 2e. Mº Bourse. New and secondhand books, including musty leather-bound volumes on Paris and France.

L'Introuvable, 25 rue Juliette-Dodu, 10e. Mº Colonel-Fabien. Tues–Sat 11am–1pm & 3–7pm. All sorts stocked, including some rare editions.

Gibert Jeune, see above.

Librairie St-Georges, 50 rue St-Georges, 9e. Mº St-Georges. Mon–Fri 10am–12:30pm & 2–7pm. Interesting antiquarian bookshop.

Plaisir du Texte, 8 rue des Fossés-St-Jacques, 5e. Mº Luxembourg. Classics and modern literature, French and foreign. Plus some rare numbers.

Specialist Bookshops

African/Third World

L'Harmattan, 16 rue des Écoles, 5e. Mº Maubert-Mutualité. 10am–12:30pm & 1:30–7pm. Excellent, very knowledgeable bookshop, especially good for Arab/North African literature (in French).

Art and Architecture

Artcurial, 9 av Matignon, 8e. Mº Franklin-Roosevelt. Mon–Sat 10:30am–7:15pm; closed two weeks in Aug. French and foreign art books, plus a gallery.

Librairie du Musée des Arts Décoratifs, 107 rue de Rivoli, 1er. Mº Palais-Royal. 12:30–6pm. Design, posters, architecture, graphics, etc.

Librairie du Musée d'Art Moderne de la Ville de Paris, Palais de Tokyo, 11 av du Président-Wilson, 16e. Mº Iéna. Tues–Sun 10am–5:30pm. Specialist publications on modern art, including foreign works.

Librairie de l'École des Beaux Arts, 13 quai Malaquais, 6e. Mº St-Germain-des-Prés. Mon–Fri 10am–6pm; closed Aug. Beaux Arts publications, plus posters, postcards, etc.

Librairie du Musée du Louvre, place du Carrousel, 1er. Mº Palais-Royal–Musée-du-Louvre. 9:30am–10pm; closed Tues.

Autographs

Librairie de l'Abbaye, 27 rue Bonaparte, 6e. Mº St-Germain-des-Prés. Tues–Sat 10am–12:30pm & 2–7pm; closed Aug. Signatures of the famous. Good for a browse.

Comics/*Bandes dessinées*

Album, 60 rue Monsieur-le-Prince, 6e. Mº Odéon. Also at 6–8 rue Dante, 5e (Mº Maubert-Mutualité). Tues–Sat 10am–8pm. Some of the rarest editions and original artwork.

Boulinier, 20 bd St-Michel, 6e. Mº St-Michel. Mon–Sat 10am–7:30pm. New, secondhand, and long out-of-print.

La Terrasse de Gutenberg, 9 rue Emilio-Castelar, 12e. Mº Ledru-Rollin. Mon 2–7pm, Tues–Sun 10am–7:30pm. Excellent collection of fine and graphic art, including *bandes dessinées*, plus photographs, postcards, and general books.

Feminist

La Fourmi Ailée, 8 rue du Fouarre, 6e. Mº Maubert-Mutualité. Left-wing bookshop and *salon de thé,* stocking most feminist reviews.

Librairie Anima, 3 rue Ravignan, 18e. Mº Abbesses.

Des Femmes Librairie-Galerie, 74 rue de Seine, 6e. Mº Odéon. The bookshop of *Psyche et Po*, a women's sect antagonistic to mainstream and all other types of feminism save its own—a contrary, convoluted, and mainly incomprehensible combination of messianic politics and Lacanian psychoanalysis.

Gay and Lesbian

Les Mots à la Bouche, 6 rue Ste-Croix-de-la-Bretonnerie, 4e. Mº St-Paul. Mon–Sat 11am–8pm. Literature, psychology, etc: books and magazines—some in English. Includes some lesbian literature.

Kiosque Forum, 10 rue Pierre-Lescot, 1er. Mº Châtelet-Les Halles. Daily 8am–midnight. Newsagents carrying a wide range of gay and lesbian literature.

Leftist Avant-garde

Actualités, 38 rue Dauphine, 6e. Mº Odéon. Mon 2–6pm, Tues–Fri 11am–1pm & 2–7pm, Sat noon–7pm. Literature, philosophy, *bandes dessinées,* etc.

Librairie du Monde Libertaire, 145 rue Amelot, 11e. Mº République. The anarchist bookshop.

Parallèles, 47 rue St-Honoré, 1er. Mº Châtelet-Les Halles. Mon–Sat 10am–7pm. The place to go for green, feminist, anti-racist, 57 brands of socialist publications: carries most of the "underground" press and info on current events, demos, etc. Good too on music and comics.

Performing Arts

Librairie Bonaparte, 39 rue Bonaparte, 6e. Mº St-Germain-des-Prés. Mon–Sat 11am–1pm & 3:30–7pm; closed Aug. Exhaustive stock of books on ballet, theater, opera, puppets, music hall, *chansonniers*, etc.

Clair Obscur, 161 rue St-Martin, 3e. Mº Rambuteau. Tues–Sat 11am–7pm. Wonderful film fanatics' stuff: stacks of movie-star stills and posters. Books on cinema and theater, plus masks and puppets.

Les Feux de la Rampe, 2 rue de Lynes, 7e. Mº Bac. Tues–Sat 11am–1pm & 2:15–7pm; closed three weeks in July and Aug 15. Books, scripts, photos, etc.

Librairie du Spectacle, 39 rue de Seine, 6e. Mº Odéon. Mon–Sat 11am–12:30pm & 2–7pm. Attractive window display—pics, books, masks.

Poetry

L'Arbre Voyageur, 55 rue Mouffetard, 5e. Mº Monge. Tues–Thurs 11am–8pm, Fri & Sat 11am–midnight. Poetry from all over the world, plus readings, discussions, and exhibitions.

L'Envers du Miroir, 19 rue de Seine, 6e. Mº Mabillon. Tues–Sat noon–7:30pm; closed Aug. Some fine and rare editions of modern poetry, as well as periodicals.

Le Pont Traversé, 62 rue de Vaugirard, 6ᵉ. Mᵒ St-Sulpice. Tues–Sat noon–7pm. Modern French poetry, surrealist works, etc in a very attractive old shop.

Travel

L'Astrolabe, 46 rue de Provence, 9ᵉ. Mᵒ Le Peletier. Mon–Sat 10am–7pm. Every conceivable map, French and foreign; guidebooks; climbing and hiking guides; sailing, natural history, etc.

Institut Géographique National (IGN), 107 rue La Boétie, 8ᵉ. Mᵒ Miromesnil. Mon–Fri 8am–6:50pm, Sat 10am–12:30pm & 1:45–5:20pm. The French Ordnance Survey: the best for maps of France and the entire world, plus guidebooks, GR route descriptions, satellite photos, day packs, map holders, etc.

Ulysse, 26 rue St-Louis-en-l'Île, 4ᵉ. Mᵒ Sully-Morland. Tues–Sat 2–8pm. Travel books, maps, guides.

Clothes

There may be no way you can get to see the haute couture shows (see box below), but nothing prevents you trying on fabulously expensive creations by famous couturiers in rue du Faubourg-St-Honoré, av François-1er, and av Victor-Hugo—apart from the intimidating scorn of the assistants and the awesome chill of the marble portals. Likewise, you can treat the **younger designers** around place des Victoires and in the Marais and Saint-Germain area as sightseeing. The current darling of the glitterati is **Azzedine Alaïa**, for whom the likes of Marie Helvin model for free. He is to fashion what Jean Nouvel is to architecture and Philippe Starck to interior design—together they form the triumvirate of Paris style.

   Ends of lines and **old stock** of the couturiers are sold all year round in discount shops listed below. For **clothes to buy** without the fancy labels the best area is **the 6ᵉ**: around rue de Rennes, rue de Sèvres and, in particular, rue St-Placide and rue St-Dominique in the neighboring 7ᵉ. The **department stores** *Galeries Lafayette* and *Au Printemps* have good selections of designer *prêt-à-porter*; the **Forum des Halles** is chockablock with clothes shops but at less competitive prices; and individual boutiques are taking over more and more of the **Marais** and the **Bastille** around rue de la Roquette.

   The Les Halles end of rue Rivoli has plenty of chain stores, including a *Monoprix* supermarket for essentials, or you can get even better bargains in the **rag-trade district** around place du Caire or **place de la République**, with a *Printemps* on the north side, *Tati* on the south, and the adjacent rues Meslay and Notre-Dame-de-Nazareth full of **shoe and clothes shops** respectively. **For jewelry**—gems and plastic—try rue du Temple and rue Montmorency.

   The **sales** take place in January and July, with up to forty percent reductions on designer clothes. This still leaves prices running into thousands of francs, but if you want to blow out on something bizarre and beautiful these are the months to do it. The sales in the more run-of-the-mill shops don't offer significant reductions.

   The common signs **vente en gros** and **vente en détail** or **vente aux particuliers** mean wholesale and retail, respectively.

Discount

The highest concentration of shops selling end-of-line and last year's models at thirty to fifty percent reductions are in rue d'Alésia in the 14ᵉ and rue St-Placide in the 6ᵉ. Though before you get too excited, remember that twenty percent off 5000F still leaves a hefty bill. Not that all items are as expensive as that. The best time of year to join the teeming masses is after the new collections have come out in January and October.

Azzedine Alaïa, 60 rue de Bellechasse, 7ᵉ. Mᵒ Varenne. Mon–Sat 10am–6:30pm. His creations at half-price.

Bil Toki, 42 rue des Plantes, 14ᵉ. Mᵒ Alésia. Mon 2–7:15pm, Tues–Sat 10:15am–7:15pm. Agnès B ends of lines.

Cacharel Stock, 114 rue d'Alésia, 14ᵉ. Mᵒ Alésia. Mon 2–7:30pm, Tues–Sat 10am–7:30pm. 30–40 percent off last season's stock. Men, women, and kids.

Dorothée Bis, 76 rue d'Alésia, 14ᵉ. Mᵒ Alésia. Mon 2–7pm, Tues–Sat 10:15am–7pm. 25 percent discount. Women and kids.

Stock 2, 92 rue d'Alésia, 14ᵉ. Mᵒ Alésia. Mon–Sat 10am–7pm. 30 percent reductions on Daniel Hechter's ends of lines.

Le Mouton à Cinq Pattes, 8 & 18 rue St-Placide, 6ᵉ, and **L'Annexe** (for men) at no. 48. Mᵒ Sèvres-Babylone. Mon 2–7pm, Tues–Sat 10am–7pm. Discounts on a wide range of big names.

Jean-Louis Scherrer Stock, 29 av Ledru-Rollin, 12ᵉ. Mᵒ Gare-de-Lyon. Summer Sun–Fri 10am–7pm, winter Mon & Tues and Thurs–Sat 10am–7pm. 50–60 percent off last season's clothes and up to 80 percent off older ones.

Toutes Griffes Dehors, 76 rue St-Dominique, 7e (Mᵒ Latour-Maubourg) and 84 rue de Sèvres, 6e (Mᵒ Duroc). Ends of lines from Guy Laroche among others.

Secondhand and Rétro

Rétro means period clothes, mostly unsold factory stock from the 1950s and 1960s, though some shops specialize in expensive high fashion articles from as far back as the 1920s. Plain **secondhand** stuff is referred to as *fripe*—which tends not to be especially interesting, dominated by the US combat jacket style. The best place to look is probably the Porte de Montreuil flea market (see p.202).

THE HAUTE COUTURE SHOWS

Invitations to the **January** and **July haute couture shows** go out exclusively to the elite of the world's fashion editors and to the 2500 or so clients for whom price tags between 100,000 and 1 million francs for a dress represents a mere day or week or two's unearned income. *Hello*, *Ola* and the like have a field-day as the top hotels, restaurants, and palace venues disgorge famous bodies cloaked in famous names. Mrs Ex-Trump thrills the press by saying husbands come and go but couturiers are worth hanging onto, and every arbiter of taste and style maintains the myth that fashion is the height of human attainment.

The truth, of course, is that the catwalks and the clientele are there to promote more mass-consumed products and the recession is beginning to bite. 1991 was a near-disaster with the Gulf Princess sector of the market keeping a low profile and the Americans too frightened of bombs on Concorde to attend. The designer Valentino responded with a dress inscribed with "Peace" in twelve languages.

THE BIG NAMES IN PARIS FASHION

Prices at Paris's big-name fashion emporia are well into the stratosphere. The addresses below are those of the main or most conveniently located shops.

Agnès B, 6 rue du Jour, 1er. M^o Châtelet-Les Halles.

Azzedine Alaïa, 18 rue de la Verrerie, 4e. M^o Hôtel-de-Ville.

Giorgio Armani, 6 & 25 place Vendôme, 1er. M^o Opéra.

Balenciaga, 10 av George-V, 8e. M^o Alma-Marceau.

Balmain, 44 rue François-1er, 8e. M^o George-V.

Anne-Marie Beretta, 24 rue St-Sulpice, 6e. M^o St-Sulpice.

Cacharel, 5 place des Victoires, 1er. M^o Bourse.

Pierre Cardin, 14 place François-1er, 8e. M^o Franklin-Roosevelt.

Carven, 6 rond-point des Champs-Élysées, 8e. M^o Franklin-Roosevelt.

Castelbajac, 31 place du Marché-St-Honoré, 1er. M^o Pyramides.

Cerruti 1881, 15 place de la Madeleine, 8e. M^o Madeleine.

Chanel, 31 rue Cambon, 1er. M^o Madeleine.

Chloé, 60 rue du Faubourg-St-Honoré, 8e. M^o Madeleine.

Comme des Garçons, 42 rue Étienne-Marcel, 2e. M^o Châtelet-Les-Halles.

Courrèges, 40 rue François-1er, 8e. M^o George-V.

Dior, 30 av Montaigne, 8e. M^o Franklin-Roosevelt.

Dorothée Bis, 46 rue Étienne-Marcel, 1er. M^o Châtelet-Les Halles.

Louis Féraud, 88 rue du Faubourg-St-Honoré, 8e. M^o Madeleine.

J-P Gaultier, 6 rue Vivienne, 2e. M^o Bourse.

Givenchy, 3 & 8 av George-V, 8e. M^o Alma-Marceau.

Grès, 17–21 rue du Faubourg-St-Honoré, 8e. M^o Concorde.

Daniel Hechter, 12 rue du Faubourg-St-Honoré, 8e. M^o Concorde.

Kenzo, 3 place des Victoires, 1er. M^o Bourse.

Emanuelle Khan, 2 rue de Tournon, 6e. M^o Odéon.

Christian Lacroix, 73 rue du Faubourg-St-Honoré, 8e. M^o Concorde.

Karl Lagerfeld, 19 rue du Faubourg-St-Honoré, 8e. M^o Concorde.

Lanvin, 22 rue du Faubourg-St-Honoré, 8e. M^o Concorde.

Ted Lapidus, 35 rue François-1er, 8e. M^o Franklin-Roosevelt.

Guy Laroche, 29 av Montaigne, 8e. M^o Alma-Marceau.

Isse Miyake, 3 place des Vosges, 4e. M^o St-Paul.

Claude Montana, 31 rue de Grenelle, 6e. M^o Sèvres-Babylone.

Hanae Mori, 17–19 av Montaigne, 8e. M^o Alma-Marceau.

Thierry Mugler, 10 place des Victoires, 2e. M^o Bourse.

Per Spook, 18 av George-V, 8e. M^o Alma-Marceau.

Paco Rabanne, 7 rue du Cherche-Midi, 6e. M^o Sèvres-Babylone.

Georges Rech, 54 rue Bonaparte, 6e. M^o St-Germain-des-Prés.

Nina Ricci, 39 av Montaigne, 8e. M^o Alma-Marceau.

Sonia Rykiel, 70 rue du Faubourg-St-Honoré, 8e. M^o Concorde.

Saint-Laurent, 5 av Marceau, 16e. M^o Alma-Marceau.

Jean-Louis Scherrer, 51 av Montaigne, 8e. M^o Franklin-Roosevelt.

Junko Shimada, 54 rue Étienne-Marcel, 1er. M^o Châtelet-Les Halles.

Ungaro, 2 av Montaigne, 8e. M^o Alma-Marceau.

Valentino, 17–19 av Montaigne, 8e. M^o Alma-Marceau.

Yamamoto, 25 rue du Louvre, 1er. M^o Rivoli.

Derrière les Fagots, 8 rue des Abbesses, 18e. Mo Abbesses. Tues–Sat 11:30am–7:30pm. Hats, gloves, bags, scarves, Burberrys, and ball gowns. Reasonable prices.

Fuchsia, corner of rues St-Paul & l'Ave-Maria, 4e. Mo St-Paul. Noon–7:30pm. Lacy underwear and slinky dresses from 1900 to 1930—expensive.

Halles aux Fringues, 16 rue de Montreuil, 11e. Mo Faidherbe-Chaligny. 10am–7pm. Classy 1940–60 clothes, hats of all descriptions, and kimonos.

Rag Time, 23 rue du Roule, 1er. Mo Rivoli. Mon–Sat 2–7:30pm. A veritable museum of superb dresses and high fashion articles from the Twenties to the Fifties. Expensive.

Réciproque, 95, 101 & 123 rue de la Pompe, 16e. Mo Pompe. Tues–Sat 10am–6:45pm. Haute couture: for women at no. 95; accessories and coats for men at no. 101; more accessories and coats for women at no. 123.

Rétro Activité, 38 rue du Vertbois, 3e. Mo Temple. Tues–Sat noon–7pm. Dresses from 1930s to 1960s and men's suits from Fifties and Sixties—unbelievably cheap.

Tati

Tati is in a class by itself, the cheapest of cheap clothes stores and always thronged with people. Addresses are: 2–30 bd Rochechouart, 18e (Mo Barbès-Rochechouart); 140 rue de Rennes, 6e (Mo St-Placide); and 13 place de la République, 11e (Mo République).

Department Stores and Hypermarkets

The two largest **department stores**, *Printemps* and *Galeries Lafayette*, are right next door to each other near the St-Lazare station and between them there's not much they don't have. Less enticing for its wares perhaps, but a visual knockout, is the newly renovated **Samaritaine**.

In addition, Paris has its share of **hypermarkets**—giant shopping complexes—of which the *Forum des Halles* in the 1er, the *Centre Maine-Montparnasse* in the 14e, and the *Quatre-Saisons* in La Défense are the biggest.

Bazar de l'Hôtel de Ville, 52–64 rue de Rivoli, 4e. Mo Hôtel-de-Ville. Mon, Tues, Thurs & Fri 9am–6:30pm, Wed 9am–10pm, Sat 9am–7pm. Only two years younger than the *Bon Marché* and noted in particular for its do-it-yourself department and cheap self-service restaurant overlooking the Seine.

Au Bon Marché, 38 rue de Sèvres, 7e. Mo Sèvres-Babylone. Mon–Sat 8:30am–8:30pm. Paris's oldest department store, founded in 1852. The prices are lower on average than at the chicer *Galeries Lafayette* and *Printemps*, and the tone is more mass-market middle class. It has an excellent kids' department and an alluring food hall.

Galeries Lafayette, 40 bd Haussmann, 9e. Mo Havre-Caumartin. Mon–Sat 9:30am–6:45pm. The store's forte is, above all, high fashion. Two complete floors are given over to the latest creations by leading designers for men, women, and children. Then there's household stuff, tableware, furniture, a host of big names in men and women's accessories, a huge *parfumerie*, etc—all under a superb 1900 dome.

Au Printemps, 64 bd Haussmann, 9e. Mo Havre-Caumartin. Mon–Sat 9:35am–7pm. Books, records, a *parfumerie* even bigger than the rival *Galeries Lafayette*, excellent fashion department for women—less so for men.

La Samaritaine, 75 rue de Rivoli, 1er. Mo Rivoli. Mon, Wed, Thurs & Sat 9:30am–7pm, Tues & Fri 9:30am–8:30pm. The biggest of the department stores, spread over three buildings, whose boast is to provide anything anyone could possibly want. It aims down-market of the previous two. *Magasin 3* is wholly devoted to sport. Superb view of the Seine from the tenth-floor terrace—closed from October to March.

Food

Food markets are detailed in the final section of this chapter. These listings are for the **specialist places**, palaces of gluttony, many of them, and some with prices to match. The equivalents of London's famous Harrods' food hall are to be found at *Fauchon's* and *Hédiard's*, on place de la Madeleine: each has exhibits to rival the best of the capital's museums. Among smaller collections, don't miss *Poilâne's*—the world's most sought-after bakery, the *Barthélémy* cheese shop, *La Maison de l'Escargot,* or the amazing provincial confectioneries of *Specialtés de France.* Wines are most startlingly extensive at the English-run *La Cave de la Madeleine.*

Buying food with a view to **economic eating**, you will be invariably best off shopping at the **street markets or supermarkets**—though save your bread-buying at least for the local *boulangerie* and let yourself be tempted once in a while by the apple *chaussons, pains aux raisins, pains au chocolat, tartes aux fraises,* and countless other goodies. Useful **supermarkets** with branches throughout the city are *Félix Potin, Prisunic,* and *Monoprix.* Cheapest of all but with very limited choice are *Franprix, Ed-Discount,* and *As-Eco* (11 rue Brantôme, 3ᵉ; Mᵒ Rambuteau) which stays open till 1am.

The Palaces . . .

Fauchon, 26 place de la Madeleine, 8ᵉ. Mᵒ Madeleine. Mon–Sat 9:40am–10pm. Carries an amazing range of super-plus groceries, almost anything you can think of. Just the place for presents of tea, jam, truffles, chocolates, exotic vinegars and mustards, etc. They also have an extensive wine cellar and a self-service.

Hédiard, 21 place de la Madeleine, 8ᵉ. Mᵒ Madeleine. Mon–Sat 9:15am–11pm. Since 1850, the aristocrat's grocer, with sales staff as deferential as servants, as long as you don't try to reach down items for yourself. Among the other branches are those at 126 rue du Bac, 7ᵉ; 106 bd de Courcelles, 17ᵉ; and Forum des Halles, level-1.

. . . and a Few Specialists

Bread

Ganachaud, 150–154 rue de Ménilmontant, 20ᵉ. Mᵒ Pelleport. Tues 2:30–8pm, Wed–Sat 7:30am–8pm, Sun 7:30am–1:30pm; closed Aug. Special for its wide range of traditional cakes and different types of bread.

Poilâne, 8 rue du Cherche-Midi, 7ᵉ. Mᵒ Sèvres-Babylone. Mon–Sat 7:15am–8:15pm. Also at 49 bd de Grenelle, 7e (Mᵒ Dupleix; Tues–Sun 7:15am–8:15pm). Bakes to ancient and secret family recipes, but there is always a line.

Poujauran, 20 rue Jean-Nicot, 7ᵉ. Mᵒ Latour-Maubourg. Mon–Sat 8am–8:30pm; closed Aug. The shop has its original painted glass panels and serves exquisite nut, olive, and raisin bread.

Charcuterie

Divay, 50 rue du Faubourg-St-Denis, 10ᵉ. Mᵒ Château-d'Eau. Tues–Sat 7:30am–1pm & 4–7:30pm, Sun 7:30am–1pm. *Foie gras, choucroute, saucisson,* and such.

Aux Ducs de Gascogne, 4 rue du Marché-St-Honoré, 1ᵉʳ. Mᵒ Pyramides. There are farther branches at 112 bd Haussmann, 8ᵉ (Mᵒ St-Augustin), and 29 rue des Martyrs, 9ᵉ (Mᵒ Notre-Dame-de-Lorette). Opening hours are Mon–Sat 10am–7pm; closed Aug. An excellent chain with numerous southwestern products like preserved fruits in Armagnac, *foie gras,* conserves, hams, and all the rest.

Goldenberg's, 7 rue des Rosiers, 4ᵉ. Mº St-Paul. Sun–Fri 9am–midnight, Sat 9am–2am. Superlative Jewish deli and restaurant.

Labeyrie, 6 rue Montmartre, 1ᵉʳ. Mº Châtelet-Les Halles. Mon–Sat 7am–6pm. Specialist in products from the Landes region: Bayonne hams, goose and duck pâtés, conserves, etc.

Maison de la Truffe, 19 place de la Madeleine, 8ᵉ. Mº Madeleine. Mon–Sat 9am–8pm. Truffles, of course, and more from the Dordogne and Landes.

Cheese

Androuet, 41 rue d'Amsterdam, 8ᵉ. Mº Liège. Tues–Sat 10am–7pm. A huge selection including foreign cheeses.

Barthélémy, 51 rue de Grenelle, 7ᵉ. Mº Bac. Tues–Sat 8:30am–1pm & 4–7:30pm, closed Aug. Purveyors of cheeses to the rich and powerful; orders can be faxed.

Carmès et Fils, 24 rue de Lévis, 17ᵉ. Mº Villiers. Tues–Sat 8:30am–1pm & 4–7:30pm, Sun 8:30am–1pm; closed Aug. In the rue de Lévis market.

Maison du Fromage, 62 rue de Sèvres, 6ᵉ. Mº Sèvres-Babylone. Tues–Sat 9am–2pm & 4–8:30pm, Sun 9am–2pm; closed Aug. Specializes in goat, sheep, and Alpine cheeses.

Chocolates and Pâtisserie

Debauve and Gallais, 30 rue des Saints-Pères, 6ᵉ. Mº St-Germain-des-Près. Tues–Sat 10am–7pm; closed Aug. A beautiful and ancient shop, specializing since time began in chocolate and elaborate sweets.

À la Mère de Famille, 35 rue du Faubourg-Montmartre, 9ᵉ. Mº Le Peletier. Mon–Sat 7:30am–1:30pm & 3–7pm. An eighteenth-century *confiserie* serving marrons glacés, prunes from Agen, dried fruit, sweets, chocolates, and even some wines.

La Petite Fabrique, 12 rue St-Sabin, 12ᵉ. Mº Bastille. Mon–Sat 10:30am–7:30pm. Beautiful homemade chocolates, especially the bars, nuts, nougat, and the dark stuff, all elegantly wrapped.

Ladurée, 16 rue Royale, 8ᵉ. Mº Madeleine. Mon–Sat 8:30am–7pm; closed Aug. Delectable and pricey patisseries.

Le Moule à Gâteaux—chain of good *pâtisseries.* Addresses include 17 rue St-Louis-en-L'Île, 4e (Mº Pont-Marie); 111 rue Mouffetard, 5e (Mº Censier-Daubenton); 17 rue Daguerre, 14e (Mº Denfert-Rochereau); 25 rue de Lévis, 17e (Mº Villiers); 53 rue des Abbesses, 18e (Mº Abbesses). All are open Tues–Sun 8am–7:30pm.

Herbs, Spices, and Dried Foods

Aux Cinq Continents, 75 rue de la Roquette, 11ᵉ. Mº Bastille. Mon–Fri 10am–1pm & 3:30–8pm, Sun 10am–1pm. Boxes, trays, sacks of rice, pulses, herbs, spices, tarama, vine leaves, etc, from the world over, plus alcohol.

Izraêl, 30 rue François-Miron, 4ᵉ. Mº St-Paul. Tues–Sat 9:30am–1pm & 2:30–7pm; closed Aug. Another cosmopolitan emporium of goodies from all around the globe.

Kitchen Equipment

Au Bain Marie, 10 rue Boissy d'Anglas, 8ᵉ. Mº Concorde. Mon–Sat 10am–7pm. An Aladdin's cave of things for the kitchen: pots, pans, books, antiques, napkins.

E Dehillerin, 51 rue Jean-Jacques-Rousseau, 1ᵉʳ. Mº Châtelet-Les Halles. Mon–Sat 8am–12:30pm & 2–6pm. Laid out like a traditional ironmonger's: no fancy displays, prices buried in catalogues, but good quality stock at reasonable prices.

MORA, 13 rue Montmartre, 1ᵉʳ. Mº Châtelet-Les Halles. Mon–Fri 8:30am–noon & 1:30–5:45pm, Sat 8:30am–noon. An exhaustive collection of tools of the trade for the top professionals.

Salmon, Seafood, and Caviar

In addition to the establishments below, more caviar, along with truffles, *foie gras*, etc are to be found at the lower end of rue Montmartre by the Forum des Halles in the 1er.

Comptoir de Saumon et Cie, 60 rue François-Miron, 4e. Mº St-Paul. Tues–Sat 10:30am–1:30pm & 3:30–8pm; closed second half of August. A Norwegian shop full of salmon and other fishy things from the North, at better prices than elsewhere.

Caviar Kaspia, 17 place de la Madeleine, 8e. Mº Madeleine. Mon–Sat 9:30am–12:30am. Blinis, smoked salmon, and Beluga caviar.

Petrossian, 18 bd de Latour-Maubourg, 7e. Mº Latour-Maubourg. Mon–Sat 9am–1pm & 2:30–7pm. More gilt-edge fish eggs.

Snails

La Maison de l'Escargot, 19 rue Fondary, 15e. Mº Dupleix. Tues–Sun 8:30am–8pm; closed mid-July to end of Aug. They even sauce them and re-shell them while you wait. Of interest to zoologists as well as gourmets. The establishment has a snails-only restaurant opposite at no. 70 (around 50F).

Vegetarian

Diététique DJ Fayer, 45 rue St-Paul, 4e. Mº St-Paul. Tues–Sat 9:30am–1pm & 3–7:30pm. Dietary, macrobiotic, vegetarian . . . one of the city's oldest specialists.

Wine

La Cave du Moulin Vieux, 4 rue de la Butte-aux-Cailles, 14e. Mº Place d'Italie. 10am–12:30pm & 3:30–7:30pm. Small but excellent selection of wines bought directly from *vignerons* which you can buy *en vrac* (from the barrel). The proprietors are very helpful and friendly.

Les Caves St-Antoine, 95 rue St-Antoine, 4e. Mº St-Paul. 10am–12:30pm & 3:30–7:30pm. Another small amicable outfit.

Les Caves de la Madeleine, Cité Berryer, 25 rue Royale, 8e. Mº Madeleine. Mon–Fri 9am–7pm, Sat 9am–1pm. A suit and tie and an upper-class English accent would go down well here. It may be expensive but is definitely one of the best-stocked cellars in Paris. If you want to discuss your purchase, the proprietor is Steven Spurrier of wine bar fame and three of his "boys" are English.

Michel Renaud, 12 place de la Nation, 12e. Mº Nation. Mon 2–8:30pm, Tues–Sat 9am–1pm & 2–8:30pm, Sun 9am–1pm. The other end of town and the other end of the scale from the Madeleine *caves*—superb value French and Spanish wines (drinkable bargains at under 10F a bottle), champagnes, and Armagnac.

Le Baron Rouge, 91 rue Théophile-Roussel, 12e. Mº Ledru-Rollin. Tues–Sat 10am–2pm & 5–9:30pm, Sun 10am–2pm. A good selection of dependable lower-range French wines.

Music

Records, cassettes, and **CDs** are not a particularly cheap buy in Paris, but you may come across selections that are novel enough to tempt you. Like the live music to be heard, Brazilian, Caribbean, Antillais, African, and Arab albums that would be **specialist** rarities elsewhere, as well as every kind of **jazz,** abound in Paris. Secondhand bargains can be scratchy treats—anything from the Red Army choir singing the *Marseillaise* to African drummers on skins made from spider ovaries. The **flea markets**, St-Ouen especially, and the *bouquinistes* along the Seine are good places to look for old records. In the **classical** department, the choice of interpretations is very generous and un-xenophobic. For all new and mainstream records, *FNAC* usually has the best prices.

Also listed below are a couple of **bookshops** selling sheet music, scores, and music literature, and some that sell instruments. Victor-Massé, Douai, Houdon, bd Clichy, and other streets in the Pigalle area are full of instrument and sound system shops (guitarists will enjoy a look in at 16 rue V-Massé, 9e—afternoons only—where François Guidon builds jazz guitars for the greats and the gifted amateurs). The *Cité de la Musique*, soon to open in La Villette, will have a whole range of shops devoted to all things musical.

Blue Moon, 7 rue Pierre-Sarrazin, 6e. Mº Odéon. Mon–Sat 11am–7pm. Exclusive imports from Jamaica and Africa: ska and reggae.

Bonus Beat, 1 rue Keller, 11e. Mº Bastille. Tues–Sat 1–9pm. Specialists in house, including acid, hip-hop, and rap.

Crocodisc, 42 rue des Écoles, 5e. Mº Maubert-Mutualité. Tues–Sat 11am–7pm. Folk, Oriental, Afro-Antillais, funk, reggae, soul, country, new, and secondhand. Some of the best prices in town.

Crocojazz, 64 rue de la Montagne-Ste-Geneviève, 5e. Mº Maubert-Mutualité. Tues–Sat 11am–1pm & 2–7pm. Jazz, blues, and gospel: mainly new imports.

Le Disque Arabe, 116bis bd de la Chapelle, 18e. Mº Porte-de-la-Chapelle. Mon–Sat 10am–8pm. Good range of Arab music. Also at 125 bd de Ménilmontant (Mº Ménilmontant; same hours).

Dream Store, 4 place St-Michel, 6e. Mº St-Michel. Mon 2–7pm, Tues–Sat 10am–7pm. Good discounted prices on blues, jazz, rock, folk, and classical.

FNAC Musique, 4 pl de la Bastille, 12e (next to opera house). Mº Bastille. Mon, Tues, Thurs & Sat 10am–8pm, Wed & Fri 10am–10pm. Extremely stylish shop in black, gray, and chrome with computerized catalogues, every variety of music, books, and a concert booking agency. New branch planned for 24 bd des Italiens, 9e, with a greater emphasis on rock and popular music (phone above on ☎43.42.04.04 to check). The other *FNAC* shops (see above under books) also sell music and hi-fi.

Hamm, 135 rue de Rennes, 6e. Mº St-Placide. Mon 11am–7pm, Tues–Sun 10am–7pm; closed Sun & Mon in July and Aug. The biggest general music shop in Paris, selling instruments new and old, sheet music, scores, manuals, librettos, etc.

Librairie Musicale de Paris, 68bis rue Réaumur, 3e. Mº Réaumur-Sébastopol. Mon–Sat 10am–12:45pm & 2–7pm. Huge selection of books, on music and of music: Baroque oratorios to heavy metal.

Lutherie Ancienne Moderne, 4 rue Elzévir, 3e. In an ancient house, the selling, buying, and restoration of stringed instruments goes on.

New Rose, 6 rue Pierre-Sarrazin, 6e. Mº Odéon. Mon–Sat 11am–7:15pm. Good for indies, including its own label—mainly new wave.

Parallèles, 47 rue St-Honoré, 1er. Mº Châtelet-Les Halles. A bookshop (see p.193), which also sells records.

Paris Musique, 10 bd St-Michel, 6e. Mº St-Michel. Mon–Sat 10am–8pm, Sun 2–9pm. Secondhand, bootlegs, and new—jazz, classical, and rock.

Virgin Megastore, 56–60 av des Champs-Élysées, 8e. Mº Franklin-Roosevelt. Mon–Thurs 10am–midnight, Fri & Sat 10am–1am, Sun 2pm–midnight. *Virgin* has trumped all Paris music shops. It's the biggest and the trendiest. Also concert booking agency.

Sport

La Boutique Gardien du But, 89ter rue de Charenton, 12e. Mo Gare-de-Lyon. *The Goalkeeper:* a very friendly, young shop specializing in French soccer. Stock includes shirts of every French club.

Le Ciel est à Tout le Monde, 10 rue Gay-Lussac, 5e. Mo Luxembourg. Also at 7 av Trudaine, 9e (Mo Anvers). Mon–Sat 10:30am–7pm; closed Mon in Aug. The best kite shop in Europe also sells frisbees, boomerangs, and anything else that flies without a motor.

La Gazelle, 47–49 bd Jean-Jaurès, Boulogne. Mo Boulogne-Jean-Jaurès. Tues–Sat 9am–noon & 2–7pm. Traditional bike enthusiasts' shop: hand-built racers, mountain bikes, etc.

La Haute Route, 33 bd Henri-IV, 4e. Mo Bastille. Mon 2–7pm, Tues–Sat 9:30am–1pm & 2–7pm. Skiing and mountaineering equipment principally: to rent, to buy—new and second-hand.

La Maison du Vélo, 8 rue de Belzunce, 10e. Mo Gare-du-Nord. Tues–Sat 10am–7pm. Specialists in mountain bikes, with some tourers and racers thrown in.

Marathon, 29 rue de Chazelles, 17e. Mo Monceau. Specialists in running shoes. The shop is owned by an experienced marathon runner.

La Roue d'Or, 7 rue de la Fidelité, 10e. Mo Gare-de-l'Est. Mon–Fri 9am–12:30pm & 2–6:30pm; closed Aug. Another cycling enthusiast.

Au Vieux Campeur, 2 rue de Latran, 5e. Mon 2–7pm, Tues–Fri 9:30am–8:30pm, Sat 9:30am–8pm. Maps, guides, climbing, hiking, ski gear, camping, and mountain bikes—plus kids' climbing wall. With its various mushrooming departments the shop now occupies half the *quartier*.

MARKETS

Several of the markets which we list below are described in the text of Chapters One, Two, and Three. These, however, are the details—and the highlights. The map on pages 204–205 shows the location of them all.

Flea Markets (*Marchés aux Puces*)

Paris has three main **flea markets**—of ancient descent—gathered about the old gates of the city. No longer the haunts of the flamboyant gypsies and petty crooks of literary tradition, they are nonetheless good entertainment and if you go early enough you might just find something special. Some of the food markets have spawned secondhand clothes and junk stalls, notably the place d'Aligre in the 12e and the place des Fêtes in the 20e.

Carreau du Temple, between rue Perrée and rue du Petit-Thouars, 3e. Mo Temple. Tues–Fri until noon, Sat & Sun until 1pm. Specializes in plain and practical new clothes.

Marché St-Pierre, 2 rue Charles-Nodier, 18e. Mo Anvers. Mon–Fri 9:30am–6:30pm. More clothes and fabrics in particular.

Porte de Montreuil, 20e. Mo Porte-de-Montreuil. Sat, Sun & Mon 7am–7pm. Best of the flea markets for secondhand clothes—cheapest on Mondays when leftovers from the weekend are sold off.

Porte de Vanves, 14e (av Georges-Lafenestre/av Marc-Sangnier). Mo Porte-de-Vanves. Sat & Sun 7am–7pm. The obvious choice for bric-à-brac searching, with amateurs spreading wares on the sidewalk as well as the professional dealers. See account on p.99.

St-Ouen/Porte de Clignancourt, 18ᵉ. Mᵒ Porte de Clignancourt. Sat, Sun & Mon 7:30am–7pm. The biggest and most touristy, with stalls selling clothes, shoes, records, books, and junk of all sorts as well as expensive antiques. Trading usually starts well before the official opening hour—as early as 5am. For a detailed description see p.119.

Flowers and Birds

Paris used to have innumerable **flower markets** around the streets, but today just the three listed below remain. Throughout the week, however, there's also the heavy concentration of plant and pet shops along the quai de la Megisserie between Pont Neuf and Pont au Change.

Place Lépine, Île de la Cité, 1ᵉʳ. Daily 8am–7:30pm. This flower market transforms into a (rather unappealing) **bird and pet** market every Sunday.

Place de la Madeleine, 8ᵉ. Tues–Sun 8am–7:30pm. Flowers and plants.

Place des Ternes, 8ᵉ. Tues–Sun 8am–7:30pm. Flowers and plants.

Books and Stamps

As well as the specialized book markets listed below, you should of course remember the wide array of books and all forms of printed material on sale from the **bouquinistes** who hook their green padlocked boxes onto the **riverside quais** of the Left Bank (see p.82).

Paris's **stamp market** is at the junction of avenues Marigny and Gabriel, on the north side of place Clemenceau in the 8ᵉ (Thurs, Sat, Sun & hols 10am–dusk).

Marché aux Cartes Postales Anciennes, Marché St-Germain, 3ter rue Mabillon, 6ᵉ. Mᵒ Mabillon. Wed & Thurs 9am–1pm & 4–6:30pm. Old postcards.

Marché du Livre Ancien et d'Occasion, Pavillon Baltard, Parc Georges-Brassens, rue Brancion, 15ᵉ. Mᵒ Porte de Vanves. Sat & Sun 9am onwards. Secondhand and antiquarian books (see p.99).

Marché aux Vieux Papiers de St-Mande, av de Paris. Mᵒ St-Mande. Wed 10am–6pm. Old books, postcards, and prints.

Food Markets

The **mainly-for-food street markets** provide one of the capital's more exacting tests of willpower. At the top end of the scale, there are the Satanic arrays in **rue de Lévis** in the 17ᵉ and **rue Cler** in the 7ᵉ, both of which are more market street than street market, with their stalls mostly metamorphosed into permanent shops. More for ordinary mortals, the real street markets include a tempting scattering in the **Left Bank—rue de Buci** (the most photographed) near St-Germain-des-Prés, **rue Mouffetard**, **place Maubert**, and **place Monge**. Bigger ones at **Montparnasse in bd Edgar-Quintet** and opposite Val-de-Grâce in **bd Port-Royal**, the biggest in **rue de la Convention** in the 15ᵉ.

For a different feel—and more unfamiliar goods—it's well worth taking a look at the Mediterranean/Oriental displays in **bd de Belleville** and **rue d'Aligre**.

MARKETS

FLEA MARKETS:
A. Puces St-Ouen
   (Porte de Clignancourt)
B. Belleville: Places des Fêtes
C. Carreau du Temple
D. Porte de Montreuil
E. Place d'Aligre
F. Porte de Vanves

SPECIALIST MARKETS:
G. Place des Ternes (flowers)
H. Stamp Market
 I. Place de la Madeleine (flowers)
J. Quai de la Mégosseroe (plants & pets)
K. Place Lépine (flowers)
L. Seine Quais (books)
M. Marché aux Livres (books)

STREET MARKETS:
1. Rue de Lévis
2. Rue Cler
3. Convention
4. Edgar Quinet
5. Raspail
6. St-Germain
7. Buci
8. Garnes
9. Mouffetard
10. Monge
11. Port Royal
12. Montorgueil
13. Enfants-Rouges
14. Porte St-Martin
15. Sécretan
16. Place des Fêtes

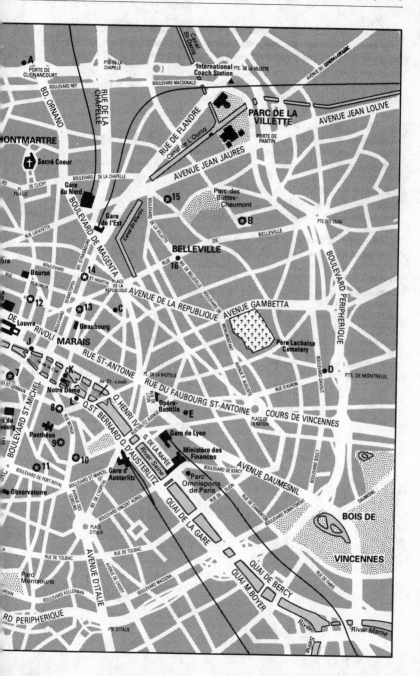

Markets usually **start between 7am and 8am** and tail off mid-afternoon. The **covered markets** have specific opening hours, which are given below along with details of locations and days of operation.

Place d'Aligre , 12ᵉ. Mᵒ Ledru-Rollin. Tues–Sat.

Belleville, bd de Belleville, 20ᵉ. Mᵒ Belleville/Ménilmontant. Tues & Fri.

Buci, rue de Buci and rue de Seine, 6ᵉ. Mᵒ Mabillon. Tues–Sun.

Carmes, place Maubert, 5ᵉ. Mᵒ Maubert-Murualité. Tues, Thurs & Sat.

Rue Cler, 7ᵉ. Mᵒ École-Militaire. Tues–Sat.

Convention, rue de la Convention, 15ᵉ. Mᵒ Convention. Tues, Thurs & Sun.

Edgar-Quinet, bd Edgar-Quinet, 14ᵉ. Mᵒ Edgar-Quinet. Wed & Sat.

Enfants-Rouges, 39 rue de Bretagne, 3ᵉ. Mᵒ Filles-du-Calvaire. Tues–Sat 8am–1pm & 4–7:30pm, Sun 8am–1pm.

Rue de Lévis, 17ᵉ. Mᵒ Villiers. Tues–Sun.

Monge, place Monge, 5ᵉ. Mᵒ Monge. Wed, Fri & Sun.

Montorgueil, rue Montorgueil and rue Montmartre, 1ᵉʳ. Mᵒ Châtelet-Les Halles/Sentier. Daily.

Mouffetard, rue Mouffetard, 5ᵉ. Mᵒ Censier-Daubenton. Daily.

Porte-St-Martin, rue du Château-d'Eau, 10ᵉ. Mᵒ Château-d'Eau. Tues–Sat 8am–1pm & 4–7:30pm, Sun 8am–1pm.

Port-Royal, bd Port-Royal, near Val-de-Grâce, 5ᵉ. Mᵒ Porte-Royale. Tues, Thurs & Sat.

Raspail, bd Raspail, between rue du Cherche-Midi and rue de Rennes, 6ᵉ. Mᵒ Rennes. Tues & Fri.

Secrétan, av Secrétan/rue Riquet, 19ᵉ. Mᵒ Bolivar. Tues–Sat 8am–1pm & 4–7:30pm, Sun 8am–1pm.

Saint-Germain, rue Mabillon, 6ᵉ. Mᵒ Mabillon. Tues–Sat 8am–1pm & 4–7:30pm, Sun 8am–1pm.

Tang Frères, 48 av d'Ivry, 13ᵉ. Mᵒ Tolbiac. Tues–Sun 9am–7:30pm. Not really a market, but a vast emporium of all things Oriental, where speaking French will not help you discover the nature and uses of what you see before you. In the same yard there is also a Far Eastern flower shop.

Ternes, rue Lemercier, 17ᵉ. Mᵒ Ternes. Tues–Sat 8am–1pm & 4–7:30pm, Sun 8am–1pm.

CHAPTER EIGHT

DRINKING AND EATING

The French never separate the major pleasures of **food and drink**, and with tens of thousands of establishments specializing in various combinations of the two, your choice of a meal, a snack, a glass of wine, or a cup of coffee could be overwhelming. The different **restaurants, wine bars, cafés**, and so forth are listed here under the same subheadings as are used to divide Chapters One to Three. For each area, they have been arranged in three price categories in alphabetical order, and you'll find cross references for **ethnic, vegetarian**, and **late-night** possibilities at the end of the chapter. For a **general introduction** to the business and some assistance with vocabulary and how to go about getting what you want, turn to the "Food and Drink" section of *Basics* (p.13).

Cafés

Cafés are all over the place: big ones, small ones, scruffy ones, stylish ones, snobby ones, arty ones. Crossroads and intersections are where they chiefly like to congregate, often side by side with the look-alike brasseries.

The most enjoyable are often ordinary, local places, but there are particular areas which café-lizards head for. **Boulevards Montparnasse** and **St-Germain** on the Left Bank are favored ones. There you'll find the *Select, Coupole, Closerie des Lilas, Deux Magots*, and *Flore*—the erstwhile hangouts of Apollinaire, Picasso, Hemingway, Sartre, de Beauvoir, and most other literary–intellectual figures of the last six decades. Most of them are still frequented by the big, though not yet legendary, names in the Parisian world of art and letters, cinema, politics, and thought, as well as by their hangers-on and other lesser mortals.

The location of other lively **Left Bank café concentrations** is determined by the geography of the university. Art students from the Beaux Arts school patronize the old-time *La Palette* on the corner of rue Jacques-Callot. Science students gravitate toward the cafés in rue Linné by the Jardin des Plantes. The Humanities gather in the place de la Sorbonne and rue Soufflot. And all the world—especially non-Parisians—finds its way to the place St-André-des-Arts and the downhill end of bd St-Michel.

The **Bastille** is another good area to tour—now livelier than ever as the new Opéra and rocketing property values bring headlong development. The same is true of **Les Halles**, though the latter's trade is principally among transient out-of-towners up for the bright lights. The much-publicized *Café Costes* and its rival, the *Café Beaubourg*, are here, Meccas of the self-conscious and committed trendies (*branchés*—plugged in—as they're called in French).

All the main squares and boulevards have cafés spreading out onto the sidewalks, which are always more expensive than those a little removed from the thoroughfares. Addresses in the more upmarket or touristy *arrondissements* set **prices** soaring. The Champs-Élysées and rue de Rivoli, for instance, are best avoided, at double or triple the price of a Belleville, Villette, or lower 14e café.

Champs-Élysées

Le Fouquet's, 99 av des Champs-Élysées, 8e. Mº George-V. 9–2am. A long-established and expensive watering-hole for aging stars, rich Lebanese, and anyone else who has anything to hide behind dark glasses.

Virgin Megastore Café, 52 av des Champs-Élysées, 8e. Mº Franklin-Roosevelt. Daily 10am–8pm. As popular as the new store; coffee and snacks, or meals for around 150F.

The Passages and Right Bank Commerce

Le Bar de l'Entracte, on the corner of rue Montpensier and rue Beaujolais, 1er. Mº Palais-Royal–Musée-du-Louvre. Tues–Sat 10am–2am. Theater people, bankers, and journalists come for quick snacks of *gratin de pomme de terre* and Auvergnat ham, in this almost traffic-free spot. Fills up to bursting during the intervals at the *Palais-Royal* theater just down the road.

La Chope du Croissant, corner of rue du Croissant and rue Montmartre, 2e. Mº Montmartre. On July 31, 1914 the Socialist leader Jean Jaurès was assassinated here for his antiwar activities. The table he was sitting at still remains.

Café de la Comédie, 153 rue Rivoli, 1er. Mº Palais-Royal–Musée-du-Louvre. Tues–Sun 10am–midnight. Small café opposite the Comédie Française, with a mirror painted with theatrical scenes at the back.

Le Grand Café, 40 bd des Capucines, 9e. Mº Opéra. A favorite all-nighter.

Café de la Paix, 12 bd des Capucines, 9e. Mº Opéra. Open until 2am. On place de l'Opéra, it is decorated in the sumptuous, vulgar Imperial style perfected by Garnier, architect of the Opéra. It has a fast restaurant as well, *Relais Capucines*. The prices are certainly not the cheapest around.

Les Halles to Beaubourg

Café Beaubourg, 43 rue St-Merri, 4e. Mº Rambuteau. Until 2am. Post-modernist clone of the *Café Costes*. It's expensive and the service is sour. It shares its rival's bathroom fetish.

Le Cochon à l'Oreille, 15 rue Montmartre, 1er. Mº Châtelet-Les Halles/Étienne-Marcel. Mon–Sat only. This classic little café with raffeta chairs outside and pictures in ceramic tiles inside opens at 4am for the local fishmongers and meat traders.

Le Comptoir, 14 rue Vauvilliers, 1er. Mº Châtelet-Les Halles/Louvre-Rivoli. An ancient bistro turned fashionable café, serving *tapas* and other snacks.

Café Costes, 4 rue Berger, 1er. Mº Châtelet-Les Halles. Tedious, overpriced, shallow, and ugly. The design of the bathrooms is original but has failed to take account of the effect water smears have on glass.

Le Petit Marcel, 63 rue Rambuteau, 3e. Mº Rambuteau. Mon–Sat, until 2am. Speckled tabletops, mirrors and Art Nouveau tiles, cracked and faded ceiling, and about eight square meters of drinking space. Friendly barman and "local" atmosphere.

La Pointe St-Eustache, 1 rue Montorgueil, 1er. Mº Les Halles. Alongside the church of St-Eustache, it has the advantage of being just an ordinary café-brasserie on the edge of the Les Halles hype.

The Marais and Île St-Louis

Ma Bourgogne, 19 place des Vosges, 3e. Mº St-Paul. A quiet and agreeable stopover on the corner of the square—with decent meals too.

L'Oiseau Bariolé, 16 rue Ste-Croix-de-la-Bretonnerie, 4e. Mo Hôtel-de-Ville. Open until 2am. Small and friendly, surreal paintings on glass, full of Americans. *Plats du jour,* salads, Breton cider, omelettes.

Au Petit Fer à Cheval, 30 rue Vieille-du-Temple, 4e. Mo St-Paul. Noon–1am. Small classic friendly café with *plats du jour* for 50–65F.

Le Taxi Jaune, 13 rue Chapon, 3e. Mo Arts-et-Métiers. Mon–Sat until 2am. An ordinary café, made special by the odd poster, good taped rock and new wave music, food until 11:30pm, and the occasional concert.

Le Temps des Cérises, 31 rue de la Cerisaie, 4e. Mo Bastille. It is hard to say what it is so appealing about this café, with its dirty yellow décor, old posters, and prints of *vieux Paris,* save that the *patronne* knows most of the clientele, who are young, relaxed, and not the dreaded *branchés.* There's a cheap *menu fixe* at lunchtime.

Trocadéro to Les Invalides

Au Bon Accueil, 15 rue Babylone, 7e. Mo Sèvres-Babylone. A cosy characterful old-timer, right next door to a good lunchtime restaurant, *Au Babylone.*

Kléber, place du Trocadéro, 16e. Mo Trocadéro. Open until dawn. Good for cinematic views of the Eiffel Tower catching the first light or morning mist filling the valley of the Seine.

Quartier Latin

Café de Cluny, corner of bd St-Michel and bd St-Germain, 5e. Mo St-Michel. Open until 2am. Very crowded, but a convenient meeting place. Go upstairs for some peace and quiet.

La Chope, place de la Contrescarpe, 5e. Mo Monge. Hemingway was a regular and Juliette Greco and George Brassens used to sing here. Now swamped by tourists in summer but perfect for sunny winter days.

Café Notre-Dame, corner of quai St-Michel and rue St-Jacques, 5e. Mo St-Michel. With a view right across to the cathedral. Lenin used to drink here.

La Périgordine, corner of quai des Grands-Augustins and place St-Michel, 5e. Mo St-Michel. A classic cane-chaired corner café, big and busy.

Polly Magoo, 11 rue St-Jacques, 5e. Mo St-Michel/Maubert-Mutualité. A scruffy all-nighter frequented by chess addicts.

St-Germain

Le Bonaparte, corner rue Bonaparte and place St-Germain. Mo St-Germain-des-Prés. Meeting place for the *quartier*'s intellectuals, quieter and less touristy than *Deux Magots* or *Flore.*

Café de la Mairie, place St-Sulpice, 6e. Mo St-Sulpice. A peaceful, pleasant, youthful café on the sunny north side of the square.

Les Deux Magots, 170 bd St-Germain, 6e. Mo St-Germain-des-Prés. Open until 2am; closed Aug. Right on the corner of place St-Germain-des-Prés, it too owes its reputation to the *intellos* of the Left Bank, past and present. In summertime it picks up foreigners seeking the exact location of the spirit of French culture, and street musicians galore play to the packed terrace.

Le Flore, 172 bd St-Germain, 6e. Mo St-Germain-des-Prés. Open until 2am; closed July. The great rival and immediate neighbor of *Deux Magots*, with a very similar clientele.

Le Mandarin, 148 bd St-Germain, 6e. Mo Mabillon. Berthillon ices.

Le Mazet, 6 rue St-André-des-Arts, 6e. Mo Odéon. 10am–2am; Fri and Sat until 3:30am; closed Sun. A well-known hangout for street musicians (with a lock-up for their instruments) and heavy drinkers. What about a *bière brûlée* for an evil concoction—it's flambéed with gin.

Au Petit Suisse, place Claudel, 6e. Mo Luxembourg. An attractive small café on the corner of rue de Médicis by some excellent antiquarian bookshops.

Sam Kearney's, rue Princesse, 6e. Mo Mabillon. An American café-bar.

Montparnasse to the Cité Universitaire

Le Boulevard, 73 bd du Montparnasse, 6ᵉ. Mᵒ Montparnasse. Gorgeous, grotesque ices and cheaper than the neighbors.

Le Chien Qui Fume, 19 bd du Montparnasse, 14ᵉ. Mᵒ Duroc/Falguière. Named after a real dog, it's an old and ordinary café—a refuge from its tourist-haunted famous neighbors.

La Coupole, 102 bd de Montparnasse, 14ᵉ. Mᵒ Montparnasse. Open until 2am; closed Aug. Still the haunt of the chic and successful. Café, bar, and restaurant—dancing, too, in the afternoons and evenings.

Le Dôme, 108 bd du Montparnasse, 6ᵉ. Mᵒ Vavin. Tues–Sun until 1am. Its reputation is the same as the above, but it has become more of a restaurant than café nowadays. Drinks only on the terrace.

La Rotonde, 105 bd du Montparnasse, 6ᵉ. Mᵒ Vavin. Another of the Montparnasse grand old names, with the names of the departed famous on the menu: Lenin, Trotsky, etc.

Le Select, 99 bd du Montparnasse, 6ᵉ. Mᵒ Vavin. Open until 3am. The least spoiled of the Montparnasse cafés and more of a traditional café than the rest.

Montmartre and the 9ᵉ

Le Pigalle, 22 bd de Clichy, 9ᵉ. Mᵒ Pigalle. 24hr bar, brasserie, and *tabac*. A classic, complete with 1950s decor. Closed at the time of writing, but keep an eye out for its reopening.

Canal St-Martin and La Villette

Café de la Ville, Parc de la Villette, between the Grande Salle and the Zenith, 19ᵉ. Mᵒ Porte-de-Pantin/Corentin-Cariou. Open in summer only. In one of the Tschumi follies with interior design by Starck.

Bastille to Vincennes

Le Clown, 114 rue Amelot, 11ᵉ. Mᵒ Filles-du-Calvaire. Rendezvous for professional circus artistes.

Iguana, corner of rue de la Roquette and rue Daval, 11ᵉ. Mᵒ Bastille. Mon–Sat 10am–midnight. A place to be seen in. Colonial fans and trellises, brushed bronze bar counter, and clientele reading récherché art reviews.

Café de L'Industrie, 16 rue St-Sébastien, 11ᵉ. Mᵒ Bastille/Bréguet-Sabin. Mon–Sat 9am–2am. Rugs on the floor around solid old wooden tables, miscellaneous objects on the walls, and a young unpretentious crowd enjoying the lack of chrome, minimalism, or Philippe Starck. One of the best Bastille addresses. *Plats du jour* from 35–40F.

Le Petit Lappe, 20 rue de Lappe, 11ᵉ. Mᵒ Bastille. A simple café with a beautifully painted exterior, opposite the *Chapelle des Lombards*.

Bars

Though cafés are called *bars* or *cafés* without distinction, some drinking places are definitely more **bar-ish**, with cocktails, music, and sometimes a transatlantic, gay, or starlet flavor. All of them serve coffee though, as well as food.

Champs-Élysées

Hôtel Crillon, 10 place de la Concorde, 8ᵉ. Mᵒ Concorde. Noon–2am. Very classy surroundings where English rock stars in Paris are likely to drink after their gigs.

The Passages and Right Bank Commerce

La Champsmeslé, 4 rue Chabanais, 2ᵉ. Mᵒ Pyramides. Mon–Sat 6pm–2am. A lesbian bar with some gay men, and a back room reserved for women; not very friendly to outsiders. Cocktails, picture/photo exhibitions, and Thurs night cabaret.

Harry's New York Bar, 5 rue Daunou, 2ᵉ. Mᵒ Opéra. 10:30am–4am. A cramped little place, frequented by Fitzgerald and Hemingway in their time, and now by lots of posthumous groupies and upper-class twits.

Tigh Johnny, 55 rue Montmartre, 2ᵉ. Mᵒ Sentier. Daily 4pm–1:30am, last orders 12:30am. A mostly Irish clientele at this bar that serves a reasonably priced Guinness and sometimes has impromptu Celtic bands.

Les Halles to Beaubourg

Broad Café, 13 rue de la Ferronnerie, 1ᵉʳ. Mᵒ Châtelet-Les Halles. 5pm–3am. Cocktails, snacks; a favorite gay pickup place.

Conways, 73 rue St-Denis, 10ᵉ. Mᵒ Châtelet-Les Halles. Open until 1am. A New York-style bar with photos of boxers and gyms on the walls and transatlantic food in the restaurant. Sunday brunch. A relaxed, friendly atmosphere without being stuffy or dull. An oasis in the Les Halles neighborhood. Reasonable prices without being cheap.

The James Joyce, 5 rue du Jour, 1ᵉʳ. Mᵒ Châtelet-Les Halles. Noon–3:30pm & 7pm–1am. This might be authentic Irish paraphernalia—*Freeman's Journal* and pics of Dublin on the wall, but on the edge of Les Halles it's a bit pretentious. Jazz some weekend evenings.

The Marais and Île St-Louis

Bar Hôtel Central, 33 rue Vieille-du-Temple, 4ᵉ. Mᵒ St-Paul. Noon–2am. One of the most popular gay bars in the Marais; women excluded.

Le Duplex, 25 rue Michel-le-Comte, 3ᵉ. Mᵒ Rambuteau. 8pm–2am. Young gay bar with an arty and friendly atmosphere.

La Perla, 23 rue du Pont-Louis-Philippe, 4ᵉ. Mᵒ St-Paul. Noon–2am. Mexican specialties in a spacious trendy corner café. The tequila cocktails are good (average price 48F); there are snacks from 14 to 27F, and meals too, though these are best avoided.

Le Swing, 42 rue Vieille-du-Temple, 4ᵉ. Mᵒ Hôtel-de-Ville. Noon–2am. Gays and heteros. Newspapers to read and early rock 'n' roll in the background.

Quartier Latin

Le Crocodile, 6 rue Royer-Collard, 5ᵉ. Mᵒ Luxembourg. Mon–Sat 10:30am–2am; closed Aug. Small, cosy, old-fashioned bar, where a stooped old proprietor fixes cocktails to the sounds of the Kinks and the Beatles.

Le Piano Vache, 8 rue Laplace, 5ᵉ. Mᵒ Cardinal-Lemoine. Long-established student bar with canned music and relaxed atmosphere.

Montparnasse to the Cité Universitaire

Ciel de Paris, Tour Montparnasse, 33 av du Maine, 15ᵉ. Mᵒ Montparnasse. Noon–2am. Popular with tourists, the bar has a tremendous view over the western part of the city and into the setting sun. Better to go to the bar than take the tour—no charge for the elevator.

La Closerie des Lilas, 171 bd du Montparnasse, 6ᵉ. Mᵒ Port-Royal. Noon–2am. A classy, arty, fashionable bar with good cocktails. No bum's paradise—it's pricey. The tables are name-plated after celebrated habitués, and there's a pianist in residence.

Parc Monceau to Batignolles

L'Endroit, 67 place Félix-Lobligeois, 17ᵉ. Mᵒ Batignolles/Brochant. Noon–2am. An upscale late-night bar serving the local trendies.

Montmartre and the 9^e

Le Dépanneur, 27 rue Fontaine, 9e. M^o Pigalle. A relaxed and fashionable all-night bar in black and chrome. Tequila the specialty. Just off place Pigalle.

Canal St-Martin and La Villette

L'Opus, 167 quai de Valmy, 10e. M^o Château-Landon. 7:30pm–2am. A stylish modern-chintzy atmosphere in a barn-like space used by British officers in World War I as their mess. Listen to live classical music (from 10pm) while you sip your cocktails—or dine, in the rather expensive restaurant. Drinks 65–80F average, plus 50F surcharge for the music.

Belleville, Ménilmontant , and Charonne

La Mouette Rieuse, 66 place de la Réunion, Charonne, 20e. M^o Alexandre-Dumas/Maraîchers. Tues–Sat 7pm–midnight, Sun 11am–2pm. A cooperative outfit, battling against encroaching gentrification. Live music (jazz and *chansons*) on Fri and Sat nights; various cultural activities the rest of the week.

Bastille to Vincennes

Café de la Plage, 59 rue de Charonne, 11e. M^o Bastille. Tues–Sun 10am–2pm. A multi-racial clientele and as many women as men in this low-ceilinged, friendly, and youthful bar above a jazz club.

Tapas Nocturnes, rue de Lappe, 11e. M^o Bastille. Mon–Sat 7:30pm–2am. *Tapas* bar (25–35F a go); small, packed, and high-spirited. Occasional live flamenco.

The 13^e

Le Merle Moqueur, 11 rue des Buttes-aux-Cailles, 13^e. M^o Place-d'Italie/Corvisart. 9pm–1am. A workers' co-op bar with jazz on Monday night and popular French songs every Thursday.

Wine bars

Revitalized, ironically, by the English, **wine bars** are once more an established part of the Paris scene. The attention to wine is serious and scholarly and the object of the exercise is to make really good or interesting wines available by selling them by the glass. Traditional *bistrots à vin* like *Le Rubis* and *La Tartine* cater to everyone, but the newer generation have a distinctly yuppieish flavor, and are not cheap—nor is the food they serve.

Champs-Élysées

Ma Bourgogne, 133 bd Haussmann, 8e. M^o Miromesnil. Mon–Fri 7am–8:30pm; closed Aug. Not the establishment on the place des Vosges, but a place for pre-siesta glasses of Burgundy; *plats du jour* as well, and meals at 150–200F.

L'Écluse, rue Mondétour, 1er (M^o Étienne-Marcel) and 64 rue François-1er, 8e (M^o Franklin-Roosevelt). See under "Quartier Latin."

The Passages and Right Bank Commerce

Blue Fox, Cité Berryer, 25 rue Royale, 8e. M^o Madeleine. Mon–Sat noon–2:30pm & 7–11pm. Run by English wine expert, Mark Williamson. The food and wines are excellent, and not too expensive.

Aux Bons Crus, 7 rue des Petits-Champs, 1ᵉʳ. Mᵒ Palais-Royal. Closed Sun. A relaxed workaday place, with blue collars and white, and much cheaper than the neighbors. A *plat*, cheese, and a quarter of Bordeaux comes to about 60F.

Cave Drouot, 8 rue Drouot, 9ᵉ. Mᵒ Richelieu-Drouot. Mon–Fri 7:30am–9pm, closed July 14–Sept 1. By the Drouot auction rooms. Excellent wines and a reasonably priced restaurant with *plats du jour* and *charcuterie*.

L'Écluse, 15 place de la Madeleine, 8ᵉ. Mᵒ Madeleine. See under "Quartier Latin."

Le Rubis, 10 rue du Marché-St-Honoré, 1ᵉʳ. Mᵒ Pyramides. Mon–Fri 7am–10pm; closed three weeks in Aug. One of the oldest wine bars, it enjoys a reputation for having among the best wines, plus excellent snacks and *plats du jour*. Very crowded. Glasses of wine for 4F, 5F, and 7.50F.

Willi's, 13 rue des Petits-Champs, 1ᵉʳ. Mᵒ Bourse. Mon–Sat 11am–10pm. The standard bearer of the new generation of wine bars, with a rich selection of wines, especially from the Rhône region.

The Marais and Île St-Louis

Le Coude-Fou, 12 rue du Bourg-Tibourg, 4ᵉ. Mᵒ Hôtel-de-Ville. Noon–4pm & 6pm–midnight; closed Sun lunchtime. Good Côtes-du-Rhône and Loire wines with *charcuterie* and cheese to match in a very relaxed setting. Around 100F for a full feed.

Le Rouge Gorge, 8 rue St-Paul, 4ᵉ. Mᵒ St-Paul. Tues–Sun noon–11:30pm. The young and enthusiastic clientele sip familiar wines and snack on *chèvre chaud*, smoked salmon salad, or tuck into more substantial fare (*plats du jour* around 60F) while listening to jazz or classical music.

La Tartine, 24 rue de Rivoli, 4ᵉ. Mᵒ St-Paul. Wed–Mon until 10pm, closed Aug and Christmas. The genuine 1900s article, which still cuts across class boundaries in its clientele. A good selection of affordable wines, plus excellent cheese, and *saucisson* with *pain de campagne*.

Île de la Cité

Taverne Henri IV, 13 place du Pont-Neuf, 1ᵉʳ. Mᵒ Pont-Neuf. Mon–Fri 11:30am–9:30pm; closed Aug 15–Sept 15. Another of the good older bars, opposite Henri IV's statue. Yves Montand used to come here when Simone Signoret lived in the adjacent place Dauphine. Full of lawyers from the Palais de Justice. The food is good but a bit pricey.

Quartier Latin

L'Écluse, 15 quai des Grands-Augustins, 6ᵉ. Mᵒ St-Michel. Noon–2am. Forerunner of the new generation of wine bars, with decor and atmosphere in authentic traditional style—just lacking the crude types to spit on the floor. Small and intimate: a very agreeable place to sit and sip. It has spawned several offspring; see under **Champs-Élysées**.

Café de la Nouvelle Mairie, 19 rue des Fossés-St-Jacques, 5ᵉ. Mᵒ Luxembourg. Mon–Fri 10:30am–8:30pm. A small, sawdusted bar in a quiet Latin Quarter street close to the Panthéon, with good wines, *saucisson*, and sandwiches. Three or four tables on the street. A perfect place for serious discussion.

St-Germain

Chez Georges, 11 rue des Canettes, 6ᵉ. Mᵒ Mabillon. Tues–Sat noon–2am; closed July 14–Aug 15. Another attractive place in the spit-on-the-floor mode, with its old shop front still intact in a narrow leaning street off place St-Sulpice.

Le Petit Bacchus, 13 rue du Cherche-Midi, 6ᵉ. Mᵒ Sèvres-Babylone. Tues–Sat 9am–7:30pm. Elegant, quiet situation for elegant, quiet people. Another Steven Spurrier outfit with a changing selection of wines and snacks. Opposite *Poilâne*'s bakery.

Au Sauvignon, 80 rue des Sts-Pères, 6e. Mo Sèvres-Babylone. Mon–Sat 9am–10pm; closed holidays and Aug. Very small and decorated with German shepherd posters and murals. A relaxed, unpretentious atmosphere.

Montparnasse to the Cité Universitaire

Au Père Tranquille, 30 av du Maine, 15e. Mo Montparnasse/Denfert-Rochereau. Tues–Sat 10am–8pm. Pleasant little place close to the Montparnasse tower.

Le Rallye, 6 rue Daguerre, 14e. Mo Denfert-Rochereau. Tues–Sat until 8pm; closed Aug. A good place to recover from the catacombs or Montparnasse cemetery. The patron offers a bottle for tasting; gulping the lot would be considered bad form. Good cheese and *saucisson*.

Montmartre and the 9e

Aux Négociants, 27 rue Lambert, 18e. Mo Château-Rouge. Mon–Fri 11:30am–9pm, closed July 15–Aug 15. Cheap good wines and snacks. Popular with journalists and not at all snobby.

Belleville, Ménilmontant, and Charonne

Le Baratin, 3 rue Jouye-Rouve, 20e. Mo Pyrénées. Wed 11am–9pm, Thurs–Sat 11am–1:30am, Sun 5pm–1:30am. A good mix of people and a friendly atmosphere. Good wines from Cahors and *plats du jour* from 25 to 50F.

Les Envierges, 11 rue des Envierges, 20e. Mo Pyrénées. Tues–Sun noon–8:30pm (late opening Wed & Thurs); closed Aug. Another new wine bar in this changing *quartier*, with a wide choice of middle-range wines.

Bastille to Vincennes

Le Baron Rouge, 1 rue Théophile-Roussel, 12e. Mo Ledru-Rollin. Tues–Sat 9:30am–1:30pm & 4:30–7:30pm, Sun 9:30am–1:30pm. A crowded and popular bar, serving cheese, *charcuterie*, and wines to taste—but will leave you enough money for bargains at the nearby place d'Aligre market.

Jacques-Mélac, 42 rue Léon-Frot, 11e. Mo Charonne. Mon, Wed & Fri 9am–7:30pm, Tues & Thurs 9am–10pm. Some way off the beaten track but a highly reputed bar whose *patron* even makes his own wine—the solitary vine winds around the front of the shop (harvest celebrations at the start of Sept). You can buy others' wines at very reasonable prices by the bottle or the glass, accompanied by Auvergnat specialties (*plats du jour* 40–50F).

Beer Cellars and Pubs

As their names and decor suggest, **beer-drinking** establishments owe their inspiration chiefly to their cross-Channel cousins and the Belgians. Most stock at least some British draft beers and a host of international bottles.

Champs-Élysées

Pub Winston Churchill, 5 rue Presbourg, 16e. Mo Étoile. Mon–Fri 9am–2am, Sat & Sun 9am–2:30am. Edwardian brass and paneling. Hot English-style breakfast, and roast beef and Yorkshire pudding at lunchtime—reasonable prices.

The Passages and Right Bank Commerce

Kitty O'Shea's, 10 rue des Capucines, 2e. Mo Opéra. Noon–1:30am. An Irish pub with excellent Guinness and Smithwicks and a favorite haunt of the Irish expats. The *John Jameson* restaurant upstairs serves high-quality Gaelic fare, including seafood flown in from Galway, at a price.

La Micro-Brasserie, 106 rue de Richelieu, 2ᵉ. Mᵒ Richelieu-Drouot. A fashionable newcomer, brewing its own beer on the spot.

Les Halles to Beaubourg

Gambrinus, 62 rue des Lombards, 1ᵉʳ. Mᵒ Châtelet-Les Halles. The king of beer: his hall installed in the crypt of a thirteenth-century chapel, with thirty ceramic fonts for pulling draft beers.

Guinness Tavern, 31 rue des Lombards, 1ᵉʳ. Mᵒ Châtelet. 6pm–4am. Music (piano and live folk, jazz, rock Mon, Tues, and Thurs) and Guinness.

Le Sous-Bock, 49 rue St-Honoré, 1ᵉʳ. Mᵒ Châtelet-Les Halles. 11am–5am. Hundreds of bottled beers and simple, inexpensive food. Frequented by night owls.

Au Trappiste, 4 rue St-Denis, 1ᵉʳ. Mᵒ Châtelet. Daily until 2am. Numerous draft beers include *Jenlain*, France's best known *bière de garde*, Belgian *Blanche Riva*, and *Kriek* from the *Mort Subite* (Sudden Death!) brewery—plus mussels and *frites* and various *tartines*.

Quartier Latin

Académie de la Bière, 88bis bd Port-Royal, 5ᵉ. Mᵒ Port-Royal. Mon–Sat until 2am; closed Aug. More than 120 beers from 22 countries. Also food—good mussels and fries, Belgian cheeses, and *charcuterie*.

La Gueuze, 19 rue Soufflot, 5ᵉ. Mᵒ Luxembourg. Comfy surroundings—lots of wood and stained glass. Kitchen specials are *pierrades*: dishes cooked on hot stones. Numerous bottles and several drafts, including cherry beer. Close to the university with lots of student habitués.

Mayflower Pub, 49 rue Descartes, 5ᵉ. Mᵒ Cardinal-Lemoine. All-nighter. International beers and loads of students.

Le Violon Dingue, 46 rue de la Montagne-Ste-Geneviève, 5ᵉ. Mᵒ Maubert-Mutualité. Daily 6pm–1am. A long dark student pub, noisy and friendly.

St-Germain

Bedford Arms, 17 rue Princesse, 6ᵉ. Mᵒ Mabillon. Tues–Sun until dawn. Darts and Guinness.

London Tavern, 3 rue du Sabot, 6ᵉ. Mᵒ St-Sulpice. Mon–Fri 10am–2am, Sat 10am–3am, Sun 6pm–2am. Watney's and Heineken, plus piano (Sun from 6pm, other days from 9pm).

La Pinte, 13 carrefour de l'Odéon, 6ᵉ. Mᵒ Odéon. 6:30pm–2am; closed Aug. Boozy and crowded, with piano and jazz.

Pub Saint-Germain, 17 rue de l'Ancienne-Comédie, 6ᵉ. Mᵒ Odéon. Open 24 hours. 21 draft beers and hundreds of bottles. Huge and crowded. Hot food at mealtimes, otherwise cold snacks. For a taste of "real" French beer try *ch'ti* (*patois* for northerner), a *bière de garde* from the Pas-de-Calais.

La Taverne de Nesle, 32 rue Dauphine, 6ᵉ. Mᵒ Odéon. 7am–5am. Vast selection of beers. Full of local nightbirds.

Twickenham, 70 rue des Sts-Pères, 6ᵉ. Mᵒ Sèvres-Babylone. Mon–Fri noon–2am, Sat 7pm–2am. Rugby and publishers' pub. Lots of wood and brass.

Parc Monceau to Batignolles

Bar Belge, 75 av de St-Ouen, 17ᵉ. Mᵒ Guy-Môquet. Tues–Sun 3:30pm–1am. Belgian beers.

Montmartre and the 9ᵉ

Au Général La Fayette, 52 rue La Fayette, 9ᵉ. Mᵒ Le Peletier. Mon–Fri 11am–2am, Sat 3pm–2am. A dozen drafts, including Guinness, and many more bottled. Belle Époque decor, mixed clientele, and very pleasant, quiet atmosphere. *Plats du jour*.

Salons de Thé, Snacks, and Ice Cream

Tea room does not quite conjure up the chic and refined atmosphere of the *salons de thé* that crop up both in established *BCBG* haunts and wherever a new part of town has been gentrified. The oldest is *Angélina's* with its marble cake-frosting exterior. More relaxed and exotic are *La Pagode* and *La Mosquée*, in the two least Parisian buildings of the city. **Snacks and light midday meals** are easy to find and unlikely to disappoint.

As well as the places listed below, there are all the cafés and *brasseries* to choose from. The classier cafés sell confections of cake and **ice cream**, as do the drugstores; the supreme sorbet experience is *Berthillon's* in the Île St-Louis.

Salons de Thé

The Passages and Right Bank Commerce

Angélina, 226 rue de Rivoli, 1er. Mº Tuileries. l0am–7pm; closed Aug. A long-established gilded cage for the well-coiffed to sip the best hot chocolate in town, plus *pâtisseries* and other desserts of the same high quality.

Daru, 19 rue Daru, 8e. Mº Ternes. A Russian tea room next to the Russian Orthodox church, with Danish salmon, caviar, and vodka on the menu . . . so not cheap. See also under "Restaurants."

A Priori Thé, 35–37 galerie Vivienne, 2e. Mº Bourse. Mon–Sat noon–7pm. Sip your tea outside but under cover in the watery lighting of a *passage*. Snacks are 100F.

Ladurée, 16 rue Royale, 9e. Mº Madeleine. Mon–Sat 8:30am–7pm; closed Aug. For the dainty and affected. Best to buy the chocolate and coffee macaroons to take out.

Pantera, 2 impasse Gomboust, 1er. Mº Pyramides. Chocolate blow-out in modernist salon.

Rose Thé, 91 rue St-Honoré, 1er. Mº Louvre-Rivoli. Mon–Fri noon–7pm. Calm and tranquil, in a courtyard of antique shops and faded bric-à-brac. Teas, milkshakes, *tartes aux fruits*, salads, etc. Reasonable prices.

The Marais and Île St-Louis

Berthillon, 31 rue St-Louis-en-l'Île, 4e. Mº Pont-Marie. Wed–Sun l0am–8pm. The very best ice creams and sorbets made and sold here on the Île St-Louis. Also available at *Lady Jane* and *Le Flore-en-l'Île*, both on quai d'Orléans, as well as four other island sites listed on the door.

Dattes et Noix, 4 rue du Parc-Royal, 3e. Mº Chemin-Vert. Noon–midnight. Not the most appealing of decors, but good cakes and salads.

L'Ébouillanté, 6 rue des Barres, 4e. Mº Hôtel-de-Ville. Tues–Sun noon–9pm. Very small, with reasonable prices and simple fare—chocolate cakes and *pâtisseries* as well as savory dishes. *Plats du jour* for 60F.

Eurydice, 10 place des Vosges, 4e. Mº Chemin-Vert. Winter Wed–Sun noon–7pm, summer Wed–Sun noon–10pm. On the east side of the *place* and desirable for the summer tables under the arcade, if you can get one. Cakes, salads, meat dishes, and seafood, with an Eastern European touch, and the possibility of accompanying vodka. Brunch on Sunday.

Le Loir dans la Théière, rue des Rosiers, 4e. Mº St-Paul. Tues–Sat noon–7pm, Sun 11am–7pm; closed Aug. The name means dormouse in the teapot and the best thing about the place is the mural of the Mad Hatter's tea party. Sunday brunch, midday *tartes* and omelettes, fruit teas of every description, and cakes all day.

Marais Plus, 20 rue des Francs-Bourgeois, 3e. Mº St-Paul. Mon–Sat 9am–midnight, Sun 9am–7pm. Breakfasts, brunches (80F), and teas and cakes all day long at this pleasant arty bookshop.

Île de la Cité

Fanny Tea, 20 place Dauphine, 1er. Mº Pont-Neuf. Tues–Sun 1–7:30pm; closed Aug. Snacks as well as tea and cakes. Very small. In summer, tables outside in the beautiful seventeenth-century *place*.

Trocadéro to Les Invalides

La Pagode, 57bis rue de Babylone, 7e. Mº François-Xavier/Sèvres-Babylone. 4–10pm. A real-life pagoda (see p.248)—one of the most beautiful buildings in Paris in which to have tea. Tables in the Chinese garden in summer.

Quartier Latin

Café de la Mosquée, 39 rue Geoffroy-St-Hilaire, 5e. Mº Monge. Mon–Thurs, Sat & Sun 10am–9:30pm. In fine weather you can drink mint tea beside a fountain and assorted fig trees in the courtyard of this Paris mosque—a delightful haven of calm. The interior of the *salon*, on the other hand, is a little gloomy.

La Fourmi Ailée, 8 rue du Fouarre, 5e. Mº Maubert-Mutualité. Noon–7pm; closed Tues. Simple, light fare—including brunch on Saturdays and Sundays—in this feminist bookshop-cum–*salon-de-thé*.

La Passion du Fruit, 71 quai de la Tournelle, 5e. Mº Maubert-Mutualité. Mon & Tues 6pm–1:30am, Wed–Sun noon–1:30am. An attractive *terrasse* opposite Notre-Dame with a few tables in the garden, serving juice, sorbets, salads, milkshakes, and teas—all of fruit.

St-Germain

À la Cour de Rohan, 59–61 rue St-André-des-Arts, 6e. Mº Odéon. Tues–Fri noon–7pm, Sat & Sun 3–7pm; closed Aug. A genteel, chintzy drawing-room atmosphere in a picturesque eighteenth-century alley. Cakes, *tartes*, poached eggs, etc. Close to bd St-Germain.

Montparnasse to the Cité Universitaire

JeThéMe, 4 rue d'Alleray, 15e. Mº Vaugirard. Mon–Sat noon–7pm; closed Aug. Obnoxious name and nostalgic decor, and the usual sweets, salads, and snacks, served at reasonable prices and with rare grace. Also sells coffee, tea, and chocolate to take away.

The 15e

La Passion du Fruit, 31 av de Suffren, 7e. Mº Bir-Hakeim. Mon & Tues 6pm–1:30am, Wed–Sun noon–1:30am. See entry under "Quartier Latin" above.

Auteuil and Passy

Le Coquelin Aîné, 67 rue de Passy, 16e. Mº Muette. Tues–Sat 9am–6:30pm. Right on place Passy, meeting place of gilded youth and age. Excellent salads, *tartes,* cakes. Not for paupers.

Bastille to Vincennes

Shake, 16 rue Daval, 11e. Mº Bastille. Mon–Fri 12:30–5:30pm & 8pm–midnight, Sat 7pm–2am. Salads, quiches, cakes, and Périgordian *plats du jour* for under 80F in a tiny, stylish salon.

Snacks

Paris does, of course, have its quota of outlets for the fast-food chains, which unfortunately are pretty much the same as those to be found in any of the western world's major cities. There are also innumerable **street sandwich stands**, especially around the big stations, which are probably the best bet of all for a cheap and filling snack.

In this section we've aimed to cover the more unusual and hard-to-find options for those times when you don't want—or can't face—a full meal. Eastern European delicatessens and sandwich bars make a particularly welcome change.

We've also included **late-night** establishments, such as the three **drugstores** around av des Champs-Élysées and bd St-Germain, and those which cater to all ranges simultaneously, where one person can eat something substantial while a companion just sips at a coffee.

Champs-Élysées

La Boutique à Sandwiches, 12 rue du Colisée, 8e. Mº St-Philippe-du-Roule. Mon–Sat 11:45am–11:30pm; closed Aug. The best sandwiches in town, though certainly not the cheapest. If you go for something like the *maison*'s specialty—the German shepherd *pickelfleish*—you're getting a whole meal, and paying for it.

Fauchon, 24 place de la Madeleine, 8e. Mº Madeleine. Mon–Sat 9:45am–6:30pm. Narrow and uncomfortable counters at which to gobble wonderful *pâtisseries*, *plats du jour*, and sandwiches—at a price.

Lord Sandwich, 276 rue St-Honoré, 1er (Mº Palais-Royal) and 134 rue du Faubourg-St-Honoré, 8e (Mº St-Philippe-du-Roule). Mon–Fri 11am–5pm. A New York-style choice of bread and filler combinations.

Drugstore Elysées, 133 av des Champs-Élysées, 8e. Mº Étoile. 9am–2am. **Drugstore Matignon**, 1 av Matignon, 8e. Mº Franklin-Roosevelt. 10am–2am. All day salads, sandwiches, *plats du jour,* full-blown meals, and huge, delicious desserts are available from the three drugstores (see "St-Germain" below), along with books, newspapers, tobacco, and a multitude of fripperies. Prices are reasonable and the food much better than the decor would suggest.

The Passages and Right Bank Commerce

Jarmolinska, 272 rue St-Honoré, 1er. Mº Palais-Royal. Mon–Sat 9am–7pm. Polish delicatessen—to eat here or take out: blinis, potato pancakes, herring in dill and cream, borscht. 72F menu.

Lina's Sandwiches, 50 rue Étienne-Marcel, 2e. Mº Étienne-Marcel. Mon–Sat 9:30am–5pm. A spacious, stylish place for your designer shopping break. A sandwich, glass of wine, and cake will set you back 65F.

Monoprix, 23 av de l'Opéra, 1er. Mº Pyramides. Top-floor self-service; crowded, but good value. Open evenings as well.

Osaka, 1 impasse Gomboust, 1er. Mº Pyramides. Mon–Sat 11am–7:30pm, Sun noon–7pm. Japanese snacks, and groceries. Lunchtime menus 100F and 150F.

La Patata, 25 bd des Italiens, 2e. Mº Opéra. Daily 11am–midnight. Dedicated to the baked potato with all the possible fillings. From 40F to 80F.

Ramen-Tei, 163 rue St-Honoré, 1er. Mº Palais-Royal. 11:30am–1am. Japanese snack bar without a trace of Frenchness. Pay before you eat and take pot-luck-style.

Les Halles to Beaubourg

Self-Service de la Samaritaine, 2 quai du Louvre, 1ᵉʳ. Mᵒ Pont-Neuf. Mon–Sat 11:30am–6pm. In the number two *magasin*. More for the view over the Seine than the food.

The Marais and Île St-Louis

La Crêpe St-Louis, 86 rue St-Louis-en-l'Île, 4ᵉ. Mᵒ Pont-Marie. Noon–midnight. Breton *crêpes* with cider.

Sacha Finkelsztajn and **Florence Finkelsztajn**, 27 rue des Rosiers, 4ᵉ (Wed–Sun 9:30am–1:30pm & 3–7:30pm) and 24 rue des Écouffes, 4ᵉ (Mon & Thurs–Sun 9:30am–1:30pm & 3–7:30pm). Both Mᵒ St-Paul. Gorgeous East European breads, cakes, gefilte fish, eggplant purée, tarama, blinis, and borscht to take away.

Fous du Sandwich, 27 rue St-Louis-en-l'Île, 4ᵉ. Mᵒ Pont-Marie/Sully-Morland. Tues–Fri 11:30am–3pm, Sat & Sun 11am–6pm. Soup, sandwich, and dessert for 49F in a new outfit that hasn't quite got its act together. Lovely hazelnut bread; best fillers are Bayonne ham or smoked salmon.

Fleur de Lotus, 2 rue du Roi-de-Sicile, 4ᵉ. Mᵒ St-Paul. 10am–9pm. Cheap Vietnamese dishes, heated up while you wait—to take out or eat on the premises.

Restaurant du Musée Picasso, Hôtel Salé, 5 rue de Thorigny, 3ᵉ. Mᵒ St-Sébastien. l0am–5:15pm. You may have to wait for a table. Reasonable prices and reliable lunchtime fare.

L'Oiseau Bariolé, 16 rue Ste-Croix-de-la-Bretonnerie, 4ᵉ. Mᵒ Hôtel-de-Ville. Open until 2am. Small and friendly, surreal paintings on glass, full of Americans. *Plats du jour,* salads, Breton cider, omelettes.

Le Roi Falafel, 34 rue des Rosiers, 4ᵉ. Mᵒ St-Paul. Take-out Egyptian. 17F and 20F snacks.

Yahalom, 22–24 rue des Rosiers, 4ᵉ. Mᵒ St-Paul. Kosher falafel 20F; *plats du jour* 40F.

Trocadéro to Les Invalides

Palais de Tokyo, 13 av du Président-Wilson, 16ᵉ. Mᵒ Iéna/Alma-Marceau. Good food in the museum snack bar.

St-Germain

Drugstore Saint-Germain, 149 bd St-Germain, 6ᵉ. Mᵒ St-Germain-des-Prés. l0am–2am. See "Champs-Élysées" above.

La Table d'Italie, 69 rue de Seine, 6ᵉ. Mᵒ Mabillon/St-Germain-des-Prés. Italian pasta, snacks, etc at the counter, plus a grocery selling pasta and other Italian delicatessen products.

Canal St-Martin and La Villette

Le Croixement, Parc de la Villette, 19e, by the bridge over the canal. Mᵒ Porte-de-Pantin/Corentin-Cariou. Noon–8pm. Not the best food, but a great place to rest on a sunny day. *Plats du jour* for 60F.

Belleville, Ménilmontant, and Charonne

Le Pavillon du Lac, Parc des Buttes-Chaumont, 19ᵉ. Mᵒ Buttes-Chaumont. Noon–3pm. Tranquil, if rather overpriced, stopoff for steak tartare and fries and Berthillon ice creams. 250F for a full meal.

Aux Rendez-vous des Amis, 10 av Père-Lachaise, 20ᵉ. Mᵒ Gambetta. Mon–Sat noon–2:30pm; closed last two weeks of Aug. Unprepossessing surroundings for satisfying post-cemetery munchies; around 80F.

LATE-NIGHT PARIS

CAFÉS AND SNACKS

Le Cochon à l'Oreille, 15 rue Montmartre, 1er. *Opens* at 4am. p.208.

Drugstore Élysées, 133 av des Champs-Élysées, 8e (p.218); **Drugstore Matignon**, 1 av Matignon, 8e (p.218); and **Drugstore Saint-Germain**, 149 bd St-Germain, 6e (p.219). All until 2am.

Le Grand Café, 40 bd des Capucines, 9e. All-nighter. p.208.

Kléber, place du Trocadéro, 16e. Until dawn. p.209.

Le Mazet, 6 rue St-André-des-Arts, 6e. Until 2am; Fri & Sat until 3:30am. p.209.

Le Pigalle, 22 bd de Clichy, 9e. 24-hr. p.210.

Polly Magoo, 11 rue St-Jacques, 5e. All-nighter. p.209.

Le Select, 99 bd du Montparnasse, 6e. Until 3am. p.210.

BARS AND BEER CELLARS

Bedford Arms, 17 rue Princesse, 6e. Until dawn. p.215.

Broad Café, 13 rue de la Ferronnerie, 1er. Until 3am. p.211.

Le Dépanneur, 27 rue Fontaine, 9e. All-nighter. p.212.

Guinness Tavern, 31 rue des Lombards, 1er. Until 4am. p.215.

Harry's New York Bar, 5 rue Daunou, 2e. Until 4am. p.211.

Mayflower Pub, 49 rue Descartes, 5e. All-nighter. p.215.

Pub Saint-Germain, 17 rue de l'Ancienne-Comédie, 6e. 24-hr. p.215.

Le Sous-Bock, 49 rue St-Honoré, 1er. Until 5am. p.215.

La Taverne de Nesle, 32 rue Dauphine, 6e. Until 5am. p.215.

RESTAURANTS

Aux Artistes, 63 rue Falguière, 15e. Until 12:30am. p.227.

Baalbeck, 16 rue Mazagran, 10e. Until 1am. p.223.

Bistro de la Gare, 73 Champs-Élysées, 8e (p.222) and several other locations. Until 1am.

Le Bistro Romain, 122 Champs-Élysées, 8e (p.222) and several other locations. Until 1am.

Bofinger, 3–7 rue de la Bastille, 3e. Until 1am. p.232.

Chez Maria, 16 rue du Maine, 14e. Until 1am. p.228.

La Coupole, 102 bd du Montparnasse, 14e. Until 2am. p.228.

La Criée, 31 bd Bonne-Nouvelle, 2e (p.222) and 54 bd Montparnasse, 15e (p.227). Until 1am.

Aux Deux Saules, 91 rue St-Denis, 1er. Until 1am. p.223.

Flo, 7 cours des Petites-Écuries, 10e. Until 1:30am. p.230.

Hippopotamus, 1 bd des Capucines, 9e (p.223) and 12 av du Maine, 15e (p.228). Until 1am.

Julien, 16 rue du Faubourg-St-Denis, 10e. Until 1:30am. p.230.

Lipp, 151 bd St-Germain, 6e. Until 2am. p.227.

Le Muniche, 27 rue de Buci, 6e. Until 3am. p.226.

L'Oustalou/Gladines, 30 rue des Cinq-Diamants, 13e. Until 2am. p.232.

Le Petit Zinc, 25 rue de Buci, 6e. Until 3am. p.227.

Le Petit Prince, 12 rue Lanneau, 5e. Until 12:30am. p.225.

Au Pied de Cochon, 6 rue Coquillière, 1er. 24-hr. p.223.

Terminus Nord, 23 rue de Dunkerque, 10e. Until 12:30am. p.230.

Thaï Yen, 5 rue de Belleville, 20e. Until 1am. p.231.

Le Vaudeville, 29 rue Vivienne, 2e. Until 2am. p.223.

Restaurants and Brasseries

Contrary to what you might expect, eating out in Paris need not be an enormous extravagance. There are numerous **fixed price menus under 80F** providing simple but well-cooked fare, and at *Casa Miguel* you can still have a whole meal for a mere 5F. Paying a little **more than 80F** gives you the chance to try out a greater range of dishes and once **over 150F** you should be getting some serious gourmet satisfaction. Our classification into these three main categories is based on the cheapest fixed-price menu available, and doesn't include drink. If you choose from the *carte*, bear in mind that you may well boost the bill into the next price category.

Anyone in possession of an International Student Card or *Carte Jeune* (for which you have to be under 26) is eligible to apply for tickets for the **university restaurants** under the direction of *CROUS de Paris*. A list of addresses, which includes numerous cafeterias and brasseries, is obtainable from their offices at 39 av Georges-Bernanos, 5e (Mº Port-Royal). The meal tickets, however, come in units of ten and are only obtainable from and valid for each particular restaurant—worthwhile if you are not bothered by the restrictions, for you get a square meal for little more than 20F.

The latest **time** at which you can walk into a restaurant and order is usually about 9:30 or 10pm, though once ensconced, of course, you can often remain well into the night. Hours are stated in the listings below and unusually, or specifically, **late-night** places are included in the box opposite.

Ethnic restaurants, of which there are a great many in Paris, are listed below in their price category with full details, and also in the box on p.233 according to the origin of the food they serve. They do not have the prominence in French dining habits of, for example, Indian cuisine in British, because of the strength of France's own cooking traditions, and they should not be regarded as intrinsically cheap alternatives to the home-grown product. Usually they're not.

PARIS FOR VEGETARIANS

Vegetarians will find that French chefs have not yet caught on to the idea that tasty and nutritious meals do not need to be based on meat or fish. Consequently the chances of finding vegetarian main dishes on the menus of regular restaurants are not good. No need to despair, however. Even if you don't eat fish, it is possible to make up a vegetarian meal from the menu of even the most meat-oriented *brasserie* by choosing dishes from among the appetizers (*crudités*, for example, are nearly always available) and soups, or by asking for an omelette.

As far as specifically **vegetarian restaurants** are concerned, the list is brief. All the establishments listed below are reviewed in the pages which follow.

Aquarius, 54 rue Ste-Croix-de-la-Bretonnerie, 4e. p.224.

Country Life, 6 rue Daunou, 2e. p.222.

Au Grain de Folie, 24 rue La Vieuville, 18e. p.229.

La Macrobiothèque, 17 rue de Savoie, 6e. p.226.

Piccolo Teatro, 6 rue des Écouffes, 4e. p.224.

Restaurant Végétarien Lacour, 3 rue Villedo, 1er. p.223.

Tripti-Kulai, 2 place du Marché Ste-Cathérine, 4e. p.224.

Champs-Élysées

UNDER 80F

Bistro de la Gare, 73 av des Champs-Élysées, 8e. ☎43.59.67.83. Mo Franklin-Roosevelt. Daily noon–3pm & 6pm–1am. The food is okay, if somewhat plastic. Good for a quick and convenient meal, not for quiet intimacy. Menus at 57F and 74F; *carte* up to 150F. Part of a chain.

Le Bistro Romain, 122 av des Champs-Élysées, 8e. ☎43.59.93.31. Mo George-V. Also place Victor-Hugo, 16e. ☎45.00.65.94. Mo Victor-Hugo. Daily until 1am. A slightly more upmarket, vaguely Italian, version of the *Bistro de la Gare*. Menus at 57F and 74F. Okay for a quick meal, but not recommended for intimate chats.

Chez Mélanie, 27 rue du Colisée, 8e. ☎43.59.42.76. Mo Franklin-Roosevelt. Mon–Fri 11:30am–3pm. Simple French classic details in a tiny resto on the third floor.

UNDER 150F

Le Daru, 19 rue Daru, 8e. ☎42.27.23.60. Mo Courcelles. Mon–Fri noon–11pm. This is where aged aristocratic Russian exiles come after services at the Orthodox Russian church opposite. Beef Stroganoff, borscht, pickled herring, shashliks for around 150F.

La Fermette Marbeuf, 5 rue Marbeuf, 8e. ☎47.20.63.53. Mo Franklin-Roosevelt. Daily until 11:30pm. Try to eat in the tiled and domed inner room, where the original Art Nouveau decor has been restored. A rather well-heeled, bourgeois clientele, foreign as well as French, but not stuffy. A good inclusive menu for 150F; *carte* up to 300F.

Pépita, 21 rue Bayard, 8e. ☎47.23.58.49. Mo Franklin-Roosevelt. Mon–Fri noon–3pm & 7:30–10pm. The zinc counter and trestle tables are usually packed at lunchtime, but meals are served at great speed and lingering over coffee is not encouraged. A rare cheapie for this area—around 100F.

OVER 150F

Fouquet's, 99 av des Champs-Élysées, 8e. ☎47.23.70.60. Mo George-V. Daily until midnight. A classic name, like *Maxim's*, and outrageous for the price—350F—but you're paying for the past and present clientele, the *terrasse* on the Champs-Élysées, and the snobbishness of the whole affair.

Prince de Galles, 33 av George V, 8e. ☎47.23.55.11. Mo George-V. Daily noon–2:30pm & 7–10:30pm. A choice of three entrées, three main courses, and three desserts in very classy surroundings for under 200F—so long as you only drink water.

Yakitori, 24 rue Marbeuf, 8e. ☎42.25.60.01. Mo Franklin-Roosevelt. Mon–Sat noon–2:15pm & 7–10:45pm. The most upmarket sushi bar of this chain—you may prefer the *Sushi Bar* next door which only serves raw fish. The standard *Yakitori* meal is lemon grass soup, sushi, and spiced grills. Around 200F.

The Passages and Right Bank Commerce

UNDER 80F

Le Bistro Romain, 9 bd des Italiens, 2e. ☎42.97.49.55. Mo Richelieu-Drouot. See under "Champs-Élysées."

Country Life, 6 rue Daunou, 2e. ☎42.97.48.51. Mo Opéra. Mon–Fri 11:30am–2:30pm only. Vegetarian soup, hors d'oeuvres, lasagne, and salad for under 60F. No alcohol, no smoking.

La Criée, 31 bd Bonne-Nouvelle, 2e. ☎42.33.32.99. Mo Strasbourg-St-Denis. Daily until 1am. Part of a good seafood and fish chain, with menus at 69F and 85F.

Drouot, 103 rue de Richelieu, 2e. ☎42.96.68.23. Mo Richelieu-Drouot. Daily noon–3pm & 6:30–10pm. Admirably cheap and good food, served at a frantic pace, in an Art Nouveau decor. Same management as the better-known *Chartier* in the 9e (see below).

Foujita, 45 rue St-Roch, 1er. ☎42.61.42.93. Mº Palais-Royal–Musée-du-Louvre. Mon–Sat noon–10pm. One of the cheaper but best Japanese restaurants as evidenced by the numbers of Japanese eating here. Quick and crowded; soup, sushis, rice, and tea for 60F.

L'Incroyable, 26 rue de Richelieu, 1er. ☎42.96.24.64. Mº Palais-Royal. Tues–Thurs lunchtime & 6:30–8:30pm, Sat & Mon lunchtime only; closed Sun & two weeks at Christmas. Hidden in a *passage*, this tiny restaurant serves decent meals for 45F at midday and 55F in the evening.

Restaurant Végétarien Lacour, 3 rue Villedo, 1er. ☎42.96.08.33. Mº Pyramides. Mon–Fri noon–3pm. Vegetarian lunches for under 50F.

UNDER 150F

Aux Crus de Bourgogne, 2 rue Bachaumont, 2e. ☎42.33.48.24. Mº Sentier. Good Burgundy *cuisine*, including lobster at reasonable prices.

Hippopotamus, 1 bd des Capucines, 9e. ☎47.42.75.70. Mº Opéra. 11:30am–3pm & 6:30pm–1am. A quick service chain for meat-eaters. Somewhat characterless, but the food is reasonable. There is a menu at 57F, but you really need to reckon on about 120F.

Restaurant Jhelum, 30 rue St-Marc, 2e. ☎42.96.99.43. Mº Richelieu-Drouot. Daily until 11:30pm. Indian and Pakistani food, with several vegetarian dishes—served behind a spectacularly wrought façade, done up like a Kashmiri houseboat. Menu at 93F (65F at lunchtime only); *carte* around 180F.

Le Vaudeville, 29 rue Vivienne, 2e. ☎42.33.39.31. Mº Bourse. Until 2am. A lively late-night *brasserie*—where it's often necessary to wait in line—with good food and an attractive marble-and-mosaic interior. Menu at 103F, without service.

Yakitori, 34 place du Marché-St-Honoré, 2e. ☎42.61.03.54. Mº Pyramides. Mon–Sat only. Crowded Japanese with fast service: menus at 72F, 89F, and 120F.

OVER 150F

Baalbeck, 16 rue Mazagran, 10e. ☎47.70.70.02. Mº Bonne-Nouvelle. Noon–3pm & 8pm–1am. Much liked by the moneyed refugees, a Lebanese restaurant with dozens of appetizers. For 400F you can have a representative selection for four, with *arak* to drink. Sticky Levantine/ Turkish cakes too. Very busy, so make a reservation or go early.

Le Grand Véfour, 17 rue de Beaujolais, 1er. ☎42.96.56.27. Mº Pyramides. Mon–Fri 12:30–2pm & 7:30–10pm, Sat 7:30–10pm. The carved wooden ceilings, frescoes, velvet hangings and late eighteenth-century chairs haven't changed since Napoléon brought Josephine here. The lunchtime menu for 305F is a cinch for the luxury cuisine served here. Go *à la carte* and the bill will top 700F.

Les Halles to Beaubourg

UNDER 80F

Bistro de la Gare, 30 rue St-Denis, 1er. Mº Châtelet-Les Halles. Daily noon–3pm & 6pm–1am. See under "Champs-Élysées."

Aux Deux Saules, 91 rue St-Denis, 1er. ☎42.36.46.57. Mº Châtelet-Les Halles. Daily until 1am. Cheap if unexciting fare. A leftover from the days of the market. The tilework representing same is the best feature.

Le Petit Ramoneur, 74 rue St-Denis, 1er. ☎42.36.39.24. Mº Châtelet-Les Halles. Mon–Fri until 9:30pm. Elbow-rubbing cheapie in good bistro tradition, with cheap wine that's better than table wine. Crowded, but a welcome and genuine relief in Les Halles.

OVER 150F

Au Pied de Cochon, 6 rue Coquillière, 1er. ☎42.36.11.75. Mº Châtelet-Les Halles. Open 24 hours. For extravagant middle-of-the-night pork chops and oysters. Top of the price range.

The Marais and Île St-Louis

UNDER 80F

Aquarius, 54 rue Ste-Croix-de-la-Bretonnerie, 4ᵉ. ☎48.87.48.71. Mᵒ St-Paul/Rambuteau. Mon–Sat noon–9:45pm. Austere vegetarian restaurant: no alcohol, no smoking.

Bistro du Marais, 15 rue Ste-Croix-de-la-Bretonnerie, 3ᵉ. Mᵒ St-Paul. A pleasant cheap local.

Piccolo Teatro, 6 rue des Écouffes, 4ᵉ. ☎42.72.17.79. Mᵒ St-Paul. Noon–3pm & 7:15–11pm. A vegetarian restaurant with *assiette végétarienne* at 58F; lunch menu at 49F, evening at 70F.

Le St-Regis, 92 rue St-Louis-en-l'Île, 4ᵉ. Mᵒ Pont-Marie. The one unpretentious brasserie on the Île St-Louis, with *plats du jour* for 58F.

Tripti-Kulai, 2 place du Marché Ste-Cathérine, 4ᵉ. Mᵒ St-Paul. Mon & Thurs noon–6pm; Tues, Wed, Fri & Sat noon–11pm (reservations only on Sat). *Salon de thé* in the afternoon. A friendly, accommodating vegetarian place, with organic fruit and vegetables; English spoken.

UNDER 150F

Goldenburg's, 7 rue des Rosiers, 4ᵉ. ☎48.87.20.16. Mᵒ St-Paul. Daily until 11pm. The best-known Jewish restaurant in the capital; its borscht, blinis, potato strudels, *zakovski,* and other central European dishes are a treat.

Le Gourmet de l'Île, 42 rue St-Louis-en-l'Île, 4ᵉ. ☎43.26.79.27. Mᵒ Pont-Marie. Wed–Sun noon–2pm & 7–10pm. A bargain four-course menu for 110F, including wonderful stuffed mussels.

Auberge de Jarente, 7 rue Jarente, 4ᵉ. ☎42.77.49.35. Mᵒ St-Paul. Tues–Sat noon–2:30pm & 6:30–10:30pm. A hospitable and friendly Basque restaurant, serving excellent *cassoulet*, hare stew, king prawns in whiskey, and *magret de canard*. 100–200F.

Le Ravaillac, 10 rue du Roi-de-Sicile, 4ᵉ. Mᵒ St-Paul. Mon 7–10:30pm, Tues–Sat noon–3pm & 7–10:30pm; closed Aug. A Polish restaurant whose specialties include meat *perushkis,* beef Stroganoff, and *choucroute*. Excellent quality for the price—around 100F.

OVER 150F

Anahi, 49 rue Volta, 3ᵉ. ☎48.87.88.24. Mᵒ Arts-et-Métiers. 7:30pm–midnight; closed Wed. A restaurant specializing in South American cuisine: *empanadas, cururu de camerao,* Argentinian grills.

Au Franc Pinot, 1 quai de Bourbon, 4ᵉ. ☎43.29.46.98. Mᵒ Pont-Marie. Tues–Sat until 11pm. *Nouvelle cuisine* and high-class wines at high prices, but still a bargain for this kind of cooking and for the seventeenth-century surroundings. Reserve well in advance.

La Petite Chaumière, 41 rue des Blancs-Manteaux, 4ᵉ. ☎42.72.13.90. Mᵒ Rambuteau. Mon–Sat until 10pm, Sun evenings only; closed Aug. Wonderful seafood dishes and other original recipes based on classic sauces, cooked by one of the best women chefs in Paris.

Trocadéro to Les Invalides

UNDER 80F

Au Babylone, 13 rue de Babylone, 7ᵉ. ☎45.48.72.13. Mᵒ Sèvres-Babylone. Mon–Sat lunchtime only; closed Aug. Lots of old-fashioned charm and a good menu at 75F.

Germaine, 30 rue Pierre-Leroux, 7ᵉ. ☎42.73.28.34. Mᵒ Vaneau. Mon–Fri lunchtime & 6:30–9pm, Sat lunchtime only; closed Aug. Very cheap and good—50F-ish—and consequently very popular and crowded.

UNDER 150F

L'Ami Jean, 27 rue Malar, 7ᵉ. 47.05.86.89. Mᵒ Latour-Maubourg. Mon–Sat lunchtime & 7–10:30pm. Nice ambience and good Basque food for around 130–150F.

Aux Délices de Széchuen, 40 av Duquesne, 7ᵉ. ☎43.06.22.55. Mᵒ St-François-Xavier. Tues–Sun until 10:30pm; closed Dec 23–31 & July 29–Aug 27. High quality and reasonably priced Chinese food served to the elegant inhabitants of an elegant *quartier*. A menu at 87F on weekdays; *carte* around 200F.

Escale de Saigon, 24 rue Bosquet, 7ᵉ. ☎45.51.60.14. Mᵒ École-Militaire. A small and inexpensive local Vietnamese.

Au Pied de Fouet, 45 rue de Babylone, 7ᵉ. Mon–Fri 2–4pm & 7–8:50pm, Sat 2–4pm; closed Aug. Good food and a great little place—little being the operative word: there are just four tables and no reservations. No good being shy about your French here.

Thoumieux, 79 rue St-Dominique, 7ᵉ. ☎47.05.49.75. Mᵒ Latour-Maubourg. Lunchtime & 7–11:30pm. A large and popular establishment in this rather elegant district, with a menu at 52F—otherwise you have to be careful to get away with less than 150F.

Quartier Latin

UNDER 80F

Le Baptiste, 11 rue des Boulangers, 5ᵉ. ☎43.25.57.24. Mᵒ Jussieu. Mon–Fri lunchtime & 7:30–10:30pm, Sat 7:30–10:30pm; closed last week in Dec. Noisy, friendly, and full of students. Menus under 60F.

La Criée, 15 rue Lagrange, 5ᵉ. ☎43.54.23.57. Mᵒ Maubert-Mutualité. See under "Passages and Right Bank Commerce."

Aux Savoyards, 14 rue des Boulangers, 5ᵉ. ☎46.33.53.78. Mᵒ Jussieu. Mon–Fri until 10:30pm, Sat lunchtime only; closed holidays and Aug. A delightfully friendly and wholesome place, but on the map and likely to be packed. 59F all included.

Bistro de la Sorbonne, 4 rue Toullier, 5ᵉ. ☎43.54.41.49. Mᵒ Luxembourg. Mon–Sat until 11pm. Help-yourself appetizers and salads, good ices and *crêpes flambées*. Copious portions. Crowded and attractive student ambience. 65F menu at lunchtime, including wine and service; 95F in the evening.

Tashi Delek, 4 rue des Fossés-St-Jacques, 5ᵉ. ☎43.26.55.5. Mᵒ Luxembourg. Lunchtime and until 10:30pm. An enjoyable Tibetan restaurant—run by refugees—where you can eat for as little as 50F, without wine.

La Vallée des Bambous, 35 rue Gay-Lussac, 5ᵉ. ☎43.54.99.47. Mᵒ Luxembourg. Open until 10:30pm; closed Tues & Aug. You usually have to wait in line for this popular Chinese restaurant. An excellent value menu at 48F all included, otherwise around 150F.

UNDER 150F

Le Jardin des Pâtes, 4 rue Lacépède, 5ᵉ. ☎43.31.50.71. Mᵒ Monge. Tues–Sun lunchtime & 7–10:30pm. A fresh and attractive pasta specialist—all homemade. Around 100F.

Le Liban à la Mouff, 18 rue Mouffetard, 5ᵉ. ☎47.07.30.72. Mᵒ Monge. A pleasant and unusually cheap Lebanese restaurant. 90–120F.

Perraudin, 157 rue St-Jacques, 5ᵉ. ☎46.33.15.75. Mᵒ Luxembourg. Mon 7:30–10:15pm, Tues–Fri lunchtime & 7:30–10:15pm, Sun lunchtime only. A well-known traditional bistro with a menu at 59F; *carte* around 100F.

Le Petit Prince, 12 rue Lanneau, 5ᵉ. ☎43.54.77.26. Mᵒ Maubert-Mutualité. Evenings only, until 12:30am. Good food in a restaurant full of Latin Quarter charm in one of the *quartier*'s oldest lanes. Menus at 72F and 98F.

Pizzeria Roma, 79 rue du Cardinal-Lemoine, 5ᵉ. Mᵒ Cardinal-Lemoine. An excellent, unpretentious Italian joint, right by the place de la Contrescarpe.

Restaurant A, 5 rue de Poissy, 5ᵉ. ☎46.33.85.54. Mᵒ Cardinal-Lemoine. Tues–Sun until 11pm. Good and unusual Chinese dishes. Menu at 98F; *carte* 200F plus.

Yakitori, 10 rue Boutebrie, 5ᵉ. ☎46.33.45.92. Mᵒ St-Michel. Mon–Sat only. See under "Passages and Right Bank Commerce."

OVER 150F

Brasserie Balzar, 49 rue des Écoles, 5ᵉ. ☎43.54.13.67. Mᵒ Maubert-Mutualité. Daily until 12:30am; closed Aug. A traditional literary-bourgeois *brasserie*, frequented by the intelligentsia of the Latin Quarter.

Sud-Ouest, 40 rue de la Montagne-Ste-Geneviève, 5ᵉ. ☎46.33.30.46. Mᵒ Maubert-Mutualité. Mon–Sat until 10:30pm; closed Aug. Serious and heavy eating: specializes in *cassoulet* and the cuisine of the southwest, with menus at 150F and 190F.

St-Germain

UNDER 80F

Restaurant des Arts, 73 rue de Seine, 6ᵉ. Mᵒ St-Germain-des-Prés. Mon–Thurs all day, Fri lunchtime only; closed Aug. Menu at 62F including service. A small, crowded, friendly place with simple, homey fare. Young and old, both well-heeled and not at all.

Restaurant des Beaux-Arts, 11 rue Bonaparte, 6ᵉ. ☎43.26.92.64. Mᵒ St-Germain-des-Prés. Daily lunchtime and evening until 11pm. The traditional hangout of the art students from the Beaux-Arts across the way. Menu at 60F including wine. The choice is wide, the portions generous, and the lines long in high season; the atmosphere is generally good, though the waitresses can get pretty irritable.

Le Bistro de la Gare, 1 rue du Four, 6ᵉ. ☎43.25.87.76. Mᵒ Mabillon. See under "Champs-Élysées."

La Macrobiothèque, 17 rue de Savoie, 6ᵉ. ☎43.25.04.96. Mᵒ St-Michel. Lunchtime and 7–10pm. A good macrobiotic restaurant with a wholesome pine-and-fern feel.

Orestias, 4 rue Grégoire-de-Tours, 6ᵉ. ☎43.54.62.01. Mᵒ Odéon. Mon–Sat lunchtime & evening until 11:30pm. A mixture of Greek and French cuisine. Good helpings and very cheap—with a menu at 42F.

Le Petit Mabillon, 6 rue Mabillon, 6ᵉ. ☎43.54.08.41. Mᵒ Mabillon. Mon evening until 11:30pm, Tues–Sat lunchtime & evening until 11:30pm; closed mid-Dec to mid-Jan. Decent and straightforward Italian menu for 72F.

Le Petit Vatel, 5 rue Lobineau, 6ᵉ. ☎43.54.28.49. Mᵒ Mabillon. Mon–Sat lunchtime and 7pm–midnight, Sun 7pm–midnight. A tiny, friendly place with good plain home-cooking, including a vegetarian *plat*—for around 60F.

UNDER 150F

L'Alsace à Paris, 9 place St-André-des-Arts, 6ᵉ. ☎43.26.21.48. Mᵒ St-Michel. A very busy *brasserie* right on the *place*, with menus at 99F and 140F—though you can eat more cheaply by being selective.

Le Katyouschka, 9 rue de l'Éperon, 6ᵉ. ☎43.54.47.02. Mᵒ Odéon. Tues–Fri all day until 10:30pm, Sat & Mon evenings only; closed three weeks in Aug. Taramasalata, caviar, blinis, salmon, borscht, and vodka—cheaper than at most White Russian places. Menus at 75F (lunchtime) and 120F.

La Maison de la Lozère, 4 rue Hautefeuille, 6ᵉ. ☎43.54.26.64. Mᵒ St-Michel. Tues–Sat until l0:30pm, Sun lunchtime only; closed Aug and the last week in Dec. A scrubbed-wood restaurant serving up the cuisine, cheeses, etc of the Lozère *département*. Menus at 79F (lunchtime only during the week), 99F, and 120F, including wine. Crowded with office workers at lunchtime.

Le Muniche, 27 rue de Buci, 6ᵉ. ☎46.33.62.09. Mᵒ Mabillon. Noon–3am. A crowded old-style *brasserie* specializing particularly in seafood, smack in the middle of the St-Germain night scene. Menu at 137F; *carte* 250F.

Le Petit Saint-Benoît, 4 rue Saint-Benoît, 6ᵉ. ☎42.60.27.92. Mᵒ St-Germain-des-Prés. Mon–Fri lunchtime & 7–l0pm. A simple, genuine, and very appealing local restaurant. Serves solid traditional fare in a brown-stained, aproned atmosphere—for about 90F.

Le Petit Zinc, 25 rue de Buci, 6ᵉ. ☎43.54.79.34. Mᵒ Mabillon. Noon–3am. Excellent traditional food, especially seafood, in the middle of the Buci street market. Menu at 137F; *carte* 250F.

Polidor, 41 rue Monsieur-le-Prince, 6ᵉ. ☎43.26.95.34. Mᵒ Odéon. Mon–Sat until 1am; Sun until 11pm. A traditional bistro, whose visitors' book, they say, boasts more of history's big names than all the glittering palaces put together. Not as cheap as it was in James Joyce's day but good food and great atmosphere. Lunches at 50F, otherwise 80–100F.

Village Bulgare, 8 rue de Nevers, 6ᵉ. ☎43.25.08.75. Mᵒ Odéon/Pont-Neuf. Try the Bulgarian specialty, *cirène au four* (baked sheep's milk cheese with vegetables), yogurt, and Gamza wine. Around 150F.

OVER 150F

Aux Charpentiers, 10 rue Mabillon, 6ᵉ. ☎43.26.30.05. Mᵒ Mabillon. Mon–Sat until 11:30pm, closed holidays. A friendly, old-fashioned place belonging to the *Compagnons des Charpentiers* (Carpenters' Guild), with appropriate decor of roof-trees and tie beams. Traditional *plats du jour* are their forte. Around 180F.

Drugstore Saint-Germain, 149 bd St-Germain, 6ᵉ. Until 2am. The best of the drugstores for food. Basics like *steack tartare* and *langoustines* done to a T.

Lipp, 151 bd St-Germain, 6ᵉ. ☎45.48.53.91. Mᵒ St-Germain-des-Prés. Until 2am; closed mid-July to mid-Aug. A 1900s *brasserie*, one of the best-known establishments on the Left Bank, haunt of the successful and famous. Rather more welcoming now that its sour old owner has died and been replaced by a niece. 180–200F.

Montparnasse to the Cité Universitaire

UNDER 80F

Aux Artistes, 63 rue Falguière, 15ᵉ. ☎43.22.05.39. Mᵒ Pasteur. Mon–Fri lunchtime & 7:15pm–12:30am, Sat 7:15pm–12:30am only. An old-time cheapie that has seen many a poor artist in its time. Still crowded and popular, serving a menu at 68F.

Le Berbère, 50 rue de Gergovie, 14ᵉ. ☎45.42.10.29. Mᵒ Pernety. Daily, lunchtime & evenings until 10pm. A very unprepossessing place decor-wise, but serves wholesome, unfussy, and cheap North African fare.

Le Biniou, 3 av du Général-Leclerc, 14ᵉ. ☎43.27.20.40. Mᵒ Denfert-Rochereau. Lunchtime & 6:45–10pm. A big variety of delicious *crêpes*.

Bistro de la Gare, 59 bd du Montparnasse, 6ᵉ. Mᵒ Montparnasse. Daily noon–3pm & 6pm–1am. See under "Champs-Élysées."

Bistro Romain, 103 bd du Montparnasse, 6ᵉ. ☎43.25.25.25. Mᵒ Vavin. See under "Champs-Élysées."

La Criée, 54 bd Montparnasse, 15ᵉ. ☎42.22.01.81. Mᵒ Montparnasse. See under "The Passages and Right Bank Commerce."

Au Rendez-vous des Camioneurs, 34 rue des Plantes, 14ᵉ. 45.40.43.36. Mᵒ Alésia. Mon–Fri lunchtime & 7–9:30pm; closed Aug. No truck drivers any more, but good food for around 80F. Wise to reserve.

Café-Restaurant à l'Observatoire, 63 av Denfert-Rochereau, 14ᵉ. Mᵒ Denfert-Rochereau. Mon–Sat only. A straightforward quick eating place with *steack frites* and the like at their most basic and best. Very crowded at lunchtime.

UNDER 150F

Bergamote, 1 rue Niepce, 14ᵉ. ☎43.22.79.47. Mᵒ Pernety. Tues–Sat lunchtime & evenings until 11pm; closed Aug. A small and *sympa* bistro-style restaurant, in a quiet ungentrified street off rue de l'Ouest. Only about ten tables; you need to reserve weekends. There's a 99F menu at lunchtime, 120 in the evening; *carte* around 160F.

Hippopotamus, 12 av du Maine, 15ᵉ. ☎45.48.59.35. Mᵒ Falguière. See under "The Passages and Right Bank Commerce."

Chez Maria, 16 rue du Maine, 14ᵉ. ☎43.20.84.61. Mᵒ Montparnasse. Evenings only, 8:30pm–1am. *Zinc* bar, candlelight, posters, paper tablecloths—an intimate gloom that appeals to arty theater creatures after hours. Very pleasant. Around 150F.

La Route du Château, 123 rue du Château, 14ᵉ. ☎43.20.09.59. Mᵒ Pernety. Mon lunchtime only, Tues–Sat lunchtime and evenings until 12:30am; closed Aug. Linen tablecloths, a rose on your table, an old-fashioned bistro atmosphere. The food is good and interesting—getting pricey on the *carte* (well over 150F); menu at 75F.

Yakitori, 64 rue du Montparnasse, 14ᵉ. ☎43.20.27.76. Mᵒ Edgar-Quinet. Daily until 11pm. Japanese: *brochettes* served with a variety of piquant sauces. See under "The Passages and Right Bank Commerce."

N'Zadette M'Foua, 152 rue du Château, 14ᵉ. ☎43.22.00.16. Mᵒ Pernety. Mon–Sat evenings, until midnight. A small and tasty Congolese—*manioc*, *maboké*, etc. Reservations required weekends. Menu at 85F.

OVER 150F

La Coupole, 102 bd du Montparnasse, 14ᵉ. ☎43.20.14.20. Mᵒ Vavin. Breakfast 7:30–10:30am, lunch noon–2am. One of the best *brasserie* menus in perhaps the most famous and enduring arty-chic Parisian hangout. Recently and lavishly renovated by the prince of Paris's turn-of-the-century *brasseries*, Jean-Paul Bucher of *Flo* and *Julien* fame (see under "Montmartre and the 9ᵉ") . . . but it ain't the same, say the old habitués.

Pavillon Montsouris, 20 rue Gazan, 14ᵉ. ☎45.88.38.52. RER Cité-Universitaire. 12:15am–2:30pm & 7:45–10:30pm. A special treat for summer days, sitting on the terrace overlooking the park, choosing from a menu featuring truffles, *foie gras*, and the divine *pêche blanche rôtie à la glace vanille*. Around 250F.

The 15ᵉ

UNDER 80F

Le Commerce, 51 rue du Commerce, 15ᵉ. ☎45.75.03.27. Mᵒ Émile-Zola. Daily 11am–3pm & 6:30–10pm. A long-established cheap restaurant catering to *le petit peuple*. Still varied, nourishing, and cheap.

Sampieru Corsu, 12 rue de l'Amiral-Roussin, 15ᵉ. Mᵒ Cambronne. Mon–Fri lunchtime & 7–9:30pm. A fantastic, albeit simple, little place whose *patron* feeds the unemployed for nothing and expects others to contribute according to their means. The minimum charge is 31F.

Auteuil and Passy

OVER 150F

Le Mouton Blanc, 40 rue d'Auteuil, 16ᵉ. ☎42.88.02.21. Mᵒ Église d'Auteuil. Good traditional food at around 120F. The establishment was once patronized by Molière, Racine, La Fontaine, and other literary aces of the time. It is now an agreeable local place for the *quartier*'s well-off residents.

Bois de Boulogne

OVER 150F

Café de la Jatte, 67 bd de Levallois, Île de la Jatte. ☎47.45.04.20. Mᵒ Pont-de-Levallois. The locale is unbeatable, in a converted riding school on a leafy street lined with small workshops and idiosyncratic houses on an island in the Seine. The clientele is rich and elegant. The food is excellent—*carte* is upwards of 200F, but there is a lunchtime menu at 85F—and the staff, both male and female, just as appealing.

La Guinguette de Neuilly, 12 bd de Levallois, Île de la Jatte. ☎46.24.25.04. M° Pont-de-Levallois. Crowded with the same well-heeled, well-fed set as the other Jatte establishments. Excellent food—best on a sunny day at one of the outside tables.

Parc Monceau to Batignolles

UNDER 80F

Le Bistro Romain, 9 av des Ternes, 17ᵉ. ☎47.64.17.38. M° Ternes. See under "Champs-Élysées."

Natacha, 35 rue Guersant, 17ᵉ. ☎45.74.23.86. M° Porte-Maillot. Mon–Fri all day until 11pm, Sat evening only. A bit out of the way, beyond the place des Ternes, but a great bargain. For 85F, you help yourself to hors-d'oeuvres and wine, with three other very respectable courses to follow.

Port de Pidjiguiti, 28 rue Etex, 18ᵉ. ☎42.26.71.77. M° Guy-Môquet. Tues–Sun only. Very pleasant atmosphere and excellent food for about 80F. It is run by a village in Guinea-Bissau, whose inhabitants take turns in staffing the restaurant; the proceeds go to the village. Good value wine list.

Sangria, 13 bis rue Vernier, 17ᵉ. ☎45.74.78.74. M° Porte-de-Champerret. Like *Natacha*, for 85F you can help yourself to appetizers and wine in addition to enjoying three other courses. Very popular and crowded.

UNDER 150F

L'Entrecôte, 271 bd Péreire, 17ᵉ. M° Porte-Maillot. An old bourgeois favorite, with a fixed menu which basically consists of steak, fries, and salad for around 120F. There's no great atmosphere, but nonethless it's extremely popular for its excellent food and very quick service.

Montmartre and the 9ᵉ

UNDER 80F

Casa Miguel, 48 rue St-Georges, 9ᵉ. M° St-Georges. Mon–Sat noon–1pm & 7–8pm, Sun noon–1pm. A meal with wine for an unbelievable 5F, and there's always a line.

Chartier, 7 rue du Faubourg-Montmartre, 9ᵉ. ☎47.70.86.29. M° Montmartre. Until 9:30pm. Brown linoleum floor, dark-stained woodwork, brass hat racks, clusters of white globes suspended from the high ceiling, mirrors, waiters in long aprons—the original decor of a turn-of-the-century soup kitchen. Worth seeing and, though crowded and rushed, the food is not bad at all.

Fouta Toro, 3 rue du Nord, 18ᵉ. ☎42.55.42.73. M° Marcadet-Poissonniers. 8pm–1am; closed Tues. A tiny, crowded, welcoming Senegalese diner in a very scruffy run-down alley. No more than 60F all included. Unless you come at the 8pm opening time or after about 10:30pm you'll certainly have to wait.

Au Grain de Folie, 24 rue La Vieuville, 18ᵉ. M° Abbesses. Evenings only, until 10:30pm. Good, unpretentious vegetarian cheapie.

UNDER 150F

Le Maquis, 69 rue Caulaincourt, 18ᵉ. ☎42.59.76.07. M° Lamarck-Caulaincourt. Tues–Sat until 10pm. There's a lunchtime menu for 59F; *carte* around 180F. A gently elegant and courteous place.

Chez Ginette, 101 rue Caulaincourt, 18ᵉ. ☎46.06.01.49. M° Lamarck-Caulaincourt. Mon–Sat lunchtime & 7:30–11:30pm; closed Aug. Good food in a traditionally "Parisian" environment, with a pianist in the evening. *Carte* around 150F; lunchtime menu at 75F.

OVER 150F

Les Chants du Piano, 10 rue Lambert, 18ᵉ. ☎46.06.37.05. Mº Château-Rouge. Tues–Sat lunchtime & evenings until 11pm; Sun lunchtime only, Mon evenings only; closed last fortnight in Aug. Really good food and beautiful decor. Menus at 149F and 229F.

Flo, 7 cours des Petites-Écuries, 10ᵉ. ☎47.70.13.59. Mº Château-d'Eau. Until 1:30am. A handsome old-time *brasserie*, all dark-stained wood, mirrors, and glass partitions in an attractive courtyard off rue du Faubourg-St-Denis. You eat elbow-to-elbow at long tables served by waiters in ankle-length aprons. Excellent food and thoroughly enjoyable atmosphere.

Julien, 16 rue du Faubourg-St-Denis, 10ᵉ. ☎47.70.12.06. Mº Strasbourg-St-Denis. Until 1:30am. Part of the same enterprise as *Flo*, with an even more splendid original decor. Same good German shepherd—vaguely Germanic—cuisine; same prices and similarly crowded.

Au Petit Riche, 25 rue Le Peletier, 9ᵉ. ☎47.70.68.68. Mº Richelieu-Drouot. Mon–Sat until 12:15am, closed second half of Aug. A long-established restaurant with a mirrored 1900s interior. Prompt and attentive service, good food—a menu at 110F (more like 130–140F with extras). A bit stuffy.

À la Pomponnette, 42 rue Lepic, 18ᵉ. ☎46.06.08.36. Mº Blanche. Tues–Sat lunchtime & evenings until 9:30pm, Sun evenings only; closed Aug. A genuine old Montmartre bistro, with posters, drawings, zinc-top bar, nicotine stains, etc. The food is excellent, but will cost you not a penny less than 200F.

Terminus Nord, 23 rue de Dunkerque, 10ᵉ. ☎42.85.05.15. Mº Gare-du-Nord. Daily until 12:30am. A magnificent 1920s *brasserie* where a full meal costs around 200F but where you could easily satisfy your hunger with just a main course—an excellent steak, for example—and still enjoy the decor for considerably less money.

Canal St-Martin and La Villette

OVER 150F

Au Ras du Pavé, 15 rue du Buisson-St-Louis, 10ᵉ. ☎42.01.36.36. Mº Colonel-Fabien. Tues–Sat noon–2:30pm & 8–10:30pm. Classic French dishes. Keep your head and you'll keep the bill under 200F.

Belleville, Ménilmontant, and Charonne

UNDER 80F

Au Trou Normand, 9 rue Jean-Pierre Timbaud, 11ᵉ. ☎48.05.80.23. Mº République. Mon–Fri lunchtime & evenings until 9:30pm, Sat lunchtime only; closed Aug. A very pleasant cheap local bistro.

UNDER 150F

Astier, 44 rue Jean-Pierre Timbaud, 11ᵉ. ☎43.57.16.35. Mº Parmentier. Mon–Fri until 10pm; closed Aug, two weeks in May, and two weeks at Christmas. A very good and very popular restaurant. Essential to reserve. Menu at 115F.

Égée, 19 rue de Ménilmontant, 20ᵉ. ☎43.58.70.26. Mº Ménilmontant. Noon–2:30pm & 7:30–11:30pm. Greek and Turkish specialties served with fresh homemade bread. 42F lunch menu—*à la carte meals* (without wine) can be had for under 100F.

Mère-Grand, 20 rue Orfila, 20ᵉ. ☎46.36.03.29. Mº Gambetta. Mon–Fri noon–2:30pm & 7–9:30pm; closed July. Very popular classic bistro with a limited choice of dependable peasant dishes. Lunchtime menus of 46F and 98F, evening menus 70F and 129F.

Chez Justine, 96 rue Oberkampf, 11ᵉ. ☎43.57.44.03. Mº St-Maur. Mon lunchtime only, Tues–Sat lunchtime and evenings; closed Aug. Good traditional cooking at very reasonable prices. Menus at 74F and 118F.

L'Occitanie, 96 rue Oberkampf, 11ᵉ. ☎48.06.46.98. Mᵒ St-Maur. Mon–Fri lunchtime and evenings, Sat evenings only; closed July. Copious homey food from the southwest, in a simple, friendly atmosphere. Menus under 100F.

Le Pacifique, 35 rue de Belleville, 20ᵉ. ☎42.49.66.80. Mᵒ Belleville. 11am–1am. A huge Chinese eating house with variable culinary standards. The 100F menu, wine included, is good value, though.

Chez Roger, 145 rue d'Avron, 20ᵉ. ☎43.73.55.47. Mᵒ Porte-de-Montreuil. Mon & Fri–Sun 12:30–2pm & 7:30–9pm, Tues 12:30–2pm. Mirrors, red-checked tablecloths, and old-time favorites such as *gigot d'agneau,* rabbit in wine sauce, and pigs' trotters. 120F menu.

Le Royal Belleville, 19 rue Louis-Bonnet, 11ᵉ (☎43.38.22.72) and **Le Président** (☎47.00.17.18; the floor above—entrance on rue-du-Faubourg-du-Temple). Mᵒ Belleville. 11am–2am. A dramatic blood-red double staircase leads up to *Le Président*, the more expensive of these two cavernous Chinese restaurants. You go for the atmosphere and decor rather than the food, though the spring rolls and rum banana fritters are acceptable. The Thai dishes at *Le Président* are not very special. Between 100F and 150F.

Aux Tables de la Fontaine, 3 rue des Trois-Bornes. ☎43.57.26.00. Mᵒ Parmentier. Mon–Fri lunchtime and evenings, Sat evenings only; closed Aug. Opposite *Astier's*, which it resembles, on the corner of a cobbled shady *place*. Excellent uncomplicated fare at very good prices.

Taverna Restaurant, 50 rue Piat, 20ᵉ. ☎40.33.07.20. Mᵒ Pyrénées. A homey and friendly local Turkish restaurant close to the Parc de Belleville. Around 90F including wine.

Thaï Yen, 5 rue de Belleville, 20ᵉ. ☎42.41.44.16. Mᵒ Belleville. 11:30am–1am. You can admire the koi carps like embroidered satin cushions idling around their aquarium while you wait for the copious soups and steamed specialties.

Chez Vincent, 60 bd Ménilmontant, 20ᵉ. ☎46.36.07.67. Mᵒ Père-Lachaise. Mon–Thurs lunchtime & 7–9:45pm, Fri & Sat 7–9:45pm only; closed Aug. Good filling food with wine included on the 58F and 70F lunch menus and 98F and 115F evening menus.

OVER 150F

Au Pavillon Puebla, Parc des Buttes-Chaumont, 19ᵉ. ☎42.08.92.62. Mᵒ Buttes-Chaumont. Mon–Fri noon–10pm. Luxury cuisine in an old hunting lodge. Poached lobster, stuffed baby calimari, duck with *foie gras,* and spicy oyster raviolis are some of the *à la carte* delights. Around 400F. Lunchtime menu at 200F.

Bastille to Vincennes

UNDER 80F

Palais des Femmes, 94 rue de Charonne, 11ᵉ. Mᵒ Faidherbe-Chaligny. Daily 11:45am–12:45pm & 6:30–8pm. The canteen of the women's hostel, run separately and open to all. Perfectly acceptable for a bill of less than 50F.

Chez Robert, 80 bd Richard-Lenoir, 11ᵉ. ☎48.05.07.73. Mᵒ Richard-Lenoir, St-Ambroise. Daily noon–2:15pm & 7–9pm. A leftover from the pre-Opéra days when this was a *quartier populaire*. Simple and satisfying fare; 49F and 72F menus.

UNDER 150F

Chardenoux, 1 rue Jules-Vallès, 11ᵉ. ☎43.71.49.52. Mᵒ Charonne. Mon–Fri noon–2:30pm & 8–11pm, Sat 8–11pm; closed Aug. An authentic oldie, with engraved mirrors dating back to 1900, that still serves solid meaty fare at a very reasonable price. Menus at 120F and 150F, the last including wine.

La Mansouria, 11 rue Faidherbe-Chaligny, 11ᵉ. ☎43.71.00.16. Mᵒ Faidherbe-Chaligny. Mon & Thurs–Sun lunchtime and evenings until 11pm, Tues & Wed evenings only; closed for a fortnight in Aug. An excellent Moroccan restaurant, with the cheapest menu at 97F; otherwise around 150F.

Nini Peau d'Chien, 24 rue des Taillandiers, 11ᵉ. ☎47.00.45.35. Mᵒ Bastille. Daily noon–2:30pm & 7:30–midnight. The charm of the two proprietors makes up for the lax service and very mediocre main courses at this boisterous and well-heeled gay and lesbian restaurant. Good appetizers include a very light and tasty *terrine craillée de St-Jacques* and *amourettes* (spinal marrow). Around 130F.

OVER 150F

Bofinger, 3–7 rue de la Bastille, 3ᵉ. ☎42.72.87.82. Mᵒ Bastille. Daily until 1am. A well-established and popular turn-of-the-century *brasserie*, serving the archetypal fare of *sauerkraut* and seafood. Menu at 155F, otherwise over 200F.

Le Train Bleu, 1st floor, Gare de Lyon, 20 bd Diderot, 12ᵉ. ☎43.43.09.06. Mᵒ Gare-de-Lyon. Daily until 10pm. You pay not for the food but the ludicrous *fin-de-siècle* stucco and murals of popular train destinations.

The 13ᵉ

UNDER 150F

Hawaï, 87 av d'Ivry, 13ᵉ. ☎45.86.91.90. Mᵒ Tolbiac. 11am–10pm; closed Thurs. Everyday Vietnamese food, well appreciated by the locals. Particularly good Tonkinese soups, dim sum, and brochettes. Around 100F.

L'Oustalou/Gladines, 30 rue des Cinq-Diamants, 13ᵉ. ☎45.83.53.34. Mᵒ Corvisart. Tues–Sun 7:30am–2am. Sometimes empty, sometimes bursting, this small corner bistro is always welcoming. Excellent wines and dishes from the southwest. The mashed/fried potato is a must and goes best with *magret de canard*. Around 100F.

Phuong Hoang, Centre Commercial Mercure, 52 rue du Javelot, 13ᵉ. ☎45.84.75.07. Mᵒ Tolbiac. Mon–Fri noon–2:30pm & 7–11:30pm. Like most of its neighbors this is a family business and the quality varies depending on which uncle, nephew, or niece is at the stove that day. Vietnamese, Thai, and Singapore specialties on lunch menus at 50F and 68F; evening menu 100F. If it's full or doesn't strike your fancy, try *Le Grand Mandarin* or *L'Oiseau de Paradis* nearby.

Thuy Huong, Kiosque de Choisy, 15 av de Choisy, 13ᵉ. ☎45.86.87.07. Mᵒ Porte-de-Choisy. Noon–2:30pm & 7–10:30pm; closed Thurs. Chinese and Cambodian combinations such as fish and coconut cream, crackling salad, and pancakes with mysterious spicy fillings. Around 100F.

Les Temps des Cérises, 18–20 rue de la Butte-aux-Cailles, 13ᵉ. ☎45.89.69.48. Mᵒ Place-d'Italie, Corvisart. Mon–Fri noon–2pm & 7–11pm, Sat 7–11pm. A well-established workers' co-op with elbow-to-elbow seating and a different daily choice of imaginative dishes. 52F lunch menu, 98F evening menu.

And for Splurging

If you're feeling slightly crazed—or you happen on a winning lottery ticket—there are, of course, some really spectacular Parisian restaurants. For *nouvelle cuisine* at its very best *Robuchon* (32 rue de Longchamp, 16ᵉ), *Lucas Carton* (9 place de la Madeleine, 8ᵉ), and *Taillevent* (15 rue Lamenais, 8ᵉ) are said to be the pinnacles of gastronomic experience and not just for bills that can reach 10,000F for two. *La Marée* (1 rue Daru, 8ᵉ) serves the same clientele on the classic-recipe front, and for pride of place if not so much for *plats* there's *Jules Vernes* on the second floor of the Eiffel Tower. Unfortunately, the moment's madness that might inspire you to eat in any of these restaurants would most likely come months too late for you to make reservations.

ETHNIC RESTAURANTS IN PARIS

Our selection of Paris's ethnic restaurants can only scratch the surface of what's available. **North African** places are widely distributed throughout the city; apart from rue Xavier-Privas in the Latin Quarter, where the trade is chiefly tourists, the heaviest concentration is the "Little Maghreb" district along bd de Belleville. **Indo-Chinese** restaurants are also widely scattered, with notable concentrations around av de la Porte-de-Choisy in the 13e and in the Belleville Chinatown. The **Greeks** and **Turks** are tightly corralled, in rue de la Huchette, rue Xavier-Privas, and along rue Mouffetard, all in the 5e and, frankly, a rip-off.

AFRICAN AND NORTH AFRICAN

Le Berbère, 50 rue de Gergovie, 14e. North African. p.227.

Fouta Toro, 3 rue du Nord, 18e. Senegalese. p.229.

La Mansouria, 11 rue Faidherbe-Chaligny, 11e. Moroccan. p.231.

N'Zadette M'Foua, 152 rue du Château, 14e. Congolese. p.228.

Port de Pidjiguiti, 28 rue Etex, 18e. Co-operative, run by a village in Guinea-Bissau. p.229.

INDO-CHINESE

Aux Délices de Széchuen, 40 av Duquesne, 7e. Chinese. p.225.

Escale de Saigon, 24 rue Bosquet, 7e. Vietnamese. p.225.

Hawaï, 87 av d'Ivry, 13e. Vietnamese. p.232.

Le Pacifique, 35 rue de Belleville, 20e. Chinese. p.231.

Phuong Hoang, Centre Commercial Mercure, 52 rue du Javelot, 13e. Vietnamese, Thai, and Singapore. p.232.

Restaurant A, 5 rue de Poissy, 5e. Chinese. p.225.

Le Royal Belleville and **Le Président**, 19 rue Louis-Bonnet, 11e. p.231.

Thaï Yen, 5 rue de Belleville, 20e. Thai. p.231.

Thuy Huong, Kiosque de Choisy, 15 av de Choisy, 13e. Chinese and Cambodian. p.232.

La Vallée des Bambous, 35 rue Gay-Lussac, 5e. Chinese. p.225.

TURKISH

Taverna Restaurant, 50 rue Piat, 20e. p.231.

GREEK

Égée, 19 rue de Ménilmontant, 20e. p.230.

Orestias, 4 rue Grégoire-de-Tours, 6e. p.226.

LEBANESE

Baalbeck, 16 rue Mazagran, 10e. p.223.

Le Liban à la Mouff, 18 rue Mouffetard, 5e. p.225.

TIBETAN

Tashi Delek, 4 rue des Fossés-St-Jacques, 5e. p.225.

SOUTH AMERICAN

Anahi, 49 rue Volta, 3e. Argentinian. p.224.

JEWISH

Goldenburg's, 7 rue des Rosiers, 4e. p.224.

INDIAN

Restaurant Jhelum, 30 rue St-Marc, 2e. p.223.

JAPANESE

Foujita, 45 rue St-Roch, 1er. p.223.

Yakitori, 24 rue Marbeuf, 8e (p.222); 34 place du Marché-St-Honoré, 2e (p.223); 10 rue Boutebrie, 5e (p.225); and 64 rue du Montparnasse, 14e (p.228).

RUSSIAN AND EAST EUROPEAN

Le Daru, 19 rue Daru, 8e. Russian. p.222.

Le Katyouschka, 9 rue de l'Éperon, 6e. White Russian. p.226.

Le Ravaillac, 10 rue du Roi-de-Sicile, 4e. Polish. p.224.

Village Bulgare, 8 rue de Nevers, 6e. Bulgarian. p.227.

CHAPTER NINE

MUSIC AND NIGHTLIFE

The strength of the Paris **music scene** is its diversity—a reputation gained mainly from its absorption of immigrant and exile populations. The city has no rivals in Europe for the variety of **world music** to be discovered: West and Central African, Caribbean, and Latin American sounds are represented in force both by city-based bands and by club or arena appearances by groups on tour. You can spend any number of nights sampling mixtures of salsa, calypso, reggae, and African sounds from Zaire, Congo, Senegal, and Nigeria. Algerian **raï** has come out from the immigrant ghettos, with stars like Cheb Mami gaining mainstream recognition, and there is even a local version of rap—led by such exponents as Salif Kiafa and encountered, too, on the streets or quaysides. All of which makes the French inability to produce decent rock bands a minor complaint.

Jazz fans, too, are in for a treat. Paris has long been home to new styles and old-time musicians. The *New Morning* club hosts big names from all over the world and it's not hard to fill the late hours passing from one club to another in St-Germain or Les Halles—assuming your wallet can take it. Standards, though, are high and the line-ups well varied, while the ancient cellars housing many of the clubs make for great acoustics and atmosphere.

One variety of home-grown popular music that survives is the tradition of **chansons**, epitomized by Edith Piaf and developed to its greatest heights by Georges Brassens and the Belgian Jacques Brel. This music is undergoing something of a revival. The return of the 1950s star Juliette Greco to the *Olympia* stage in January 1991 brought rapt media attention; meanwhile, the form is being contemporized by such new *chansonniers* as Alain Souchon and Serge Lama.

Classical music, as you might expect in this Neoclassical city, is alive and well and takes up twice the space of "jazz-pop-folk-rock" in the listings magazines. The Paris **Opéra** has a new palace with superb acoustics, if unpopular programming, at the Bastille. The need for advance reservations (except for the concerts held in churches) rather than the price is the major inhibiting factor here. If you're interested in the **contemporary** scene of Systems composition and the like, check out the state-sponsored experiments of Pierre Boulez at Beaubourg and Iannis Xenakis out at Issy-Les-Moulineaux.

Nightlife recommendations—for **dance clubs and discos**—are to some extent incorporated with those for rock, world music, and jazz, with which they merge. Separate sections, however, detail places that are mainly disco, and which cater to a gay or lesbian clientele.

The chapter's final section details all the **stadium venues**, where major concerts—from heavy metal to opera—are promoted.

MUSIC ON TV AND RADIO

The **TV channel** *Canal Plus* has tried to bring new popular sounds to a wider audience with its program *Rapido*—which uses mainstream pop as a basis for presenting world music.

Of the **local radio stations**, *Radio Nova* (101.5 MHz) plays a good cross section of what's new from rap to funk; *Radio Beur* (98.2 MHz) and *Radio France-Mahgreb* and *Soleil Ménilmontant* (94 MHz) have raï; *Oui* (102.3 MHz) is the all-day rock radio. The **national station** *Europe I* (104.7 MHz) has some imaginative music programming, and *France Musique* (91.3 and 91.7 MHz) carries classical, jazz, and anything really big.

Tickets and Information

The best place to get **tickets** for concerts, whether rock, jazz, *chansons*, or classical, is *FNAC Musique* (4 pl de la Bastille, 12ᵉ; Mᵒ Bastille. Mon, Tues, Thurs & Sat 10am–8pm, Wed & Fri 10am–10pm) or the *Virgin Megastore* (56–60 av des Champs-Élysées, 8ᵉ; Mᵒ Franklin-Roosevelt. Mon–Thurs 10am–midnight, Fri & Sat 10am–1am, Sun 2pm–midnight).

Most current **programs** are listed in *Pariscope* and the like. For information about African music gigs, good places to ask are the record shops *Blue Moon* (7 rue Pierre-Sarrazin, 6ᵉ; Mᵒ Odéon; Mon–Sat 11am–7pm) and *Crocodisc* (42 rue des Écoles, 5ᵉ; Mᵒ Maubert-Mutualité; Tues–Sat 11am–7pm). The two *Le Disque Arabe* shops (116bis bd de la Chapelle, 18ᵉ, Mᵒ Porte-de-la-Chapelle; and 125 bd de Ménilmontant, Mᵒ Ménilmontant; both shops open Mon–Sat 10am–8pm) are a useful starting point for checking out raï concerts, and stock a good range of Arab music.

World Music and Rock

The last few years have seen considerable diversification in the Paris clubs and rock venues, leaving the big western rock bands to play the major arenas and concentrating instead on more international sounds. Almost every club features **Latin** and **African** dance music, and big names from these worlds—in particular, **zouk** musicians from the French Caribbean, for whom Paris is a second home—are almost always in town. The divisions between world sounds are mixing more and more, too, and even "ethnically French" Parisians have produced their own rewarding hybrids, best exemplified in the Pogue-like chaos of *Les Négresses Vertes*. The **listings** overleaf provide good starting points for enjoying the range of what's on offer; the only music they don't properly cover is Algerian **raï**, whose gigs—which sometimes start a couple of *days* late—are mostly word of mouth. For up-to-the-minute advice, ask at *Le Disque Arabe* (see above) or at cassette stalls in the predominantly North African quarters of Belleville and Ménilmontant.

As for **regular French rock music**, the received wisdom is steer well clear. You really do need to be French to appreciate aging stars like Sylvie Vartan, Johnny Halliday, and Françoise Hardy. The one interesting, new, and genuinely French rock form is **Trashpop**—an amalgam of influences that is fun, funky, a bit punky, with splashes of bebop, heavy metal, and psychedelia. The videos are vital to the music, the clothes are outrageous; the names to look out for are *Niagra*, the *Wampas*, *Madhouse*, *ADX*, and *Etienne Daho*.

Music Venues

Most of the venues listed below are clubs. A few of them will have live music all week, but the majority host bands on just a couple of nights—usually Friday and Saturday, when admission prices are also hiked up.

Mainly Rock

La Cigale, 120 bd de Rochechouart, 18e. Mo Pigalle. ☎42.23.38.00. Music from 8:30pm. Rita Mitsouko, punk, indie, etc: an eclectic programming policy in an old-fashioned converted theater, long a fixture on the Pigalle scene.

City Rock Café, 13 rue Berry, 8e. Mo George V. ☎43.59.52.09. Noon–6am. Live rock'n'roll every night in the cellar below the American café of rock idol memorabilia. 50–75F entry.

Elysée Montmartre, 72 bd de Rochechouart, 18e. Mo Anvers. ☎42.52.25.15. Traditional and inexpensive Pigalle venue for alternative bands, attracting a young and excitable crowd.

Le Gibus, 18 rue du Faubourg-du-Temple, 11e. Mo République. ☎47.00.78.88. 11pm–5am; Tues–Sat, Sat only in Aug. For twenty years English rock bands on their way up have played their first Paris gig at Gibus, the Clash and Police among them. Fourteen nights of dross will turn up one decent band, but it's always hot, loud, energetic, and crowded with young Parisians heavily committed to the rock scene. It's also one of the cheaper clubs, both for admission and drinks.

La Locomotive, 90 bd de Clichy, 18e. Mo Blanche. ☎42.57.37.37. Tues–Sun 11pm–5am. Concerts start at 1am. Tues–Fri 50F; Sat & Sun 90F. Enormous hi-tech nightclub fairly new to Montmartre. Two dance floors: on one you may gyrate to the beat of a group brought over from the British club scene; the other is dedicated to rock. Crowded and popular.

New Moon, 66 rue Pigalle, 9e. Mo Pigalle. ☎45.95.92.33. Mon–Wed 10pm–dawn, Thurs–Sat 11pm–dawn. Weekdays 50F with drink; weekends 60F. An ex-lesbian cabaret, dedicated to rock, with the hip suburbanites coming in to listen to French and German bands.

Phil'One, Place de la Patinoire, 3e niveau, Parvis de la Défense. ☎47.76.44.26; opposite CNIT building; Mo RER La Défense. Thurs–Sat 10pm onwards. An unprepossessing entrance and long corridor lead to one of the best clubs in Paris—great sound system, no trendy decor, pit and gallery dance floor and tables, and quirky musical policy encompassing Antillais, African, a bit of jazz, and English and French rock, the bands a good mix of the well-established and the new.

Rex Club, 5 bd Poissonnière, 9e. Mo Montmartre. ☎42.36.83.98. Tues, Wed & Fri–Sun 8:30pm–5am; sometimes closed Wed. Live music—rock, funk, soul, raï, rap (mainly on Tues and Sat from 8pm), charging 50–100F. Disco from 11pm, 60–90F.

Rock'n'Roll Circus, 6 rue Caumartin, 9e. Mo Havre-Caumartin. A smallish club for French bands, which has adopted the name of the infamous club where Jim Morrison hung out—and perhaps died. The original *Rock'n'Roll Circus* is now the *Whisky-a-Gogo* (see overpage).

Mainly Latin and Caribbean

L'Écume, 99 rue de l'Ouest, 14e. ☎45.42.72.16. Mo Pernety. Until 3am. Live Brazilian or Caribbean music on weekends in a dark, cramped, smoky cellar—just as Paris dives are supposed to be. Space upstairs for cards, chess, and chat.

L'Escale, 15 rue Monsieur-le-Prince, 6e. ☎43.54.63.47. Mo Odéon. 11pm–4am. More Latin American musicians must have passed through here than in any other club. The dancing sounds, *salsa* mostly, are in the basement (disco on Wed), while on the ground floor every variety of South American music is given an outlet.

Mambo Club, 20 rue Cujas, 5ᵉ. ☎43.54.89.21. Mᵒ St-Michel/Odéon. Afro-Cuban and Antillais music in a seedy dive with people of all ages and nationalities.

La Plantation, 45 rue de Montpensier, 1ᵉʳ. ☎49.27.06.21. Mᵒ Palais-Royal. Tues–Sun 11pm–dawn. In spite of the reputation for welcoming everyone, the doormen are fussy, particularly if you're white. Inside, excellent Cuban, Angolan, Congolese, and Antillais music awaits you.

Les Trottoirs de Buenos Aires, 37 rue des Lombards, 1ᵉʳ. ☎42.60.44.41. Mᵒ Châtelet. Tues–Sun 9:30pm onwards. Argentinian tango is the only music performed on the stage of "the sidewalks of Buenos Aires." The bands change every two months or so; the drinks are very expensive; no one dances except professional *artistes*. But the world of music built around tango rhythms is completely transporting. Highly recommended.

Bals Musettes . . .

Balajo, 9 rue de Lappe, 11ᵉ. ☎47.00.07.79. Mᵒ Bastille. Fri, Sat & Mon 10pm–4:30am. The old-style music hall of *gai* but straight *Paris*—extravagant 1930s decor, a balcony for the orchestra above the vast dance floor, working-class Parisians in their weekend best, and the music everything to move to from mazurka, tango, waltz, cha-cha, twist, and the slurpy *chansons* of between the wars. There are disco and modern hits as well, but that's on Monday night when the kids from across town come and all the popular nostalgia disappears.

Chapelle des Lombards, 19 rue de Lappe, 11ᵉ. ☎43.57.24.24. Mᵒ Bastille. Tues–Sat 10:30pm–dawn; bands Thurs–Sat only. This erstwhile *bal musette* of the rue de Lappe still plays the occasional waltz and tango but for the most part the music is salsa, reggae, steel drums, gwo-kâ, zouk, raï, and the blues. The doormen are not too friendly but it's relatively cheap and, once inside, a good night is assured.

Le Tango, 13 rue Au-Maire, 3ᵉ. ☎48.87.54.78. Mᵒ Arts-et-Métiers. Wed–Sat 11pm–5am. The tango has been played here since the turn of the century and the decor looks as if it's retained layers from every decade since. The contrast with *Les Bains* (see below) could not be greater. No vetting here, cheap admission and drinks (obligatory cloakroom fee), people wearing whatever clothes they happen to be in and dancing with abandon to please themselves, not the adjudicators of style. Anyone asks anyone for a dance and this is no pick-up joint. The music is jazzy Latin American—salsa, calypso, and reggae.

For afternoon dancing at the bals musettes, *see "Afternoon Tangos" on p.170.*

Nightclubs and Discos

Clubs listed below are essentially **discos**, though a few have the odd live group. They come and go at an exhausting rate, the business principle being to take over a place, make a major investment in the decor, and close after two years, well in the black. As a customer, you contribute on a financial level—and in many places your ornamentation potential is equally important. Being sized up by a leather-clad bouncer acting as the ultimate arbiter of style and prosperity can be a very demeaning experience. Men generally have a harder time than women, English-speakers are at an advantage, blacks are not. The one place that doesn't discriminate and should be at the top of any disco list is *Le Palace 999*.

Les Bains, 7 rue du Bourg-l'Abbé, 3ᵉ. ☎48.87.01.80. Mᵒ Étienne-Marcel. 11:30pm–dawn. This is as posed as they come—an old Turkish bathhouse where the Stones filmed part of their *Undercover of the Night* video, now redone in the antiperspirant, passionless style pioneered for the *Café Costes*. The music is limited to the most familiar international hits—

sometimes live (usually dross) bands on a Wednesday. The decor features a plunging pool by the dance floor in which the carefree are wont to ruin their non-colorfast designer creations. It's not a place where a 500-franc note has much life expectancy. Whether you can watch this spectacle depends on the bouncers, who have their fixed ideas. If you're turned away, be thankful and head down the road to *Le Tango* (see "*Bals Musettes*," above).

Blue Moon, 160 bd St-Germain, 6e. ☎46.34.01.04. M^o St-Germain-des-Prés. The best reggae disco in town.

Bus Palladium, 6 rue Fontaine, 9e. ☎48.74.54.99. M^o Pigalle. Tues–Sun 11:30pm–dawn. A fairly tame outfit for the local kids. You'll need to be well dolled up to get in.

The Cellar, 54–56 rue de Ponthieu, 8e. M^o Franklin-Roosevelt. Until 6am. A recent addition to the scene with different kinds of music each night. No admission charge but pricey drinks.

Le Central 102, 102 av des Champs-Elysées, 8e. ☎42.89.31.41. M^o George-V. 11pm–dawn. 100F with drink. Power-station decor for the well-heeled rappers and models of Neuilly.

Le Cloître des Lombards, 62 rue des Lombards, 1er. ☎42.33.54.09. M^o Châtelet. 10:30pm–4am. More of a jazz club atmosphere though the music is definitely Caribbean.

Discophage, 11 passage du Clos-Bruneau (off 31–33 rue des Écoles), 5e, ☎43.26.31.41. M^o Maubert-Mutualité. Mon–Sat 9pm–3am, music begins at 10pm; closed Aug. A jam-packed, tiny, and under-ventilated space, but all such discomforts are irrelevant for the best Brazilian sounds you can hear in Paris.

Fantasia, Palais des Congrès, 78 bd Gouvion-St-Cyr, 17e. ☎47.58.24.46. M^o Porte-Maillot. 11pm–dawn. Multicolored strobe, tie-dye T-shirts, platform boots, beatnik hats, and crushed-velvet skirts in a ludicrously large space to be dedicated to psychedelia.

Java, 105 rue du Faubourg-du-Temple, 10e. ☎42.02.20.52. M^o Belleville. Sun & Mon 2:30–7pm *thé dansant*; live music Fri & Sat 9:30pm–5am; Tues–Thurs 11pm–4am. The old *bal musette* where Piaf made her début, now given over to Sixties music, rap, tango, et al.

Keur Samba, 79 rue la Béotie, 8e. ☎43.59.03.10. M^o Franklin-Roosevelt. Until breakfast every day. An expensive and fashionable black-and-white venue, where you need to be well-dressed. Afro-Antillais music.

La Main Jaune, Place de la Porte-Champerret, 17e. ☎47.63.26.47. M^o Porte-de-Champerret. Fri 2:30–7pm & 10pm–5am, Sat 10pm–5am. Roller-rink disco. Skate to radio hits with the schoolkids of the Beaux Quartiers. See p.174.

Le Malibu, 44 rue Tiquetonne, 2e. ☎42.36.62.70. M^o Étienne-Marcel. 8:30pm–5am. Around 150F. Black music from all over West Africa and the West Indies in a crowded basement beneath a restaurant. No strict admission policy here: blacks outnumber whites and everyone is under thirty and fairly well off.

Olivia Valère, 40 rue du Colisée, 8e. ☎42.21.51.68. M^o St-Philippe-du-Roule. 11pm–dawn. Since much is made of where the rich hang out in Paris, here is one of their haunts. Firmly on home ground, exceedingly difficult to get into, expensive, and a confirmation of one's hopeful suspicions—that these people are too snobby to indulge in enjoyment.

L'Opéra Night, 30 rue Gramont, 2e. ☎42.96.62.56. M^o Richelieu-Drouot. 11pm–5am. A cinema during the day, which is transformed to Afro-funk space every evening after the last film. Renowned for quality dancing to African and Caribbean funk, reggae, and salsa.

Le Palace 999, 8 rue du Faubourg-Montmartre, 9^e. ☎42.46.10.87. M^o Montmartre. Wed–Sun 11pm–dawn. Time was when *everyone* went to the Palace; it's still packed nightly with revelers, whether they've scraped together their week's savings or are just out to exercise the credit cards, and they all don their best party gear. Some nights it's thematic fancy dress, some nights the music is all African, other times the place is booked for TV dance shows. It's big, the bopping is good, and the clientele are an exuberant spectacle in themselves.

Whisky-a-Gogo, 57 rue de Seine 6e. ☎43.29.60.01. M^o Odéon. Nightly 11:15pm–6am. This cellar bar currently plays Manchester-style dance music to flared French youth. It occupies the site of the original *Rock'n'Roll Circus*—where Jim Morrison (see p.132) made his last earthly appearance.

Lesbian and Gay Clubs and Discos

Lesbian clubs find it hard to be exclusively female, and you may find that none of the varied atmospheres is agreeable. The pleasures of **gay men** are far better catered to, though AIDS has changed the scene and the wicked little bars with obscure backrooms around Les Halles have all but ceased to exist. Hi-tech, well-lit, sense-surround disco beat is the current style.

While the selection of gay male-oriented establishments below only scratches the surface, for gay women our listings more or less cover all that's available. Lesbians, however, are welcome in some of the predominantly male clubs. For a complete rundown, consult the *Gai-Pied Guide* (see "Gay Bookstores" in Chapter Seven).

Women

Le Caveau de la Bastille, 6 passage Thiéré, 11e. ☎47.00.55.33. M° Bastille. Tues–Sat 7pm–dawn. The clientele may be changing. If Nicole and Malika are no longer behind the bar, make a hasty exit.

Chez Moune, 54 rue Pigalle, 18e. ☎45.26.64.61. M° Pigalle. 10pm–dawn. In the red-light heart of Paris, this mixed but predominantly women's cabaret and disco may shock or delight feminists. The evening includes a strip-tease (by women) without the standard audience for such shows (any man causing the slightest fuss is kicked out). Sunday tea-dance afternoons from 4:30–8pm are strictly women-only.

Entre Nous, 17 rue Laferrière, 9e. ☎48.78.11.67. M° St-Georges. Wed & Sat only 11pm–dawn. A small women-only club with an intimate atmosphere and catholic taste in music.

Le Guet-Apens, 10 rue Descartes, 5e. ☎40.46.81.40. M° Maubert-Mutualité. Mon–Sat 11pm–2am, Sun 6–11pm. An agreeable bar, run by lesbians but fairly mixed.

Le Katmandou, 21 rue du Vieux-Colombier, 6e. ☎45.48.12.96. M° St-Sulpice. 11pm–dawn. The best-known and most upmarket of the lesbian nightclubs. Good music of the Afro-Latino variety, but not an easy place to meet people.

Le Memorie's, 78 bd Goudin-de-St-Cyr, 17e. ☎46.40.28.12. M° Porte-Maillot. Daily 11pm–dawn. A masterful *patronne* runs a tight ship in this Lebanese restaurant-turned-club. Dancing; men allowed, if they behave themselves.

Le Morocco, 9 rue Guisarde, 6e. ☎43.29.01.84. M° Mabillon. Mon–Sat 10pm–4am. Not exclusively female bar, but women predominate and the music is good.

Le New Monocle, 60 bd Edgar-Quinet, 14e. ☎43.20.81.12. M° Montparnasse. 11pm–dawn; closed Sun. This women's cabaret has been revitalized since the closing of its rival, *Le Baby Doll*. A scattering of men are allowed in every evening.

Le Soft, 7 place Pigalle, 9e. ☎42.80.64.26. M° Pigalle. Wed–Sat 11pm–dawn. Wed & Thurs 60F, Fri & Sat 90F. Cabaret and pasta. Open to all and sundry after 2am on Wednesdays.

Studio A, 51 rue de Ponthieu, 8e. ☎42.25.12.13. M° Franklin-Roosevelt. Lesbian every night, save Wednesday, when the company is mixed. 100F with drink.

Men

Bar Hôtel Central, 33 rue Vieille-du-Temple, 4e. ☎42.78.11.42. M° St-Paul. Midnight–2am. An unfrenetic men-only bar catering mainly to over-30s.

Le BH, 7 rue du Roule, 1er. M° Châtelet-Les-Halles. 10pm–6am. The downstairs rooms have been knocked into one sizable and illuminated disco, but this is still one of the cheapest gay discos in the city; exclusively male.

Le Boy, 6 rue Caumartin, 9e. ☎47.42.68.05. M° Opéra. Daily 11:30pm–dawn. *The* gay dance spot.

The Broad Connection, 3 rue de la Ferronnerie, 1er. ☎42.33.93.08. Mº Châtelet-Les Halles. Tues–Sun 10:30pm–dawn. Young, chic, and perennially popular. Next door, keeping the same hours, is the *Broad Side* cocktail bar—for quieter evenings.

Club 18, 18 rue de Beaujolais, 1er. ☎42.97.52.13. Mº Bourse. 11pm–dawn. Mainly gay male clientele in this cellar bar, with weekend cabaret.

Haute Tension, 87 rue St-Honoré, 1er; (no phone); Mº Châtelet. 11pm–dawn. Discreet and rather subdued surroundings for a hot and sweaty bar-disco—a favorite with all gay men, irrespective of style and age.

La Luna, 28 rue Keller, 11e. ☎40.21.09.91. Mº Bastille. Wed–Sun 11pm–dawn. The latest hi-tech gay Bastille. Mirrors to dance to.

Le Manhattan, 8 rue des Anglais, 5e. ☎43.54.98.86. Mº Maubert-Mutualité. 11pm–6am. Men-only club with a good funky disco.

Le Piano Zinc, 49 rue des Blancs-Manteaux, 4e. ☎42.74.32.42. Mº Rambuteau. Tues–Sun 6pm–2am. From 10pm when the piano-playing starts, this bar becomes a happy riot of songs, music hall acts, and dance, which may be hard to appreciate if you don't follow French very well. It's one of the few venues patronized by lesbians and gays together.

Le Quetzal, 10 rue de la Verrerie, 4e. ☎48.87.99.07. Mº St-Paul. Daily until 2am. Popular, crowded bar and dance floor.

Le Swing, 42 rue Vieille-du-Temple, 4e. ☎42.72.16.94. Mº St-Paul. Noon–2am. A young, cool, and unpressured gay bar where women are welcome and the music is sweet.

Jazz, Blues, and *Chansons*

Jazz has long enjoyed an appreciative audience in France, most especially since the end of World War II when the intellectual rigor and agonized musings of bebop struck an immediate chord of sympathy in the existentialist hearts of the *après-guerre*. Charlie Parker, Dizzy Gillespie, Bud Powell, Miles Davis—all were being listened to in the Fifties, when elsewhere in Europe their names were known only to a tiny coterie of fans.

Gypsy guitarist Django Rheinhardt and his partner, violinist Stéphane Grappelli, whose work represents the distinctive and undisputed French contribution to the jazz canon, had much to do with the music's popularity. But it was also greatly enhanced by the presence of many front-rank black American musicians, for whom Paris was a haven of freedom and culture after the racial prejudice and philistinism of the States. Among them were the soprano sax player Sidney Bechet, who set up in legendary partnership with French clarinetist Claude Luter, and Bud Powell, whose turbulent exile partly inspired the tenor man played by Dexter Gordon (himself a veteran of the Montana club) in the film *Round Midnight*.

Jazz is still alive and well in the city, with new venues opening all the time, where you can hear all styles from New Orleans to current experimental. Some **local names to look out for** are: saxophonists François Jeanneau, Barney Willen, Didier Malherbe, and Steve Lacey; violinist Didier Lockwood; British-born but long Paris-resident guitarist John McLaughlin; pianist Alain Jeanmarie; and bass player Jean-Jacques Avenel. All of them can be found playing small gigs, regardless of the size of their reputations. The most bizarre French jazz ensemble is a group of thirty saxophonists called Urban Sax who specialize in post-holocaust costumes and descend on stage from different directions and considerable distances. A powerful transmitter keeps them all in time as they climb down from a roof or move toward a central space. Well worth catching.

A Note on Prices

With virtually all of the **clubs** listed below—*Le Dunois* is a rare, honorable exception—expense is a real drawback to enjoyment. **Admission charges** are generally high and when they're not levied there's usually a whopping charge for your first drink.

Subsequent **drinks**, too, are absurdly priced—about twice what you'd pay in a similar club in New York—and they can have a seriously dulling effect on the atmosphere. If you consider drinking an essential accompaniment to jazz, best bring your own discreet hip flask.

Mainly Jazz

Les Alligators, 23 av du Maine, 15e. ☎42.84.11.27. Mº Montparnasse. Mon–Sat 10pm–4am. A new, plush cocktail-style bar, with jazz on the stage. French and international musicians—Lee Konitz, for example. No admission charge, but 140F first drink.

The American Center, 261 bd Raspail, 14e. ☎43.35.21.50. Mº Raspail. Sun from 6:30pm. Worth checking out for jazz and also modern dance performances.

Baiser Salé, 58 rue des Lombards, 1er. ☎42.33.37.71. Mº Châtelet. 8:30pm–4am. A bar downstairs and a small, crowded upstairs room with live music every night from 11pm—usually jazz, rhythm & blues, Latino-rock, reggae, or Brazilian.

Le Bilboquet, 13 rue St-Benoît, 6e. ☎45.48.81.84. Mº St-Germain. Mon–Sat 7pm–2:30am. A very comfortable bar/restaurant with live jazz every night—local and international stars, like baritone player Gary Smulyan. The music starts at 10:45pm. No admission charge; drinks 110F a shot. This is the street where Dexter Gordon, Miles Davis, Bud Powell, and many others played and hung out in the Fifties.

Les Bouchons, 19 rue des Halles, 1er. ☎42.33.28.73. Mº Châtelet-Les-Halles. Until 2am. This is a restaurant, with live jazz every evening—from traditional to contemporary in a room below the *brasserie* reminiscent of a gentleman's club. But, surprisingly, no admission charge and reasonably priced cocktails. A good place if you want to sit and talk.

Le Café de la Plage, 59 rue de Charonne, 11e. ☎47.00.91.60. Mº Bastille. Tues–Sun 10pm–2am. A smoky, low-ceilinged arty bar where it is easy to talk to people. Jazz in the basement.

La Closerie des Lilas, 171 bd Montparnasse, 14e. ☎43.26.70.50. Mº Port-Royal. Until 2am. Brilliant piano-playing the nights when Ivan Meyer is on. Having chosen your cocktail, you can make your musical requests and sit back in a chair that may well bear the nameplate of Trotsky, Verlaine, or André Gide.

Au Duc des Lombards, 42 rue des Lombards, 1er. ☎42.36.51.13. Mº Châtelet-Les-Halles. Until 2am. Small, unpretentious bar with performances every night from 11pm—jazz piano, blues, ballads, fusion.

Le Dunois, 108 rue du Chevaleret, 13e. ☎45.70.81.16. Mº Chevaleret. Concerts Mon–Fri & Sun 8:30–11:30pm. A new location for the *Dunois*, more modern, no stage, and a bigger bar. The musical policy still gives consistent support to free and experimental jazz. And this is one of the few places in Paris to hear improvised music, as opposed to free jazz. It's also very pleasant for being out of the Latin Quarter and Les Halles, cheap and entirely unsnobbish. When there aren't jazz concerts the space is used for musical theater, video, and shows for children.

L'Eustache, 37 rue Berger, 1er. ☎40.26.23.20. Mº Châtelet-Les Halles. Mon–Sat 11am–4am; music from 10pm. Cheap beer and very good jazz by local musicians in this young and friendly Les Halles café—cheapest good jazz in the capital.

Latitudes, 7–11 rue St-Benoît, 6e. ☎42.61.53.53. Mo St-Germain-des-Prés. Daily 6pm–2am; live jazz Thurs–Sat 10pm–2am. French and foreign stars play in the swish downstairs bar of the hotel. Around 100F for the first drink.

Lionel Hampton Bar, Hôtel Méridien, 81 bd Gouvion-St-Cyr, 17e. ☎40.68.34.34. Mo Porte-Maillot. Mon–Sat 10pm–2am. First-rate jazz venue, with big-name musicians. Inaugurated by himself, but otherwise the great man is only an irregular visitor. Drinks from 120F.

Magnetic Terrace, 2 rue de la Cossonnerie, 1er. ☎42.36.26.44. Mo Châtelet-Les Halles. Tues–Sat, music from 10:30pm. Trendy bar turned jazz club, often with big-name guest artists.

Le Merle Moqueur, 11 rue des Buttes-aux-Cailles, 13e. Mo Place d'Italie/Corvisart. 5pm–2am. A workers' co-op bar with jazz on Mondays and popular French songs every Thursday.

Le Montana, 28 rue St-Benoît, 6e. ☎45.48.93.08. Mo St-Germain-des-Prés. 9pm–6am; music from 10:30pm. Jazz, French songs . . . not one of the best venues for jazz.

New Morning, 7–9 rue des Petites-Écuries, 10e. ☎45.23.51.41. Mo Château-d'Eau. 9pm–1:30am (concerts start around 10pm). This is the place where the big international names in jazz come to play. It's not all it's cracked up to be, though. The sound is good but the décor, though spacious, is rather cold—and no marks either for the ludicrous drink prices.

Le Petit Journal, 71 bd St-Michel, 5e. ☎43.26.28.59. Mo Luxembourg. Mon–Sat 10pm–2am. A small, smoky bar, long frequented by Left Bank student types, with good, mainly French, traditional and mainstream sounds.

Le Petit Journal Montparnasse, 13 rue du Commandant-Mouchotte, 14e. ☎43.21.56.70. Mo Montparnasse. Mon–Sat 9pm–2am. Under the Hôtel Montparnasse, and sister establishment to the above, with bigger, visiting names, both French and international.

Le Petit Opportun, 15 rue des Lavandières-Ste-Opportune, 1er. ☎42.36.01.36. Mo Châtelet-Les-Halles. 9pm–3am; music from 11pm. It's worth arriving early to get a seat for the live music in the dungeon-like cellar where the acoustics play strange tricks and you can't always see the musicians. Fairly eclectic policy and a crowd of genuine connoisseurs.

Slow Club, 130 rue de Rivoli, 1er. ☎42.33.84.30. Mo Châtelet/Pont-Neuf. Tues–Sat 9:30pm–2:30am. A jazz club to bop the night away to the sounds of Claude Luter's sextet and visiting New Orleans musicians.

Le Sunset, 60 rue des Lombards, 1er. ☎40.26.46.20. Mo Châtelet-Les-Halles. Mon–Sat 9pm–5am. Restaurant upstairs, jazz club in the basement, featuring the best musicians—the likes of Alain Jeanmarie and Turk Mauro—and frequented by musicians.

Utopia, 1 rue Niepce, 14e. ☎43.22.79.66. Mo Pernety. Tues–Sat 8:30pm–dawn. No genius here, but good French blues singers interspersed with jazz and blues tapes, the people listening mostly young and studentish. No admission charge and cheap drinks. Generally very pleasant atmosphere.

Mainly *Chansons*

Le Caveau de la Bolée, 25 rue de l'Hirondelle, 6e. ☎43.54.62.20. Mo St-Michel. 9:30pm–6:30am. An ancient, ramshackle place where Parisian luminaries of the likes of Baudelaire used to go to hear their favorite singers. The music is still mainly *chansons* with occasional evenings of jazz. Affordable prices and a mainly student clientele.

Le Caveau des Oubliettes, 11 rue St-Julien-le-Pauvre, 5e. ☎45.83.41.77. Mo St-Michel. 9pm–2am. French popular music of bygone times—Piaf and earlier—sung with exquisite nostalgia in the ancient prisons of Châtelet.

Magique, 42 rue de Gergovie, 14e. ☎45.42.26.10. Mo Pernety. Wed–Sun 8pm–2am. A friendly, relaxed bar where prices are low and singer Marc Havet does his versions of French *chansons*.

Le Père Boutgras, 50 rue Montorgueil, 2e. ☎40.39.05.80. Mo Sentier. Tues–Sat 8pm–2am. A *caveau à vin et à chansons* where you can drink or dine at 8:30pm, followed by a performance of *chansons* at 10pm Tues–Thurs; Fri & Sat are more impromptu; prices are reasonable (*plats du jour* 52F), and there's no extra charge for the music.

Completely Wonderful . . .

Les Trois Mailletz, 56 rue Galande, 5ᵉ. ☎43.54.00.79. Mᵒ St-Michel. Wed–Sun 6pm–dawn. The builders responsible for Notre-Dame drank in this cellar-bar, which belies the appearance of its tiny, upstairs room. Here, Ahmed plays any tune with a dream of ease on the piano, joined by anyone with an instrument or a desire to sing. Down below, you've a chance of hearing just about anything in the course of an evening—from jazz, through *chansons*, to mad French rock'n'roll with everyone twisting on the tables. The clientele are classic Parisians—Polish *immigrés*, exiles from the eastern Mediterranean, young Americans preferring the Parisian gutter to Manhattan mod-cons, a Frenchman in love with the scornful waitress, and characters unclassified. With free admission and averagely pricey drinks, it is always packed—if you aren't immediately admitted, wait around or ask if you can return.

Classical and Contemporary Music

Paris is a stimulating environment for **classical music**—both established and contemporary. The former is well represented in concert, with numerous performances taking place in the appropriate acoustical setting of churches—often for free or very cheap—and an enormous choice of commercially promoted concerts every day of the week. Contemporary music, in the city that is home to Olivier Messiaen and Pierre Boulez, has active and permanent bases at the Beaubourg's **IRCAM** center, and, under the direction of Iannis Xenakis at **CEMAMU**, in the suburb of Issy-Les-Moulineaux.

Regular Concert Venues

The **Citè de la Musique project** at La Villette (see p.125) has given Paris two new, major concert venues. The **Conservatoire**, the national music academy, has already opened its doors on av. Jean-Jaurès (information and reservations: ☎40.40.46.46/40.40.46.47). And next door, a new **auditorium** due to be completed in 1992, and adaptable to all kind of novel configurations of instruments, will become home to *L'Ensemble Inter-Contemporain*, led by Pierre Boulez's orchestra (for more on whom, see below).

These apart, the top **auditoriums** are: *Salle Pleyel* (252 rue du Faubourg-St-Honoré, 8ᵉ; Mᵒ Ternes; ☎45.63.88.73), *Épicerie-Beaubourg* (12 rue du Renard, 4ᵉ; Mᵒ Hôtel-de-Ville; ☎42.72.23.41), *Gaveau* (45 rue de la Boétie; Mᵒ Miromesnil), *Théâtre des Champs-Élysées* (15 av Montaigne, 8ᵉ; Mᵒ Alma-Marceau; ☎47.23.47.77), and the *Théâtre Musical de Paris* (1 place du Châtelet, 1ᵉʳ; Mᵒ Châtelet; ☎42.33.44.44). **Tickets** are best bought at the box offices, though for big names you may find overnight lines, and a large number of seats are always booked by subscribers. The price range is very reasonable.

Classical concerts also take place for **free** at *Radio France* (166 av du Président-Kennedy, 16ᵉ. Mᵒ Passy; ☎45.24.15.16).

Opera

Opera, too, has had its rewards in President Mitterrand's millennial endowments. The newly constructed **Opéra-Bastille** (see p.134) is his most extravagant memento to the city and was opened, with all due pomp, in 1990. Its first performance—the obscure, six-hour-long *Les Troyens* by Berlioz—cast something of a shadow on the project's proclaimed commitment to popularizing its art. "We are audacious," was the defense of the director, Pierre Bergé, who got the job after resignations by both Daniel Barenboim and Pierre Boulez; a self-proclaimed anarchist, Bergé's former post had been running Yves St-Laurent's fashion house.

To judge the place for yourself, tickets (40–520F) can be bought Monday to Saturday 11am to 6pm on ☎40.01.16.16 or from the ticket offices (Mon–Sat 11am–6:30pm within two weeks of the performance). The cheapest seats are only available to personal callers; unfilled seats are sold at discount to students five minutes before the curtain goes up. For program details phone ☎43.43.96.96.

Rather less grand opera is also performed at the **Épicerie-Beaubourg** (in the Centre Beaubourg) and at the **Opéra-Comique** (Salle Favard, 5 rue Favard, 2e. Mº Richelieu-Drouot. ☎42.96.12.20). Both opera and recitals are also put on at the multipurpose performance halls (see final section, below).

Contemporary Music: Pierre Boulez and IRCAM

Beneath the Beaubourg arts center, the composer **Pierre Boulez** has been given space and funding to install a vast laboratory of acoustics and "digital signal processing"—a complex known as **IRCAM**. Here, amid banks of sophisticated synthesizers and computers, he and his team of scientists/technicians/musicians indulge in a "double dialectic" and study "psychoacoustics" toward "global, generalized solutions." To exactly what problems is unanswerable, but go and decide for yourself by playing around for free with tapes in the IRCAM lobby (entrance down the stairs by the Stravinsky pool on the south side of Beaubourg). If you're impressed, you might want to attend a performance by the resident *Ensemble Inter-Contemporain* (details from Beaubourg information desk).

Apart from Boulez, the main computer freaks are **Tod Machover**, also of IRCAM, and **Iannis Xenakis** at **CEMAMU** (Research Center for Mathematics and Musical Automation) in Issy-Les-Moulineaux. Xenakis's baby is the *UPIC*, a computer in which all the parameters of sound are drawn onto a graphics tablet (a kind of computerized drawing board) and then read and played by the machine.

Other Paris-based practitioners of contemporary and experimental music include **Olivier Messiaen**, at ninety the grand old man of Paris music; **Jean-Claude Eloy**, who exchanged serialism for oriental sounds; **Pascal Dusapin**, who verges into jazz; and **Luc Ferrarie**, an electro-acoustic producer of "anecdotal" sounds. Concerts by any of these luminaries are quite regular events. Check *Pariscope* etc for details.

Festivals

Festivals are plentiful in all the diverse fields that come under the far too general term of "classical." The **Festival de Musique Ancienne** takes place at the end of May and beginning of June, and focuses on a particular civilization or culture. The **Soirées de Saint-Aignan** at the Hôtel St-Aignan in May feature European music of the eighteenth and nineteenth centuries. There is also a **festival of sacred music** most years, a **Chopin festival**, a **Mozart festival**, and the *Festival de l'Orangerie de Sceaux* of chamber music all summer at the Château de Sceaux (see p.270).

For details of these and more, pick up the current year's **festival schedule** from one of the tourist offices or the Hôtel de Ville.

The Big Performance Halls

Events at any of the performance spaces listed below will be well advertised on billboards and posters throughout the city. Tickets can be obtained at the halls themselves, though it's easier to get them through agents like *FNAC* or *Virgin Megastore* (see p.235).

Le Bataclan, 50 bd Voltaire, 11ᵉ. Mᵒ Oberkampf. ☎47.00.30.12. One of the best places for visiting and native rock bands.

Forum des Halles, Niveau 3, Porte Rambuteau, 15 rue de l'Equerre-d'Argent, 1ᵉʳ· Mᵒ Châtelet. ☎42.03.11.11. Varied functions—theater, performance art, rock, etc, often with foreign touring groups.

Maison des Cultures du Monde, 101 bd Raspail, 6ᵉ; Mᵒ Rennes; ☎45.44.72:30. All the arts from all over the world and undominated for once by the Europeans.

Olympia, 28 bd des Capucines, 9ᵉ. Mᵒ Madeleine/Opéra. ☎ 47.42.25.49. An old music hall hosting occasional well-known rock groups.

Palais des Congrès, place de la Porte-Maillot, 17ᵉ. Mᵒ Porte-Maillot. ☎46.40.27.01. Opera, ballet, orchestral music, trade fairs, and the superstars of US and British rock.

Palais des Glaces, 37 rue du Faubourg-du-Temple, 10ᵉ. Mᵒ République. ☎46.07.49.93. Smallish theater used for rock, ballet, jazz, and French folk.

Palais Omnisports de Bercy, 8 bd de Bercy, 12ᵉ. Mᵒ Bercy. ☎43.41.72.04. Opera, bicycle racing, Bruce Springsteen, ice hockey, and Citroën launches—the newest multipurpose stadium with seats to give vertigo to the most level-headed, but an excellent space when used in the round.

Palais des Sports, Porte de Versailles, 15ᵉ. Mᵒ Porte-de-Versailles. ☎48.28.40.10. The Maddison Avenue Garden equivalent for seeing your favorite rock star in miniature half a mile away.

Zenith, Parc de la Villette, 211 av Jean-Jaurès, 20ᵉ· Mᵒ Porte-de-Pantin. ☎42.08.60.00/ 42.40.60.00. Seating for six-and-a-half-thousand people in an inflatable stadium designed exclusively for rock and pop concerts. The concrete column with a descending red airplane is the landmark to head for.

CHAPTER TEN

FILM, THEATER, AND DANCE

There are over 350 **films** showing in Paris in any one week, which puts moving visuals on an equal footing with the still visuals of the art museums and galleries. And they cover every place and period, with new works (excepting British movies) arriving here long before London and New York (and even big American films reach Parisian movie theaters before London's). If your French is good enough for subtitles, go and see a Senegalese, Taiwanese, Brazilian, or Finnish film that probably would never be seen in the US.

Theater can be less accessible to non-natives—especially the *café-théâtre* touted by "knowing" guide-writers—but there is stimulation in the cult of the director (Peter Brook and other exiles, as well as the French) while, transcending language barriers, there are exciting developments in **dance**, much of it incorporating **mime**, which, alas, no longer seems to have a separate status.

As for **sex shows and soft porn cabarets**, with names that conjure up the classic connotations of the sinful city—*Les Folies Bergères* or the *Moulin Rouge*—they thrive and will no doubt continue for as long as Frenchmen's culture excuses anything on the grounds of stereotyped female beauty. See p.121 for a fuller account.

Listings for all films and stage productions are detailed in *Pariscope*, etc., with brief resumés or reviews. Venues with wheelchair access will say "*accessible aux handicapés*." **Cinema tickets** rarely need to be bought in advance and are no more expensive than most Manhattan cinemas. The easiest place to get **stage tickets** is at one of the *FNAC* shops (see pp.191, 201) or at two ticket kiosks. These are at the Châtelet-Les Halles RER station (through the turnstiles, alongside *FNAC Photo-Service* and the bureau de change; Tues–Fri 12:30–7:30pm, Sat 2–7:30pm) and on place de la Madeleine, 8e (opposite no. 15; Tues–Sat 12:30–8pm, Sun 12:30–4pm). They sell same-day tickets at half price, but lines can be very long. **Prices** for the theater vary between 70F and 150F on average and there are weekday student discounts. Most theaters are closed on Monday.

Booking well in advance is essential for new productions and all shows by the superstar directors. These are sometimes a lot more expensive, quite reasonably so when they are the much-favored epics, lasting seven hours or even carrying on over several days.

FRENCH CINEMA

The French have treated cinema as an art form, deserving of state subsidy, ever since its origination with the Lumière brothers in 1895. The medium has as yet never had to bow down to TV, the seat of judgment stays in Cannes, and Paris is the cinema capital of the world.

But as far as making movies is concerned, the French have kept a low and very introverted profile over the last few years. The one exception is Jean-Paul Rappeneau's *Cyrano de Bergerac* with Gérard Dépardieu, the most expensive French film ever made, and breaking all box office expectations in America and Britain. During the 1980s style movies like *Diva* or *Subway* touched a trend but lacked all substance. Agnès Varda's *Vagabonde*, which treated the issue of unbridgeable cultures, failed to cross frontiers and was widely ignored in France. Claude Zidi's *Le Cop*, about police corruption in Paris, was by far the most enjoyable offering but atypical in its quick lightheartedness.

Meanwhile, foreign directors such as Kurosawa and Wajda have benefited from French public funds, French studios, and coproduction deals to bring out non-French language works. American-movie versions have been made of the quintessentially French novel *Les Liaisons Dangereuses*, and of the Parisian life of Henry Miller and Anaïs Nin. The top box office hits are all dominated by transatlantic imports and a quick scan down the listings for any week shows just how few solely French films are being made. But for all that, Paris remains the place to see movies, from the latest blockbuster to the least-known works of the earliest directors.

Cinema

Cinema-going in Paris is not exclusively an evening occupation: the *séances* (programs) start between 1 and 3pm at many places and continue through to the early hours. The average price is 35F; most movie theaters have lower rates on Monday, and reductions for students from Monday to Thursday. Some matinée *séances* also have discounts. All are **non-smoking**, and some have unpaid ushers who need to be tipped. Almost all of the huge selection of foreign films will be shown at some movie theaters in the original—*v.o.* in the listings as opposed to *v.f.*, which means it's dubbed into French (*v.a.* means it's the English version of an international coproduction).

Many of the movie theaters run **"festivals"** when you can pass an entire day or more watching your favorite actor/actress, director, genre, or period. The *Action* chain, the *Escurial*, and *Entrepôt* run regular feasts, as does *Le Studio 28*. As well as those, some of the foreign institutes in the city have occasional screenings, so if your favorite director is a Hungarian, a Swede, a Yugoslav, or whatever, check what's on at those countries' cultural centers. These will be listed along with other cinema-clubs and museum screenings, under *"Séances exceptionnelles"* or *"Ciné-clubs,"* and are usually cheaper than ordinary movie theaters.

An **International Festival of Women's Films** takes place at the end of March or beginning of April, organized by the *Maison des Arts* in Créteil, a southeastern suburb at the end of the Balard-Créteil métro line. 1991 was the thirteenth year of this festival, which has been very influential in promoting and encouraging works by women, particularly in France. Chinese, Russian, American, Japanese, and European films compete for the eight awards, six of which are voted for by the audiences. Program details are available from mid-March onwards, from the *Maison des Arts* (place Salvador-Allende, Créteil; Mᵒ Créteil-Préfecture; ☎49.80.18.88) or from the *Maison des Femmes* (8 Cité Prost, 11ᵉ; Mᵒ Faidherbe-Chaligny; ☎43.48.29.91).

Cinemas

Action Rive Gauche & Action Écoles, 5 and 23 rue des Écoles, 5ᵉ, Mᵒ Cardinal-Lemoine/Maubert-Mutualité; **Action Christine**, 4 rue Christine, 6ᵉ, Mᵒ Odéon/St-Michel. The *Action* chain specializes in new prints of ancient classics.

Cosmos, 76 rue de Rennes, 6ᵉ. Mᵒ St-Sulpice. Specializes in Soviet movies.

L'Escurial Panoramas, 11 bd de Port-Royal, 13ᵉ. Mᵒ Gobelins. A cinema that combines plush seats, big screen, and more art than commerce in its screening policy, this is likely to be showing something along the lines of *Eraserhead* on the small screen and the latest offering from a big name director—French, Japanese, or American—on the panoramic screen (and never dubbed).

Le Grand Rex, 1 bd Poissonnière, 2ᵉ. Mᵒ Bonne-Nouvelle. Just as outrageous as the *Pagode* (see below) but in the kitsch line, with a Metropolis-style tower blazing its neon name, 2800 seats, and a ceiling of stars and city skylines, plus flying whales and dolphins, all as a frame for the largest cinema screen in Europe. It's the good old Thirties public movie-seeing experience, though unfortunately all its foreign films are dubbed.

Kinopanarama, 60 av de la Motte-Piquet, 15ᵉ. Mᵒ La Motte-Picquet. One of the big ones, which has reintroduced organ interludes for some showings.

Lucernaire Forum, 53 rue Notre-Dame-des-Champs, 6ᵉ. Mᵒ Notre-Dame-des-Champs/Vavin. An art complex with three screening rooms, two theaters, an art gallery, bar, and restaurant, showing mainly old arty movies.

Max Linder Panorama, 24 bd Poissonnière, 9ᵉ. Mᵒ Bonne-Nouvelle. Opposite *Le Grand Rex*, this always shows films in the original, and has almost as big a screen, state-of-the-art sound, and Art Déco decor.

L'Olympic Entrepôt, 7–9 rue Francis-de-Pressensé, 14ᵉ. Mᵒ Pernety. One of the best alternative Paris movie houses, which has been keeping ciné-addicts happy for years with its three screens dedicated to the obscure, the subversive, and the brilliant, and to showing among those categories many Arab and African films. It also shows videos, satellite and cable TV, has a bookshop selling books and posters on the cinema (Mon–Sat 2–8pm), and a restaurant (noon–midnight daily).

La Pagode, 57bis rue de Babylone, 7ᵉ. Mᵒ François-Xavier. The most beautiful of all the capital's movie theaters, originally transplanted from Japan at the turn of the century to be a rich Parisienne's party place. The wall panels of the *Grande Salle* are embroidered in silk; golden dragons and elephants hold up the candelabra; and a battle between Japanese and Chinese warriors rages on the ceiling. If you don't like the films being shown you can still come here for tea and cakes (see p.217).

Le Studio des Ursulines, 10 rue des Ursulines, 5ᵉ. Mᵒ Censier-Daubenton. This was where *The Blue Angel* had its world premiere.

Le Studio 28, 10 rue de Tholozé, 18ᵉ. Mᵒ Blanche/Abbesses. In its early days, after one of the first showings of Bunuel's *L'Age d'Or*, this was done over by extreme right-wing Catholics who destroyed the screen and the paintings by Dali and Ernst in the foyer. The cinema still hosts avant-garde premieres, followed occasionally by discussions with the director, as well as regular festivals.

Utopia, 9 rue Champollion, 5ᵉ. Mᵒ Odéon. Another favorite.

Cinémathèques

For the seriously committed film-freak, the best movie venues in Paris are the three **cinémathèques**, in the *Salle Garance* on the top floor of Beaubourg (4ᵉ, Mᵒ Rambuteau; closed Tues) and the *Cinémathèque Française* in the *Musée du Cinéma* (Palais de Chaillot, corner of avs Président-Wilson and Albert-de-Mun, 16ᵉ; Mᵒ Trocadéro) and in the Palais de Tokyo (13 av du Président-Wilson, 16ᵉ; Mᵒ Trocadéro), with screenings every day. These give you a choice of over fifty different films a week, many of which would never be shown commercially, and tickets are only 20F.

The *Vidéothèque de Paris* in the Forum des Halles (see p.171) is another excellent-value venue for the bizarre or obscure on celluloid or video. Their repertoires are always based around a particular theme with some connection with Paris.

The Largest Screen

There is one cinematic experience that has to be recommended, however trite and vainglorious the film. The venue in question is **La Géode**, the mirrored globe bounced off the *Cité des Sciences* at La Villette. The 180-degree projection system is called Omnimax and works with a special camera and a 70mm horizontally progressing film. There are less than a dozen of these things in existence, and their owners are not the sort to produce brilliant films. What you get is a Readers' Digest view of outer space, great cities of the world, monumental landscapes, or whatever, on a screen wider than your range of vision into which you feel you might fall at any moment. Low-flying shots or shots from the front of moving trains, bobsleighs, cars, etc are sensational.

There are several screenings a day, but you usually need to reserve in advance (Tues–Sun 10am–9pm; tickets 45F/35F or 70F/60F for combined ticket with *Cité des Sciences*; reservations ☎46.42.13.13; Mᵒ Porte-de-la-Villette/Corentin-Cariou). The film is the same for months at a time (listed in *Pariscope*, etc under the 19ᵉ *arrondissement*) and not understanding French is a positive advantage.

Television

At the other end of the scale of screen size, there's French TV, with seven channels: two public, *Antenne 2* and *FR3*; one satellite, *La Sept*; one subscription, *Canal Plus* (with some unencrypted programs); and three commercial open broadcasts, *TF1*, *La Cinq*, and *M6*. *Canal Plus* is **the main movie channel** (and funder of the French film industry) with repeats of foreign films usually shown at least once in the original language. *FR3*'s **Sunday evening movie** (at 10:40pm) is usually an old undubbed Hollywood classic. *Antenne 2* debates cinema and cineastes in its weekly magazine *Cinéma, cinémas 2ᵉ* on Tuesday at 10:10pm.

The main French **news** comes at 8pm on *TF1*, *La Cinq*, and *Antenne 2*; and at varying times between 10 and 11:15pm on *FR3*. At 7am on *Canal Plus* (unencrypted) you can watch the American CBS evening news.

Drama

Bourgeois farces, postwar classics, Shakespeare, Racine—all these are staged with the same range of talent or lack of it that you'd find in New York or London. What you'll rarely find are the home-grown, socially concerned, and realist dramas of the sort that keep theater alive in Britain. An Edward Bond or David Edgar play crops up in translation often enough—the French equivalent hardly exists.

Samuel Beckett—who lived in Paris until his death in 1990—was the last of the great generation of French or Francophone dramatists, which included Anouilh, Genet, Camus, Sartre, Adamov, Ionesco, Cocteau. Their plays are still frequently performed. The *Huchette* has been playing Ionesco's *La Cantatrice Chauve* every night for nearly thirty years, and Genet's *Les Paravents*, that set off riots on its opening night, can now be included alongside Corneille and Shakespeare in the program of the **Comédie Française** (the national theater for the classics at 2 rue Richelieu, 1er; M° Palais-Royal; ☎40.15.00.15).

And Paris theater still has little xenophobia—foreign artists are as welcome as they've always been. In any month there might be an Italian, Mexican, German, or Brazilian production playing in the original language, or offerings by radical groups from Turkey, Iraq, China, or wherever, who have no possibilities of a home venue.

The best time of all for theater-lovers to come to Paris is for the **Festival d'Automne** from October to December, an international festival of all the performing arts, which attracts stage directors of the caliber of the American Bob Wilson and Polish Tadeusz Kantor (see p.22).

In the best contemporary work emanating from the city it is directors, not writers, who shine. This superstar breed—such as Peter Brook at the Bouffes du Nord and Ariane Mnouchkine at the Cartoucherie Théâtre du Soleil—treat playwrights as anachronisms and classic texts as packs of cards to be shuffled into theatrical moments where spectacular and dazzling sensation take precedence over speech. These are the shows to go to see: huge casts, extraordinary sets, overwhelming sound and light effects—an experience, even if you haven't understood a word.

Venues

Bouffes du Nord, 37bis bd de la Chapelle, 10ᵉ. M° Chapelle. ☎46.07.34.50. Peter Brook has made this his permanent base in Paris, where he produces such events as the nine-hour show of the Indian epic *Mahabharata*.

Cartoucherie Théâtre du Soleil, rte du Champ-de-Manoeuvre, 12ᵉ. M° Château-de-Vincennes. ☎43.74.24.08. The most memorable recent production of Russian-born Ariane Mnouchkine's workers' co-op company was the epic combination of Euripides and Aeschylus in *Les Atrides* (the House of Atreus).

Centre Dramatique National, 41 av des Grésillons, Gennevilliers. M° Gabriel-Péri. ☎47.93.26.30. Several stimulating productions have brought acclaim—and audiences—to this suburban venue in recent years.

Comédie Française, 2 rue Richelieu, 1er. M° Palais-Royal. ☎40.15.00.15. The national theater for the classics.

Galerie 55—The English Theater of Paris, 55 rue de Seine, 6e. M° Odéon/St-Germain-des-Prés. ☎43.26.63.51. Only puts on shows in English, and tends toward a middle ground between the tastes of its student, diplomatic, and business audiences. The theater is small, so you need to reserve well in advance.

Maison des Arts, Créteil (see above under "Cinema"). Serves also as a lively suburban theater.

Maison de la Culture, 1 bd Lénine, Bobigny. M° Pablo-Picasso. ☎48.31.11.45. The resident company, *MC93*, astounded theater critics and theatergoers in early 1991 by an extraordinarily successful dramatization of *De Rerum Natura—The Nature of Things*—a scientific treatise by the first-century BC Roman poet, Lucretius, using the auditorium as stage, considerable amounts of Latin, a boxing match, mime, and giant swings.

Odéon Théâtre de l'Europe, 1 place Paul-Claudel, 6e. M° Odéon. ☎43.25.70.32. Roger Planchon's Lyon-based *Théâtre National Populaire* puts on its Paris performances on the main stage, while the smaller stage, the *Petit Odéon*, hosts **foreign-language plays**. In May 1968 this theater was occupied by students and became an open parliament with the backing of its directors, Jean-Louis Barrault (of Baptiste fame in *Les Enfants du Paradis*) and Madeleine Renaud, one of the great French stage actresses. Promptly sacked by de Gaulle's Minister for Culture, they formed a new company and moved to the disused Gare d'Orsay until President Giscard's museum plans sent them packing.

Renaud-Barrault at the **Rond-Point**, av Franklin-Roosevelt, 16e. M° Franklin-Roosevelt. ☎42.56.60.70. The permanent home for the Renaud-Barrault troupe (see *Odéon* above), where their performances of Beckett are unequaled.

Théâtre des Amandiers, 7 av Pablo-Picasso, Nanterre, 92. RER Nanterre-Université and theater bus. ☎47.21.18.81. The suburban base for Patrice Chéreau's exciting productions.

Théâtre de la Bastille, 79 rue de la Roquette, 11e. M° Bastille. ☎43.57.42.14. One of the best places for new work and fringe productions.

Théâtre de la Colline, 15 rue Malte-Brun, 20e. M° Gambetta. ☎43.66.43.60. The repertoire includes epic directors' works as well as less well-established innovators.

Théâtre de la Commune, 2 rue Edouard-Poisson, Aubervilliers. M° Aubervilliers. ☎48.34.67.67. Suburban theater with an excellent reputation.

Théâtre de l'Est Parisien, 159 rue Gambetta, 20e. M° Gambetta. ☎43.64.80.80. Another good venue for innovative drama.

Théâtre National de Chaillot, Palais de Chaillot, pl du Trocadéro, 16e. M° Trocadéro. ☎47.27.81.15. The great Antoine Vitez is no more, but the mega-spectacles go on.

Dance and Mime

In the 1970s all the dancers left Paris for New York, and only **mime** remained as the great performing art of the French, thanks to the Lecoq school of Mime and Improvisation, and the famous practitioner, Marcel Marceau. Since Marceau's demise, no new pure mime artists of his stature have appeared. Lecoq foreign graduates return to their own countries while the French incorporate their skills in dance, comedy routines, and improvisation. While this cross-fertilization has given rise to new standards in performing art, it is still a pity that mime by itself is rarely seen (except on the streets, and Beaubourg's piazza in particular).

The best-known and loved French clown, Coluche, died in a motorcycle accident in 1986. Most of his acts were incomprehensible to foreigners, save jests such as starting a campaign for the presidency, for which he posed nude with a feather up his behind. A troupe of mimes and clowns who debunk the serious in literature rather than politics are *La Clown Kompanie*, famous for their Shakespearian tragedies turned into farce. Joëlle Bouvier and Régis Obadia trained both at dance school and at Lecoq's—their company *L'Equisse* combines both disciplines, takes inspiration from paintings, and portrays a dark, hallucinatory world.

The renaissance of French **dance** in the 1980s has not, on the whole, been Paris-based. Subsidies have gone to regional companies expressly to decentralize the arts. But all the best contemporary practitioners come to the capital regularly. Names to look out for are Régine Chopinot's troupe from La Rochelle, Jean-Claude Gallotta's from Grenoble, Roland Petit's from Marseille, and Dominique Bagouet's from Montpellier. The new creative choreographers based in or around Paris include Maguy Marin, Karine Saporta, François Verret, and Jean-François Duroure.

Humor, everyday actions and obsessions, social problems, and the darker shades of life find expression in the myriad current dance forms. A multi-dimensional performing art is created by the combinations of movement, mime, ballet, music from the medieval to contemporary jazz-rock, speech, noise, and theatrical effects. The Gallotta-choreographed film *Rei-Dom* opened up a whole new range of possibilities. Many of the traits of the modern epic theater are shared with dance, including crossing international frontiers.

Many of the theaters listed above under drama include both mime and dance in their programs: the *Théâtre de la Bastille* shows works by young dancers and choreographers; Maguy Marin's company is based at the Créteil *Maison des Arts* and François Verret's at the *Maison de la Culture* in Bobigny, where a prestigious competition for young choreographers is held in March; and the *Amandiers* in Nanterre hosts major contemporary works.

More experimental venues to keep an eye out for in the listings magazines, in addition to those below, are *L'Espace Kiron*, the *Théâtre Gémier*, and the rehearsal space *Ménagerie de Verre*.

Plenty of space and critical attention is also given to **tap, tango, folk, and jazz dancing**, and visiting traditional dance troupes from all over the world. There are also a dozen or so black African companies in Paris—who, predictably, find it hard to compete with Europeans (and the fashionable Japanese) for venues—several Indian dance troupes, the *Ballet Classique Khmer*, and many more from exiled cultures.

As for **ballet**, the principal stage is at the old Opéra, where the company is directed by the young Patrick Dupond, who suffered as a dancer under his predecessor's temperamental tantrums and wild unreliability. This was Rudolf Nureyev, sacked in 1990 for failing to come up with the promised program. Patrick Dupond hopes to bring back many of the best French classical dancers, including Sylvie Guillem, who stormed off under Nureyev's directorship. Paris has also lost Maurice Béjart, wooed back to his home town of Marseille, who used to run the *Ballet du XXe Siècle*. But ballet fans can still be sure of masterly performances, at the *Opéra*, the *Théâtre des Champs-Elysées*, and the *Théâtre Musical de Paris*.

The highlight of the year for dance is the *Festival International de Danse de Paris* in October and November, which involves contemporary, classical, and different national traditions. Other **festivals** combining theater, dance, mime, classical music, and its descendants include the *Festival du Marais* in June, the *Festival "Foire Saint-Germain"* in June and July, and the *Festival d'Automne* from mid-September to mid-December.

Venues

Café de la Danse, 5 passage Louis-Philippe. M° Bastille. ☎43.57.05.35. This tiny cramped space, with its hard bench seats, is renowned for innovative, if sometimes infuriatingly difficult, programs. Unfortunately, its debts are massive and the owner of the building can see more lucrative uses, so its days are numbered.

Centre Mandapa, 6 rue Wurtz, 13e. M° Glacière. ☎45.89.01.60. The one theater dedicated to traditional dances from around the world.

Le Déjazet, 41 bd du Temple, 3e. M° République. ☎48.87.97.34. Experimental dance productions, with a particular emphasis on mime.

Opéra de Paris-Garnier, place de l'Opéra, 9e. M° Opéra. ☎47.42.53.71. Now that the Bastille opera house has opened, the former opera is given over exclusively to ballet.

La Piscine, 254 av de la Division-Leclerc, Châtenay-Malabry. RER Robinson and bus #194. 46.61.14.27. *Le Campagnol* company of dance and improvisation that featured in Ettore Scola's film *Le Bal* have their own theater out here in the suburbs.

Théâtre de la Bastille, 79 rue de la Roquette, 11e. M° Bastille. ☎43.57.42.14. As well as more traditional theater (see above), there are also dance and mime performances.

Théâtre des Champs-Élysées, 15 av Montaigne, 8e. M° Alma-Marceau. ☎47.23.47.77. Forever aiming to outdo the *Opéra* with even grander and more expensive ballet productions.

Théâtre Contemporain de la Danse, 9 rue Geoffroy-l'Asnier, 4e. M° Pont-Marie. ☎42.74.44.22. Still innovative, but with more assured critical appeal than the performances at the *Café de la Danse*.

Théâtre Musical de Paris, place du Châtelet. ☎40.28.28.40. This theater, opposite the *Théâtre de la Ville*, remains a major ballet venue. It was where, in 1910, Diaghilev put on the first season of Russian ballet, assisted by Cocteau, Rodin, Proust, and others.

Théâtre de la Ville, 2 place du Châtelet, 4e. M° Châtelet. ☎42.74.22.77. The height of success for dance productions is to end up here. Karine Saporta's work is regularly played, along with modern theater classics, comedy, and concerts. Review performances at 6 or 6:30pm are excellent value at 65F/55F.

Café-Théâtre

Literally a revue, monologue, or mini-play performed in a place where you can drink, and sometimes eat, **café-théâtre** is probably less accessible than a Racine tragedy at the *Comédie-Française*. The humor or puerile dirty jokes, word-play, and allusions to current fads, phobias, and politicians can leave even a fluent French-speaker in the dark.

If you want to give it a try, the main venues are concentrated around the Marais. Tickets average around 60F and it's best to reserve in advance—the spaces are small—though you have a good chance of getting in on the night during the week.

Blancs-Manteaux, 15 rue des Blancs-Manteaux, 4e. Mo Hôtel-de-Ville/Rambuteau. ☎48.87.15.84. Somewhat cramped venue, beneath a restaurant.

Café de la Gare, 41 rue du Temple, 4e. Mo Hôtel-de-Ville/Rambuteau. ☎42.78.52.51. This may not be operating its turn-of-the-wheel admission price system any more, but it has retained a reputation for novelty.

Point Virgule, 7 rue Ste-Croix-de-la-Bretonnerie, 4e. Mo Hôtel-de-Ville/St-Paul. ☎42.78.67.03. Occasionally interesting, but more often predictable and self-regarding.

CHAPTER ELEVEN

OUT FROM THE CITY

The region around the capital—known as the **Île de France**—and the borders of the neighboring provinces are studded with large-scale **châteaux**. Many were royal or noble retreats for hunting and other leisured pursuits; some, like Versailles, were for more serious state show. The mansions and palaces themselves—**Versailles**, above all—can be tedious in the extreme. But **Vaux-le-Vicomte**, at least, is magnificent; **Fontainebleau** is pleasantly Italian; and at any of them you can get a taste of country air in the forests and parks around, and get back to Paris comfortably in a day.

But if you have limited time and even the slightest curiosity about church buildings, forget the châteaux and make instead for the cathedral of **Chartres**—which is all it is cracked up to be, and more. Also, much closer in, on the edge of the city itself, **St-Denis** boasts a cathedral second only to Notre-Dame among Paris churches. A visit to it could be combined with an unusual approach to the city: a walk back (the best direction to follow) along the banks of the **St-Denis canal**.

Whether the various **suburban museums** deserve your attention will depend on your degree of interest in the subjects they represent. Several, however, have authoritative collections: on **china** at Sèvres, **French prehistory** at St-Germain-en-Laye, **Napoléon** at Malmaison, and the **Île de France** at Sceaux. The latter, together with the **air and space museum** at Le Bourget, should give kids a good deal of pleasure, while, farther out, there's the **horse museum** at Chantilly.

Rustic riverside junketing as depicted in so many Impressionist canvases is unfortunately a thing of the past. If you are nostalgic for those apparently carefree scenes, you could recapture just a whiff of the atmosphere on the Marne at Joinville or Champigny, or perhaps the Seine island of Chatou. But the most satisfying experience is undoubtedly **Monet's** marvelous garden at **Giverny**, the inspiration for all his waterlily canvases in the Marmottan and Musée d'Orsay.

If your interest is in contemporary architecture, one of the most outrageous and startling housing experiments in Europe can be seen at the new town of **Marne-la-Vallée**. In 1992 the European **Disneyland** will open on the outskirts of this sprawling satellite town.

For want of any other obvious logic, this chapter is arranged in counterclockwise fashion, beginning with St-Denis and ending at Disneyland.

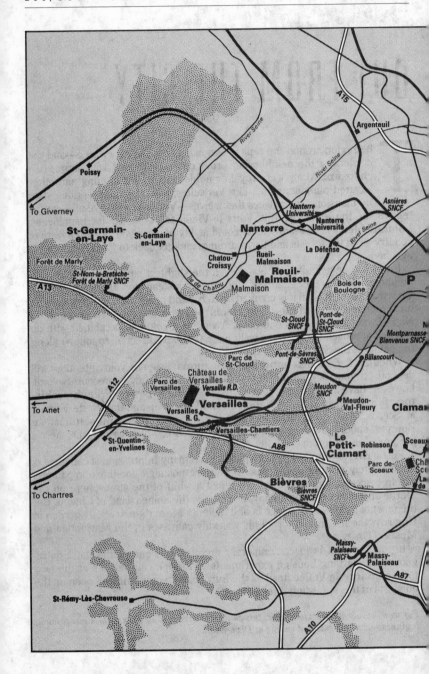

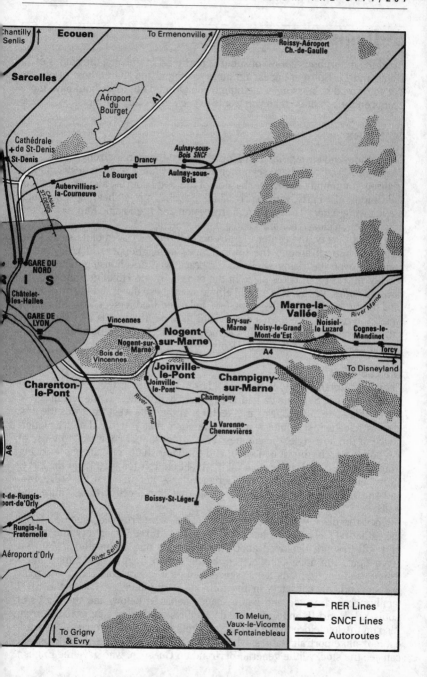

Chantilly
Senlis

Ecouen

To Ermenonville

Roissy-Aéroport
Ch.-de-Gaulle

Sarcelles

Aéroport
du
Bourget

A1

Cathédrale
de St-Denis

St-Denis

Aulnay-sous-
Bois *SNCF*

Drancy

Le Bourget

Aulnay-sous-
Bois

CANAL ST-DENIS

Aubervilliers-
la-Courneuve

GARE DU
NORD

P A R I S

Châtelet-
les-Halles

GARE DE
LYON

Vincennes

Marne-la-
Vallée

River Marne

Bry-sur-
Marne

Noisy-le-Grand
Mont-de'Est

Noisiel-
le Luzard

Cognes-le-
Mandinet

**Nogent-
sur-Marne**

Nogent-sur-
Marne

Torcy

Bois de
Vincennes

A4

To Disneyland

**Charenton-
le-Pont**

**Joinville-
le-Pont**

**Champigny-
sur-Marne**

Joinville-
le-Pont

River Marne

Champigny

A6

La Varenne-
Chennevières

t-de-Rungis-
port-d'Orly

Rungis-la-
Fraternelle

Boissy-St-Léger

Aéroport d'Orly

River Seine

To Grigny
& Evry

To Melun,
Vaux-le-Vicomte
& Fontainebleau

	RER Lines
	SNCF Lines
	Autoroutes

St-Denis and Le Bourget

Amid the amorphous sprawl of suburbs northeast of the city, the names of St-Denis and Le Bourget appear no more distinguished than a host of others. Yet you would be missing something if you ignored them, for both have more claims on the attention than you would expect, especially St-Denis.

St-Denis

Thirty-thousand-strong in 1870, one-hundred-thousand strong today, the people of **ST-DENIS** have seen their town grow into the most heavily industrialized community in France, bastion of the Red suburbs, and stronghold of the Communist Party, with nearly all the principal streets bearing some notable left-wing name. Today, though, recession and the Pacific Rim have taken a heavy toll in closed factories and unemployment.

Never a beauty, the center of St-Denis still retains traces of its small town origins, while all around the tower cranes swing hoppers of ready-mixed concrete over the rising shells of gimcrack workers' housing. The thrice-weekly **market** still takes place in the square by the Hôtel de Ville and the covered *halles* nearby. It is a multi-ethnic affair these days, and the quantity of offal on the butchers' stalls—ears, feet, tails, and bladders—shows this is not wealthy territory. The town's chief claim to fame, though, is its magnificent cathedral, close to the exit from the métro station, St-Denis Basilique—much the simplest way of getting to St-Denis.

The Cathedral

Begun by Abbot Suger, friend and adviser to kings, in the first half of the twelfth century, St-Denis cathedral is generally regarded as the birthplace of the Gothic style in European architecture. Though its west front was the first ever to have a rose window, it is in the choir that you see the clear emergence of the new style: the slimness and lightness that come with the use of the pointed arch, the ribbed vault, and the long shafts of half-column rising from pillar to roof. It is a remarkably well-lit church too, thanks to the clere-story being almost one hundred percent glass—another first for St-Denis—and the transept windows being so big that they occupy their entire end walls.

Once the place where the kings of France were crowned, since 1000 AD the cathedral has been the burial place of all but three. Their very fine **tombs and effigies** are deployed about the transepts and ambulatory (Mon–Sat 10am–5pm, Sun noon–5pm; closed during services). Among the most interesting are the enormous Renaissance memorial to François 1er on the right just beyond the entrance, in the form of a triumphal arch with the royal family perched on top and battle scenes depicted below, and the tombs of Louis XII, Henri II, and Catherine de Médicis on the left side of the church. Also on the left, close to the altar steps, Philippe the Bold's is one of the earliest look-alike portrait statues, while to the right of the ambulatory steps you can see the stocky little general, Bertrand du Guesclin, who gave the English

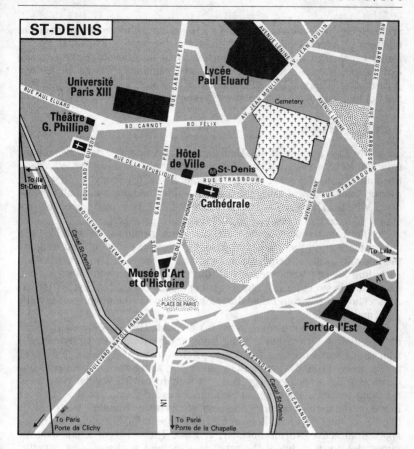

a run-around after the death of the Black Prince, and on the level above him, invariably graced by bouquets of flowers from the lunatic royalist fringe, the undistinguished statues of Louis XVI and Marie-Antoinette. And around the corner on the far side of the ambulatory is Clovis himself, king of the Franks way back in 500, a canny little German who wiped out Roman Gaul and turned it into France with Paris for a capital.

The Museum

Not many minutes' walk away on rue Gabriel-Péri is the **Musée d'Art et d'Histoire de la Ville de St-Denis** (☎42.43.05.10; Mon & Wed–Sat 10am–5:30pm, Sun 2–6:30pm; closed holidays). The quickest route is along rue de la Légion-d'Honneur, then take the third right.

The museum is housed in a former Carmelite convent, rescued from the clutches of the developers and carefully restored. The exhibits on display are not of spectacular interest, though the presentation is excellent. The **local**

archaeology collection is good and there are some interesting paintings of nineteenth- and twentieth-century industrial landscapes, including the St-Denis canal. The one unique collection is of documents relating to **the Commune**: posters, cartoons, broadsheets, paintings, plus an audiovisual presentation. There is also an exhibition of manuscripts and rare editions of the Communist poet, Paul Eluard, native son of St-Denis.

Canal St-Denis

To get to the canal—at the St-Denis end—you follow rue de la République from the Hôtel de Ville to its end by a church, then go down the left side of the church until you reach the canal bridge. If you turn left, you can **walk** all the way back **to Paris** along the towpath—about an hour and a half to Porte de la Villette. There are stretches where it looks as if you're probably not supposed to be there. Just pay no attention and keep going.

Not far from the start of the walk, past some peeling villas with lilac and cherry blossom in their unkempt gardens, you come to a cobbled ramp on the left with a cheap friendly restaurant, *La Péniche* (The Barge, needless to say). Rue Raspail leads thence to a dusty square where the town council named a side street for IRA hunger-striker Bobby Sands. Nearby, a Yugoslav runs a shop nostalgically called *Makedonia*. The whole neighborhood is calm, poor, and forgotten.

Continuing along the canal, you can't get lost. The Sacré-Coeur is visible up ahead all the way, your guiding landmark, as you pass country cottages with sunny yards open on the water, patches of greenery, sand and gravel docks, waste ground where larks rise singing above rusting bedsteads and doorless fridges, lock-keepers' cottages with roses and vegetable gardens, decaying tenements and improvised shacks as brightly painted as a Greek island house, derelict factories and huge sheds where trundling gantries load bundles of steel rods onto Belgian barges. Barge traffic is regular and the life appears attractive—to the outsider, at least. The old steel hulks slide by, gunwhales down, a dog at the prow, lace curtains at the window, a potted plant, bike propped against the cabin side, a couple of kids. But the keynote is decay and nothing looks set to last.

Le Bourget

The French were always adventurous, pioneering aviators and the name of **LE BOURGET** is intimately connected with their earliest exploits. Lindbergh landed here after his epic first flight across the Atlantic. From World War I to the development of Orly in the 1950s it was Paris's principal airport. Today it is used only for internal flights, though some of the older buildings have been turned into a fascinating **museum of flying machines**. Luckily for Le Bourget, because nothing else would bring you here.

To get there you can take the RER from Gare du Nord to DRANCY, where the Germans and the French Vichy regime had a transit camp for Jews en route to Auschwitz and where, among others, the poet Max Jacob died (a cattle wagon and a stone stele in the courtyard of a housing project commemorate the nearly 100,000 Jews who passed through here, of whom only 1518 returned). From the station (and be warned that not all trains on this line stop at Drancy) follow av Francis-de-Pressensé as far as the main road. Turn left and, by a *tabac* on the left at the first crossroads, get bus #152 to LE BOURGET/MUSÉE DE L'AIR. Alternatively, bus #350 from Gare du Nord, Gare de l'Est, Porte de la Chapelle, or #152 from Porte de la Villette.

Musée de l'Air et de l'Espace

The air and space museum (Tues–Sun 10am–5pm) occupies the old airport buildings. It consists of five adjacent hangars, the first devoted to space, with rockets, satellites, space capsules, etc. Some are mock-ups, some the real thing. Among the latter are a Lunar Roving Vehicle, the Apollo XIII command module in which James Lovell and his fellow-astronauts nearly came to grief, the Soyuz craft in which a French astronaut flew, and France's own first successful space rocket. Everything is accompanied by extremely good explanatory panels—though in French only.

The remainder of the exhibition is arranged in chronological order, starting with hangar A (the furthest away from the entrance), which covers the period 1919–39. Several record-breakers here, including the Bréguet XIX which made the first ever crossing of the South Atlantic in 1927. Also, the corrugated iron job that featured so long on US postage stamps: a Junkers F13, which the Germans were forbidden to produce after World War I and which was taken over instead by the US mail.

Hangar B shows a big collection of **World War II planes**, including a V-1 flying bomb and the Nazis' last jet fighter, the largely wooden Heinkel 162A. Incredibly, the plans were completed on September 24, 1944, and it flew on December 6. There are photographic displays and some revealing statistics on war damage in France. The destruction encompassed: two-thirds of railroad wagons, four-fifths of barges, 115 large railroad stations, nine thousand bridges, eighty wharves, and one house in twenty-two (plus one in six partially destroyed).

C and D cover the years **1945 to the present day**, during which the French aviation industry, having lost eighty percent of its capacity in 1945, has recovered to a preeminent position in the world. Its high-tech achievement is represented here by the super-sophisticated best-selling Mirage fighters, the first Concorde prototype and—symbol of national vigor and virility—the Ariane space-launcher (the two latter parked on the tarmac outside). No warheads on site, as far as we know . . . Hangar E is light and sporty aircraft.

Chantilly and Around

CHANTILLY is the kind of place you go when you think it's time you did something at the weekend, like get out and get some culture and fresh air. Château, park, museum . . . two, in fact, and one of them with a difference: it's devoted to live horses. For Chantilly is a racing lover's Mecca. Some 3000 thoroughbreds prance the forest rides each morning, and two of the season's classiest **flat races** are held here.

The town is 40km north of Paris, accessible **by train** from the Gare du Nord. The footpaths **GR11** and **12** pass through the park and forest, for a more peaceful and leisurely way of exploring this bit of country.

The Château

The Chantilly estate used to belong to two of the most powerful clans in France: first to the Montmorencys, then through marriage to the Condés. The present **château** (☎16/44.57.08.00; 10am–6pm; closed Tues) was put up in the late nineteenth century. It replaced a palace, destroyed in the Revolution, which had been built for the Grand Condé, who smashed Spanish military power for Louis XIV in 1643. It's an imposing rather than beautiful structure, too heavy for grace, but it stands well, surrounded by water and looking out in a haughty manner over a formal arrangement of pools and pathways designed by the busy Le Nôtre.

The story always told about it is of the suicide of Vatel, temperamental majordomo to the mighty and orchestrator of financier Fouquet's fateful dinner party ten years earlier in 1661 (see p.273). Wandering the corridors in the small hours, distraught because two tables had gone meatless at the royal dinner—Louis XIV was staying—Vatel bumped into a kitchen boy carrying some fish for the morrow. "Is that all there is?" "Yes," replied the boy, whereupon Vatel, dishonored, played the Roman and ran upon his sword.

The entrance to the château is across a moat past two realistic bronzes of hunting hounds. The visitable parts are all museum (same hours as the château): mainly an enormous collection of paintings and drawings. They are not well displayed and you quickly get visual indigestion from the massed ranks of good, bad, and indifferent, deployed as if of equal value. Some highlights, however, are a collection of portraits of sixteenth- and seventeenth-century French monarchs and princes in the Galerie de Logis; interesting Greek and Roman bits in the tower room called the Rotonde de la Minerve; a big series of sepia stained glass illustrating Apuleius's *Golden Ass* in the Galerie de Psyche, together with some very lively portrait drawings; and, in the so-called Santuario, some Raphaels, a Filippino Lippi, and forty miniatures from a fifteenth-century *Book of Hours* attributed to the French artist Jean Fouquet.

The museum's single greatest treasure is in the library, the Cabinet des Livres, which can be entered only in the presence of the guide. It is **Les Très Riches Heures du Duc de Berry**, the most celebrated of all Books of Hours. The illuminated pages illustrating the months of the year with representative scenes from contemporary (early 1400s) rural life—like harvesting and plowing, sheepshearing and pruning, all drawn from life—are richly colored and drawn with a delicate naturalism, as well as being sociologically interesting. Unfortunately, and understandably, only facsimiles are on display, but these give an excellent idea of the original. Sets of postcards, of middling fidelity, are on sale in the entrance. There are thousands of other fine books as well.

The Horse Museum

Five minutes' walk along the château drive, the colossal stable block has been transformed into a museum of the horse, the **Musée Vivant du Cheval** (Mon–Fri 10:30am–5:30pm, Sat, Sun & hols 10:30am–6pm). The building was erected at the beginning of the eighteenth century by the incumbent Condé prince, who believed he would be reincarnated as a horse and wished to provide fitting accommodation for 240 of his future relatives.

In the main hall horses of different breeds from around the world are stalled, with a ring for demonstrations (inquire at the ticket desk for details), followed by a series of life-size models illustrating the various activities horses are used for. In the rooms off are collections of paintings, horseshoes, veterinary equipment, bridles and saddles, a mock-up of a blacksmith's, children's horse toys (including a chain-driven number, with handles in its ears, which belonged to Napoléon III), and a fanciful Sicilian cart painted with scenes of Crusader battles. Visitors with princely ambitions might care to know that the authorities can arrange a *spectâcle*-plus-dinner party for up to five hundred guests or cocktails for a thousand.

Ecouen

ECOUEN lies midway between Chantilly and Paris, and makes a good place to stop, if you have time, on the train from the Gare du Nord. Get out at Ecouen-Ezanville, the first stop outside the high-rise suburbs if you are approaching from Paris.

The Renaissance **château** here belonged, like Chantilly, first to the Montmorencys, then to the Condés. It has been converted into the **Musée National de la Renaissance** (9:45am–12:30pm & 2–5:15pm; closed Tues). In addition to some of the original interior decoration, including frescoes and magnificent carved fireplaces, the rooms display a choice and manageable selection of Renaissance furniture, tapestries, woodcarvings, jewelry, and so forth. But you need to know you have a definite interest in the period to make it worth the effort of getting there.

Senlis and Ermenonville

An attractive old town, ten kilometers east of Chantilly, **SENLIS** (trains again from Gare du Nord, though on a different route to Chantilly) has a cathedral contemporary with Notre-Dame and all the trappings of medieval ramparts, Roman towers, and royal palace remnants to entice hordes of day-trippers and weekenders from the capital. Blood sports enthusiasts can see how the French do it at the **Musée de la Vé:nerie** (summer Wed 10am–noon, Mon & Thurs–Sun 10am–noon & 2–6pm, winter Wed 10am–noon, Mon & Thurs–Sun 10am–noon & 2–6pm).

Another dozen kilometers away is the eighteenth-century château and park of **ERMENONVILLE**, where **Rousseau** died. He was buried on an island in the lake, but not long afterwards the Revolution moved his body to the Panthéon.

Just West of Paris

Josephine Bonaparte's country house, an **island in the Seine** once frequented by the stars of Impressionism, and a **museum of prehistoric, Celtic, and Roman France**—all three places lie to the west of Paris on the RER *ligne A1*. As Saint-Germain, the furthest, is only twenty minutes away, half a day is enough to visit any of them.

Malmaison

The château of **MALMAISON** was the home of the Empress Josephine. During the 1800–1804 Consulate, Napoléon himself would drive out at weekends, though by all accounts his presence was hardly guaranteed to make the party go with a bang. Twenty minutes was all the time allowed for meals, and when called upon to sing in party games, the great man always gave a rendition of *Malbrouck s'en va-t'en guerre*, out of tune. A slightly odd choice, too, when you remember that it was Malbrouck, the Duke of Marlborough, who had given the French armies a couple of drubbings 100 years earlier. Yet according to his secretary, Malmaison was "the only place next to the battlefield where he was truly himself." After their divorce, Josephine stayed on here, occasionally receiving visits from the emperor, until her death in 1814.

The **château** (10am–12:30pm & 1:30–5:30pm; closed Tues; guided tours only; ☎47.49.20.07) is set in the beautiful grounds of the **Bois-Préau**. It's relatively small and surprisingly enjoyable. The visit includes private and official apartments, in part with original furnishings, as well as Josephine's clothes, china, glass, and personal possessions. During the Nazi occupation, the imperial chair—in the library—was rudely violated by the fat buttocks of Reichsmarschall Goering, dreaming perhaps of promotion or the conquest of Egypt. There are other Napoleonic bits in the **Bois-Préau museum** (10:30am–1pm & 2–6pm; closed Tues; same ticket as above).

The RER goes direct to RUEIL-MALMAISON, whence you have to walk. An alternative involving less walking is to get off the RER at LA DEFENSE and take bus #158A to Malmaison-Château. If you wanted to make a feature of the walk, you could go to Rueil-Malmaison and follow the GR11 footpath from the Pont de Chatou along the left bank of the Seine and into the château park.

On a high bump of ground behind the château, and not easy to get to without a car, is the 1830s fort of **Mont Valérien**. Once a place of pilgrimage, it is also the site where the Germans killed four and a half thousand hostages and Resistance people during the war. It is again a national shrine, though the memorial itself is not much to look at.

Île de Chatou

A long narrow island in the Seine, the **ÎLE DE CHATOU** was once a rustic spot where Parisians came on the newly opened railroad to row and dine and flirt at the riverside *guinguettes* (eating and dancing establishments). One of these survives, forlorn and derelict, just below the Pont de Chatou road bridge. It is the **Maison Fournaise**, a favorite haunt of Renoir, Monet,

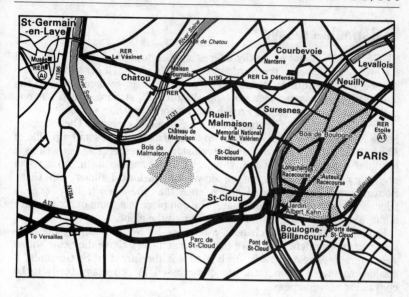

Manet, Van Gogh, Seurat, Sisley, Courbet . . . half of them in love with the proprietor's daughter, Alphonsine. One of Renoir's best-known canvases, *Le Déjeuner des Canotiers*, shows his friends lunching on the balcony. Vlaminck and his fellow-Fauves, Derain and Matisse, were also habitués. In fact, it was from here that Vlaminck set off for the 1905 *Salon des Indépendants* with the truckload of paintings that caused the critics to coin the term Fauvism.

Even now the buildings are not completely untenanted, for an elderly Algerian lives in the tumbledown outhouses at one end. But at last Chatou council is taking an interest. The elegant ironwork of the balcony has been renewed, with the help of a donation from the American Friends of the Maison Fournaise. The plan is to turn it into a restaurant once again. And it's certainly a great site, with a huge plane tree shading the riverbank and a view of the barges racing downstream on the current.

The downstream end of the island has been made into a **park**, which tapers away into a tree-lined tail hardly wider than the path. The upstream end is spooky in the extreme. A track, black with oil and ooze and littered with assorted junk, bumps along past yellowed grass and bald poplar trees to a group of ruined houses stacked with beat-up cars.

Beyond the railroad bridge a louche-looking chalet, guarded by German shepherds, stands beside the track. A concrete block saying "No Entry" in homemade lettering bars the way. If you're bold enough to ignore it, there's a view from the head of the island of the old market gardens on the right bank and the decaying industrial landscape of Nanterre on the left.

Access to the island is from the Rueil-Malmaison RER stop. Just walk straight ahead on to the Pont de Chatou. Bizarrely, there's a twice-yearly ham and antique fair on the island, which could be fun to check out (March and September).

St-Germain-en-Laye

ST-GERMAIN is not especially interesting as a town, but if you've been to the prehistoric caves of the Dordogne, or plan to go, you'll get a lot from the **Musée des Antiquités Nationales** (Wed–Sun 9am–5:15pm). It is in the unattractively renovated château (opposite the RER station), which was one of the main residences of the French court before Versailles was built.

The presentation and lighting make the visit a real pleasure. The extensive Stone Age section includes a mock-up of the Lascaux caves and a profile of Abbé Breuil, the priest who made prehistoric art respectable, as well as a beautiful collection of decorative objects, tools, and so forth. All ages of prehistory are covered, right on down into historical times with Celts, Romans, and Franks: abundant evidence that the French have been a talented arty lot for a very long time. The end piece is a room of comparative archaeology, with objects from cultures across the globe.

From right outside the château, a terrace—Le Nôtre arranging the landscape again—stretches for more than two kilometers above the Seine with a view over the whole of Paris. All behind it is the **forest of St-Germain**, a sizable expanse of woodland, but crisscrossed by too many roads to be convincing as wilderness.

Giverny and Anet

These two excursions are some way out of Paris to the west. **Monet's garden at Giverny** is really special: worth all the effort of a train ride out from Paris and then a further six kilometers by taxi, foot, or thumb. The château at Anet, twenty kilometers or so north of DREUX, is a stop worth considering if you're driving toward western Normandy from Paris, or toward Rouen from Chartres.

Giverny

GIVERNY overlooks the Seine halfway between Paris and Rouen. Monet lived here from 1883 till his death in 1926, and the gardens he laid out leading down from his house toward the river were considered by many of his friends to be his masterpiece. Each month is reflected in a dominant color, as are each of the rooms, hung as he left them with his collection of Japanese prints. May and June, when the rhododendrons flower around the lily pond and the wisteria winds over the Japanese bridge, are the best of all times to visit. But any month, from spring to autumn, is overwhelming in the beauty of this arrangement of living shades and shapes. You'll have to contend with crowds and little black boxes snapping up images of the waterlilies far removed from Monet's rendering, but there's no place like it. The gardens are open all year Tuesday to Sunday from 10am to 6pm; the house is open April to October only, during the same hours. The combined admission is 30F; entrance to the gardens alone costs 20F.

Without a car, the easiest **approach to Giverny** is by train to VERNON from Paris-St-Lazare (35min–1hr, hourly). There's no bus connection to Giverny (unless you happen on the rare and sporadic Gisors bus), so you have to take a taxi, hitch, or walk the remaining six kilometers. For the latter, cross the river and turn right on the D5; take care as you enter Giverny to take the left fork, otherwise you'll make a long detour to reach the garden entrance.

Anet

Diane de Poitiers, respected widow in the court of François 1er and powerful lover of the king's son Henri, decided that her marital home at **ANET** needed to be bigger and more comfortable. Work started with Philippe de l'Orme as the architect in charge and the designs as delicate and polished as the Renaissance could produce. Within a year Henri inherited the throne and immediately gave Diane the château of Chenonceau. But the Anet project continued, luckily for Diane, since Henri's reign was brought to an untimely end and his wife demanded Chenonceau back. Diane retired to Anet where she died. Her grandson built a chapel for her tomb alongside the château which has remained intact.

The château would have been completely destroyed by the first owner after the Revolution had it not been for a protest riot by the townspeople that sent him packing. As it is, only the front entrance, one wing, and the château chapel remain, now restored to its former glorification of hunting and feminine eroticism with the swirling floor and domed ceiling of the chapel its climax. (March–Nov: Mon & Wed–Fri 2:30–6:30pm, Sat 2–5pm, Sun & hols 10–11:30am & 2–6:30pm; Dec–Feb: Sat 2–5pm, Sun & hols 10–11:30am & 2–5pm.)

The Truth about Versailles

The **Palace of VERSAILLES** is one of the three most visited monuments in France. Truth is, however, that it is foul from every aspect—a mutated building gene allowed to run like a pounding fist for lengths no feet or eyes were made for, its decor a grotesque homage to two of the greatest of all self-propagandists, Louis XIV and Napoléon. The mirrors, in the famous Hall of, are smeared, scratched, and not the originals—for these a Breton boy is currently serving fifteen years for breaking glass with explosives. In the park, a mere two and a half square miles, the fountains only gush on selected days. The rest of the time the statues on the empty pools look as bad as gargoyles taken down from cathedral walls. It's hard to know why so many tourists come out here in preference to all except the most obvious sights of Paris. Yet they do, and the **château** is always a crush of bodies.

To **get to Versailles**, take the RER *ligne C5* to VERSAILLES-RIVE GAUCHE (40min), turn left out of the station, and immediately right to approach the palace. You can get maps of the park from the tourist office on rue des Réservoirs to the right of the palace.

The Château, Park . . . and Tea

If you're curious to visit the **château** (Tues–Sun 9:45am–5:30pm; closed hols; 23F/12F; Sun half-price and free for under-18s), you have a choice of itineraries and whether to be guided or not. Either way, the crowds won't give you much room to take your time. Other than the state apartments of the king and queen and the Hall of Mirrors, the rooms are open on a rotating basis.

If you just feel like taking a look, and a walk, **the park** (open dawn to dusk) is free and the scenery better the farther you go from the palace. There are even informal groups of trees near the lesser outcrops of royal mania, the **Grand and Petit Trianons** (Tues–Sun 9:45am–noon & 2–5:30pm, Petit Trianon afternoon only; closed hols; 10F). The fountains are turned on every Sunday from 3:30 to 5pm, May to September.

There is, too, a wonderfully snobbish place to have **tea**, the *Hôtel Palais Trianon*, where the final negotiations for the Treaty of Versailles took place in 1919. It's near the park entrance at the end of bd de la Reine and much more worthwhile than shelling out for château admission, with trayfuls of *pâtisseries* to the limits of your desire for about 60F. The style of the *Trianon* is very much that of the town in general. The dominant population is aristocratic with the pre-revolutionary titles disdainful of those dating merely from Napoléon. On Bastille Day both lots show their colors with black ribbons and ties.

Southwest: a Miscellany of Museums

Meudon, Sèvres, Biévres, and **Sceaux**, once distinct villages, have expanded into each other over the last century, spreading across the steep hills above the Seine. The heights are dominated by luxury apartments, these days, and for visitors the main attractions lie in museums: **Rodin** at Meudon, **ceramics** at Sèvres, **photography** at Biévres, and **Île de France history** at Sceaux.

Meudon-Val-Fleury

MEUDON-VAL-FLEURY, on the *C5/C7* RER lines, is the easiest accessible patch of Seine countryside. And to give a walk some purpose there is the **Villa des Brillants** (19 av Auguste-Rodin, off rue de la Belgique), the house where **Rodin** spent his last years, with an annex containing some of his maquettes, plaster casts, and other odds and ends.

From the station you make your way up the east flank of the *val*—valley—through the twisty **rue des Vignes**. You can either go up rue de la Belgique until you reach av Rodin on the left toward the top, or turn down it to the railroad embankment, go through the tunnel, and take the footpath on the right, which brings you out by the house. It stands in a big picnickable garden, where Rodin himself is buried, on the very edge of the hill looking down on the Renault works in Boulogne-Billancourt.

To the south, on the edge of Meudon's forest, is the **Musée et Jardin de Sculptures de la Fondation Jean Arp** (21 rue des Châtaigniers; Fri–Sun 2–6pm; 15F/10F). This was Jean Arp's and Sophie Taeuber's home and studio—both the house and garden have examples of their work.

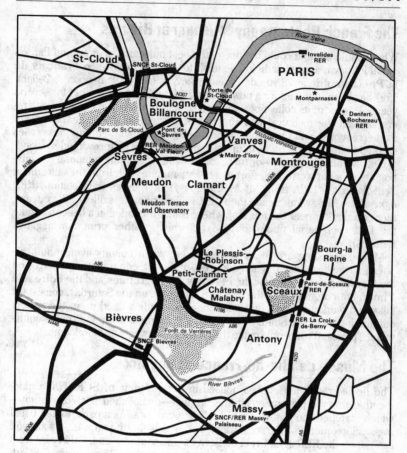

Sèvres

The **Musée National de la Céramique** in **SÈVRES** is equally easy to reach. The métro goes to Pont-de-Sèvres and the museum (10am–5:15pm; closed Tues; ☎45.34.99.05) stands just to the right of the main road, close to the riverbank. An acquired taste, maybe, but if you do have it, there is much to be savored, not just French pottery and china, but Islamic, Chinese, Italian, German, Dutch, English, etc, plus, inevitably, a comprehensive collection of Sèvres ware, as the stuff is made right here.

Close by, overlooking the river, the **Parc de St-Cloud** is good for fresh air and visual order, with a geometrical sequence of pools and fountains delineating a route down to the river and across to the city. To get there take the métro to Pont-de-Sèvres/Boulogne-Pont-de-St-Cloud, then cross the river, or take a train from St-Lazare to St-Cloud and head south.

The French Photography Museum at Bièvres

What should be (and could be) one of the best museums in or around Paris is a real letdown, as well as being fiendish to get to. The **Musée Français de la Photographie** at 78 rue de Paris in Bièvres (daily 10am–noon & 2–6pm; 15F) has been lobbying for a new building (though not a new site) for several years. At present its collection, covering the entire history of cameras, enlargers, and all the technical bits and pieces, documents and magazines, rare daguerreotypes, and thousands of photographs, is crammed into glass cases stacked in tiny rooms, or, as in the case of most of the pictures, hidden away.

Unless you're a fanatic—or there's a particularly exciting temporary exhibition on—it's not worth the effort of a twenty-minute walk from the bus stop at Petit-clamart (#190A from Mᵒ Mairie d'Issy) or Bièvres train station (RER *ligne 8* to Massy-Palaiseau, then SNCF direction Versailles). If you are, there's a marker near the bus stop where Nadar ascended in a balloon to take the first ever aerial photo in 1858 (of which neither print nor negative remains).

More interesting are the **summer fêtes**, when famous living photographers, as well as amateurs and admirers of the art, congregate in Bièvres on the first weekend in June for the **Fête des Photographes** and the **Foire à la Photo**, both organized by the museum. The *Fête*, on the Saturday, consists of talks and workshops run by professionals in studios fixed up in the rickety outbuildings. On the Sunday everyone exhibits their work and trades equipment. Thousands of people make the journey and everyone is welcome.

The Musée de l'Île-de-France at Sceaux

The Île-de-France museum is housed in the **château of SCEAUX**, a nineteenth-century replacement for the original—demolished post-Revolution—which matched the now-restored Le Nôtre grounds. As a park it's the usual classical geometry of terraces, water, and woods, but if you want a walk you can get off the RER at La-Croix-de-Berny at the southern end. Otherwise it's a five- to ten-minute walk from Parc-de-Sceaux station (15min from Denfert-Rochereau): turn left on av de la Duchesse-du-Maine, right into av Rose-de-Launay, and right again on av Le-Nôtre and you'll find the château gates on your left.

The **Musée de l'Île-de-France** (Mon & Fri–Sun 2–5pm, Wed & Thurs 10am–noon & 2–6pm; 10F, free for children of school age) evokes the Paris countryside of the *ancien régime* with its aristocratic and royal domains; of the nineteenth century, with its riverside scenes and eating and dancing places, the *guinguettes*, that inspired so many artists; and of the new towns and transport of the current age. There are models, pictures, and diverse objects: a backpack hot chocolate dispenser with a choice of two brews; 1940s métro seats; a painting of river laundering at Cergy-Pontoise alongside photos of the new town high-rise; early bicycles and a series of plates and figurines inspired by the arrival of the first giraffe in France in the 1830s. Though some of the rooms hold little excitement, most people, kids included, should find enough to make the visit worth it.

Temporary exhibitions and a summer festival of classical chamber music are held in the **Orangerie**, which, along with the **Pavillon de l'Aurore** (in the northeast corner of the park), survives from the original residence. The concerts take place on weekends, from July to October—details from the museum (☎46.61.06.71), or from the *Direction des Musées de France* (Palais du Louvre, Cours Visconti, 34 Quai du Louvre, Paris 1er; ☎42.60.39.26).

Chartres

The mysticism of medieval thought on life, death, and deity, expressed in material form by the masonry of **CHARTRES cathedral**, should best be experienced on a cloud-free winter's day. The low sun transmits the stained glass colors to the interior stone, the quiet scattering of people leaves the acoustics unconfused, and the exterior is unmasked for miles around.

The masterwork is flawed only by changes in Roman Catholic worship. The immense distance from the door to the altar which, through mists of incense and drawn-out harmonies, emphasized the distance between worshippers and worshipped, with priests as sole mediators, has been abandoned. The central altar (from a secular point of view) undermines the theatrical dogma of the building and puts cloth and boards where the colored lights should play.

A less recent change, that of allowing the congregation to use chairs, covers up the **labyrinth** on the floor of the nave—an original thirteenth-century arrangement and a great rarity, since the authorities at other cathedrals had them pulled up as distracting frivolities. The Chartres labyrinth traces a path over 200m long enclosed within a diameter of 13m, the same size as the rose window above the main doors. The center used to have a bronze relief of Theseus and the Minotaur and the pattern of the maze was copied from classical texts—the medieval Catholic idea of the path of life to eternity echoing Greek myth. During pilgrimages the chairs are removed so you may be lucky and see the full pattern.

But there are more than enough wonders to enthrall: the geometry of the building, unique in being almost unaltered since its consecration in the thirteenth century; the details of the stonework, most notably the western façade which includes the Portail Royale saved from the cathedral's predecessor destroyed by fire in 1195, the Renaissance choir screen, and the hosts of sculpted figures above each transept door; and the shining circular symmetries of the transept windows.

Among paying extras, the **crypt and treasures** can wait for another time but, crowds permitting, it's worth climbing the **north tower** (10–11:30am & 2–5:30pm, with variations). Admission hours for the main building are 7:30am to 7:30pm in summer, 7pm in winter. There are gardens at the back from where you can contemplate at ease the complexity of stress factors balanced by the flying buttresses.

If, as you're wandering around, you hear a passionate and erudite Englishman giving guided tours, that is Malcolm Miller, almost an institution in himself and a world expert on Chartres cathedral. He does two tours daily from April to November—the tourist office (see below) can provide details.

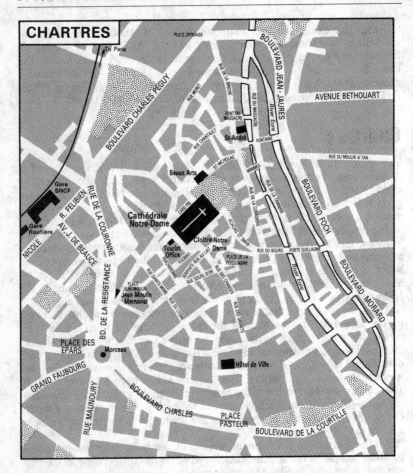

The Town

Though the cathedral is why you come here, Chartres town is not without appeal. The **Beaux Arts museum** in the former episcopal palace just north of the cathedral has some beautiful tapestries, a room full of Vlaminck, and Zurbaran's *Sainte Lucie*, as well as good temporary exhibitions (10am–noon & 2–5pm; closed Tues). Behind it, rue Chantault leads past old townhouses to the River Eure and Pont des Massacres. You can follow this reedy river lined with ancient wash-houses upstream via rue des Massacres on the right bank. The cathedral appears from time to time through the trees and, closer at hand, on the left bank is the Romanesque church of **St-André**, now used for art exhibitions, jazz concerts, and so on. Crossing back over at the end of rue de la Tannerie into rue du Bourg takes you back to the cathedral through the medieval town, decorated with details such as the carved salmon on a house on place de la Poissonerie.

The SI is on the cathedral *parvis*, at 7 Cloître Notre-Dame, and can **supply free maps** and help with **rooms** if you want to stay. Rue du Cygne is a good place to look for bars and restaurants. If you want to splash out, have a meal at *Henri IV* (31 rue Soleil-d'Or; ☎37.36.01.55; closed Mon evening & Tues), which has one of the best selections of wines in France.

Arriving at the gare SNCF (frequent trains from Paris-Montparnasse in 50–65min), av J-de-Beauce leads straight up to place Châtelet. Past all the buses on the other side of the *place*, rue Ste-Même crosses place Jean Moulin with the cathedral down to the left. Rue d'Harleville goes to the right to bd de la Résistance, a section of the main beltway around the old town. The memorial on the corner of the street and the boulevard is to **Jean Moulin**, Prefect of Chartres until he was sacked by the Vichy government in 1942. When the Germans occupied Chartres in 1940, he had refused under torture to sign a document to the effect that black soldiers in the French army were responsible for Nazi atrocities. He later became de Gaulle's number-one man on the ground, coordinating the Resistance. He died at the hands of Klaus Barbie in 1943.

Vaux-le-Vicomte and Fontainebleau

VAUX-LE-VICOMTE, 46km southeast of Paris, is one of the great **classical châteaux**. Louis XIV's finance superintendent, Nicholas Fouquet, had it built at colossal expense, using the top designers of the day—Le Vau, the royal architect, Le Brun, the painter, and Le Nôtre, the landscape gardener. The result was magnificence and precision in perfect proportion and a bill that could only be paid by someone who occasionally confused the state's account with his own. The housewarming party, to which the king was invited, was more extravagant than any royal event—a comparison which other finance ministers ensured that Louis took to heart. Within three weeks Fouquet was jailed for life on trumped-up charges and Louis carted Le Vau, Le Brun, and Le Nôtre off to Versailles to work on a gaudy and gross piece of one-upmanship.

The château (☎60.66.97.09) is open daily, except in January, from 11am until 5pm. The nearest station is at MELUN, 25 minutes by train from Gare de Lyon; however, there's no bus from the station, so call a radio cab at ☎64.52.51.50.

Fontainebleau

If you were feeling energetic, you could spend the morning at Vaux-le-Vicomte and continue by train from MELUN to **FONTAINEBLEAU**—an instructive and pleasant exercise in rapid châteaux touring. A hunting lodge from as early as the twelfth century, the château here began its transformation into a palace under François-1er in the sixteenth century. A vast, rambling place, unpretentious despite its size, it owes its distinction to a colony of Italian artists imported for the decoration—above all, Rosso Il Fiorentino, who completed the celebrated **Galerie François-1er**, a work that was seminal in the evolution of French aristocratic art and design. The gardens are equally luscious, but if you want to escape to the wilds, the surrounding **forest of Fontainebleau** is full of walking and cycling trails and its rocks are a favorite training ground for French climbers. Paths and tracks are all marked on Michelin map 196 (*Environs de Paris*).

The château, rarely overcrowded, is open daily except Tuesday from 9:30am to 12:30pm and from 2 to 5pm (half-price Sun and public hols), though some of the smaller apartments are closed on weekends. **Trains** take around 45 minutes from Gare de Lyon (25min from Melun) and there's a local bus to the gates from the train station.

In the Loops of the Marne

In the good old days of the nineteenth century, people with time, spirit, and a few *sous* would leave the city of an evening for a meal and a dance at their favorite **guinguette**. These mini-music-halls-cum-restaurants were to be found on the banks of the Seine, the Marne, the Bièvre—some of them feature in the Musée d'Orsay Impressionist collection.

One of the most beloved by Bohemians was the tree house at Robinson-Plessy, of which there's a painting at the Musée de l'Île-de-France (see p.270). It has disappeared, as have most of them, along with their surroundings of meadows, poplar-lined paths, and peasant villages. But the same combination of open-air eating, riverside views, and live music can still be had in a *guinguette* established in the 1900s: *Chez Gégène*, 162bis quai de Polangis, **JOINVILLE-LE-PONT** (March–Oct; midday *bals musettes* on weekends, noon–2pm; ☎48.83.29.43). Joinville-le-Pont is east of Paris, just across the Marne from the Bois de Vincennes (RER *ligne A2*, then buses #106 and #108 from rue J. Mermoz or walk to cross the river). Quai de Polangis runs upstream (northwards at this point). You can rent canoes or pedal boats from several places, for much better **boating** than on the Vincennes lakes.

Champigny-sur-Marne

Downstream (or three stops on the RER, then buses #208/116 or bus #108A from Joinville) is **CHAMPIGNY-SUR-MARNE**, one of the few *banlieue* addresses which feels like a place in its own right. There are tiny terraced apartment houses with wooden stairs and balconies beside the bridge; a gracefully sweet and ancient church, St-Saturnin, nestling on a cobbled square a block away from place Lénine and the central crossroads. Old and new coexist and most of the streets bear revolutionary or Resistance names. A monument up on a hill to the east (on rue du Monument) commemorates a miserable and bloody defeat during the Siege of Paris when the Parisians, led by the incompetent Ducroz, failed to break through the Prussian lines in the first sortie for several weeks.

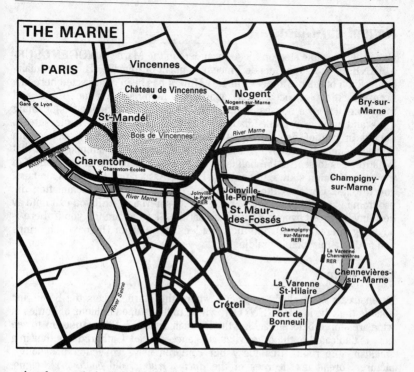

Another period of defeat, seventy years later, is the subject of the **Musée de la Résistance Nationale** (Mon & Wed–Fri 10am–5:30pm, Sat, Sun & hols 2–6pm; 18F/9F) at 88 av Marx Dormoy, reached by bus #208 from the station or the center (stop *Musée de la Résistance*). Resistance museums came back into vogue after the fortieth anniversary of the liberation of France. This one, to its credit, includes the immediate prewar period and the *Front Populaire*, acknowledges the major role of the Communists in the Resistance, and covers the Socialist reforms after the liberation. But it can't escape the need to recuperate French glory nor can it relate the dignity it accords to this resistance with other clandestine revolts whether in the past or the present.

You can rent boats from the *Centre Nautique* in Champigny (near the railroad bridge three or four kilometers upstream from the road bridge) or you can wander down the quayside path on the left bank to the **Pont de Chennevières**. There are some good riverside restaurants, too, such as *L'Écu de France*, 31 rue de Champigny (☎45.76.00.03), before you reach the Chennevières bridge; *Le Pavillon Bleu*, a genuine *guinguette* at 66 promenade des Anglais (☎48.83.10.56), farther on toward the Pont de Bonneuil on the right bank; and *La Bréteche*, 171 quai de Bonneuil (☎48.83.38.73), on the same side, past the Bonneuil bridge. The nearest RER station is La Varenne-Chennevières.

Nogent-sur-Marne

One other possible stop on these meanders of the Marne is **NOGENT-SUR-MARNE**, back by the Bois de Vincennes north of Joinville. The one remaining pavilion of the **old market at Les Halles** has been resurrected here in a bizarre setting of ocean-liner apartment high-rises on one side and mismatched prewar houses on the other. Baltard's construction, all gleaming glass and paint above the diamond-patterned brickwork, is a pleasure to behold. In front of the entrance is a "**square of bygone Paris**," replete with Wallace fountain, theater ticket kiosk, cobbles, and twirly lamppost. But that is all there is to see, as the hall is given over to private functions for most of the year—fashion shows, International Police Association balls, weapon fairs, and the like. Certain cultural events are open to all, but disseminating the program is not a high priority. From Nogent-sur-Marne RER you exit onto av de Joinville, cross over and turn left past the SI (who can tell you if there is anything interesting on), and then first left into av Victor Hugo, which brings you to the unmistakable building.

Charenton

Downstream from all these places, where the Marne meets the Seine just outside the city, is **CHARENTON**, where millions upon millions of bottles of wine are stored before reaching the Parisian throat. But the **museum** to see here is dedicated to the other vital substance—bread. Gathered together in a smallish attic room, this fussy but comprehensive collection has songs, pictures, bread tax decrees of the *ancien régime*, old *boulangerie* signs, baking trays, baskets and cupboards for bread, pieces sculpted out of dough, and the thing itself—over 4000 years old in one instance. If you're fond of museums you'll like this one. Otherwise don't bother and don't take kids along. Situated above the flour milling firm *S.A.M.* at 2bis rue Victor Hugo, the **Musée Français du Pain** is open only on Tuesday and Thursday, from 2 to 4:30pm. From Paris take the Créteil-Préfecture métro to Charenton-Écoles, exit place des Écoles: rue Victor Hugo goes down to the right of the *Monoprix* supermarket in front of you. From the Bois de Vincennes, av Cholet runs to place des Écoles from av de Grevelle on the edge of the wood, due south of Lac Daumesnil.

The New Towns and *Grands Ensembles*

Investigating life in the **suburbs** is hardly a prime holiday occupation but if you are interested in housing and urban development, or the arrogance of architects and nose-length perspectives of planners, then the "Greater Paris" new towns of the 1970s/80s, and the 1950s/60s vast housing projects known as *Grands Ensembles*, could be instructive.

Wealthy Parisians who have moved out from the *Beaux Quartiers* have always had their apartments or houses (with tennis courts and swimming pools) southwest of the city, in the garden suburbs that now stretch out beyond Versailles. Those who have been forced to move by rising rents, or who have never afforded an apartment in Paris, live, if they're lucky, in the soulless *Villes Nouvelles*, and if they're not, in the *Grands Ensembles*. These giant concrete camps were the quick-fix solution to the housing crisis brought on by population growth and city slum clearance programs in the 1950s.

The *Villes Nouvelles* became the mode in the late 1960s when the accumulating problems of high-rise low-income society first started to filter through to architects and planners. Unlike in some other cities, the Parisian new towns were grafted onto existing towns but conceived as satellites to the capital rather than places in their own right. Streets of tiny detached *pavillons* with old-time residents cower beneath buildings from another world, unfortunately the present one. As with any new town there's the unsettling reversal that the people are there because of the town and not vice versa, and the town seems to be there only because of the rail and RER lines.

Sarcelles, twelve kilometers to the north, is the most notorious of the *Grands Ensembles*. It gave a new word to the French language, "*sarcellitis*," the social disease of delinquency and despair spread by the horizons of interminable, identical, high-rise hutches. It's not worth a visit but it did teach the planners a few lessons.

La Grande Borne, Evry, and Cergy-Pontoise

A few years after Sarcelles' creation, at the end of the 1960s, the architect Emile Aillaud tried a very different approach in the *Grand Ensemble* called **LA GRANDE BORNE**. Twenty-five kilometers south of Paris and directly overlooking the Autoroute du Sud, which cuts it off from the town center and nearest rail connection of GRIGNY, it was hardly a promising site. But for once a scale was used that didn't belittle the inhabitants and the buildings were shaped by curves instead of corners. The façades are colored by tiny glass and ceramic tiles, there are inbuilt artworks—landscapes, animals, including two giant sculpted pigeons, and portraits of Rimbaud and Kafka—and the whole ensemble is pedestrian-only. To get there by public transit is a bit exhausting: train from the gare de Lyon, direction Corbeil-Essones, to Grigny-Centre, then bus or walk; but by road it's a quick flit down the A6 from Porte d'Orléans: turn off to the right on the D13 and both the first and second right will take you into the project.

Having come out this way, you could also take a look at **EVRY**, one of the five new towns in the Paris region (Evry-Courcouronnes SNCF, two stops on from Grigny). Follow the signs from Evry station to the center *commercial* and keep going through it till you surface on a walkway that bridges bd de l'Europe. This leads you into **Evry 1 housing project**, a multi-mat-colored ensemble resembling a group of ransacked wardrobes and chests-of-drawers. The architects call it pyramidal and blather on about how the buildings and the landscape articulate each other. But it's quite fun, as a monument, even if the "articulating" motifs on the façade overlooking the park are more like fossils than plants.

CERGY-PONTOISE, thirty kilometers northwest of Paris (RER *ligne A3*, Cergy-St-Christophe) has a three-kilometer highway, the *Axe Majeur*, to give it grandeur, punctuated by outrageous architectural fantasies, including a belvedere that projects a laser beam into the sky. What might attract you here, if you have a bored-child problem, is the **Parc Mirapolis**, an amusement park themed on Rabelais's giant Gargantua (see p.183). Should you fail to have the time on you, the enormous clocks on the station are hard to miss.

Marne-la-Vallée

The New Town with the most to shock or amuse, or even please, is undoubtedly **MARNE-LA-VALLÉE**, where Terry Gilliam's totalitarian fantasy *Brasil* was filmed. It starts ten kilometers east of Paris and hops for twenty kilometers from one new outburst to the next, with odd bits of wood and water in between. The RER stops from Bry-sur-Marne to the Torcy terminal (to be extended for Disneyland) are all in Marne-la-Vallée; journeys north or south from the rail line are not so easy.

You can sample the extreme with less legwork if you get off at **NOISY-LE-GRAND**, or MONT D'EST as the planners call it. You surface on the Arcades, a stony substitute for a town square, and there you have the poetic panorama of a controlled community environment. Bright blue tubing and light blue tiling on split-level walkways and spaceless concrete fencing; powder blue boxes growing plants on buildings beside gray-blue roofs of multi-angled leanings; walls of blue, walls of white, deep blue frames, and tinted glass reflecting the water of a chopped-up lake; islands linked by bridges with more blue railings ...

The two acclaimed architectural pieces in this monolith have only one thing in their favor—neither is blue in any bit. They are both low-cost housing units, they are both gigantic, quite unlike anything you're likely to have seen before, and both are unmitigatedly horrible. The **Arènes de Picasso** is in the group of buildings to the right of the RER line as you look at the lakes from the Arcades, about half a kilometer away. It's soon visible as you approach: two enormous circles like loudspeakers facing each other across a space that would do nicely for a Roman stadium. Prepare to feel as if the lions are waiting. At the other end of Mont d'Est, facing the capital, is the extraordinary semicircle, arch, and half square of *Le Théâtre et Palacio d'Abraxas*, creation of Ricardo Boffil. Ghosts of ancient Greek designs haunt the façades but proportion there is none, whether classical or any other.

Further-flung delights of Marne-la-Vallée include the mosaicked "**Totem**" **water tower** with clown and robot faces in the woods by LE LUZARD; another water tower, with plants growing through its grill cladding, at the head of bd Salvador Allende at NOISIEL MAIRIE; sympathetic small-scale housing in LE VAL MAUBOUE and, with easy access, an **RER station on a lake**, LOGNES-LE MANDINET.

Maps and information for Marne-la-Vallée as well as models and photos on view can be had from the CIVN, 3 place de l'Arche-Guédon, Torcy; bus #220 from Noisiel RER, direction Torcy, stop l'Arche-Guédon.

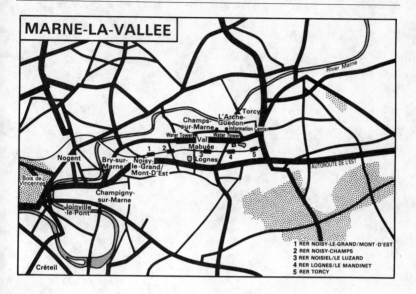

Disneyland

In spring 1992, the death warrant on European culture and civilization will have been signed as **EURO-DISNEYLAND** opens its fantasy-land gates to the public. Well, that was the French reaction.

The Disney Corporation has in fact gone out of its way to affirm that the park will be "Europe-oriented"—inspired by Loire châteaux and starring such well-known European figures as Peter Pan (who's considered English), Cinderella (she's French), and Pinocchio. However, that's just talk. In this Florida replica, the rides, the characters, the street scenes, the hotels, even the food, will be American—which is, after all, what the crowds want.

It's an enormous project, taking up a space one-fifth the size of Paris proper, privately funded with half the shares in the firm hands of Disney USA. The French government is providing the RER extension from Torcy, a new exit from the A4 motorway, and, eventually, a TGV rail link. At the moment all that is to be seen is a publicity center, topped by a witch's hat and decorated with silhouettes of Disney characters, where a gushing film of the future entertainment is screened. The cost of a taxi from Torcy RER would be an extravagance but if you're passing by car, take the Serris exit from the motorway, and you'll see the *Espace Euro-Disney* straight away. It's open Monday to Friday from 11am to 5pm, Saturday and Sunday until 7pm, and costs 10F; and you can reserve your hotel room for 1992.

PART THREE

THE
CONTEXTS

THE CITY IN HISTORY

Two thousand years of compressed history featuring riots and revolutions, shantytowns, palaces, new street plans, sanitation, and the Parisian people.

BEGINNINGS

Rome put Paris on the map as it did the rest of western Europe. When Julius Caesar's armies arrived in 52 BC, they found a Celtic settlement confined to the island in the Seine—the Île de la Cité. It must already have been fairly populous, as it had sent a contingent of eight thousand men to stiffen the Gallic chieftain Vercingétorix's doomed resistance to the invaders. Under the name of *Lutetia*, it remained a **Roman colony** for the next three hundred years, prosperous commercially because of its commanding position on the Seine trade route but insignificant politically. The Romans established their administrative center on the Île de la Cité, and their town on the Left Bank on the slopes of the Montagne Sainte-Geneviève. Though no monuments of their presence remain, except the baths by the Hôtel de Cluny and the amphitheater in rue Monge, their **street plan**, still visible in the north–south axis of rue St-Martin and rue St-Jacques, determined the future growth of the city.

When Roman rule disintegrated under the impact of **Germanic invasions** around 275 AD, Paris held out until it fell to **Clovis the Frank** in 486. In 511 Clovis's son commissioned the **cathedral of St-Etienne**, whose foundations can be seen in the *crypte archéologique* under the square in front of Notre-Dame. Clovis's own conversion to Christianity hastened the Christianization of the whole country, and under his successors Paris saw the foundation of several rich and influential monasteries, especially on the Left Bank.

With the election of **Hugues Capet, Comte de Paris**, as king in 987, the fate of the city was inextricably identified with that of the **monarchy**. The presence of the kings, however, prevented the development of the middle class, republican institutions that the rich merchants of Flanders and Italy were able to obtain for their cities. The result was recurrent political tension, which led to open **rebellion**, for instance, in 1356, when **Étienne Marcel**, a wealthy cloth merchant, demanded greater autonomy for the city. Further rebellions, fuelled by the hopeless poverty of the lower classes, led to the king and court abandoning the capital in 1418, not to return for more than a hundred years.

THE RIGHT BANK, LATIN QUARTER, AND LOUVRE

As the city's livelihood depended from the first on its river-borne trade, commercial activity naturally centered around the place where the goods were landed. This was the **place de Grève** on the **Right Bank**, where the Hôtel de Ville now stands. Marshy ground originally, it was gradually drained to accommodate the business quarter. Whence the continuing association of the Right Bank with commerce and banking today.

The **Left Bank's** intellectual associations are similarly ancient, dating from the growth of schools and student accommodation around the two great monasteries of **Ste-Geneviève** and **St-Germain-des-Prés**. The first, dedicated to the city's patron saint who had saved it from destruction by Attila's raiders, occupied the site of the present Lycée Henri IV on top of the hill behind the Panthéon. In 1215 a papal license allowed the formation of what gradually became the renowned **University of Paris**, eventually to be known as the **Sorbonne**, after Robert de Sorbon, founder of a college for poor scholars. It was the fact that Latin was the language of the schools both inside and outside the classroom that gave the district its name of **Latin Quarter**.

To protect this burgeoning city, **Philippe Auguste** (king from 1180 to 1223) built the **Louvre fortress** (remains of which are now on display in the newly excavated Cour Carrée in the Louvre museum) and a **wall**, which swung south to enclose the Montagne Ste-Geneviève and north and east to encompass the Marais. The administration of the city remained in the hands of the king until 1260 when Saint Louis ceded a measure of responsibility to the leaders of the Paris watermen's guild, whose power was based on their monopoly control of all river traffic and taxes thereon. The **city's government**, when it has been allowed one, has been conducted ever since from the **place de Grève/place de l'Hôtel de Ville**.

CIVIL WARS AND FOREIGN OCCUPATION

From the mid-thirteenth to mid-fourteenth centuries Paris shared the same unhappy fate as the rest of France, embroiled in the long and destructive **Hundred Years War** with the English. Étienne Marcel let the enemy into the city in 1357; the Burgundians did the same in 1422, when the Duke of Bedford set up his government of northern France here. **Joan of Arc** made an unsuccessful attempt to drive them out in 1429 and was wounded in the process at the Porte St-Honoré. The following year the English king, **Henry VI**, had the cheek to have himself crowned king of France in Notre-Dame.

It was only when the English were expelled—from Paris in 1437 and from France in 1453—that the economy had the chance to recover from so many decades of devastation. It received a further boost when **François 1er** decided to re-establish the royal court in Paris in 1528. Work began on **reconstructing the Louvre** and building the **Tuileries palace** for **Cathérine de Médicis**, and on transforming **Fontainebleau** and other country residences into sumptuous Renaissance palaces.

But before these projects reached completion, war again intervened, this time **civil war** between Catholics and Protestants, in the course of which Paris witnessed one of the worst atrocities ever committed against French Protestants. Some three thousand of them were gathered in Paris for the wedding of Henri III's daughter, Marguerite, to Henri, the Protestant king of Navarre. On August 25, 1572, St Bartholomew's Day, they were massacred at the instigation of the Catholic Guise family. When, through this marriage, Henri of Navarre became heir to the French throne in 1584, the Guises drove his father-in-law, Henri III, out of Paris. Forced into alliance, the two Henris laid **siege** to the city. Five years later, Henri III having been assassinated in the meantime, Henri of Navarre entered the city as king **Henri IV**. "Paris is worth a Mass," he is reputed to have said to justify renouncing his Protestantism in order to soothe Catholic susceptibilities.

The Paris he inherited was not a very salubrious place. It was overcrowded. No domestic building had been permitted beyond the limits of Philippe Auguste's twelfth-century walls because of the guilds' resentment of the unfair advantage enjoyed by craftsmen living outside the jurisdiction of the city's tax regulations. The population had doubled to around 400,000, causing acute **housing shortage** and a terrible strain on the rudimentary **water supply** and **drainage system**. It is said that the first workmen who went to clean out the city's cesspools in 1633 fell dead from the fumes. It took seven months to clean out 6420 cartloads of filth that had been accumulating for two centuries. The overflow ran into the Seine, whence Parisians drew their drinking water.

PLANNING AND EXPANSION

The first **systematic attempts at planning** were introduced by **Henri IV** at the beginning of the seventeenth century: regulating street lines and uniformity of façade, and laying out the first geometric squares. The **place des Vosges** dates from this period and the **Pont Neuf**, the first of the Paris bridges not to be cluttered with medieval houses. He thus inaugurated a tradition of grandiose public building, which was to continue to the Revolution and beyond, that perfectly symbolized the bureaucratic, centralized power of the newly self-confident state concentrated in the person of its absolute monarch.

The process reached its apogee under **Louis XIV** with the construction of the **boulevards** from the Madeleine to the Bastille, the **places Vendôme** and **Victoire**, the **Porte St-Martin** and **St-Denis** gateways, the **Invalides**,

Observatoire, and the **Cour Carrée** of the Louvre—not to mention the vast palace at **Versailles**, whither he repaired with the court in 1671. The aristocratic **hôtels** or mansions of the **Marais** were also erected during this period, to be superseded early in the eighteenth century by the **Faubourg St-Germain** as the fashionable quarter of the rich and powerful.

The underside of all this bricks and mortar self-aggrandizement was the general neglect of the living conditions of the ordinary citizenry of Paris. The center **of the city** remained a densely packed and insanitary warren of medieval lanes and tenements. And it was only in the years immediately **preceding the 1789 revolution** that any attempt was made to clean it up. The buildings crowding the bridges were dismantled as late as 1786. Pavements were introduced for the first time and attempts were made to improve the drainage. A further source of pestilential infection was removed with the emptying of the overcrowded cemeteries into the **catacombs**. One gravedigger alone claimed to have buried more than ninety thousand people in thirty years, stacked "like slices of bacon" in the charnel house of the Innocents, which had been receiving the dead of 22 parishes for 800 years.

In 1786 Paris also received its second from last ring of fortifications, the so-called **wall of the Fermiers Généraux**, with 57 *barrières* or toll gates (one of which survives in the middle of place Stalingrad), where a tax was levied on all goods entering the city.

THE 1789 REVOLUTION

The immediate cause of the revolution of 1789 was a campaign by the privileged classes of the clergy and nobility to protect their status, especially exemption from taxation, against erosion by the royal government. The **revolutionary movement**, however, was quickly taken over by the middle classes, relatively well off but politically underprivileged. In the initial phases this meant essentially the **provincial bourgeoisie**. It was they who comprised the majority of the representatives of the **Third Estate**, the "order" that encompassed the whole of French society where the clergy, who formed the first Estate, and the nobility, who formed the second. It was they who took the initiative in setting up the **National Assembly** on June 17, 1789. The majority of them would probably have been content with constitutional reforms that checked monarchical power on the English model. But their power depended largely on their ability to wield the threat of a **Parisian popular explosion**.

Although the effects of the Revolution were felt all over France and indeed Europe, it was in Paris that the most profound changes took place. Being as it were on the spot, the people of Paris discovered themselves in the Revolution. They formed the revolutionary shock troops, the driving force at the crucial stages of the Revolution. They marched on Versailles and forced the king to return to Paris with them. They stormed and destroyed the Bastille on July 14, 1789. They occupied the Hôtel de Ville, set up an insurrectionary Commune, and captured the Tuileries palace on August 10, 1792. They invaded the Convention in May 1793 and secured the arrest of the more conservative Girondin faction of deputies.

Where the bourgeois deputies of the Convention were concerned principally with political reform, the **sans-culottes**—literally, the people without breeches—expressed their **demands** in economic terms: price controls, regulation of the city's food supplies, and so on. In so doing they foreshadowed the rise of the working-class and socialist movements of the nineteenth century. They also established by their practice of taking to the streets and occupying the Hôtel de Ville a **tradition of revolutionary action** that continued through to the 1871 Commune.

NAPOLÉON— AND THE BARRICADES

Apart from some spectacular bloodletting, and yet another occupation of the city by foreign powers in 1814, Napoléon's chief legacy to France was a very centralized, authoritarian, and efficient **bureaucracy** that put Paris in firm control of the rest of the country. In Paris itself, he left his share of pompous architecture—in the **Arcs de Triomphe** and **Carrousel, rue de Rivoli** and **rue de la Paix**, the **Madeleine** and façade of the **Palais-Bourbon**, plus a further extension for the Louvre and a revived tradition of court flummery and extravagant living among the well-to-do. For the rest of the nineteenth century after his demise, France was left to fight out the contradictions and unfinished business left behind by the Revolution of 1789. And the arena in which these conflicts were resolved was, literally, the streets of the capital.

On the one hand, there was a tussle between the class that had risen to wealth and power as a direct result of the destruction of the monarchy and the old order, and the survivors of the old order, who sought to make a comeback in the 1820s under the restored monarchy of **Louis XVIII** and **Charles X**. This conflict was finally resolved in favor of the **new bourgeoisie**. When Charles X refused to accept the result of the 1830 National Assembly elections, **Adolphe Thiers**—the veteran conservative politician of the nineteenth century—led the opposition in revolt. Barricades were erected in Paris and there followed three days of bitter street fighting, known as *les trois glorieuses*, in which 1800 people were killed (they are commemorated by the column on place de la Bastille). The outcome was the election of **Louis-Philippe** as constitutional monarch, and the introduction of a few liberalizing reforms, most either cosmetic or serving merely to consolidate the power of the wealthiest stratum of the population. Radical republican and working-class interests remained completely unrepresented.

The other, and more important, major political conflict was the extended struggle between this **enfranchised and privileged bourgeoisie** and the **heirs of the 1789 sans-culottes**, whose political consciousness had been awakened by the Revolution but whose demands remained unsatisfied. These were the people who died on the barricades of July to hoist the bourgeoisie firmly into the saddle.

As their demands continued to go unheeded, so their radicalism increased, exacerbated by deteriorating **living and working conditions** in the large towns, especially Paris, as the **industrial revolution** got under way. There were, for example, twenty thousand deaths from cholera in Paris in 1832, and in 1848 sixty-five percent of the population were too poor to be liable for tax. Eruptions of discontent invariably occurred in the capital, with insurrections in 1832 and 1834. In the absence of organized parties, opposition centered on newspapers and clandestine or informal **political clubs** in the

tradition of 1789. The most notable—and the only one dedicated to the violent overthrow of the regime—was Auguste Blanqui's *Société Républicaine*.

In the 1840s the publication of the **first Socialist works** like Louis Blanc's *Organization of Labor* and Proudhon's *What is Property?* gave an additional spur to the impatience of the opposition. When the lid blew off the pot in **1848** and the **Second Republic** was proclaimed in Paris, it looked for a time as if working-class demands might be at least partly met. The provisional government included Louis Blanc and a Parisian manual worker. But in the face of demands for the control of industry, the setting up of cooperatives, and so on, backed by agitation in the streets and the proposed inclusion of men like Blanqui and Barbès in the government, the more conservative Republicans lost their nerve. The nation returned a spanking reactionary majority in the April elections. Revolution began to appear the only possible defense for the radical left. On June 23, 1848, **working-class Paris**—Poissonnière, Temple, St-Antoine, the Marais, Quartier Latin, Montmartre—rose in **revolt**. Men, women, and children fought side-by-side against fifty thousand troops. In three days of fighting, nine hundred soldiers were killed. No one knows how many of the *insurgés* died. Fifteen thousand people were arrested and four thousand sentenced to prison terms.

Despite the shock and devastation of civil war in the streets of the capital, the ruling classes failed to heed the warning in the events of June 1848. Far from redressing the injustices which had provoked them, they proceeded to exacerbate them—by, for example, reducing the representation of what Adolphe Thiers called "the vile multitude." The Republic was brought to an end in a coup d'état by **Louis Napoléon**, who within twelve months had himself crowned Emperor Napoléon III.

REWARDS OF COLONIALISM

There followed a period of **foreign acquisitions** on every continent and of **laissez-faire capitalism at home**, both of which greatly increased the economic wealth of France, then lagging far behind Britain in the **industrialization** stakes. Foreign trade trebled, a huge expansion of the railroad network was carried out, investment banks were set up, and so forth. The rewards, however, were very unevenly distributed, and the regime relied unashamedly on repressive measures—press censorship, police harassment, and the forcible suppression of strikes—to hold the underdogs in check.

The response was entirely predictable. **Opposition** became steadily more organized and determined. In 1864, under the influence of Karl Marx in London, a French branch of **the International** was established in Paris and the youthful **trade union movement** gathered its forces in a federation. In 1869 the far-from-socialist Gambetta, briefly deputy for Belleville, declared, "Our generation's mission is to complete the French Revolution."

During these nearly twenty years of the Second Empire, while conditions were ripening for the most terrible of all Parisian revolutions, the 1871 Commune, the city itself suffered the greatest ever shock to its system. **Baron Haussmann**, appointed Prefect of the Seine department with responsibility for Paris by Napoléon III, undertook the total **transformation of the city**. In love with the straight line and grand vista, he drove 85 miles of broad **new streets** through the cramped quarters of the medieval city, linking the interior and exterior boulevards, and creating north–south, east–west cross-routes. His taste dictated the **uniform gray stone façades**, mansard roofs, and six to seven stories that are the still the architectural hallmark of the Paris street today. In fact, such was the logic of his planning that construction of his projected streets continued long after his death, bd Haussmann itself being completed only in 1927.

While it is difficult to imagine how Paris could have survived without some Haussmann-like intervention, the scale of demolitions entailed by such massive redevelopment brought the direst **social consequences**. The city boundaries were extended to the 1840 fortifications where the *boulevard périphérique* now runs. The prosperous classes moved into the new western *arrondissements*, leaving the decaying older properties to the poor. These were divided and subdivided into ever smaller units as landlords sought to maximize their rents. **Sanitation** was nonexistent. Water standpipes were available only in the street. **Migrant workers** from the provinces, sucked into the city to supply capitalists' vast labor requirements, crammed into the old villages of Belleville and Ménilmontant. Many, too poor to buy furniture, lived in barely furnished digs or *demi-lits*, where the same bed was shared by several tenants on a shift basis. **Cholera and TB** were rife. Attempts to impose sanitary regulations were resisted by landlords as covert socialism. Many considered even connection to Haussmann's water mains an unnecessary luxury. Until 1870 refuse was thrown into the streets at night to be collected the following morning. When in 1884 the Prefect of the day required landlords to provide decent containers, they retorted by calling the containers by his name, *poubelle*—and the name has stuck as the French word for trash can. Far from being concerned with Parisians' welfare, Haussmann's scheme was at least in part designed to keep the workers under control. **Barracks** were located at strategic points like the place du Château-d'Eau, now République, controlling the turbulent eastern districts, and the broad **boulevards** were intended to facilitate troop movements and artillery fire. A section of the Canal St-Martin north of the Bastille was covered over for the same reason.

THE SIEGE OF PARIS AND THE COMMUNE

In September 1870 Napoléon III surrendered to Bismarck at the border town of Sedan, less than two months after France had declared war on the well-prepared and superior forces of the Prussian state. The humiliation was enough for a Republican government to be instantly proclaimed in Paris. The **Prussians** advanced and by September 19 were laying **siege** to the capital. Gambetta was flown out by hot air balloon to rally the provincial troops but the country was defeated and liaison with Paris almost impossible. Further balloon messengers ended up in Norway or the Atlantic; the few attempts at military sorties from Paris turned into yet more blundering failures. Meanwhile, the city's restaurants were forced to change menus to fried dog, roast rat, or peculiar delicacies from the zoos. For those without savings, death from disease or starvation became an ever more common though hardly novel fate. At the same time, the peculiar conditions of a city besieged gave a greater freedom to collective discussion and dissent.

The government's half-hearted defense of the city—more afraid of revolution than of the Prussians—angered Parisians, who clamored for the creation of a 1789-style Commune. The Prussians meanwhile were demanding an actual government to negotiate with. In January 1871 those in power agreed to hold **elections** for a new national assembly with the authority to surrender officially to the Prussians. A large **monarchist** majority, with Thiers at its head, was returned, again demonstrating the isolation from the countryside of the Parisian leftists, among whom many prominent old-timers, veterans of 1848 and the empire's jails, like Blanqui and Delescluze were still active.

On March 1, Prussian troops marched down the Champs-Élysées and garrisoned the city for three days while the populace remained behind closed doors in silent protest. On March 18, amid growing resentment from all classes of Parisians, Thiers's attempt to take possession of the National Guard's artillery in Montmartre (see p.118) set the barrel alight. **The Commune** was proclaimed from the Hôtel de Ville and Paris was promptly subjected to a **second siege** by Thiers's government, which had fled to Versailles, followed by all the remaining Parisian bourgeoisie.

The Commune lasted 72 days—a festival of the oppressed, Lenin called it. Socialist through and through, it had no time to implement lasting reforms. Wholly occupied with defense against Thiers it succumbed finally on May 28, 1871, after a week of **street by street warfare**, in which three thousand Parisians died on the barricades and another twenty to twenty-five thousand men, women, and children were killed in random revenge shootings by government troops. Thiers could declare with satisfaction—or so he thought—"Socialism is finished for a long time."

Among the non-human **casualties** were several of the city's landmark buildings, including the **Tuileries palace**, **Hôtel de Ville**, **Cours des Comptes** (where the Musée d'Orsay now stands), and a large chunk of the **rue Royale**.

THE *BELLE ÉPOQUE*

Physical recovery was remarkably quick. Within six or seven years few signs of the fighting remained. Visitors remarked admiringly on the teeming streets, the expensive shops, and energetic nightlife. Charles Garnier's **Opéra** was opened in 1875. Aptly described as the "triumph of molded pastry," it was a suitable image of the frivolity and materialism of the so-called **naughty Eighties and Nineties**. In 1889 the **Eiffel Tower** stole the show at the great Exposition. For the 1900 repeat, the **Métropolitain** (métro)—or *Nécropolitain*, as it was dubbed by one wit—was unveiled.

The lasting social consequence of the Commune was the confirmation of the them-and-us divide between bourgeoisie and working class. Any stance other than a revolutionary one after the Commune appeared not only feeble, but also a betrayal of the dead. None of the contradictions had been resolved. The years up to World War I were marked by the increasing **organization of the left** in response to the unstable but thoroughly conservative governments of the Third Republic. The trade union movement unified in 1895 to form the **Conféderatlon Genérale du Travail** (CGT) and in 1905 Jean Jaurès and Jules Guesde founded the **Parti Socialiste** (also known as the SFIO). On the extreme right, **Fascism** began to make its ugly appearance with Maurras's proto-Brownshirt organization, the *Camelots du Roi*, which inaugurated another French tradition, of violence and thuggery on the far right.

Yet despite—or maybe in some way because of—these tensions and contradictions, Paris provided the supremely inspiring environment for a concentration of **artists and writers**—the so-called **Bohemians**, both French and foreign—such as western culture has rarely seen. Impressionism, Fauvism, and Cubism were all born in Paris in this period, while French poets like Apollinaire, Laforgue, Max Jacob, Blaise Cendrars, and André Breton were preparing the way for Surrealism, concrete poetry, and symbolism. Film, too, saw its first developments. After World War I, Paris remained the world's art center, with an injection of foreign blood and a shift of venue from Montmartre to Montparnasse.

In the **postwar struggle for recovery** the interests of the urban working class were again passed over, with the exception of Clemenceau's eight-hour day legislation in 1919. An attempted general strike in 1920 came to nothing, and workers' strength was again weakened by the irredeemable split in the Socialist Party at the 1920 Congress of Tours. The pro-Lenin majority formed the **French Communist Party**, while the minority faction, under the leadership of Léon Blum, retained the old SFIO title.

As **Depression** deepened in the 1930s and Nazi power across the Rhine became more menacing, fascist thuggery and anti-parliamentary activity increased in France, culminating in a pitched battle outside the Chamber of Deputies in February 1934. (Léon Blum was only saved from being lynched by a funeral cortege through the intervention of some building workers who happened to notice what was going on in the street below.) The effect of this fascist activism was to unite the Left, including the Communists, led by the Stalinist Maurice Thorez, in the **Popular Front**. When they won the 1936 elections with a handsome majority in the Chamber, there followed a wave of strikes and factory sit-ins—a spontaneous expression of working-class determination to get their just deserts after a century and a half of frustration. Frightened by the apparently revolutionary situation, the major employers signed the Matignon Agreement with Blum, which provided for wage increases, nationalization of the armaments industry and partial nationalization of the Bank of France, a 40-hour week, paid annual leave, and collective bargaining on wages. These **reforms** were pushed through parliament, but when Blum tried to introduce exchange controls to check the flight of capital the Senate threw the proposal out and he resigned. The Left returned to Opposition, where it remained, with the exception of coalition governments, until 1981. Most of the Popular Front's reforms were promptly undone.

THE GERMAN OCCUPATION

During the occupation of Paris in World War II, the Germans found some sections of Parisian society, as well as the minions of the Vichy government, only too happy to hobnob with them. For four years the city suffered fascist rule with curfews, German garrisons, and a Gestapo HQ. Parisian Jews were forced to wear the star of David and in 1942 were rounded up—by other French citizens—and shipped off to Auschwitz (see pp.101, 260).

The **Resistance** was very active in the city, gathering people of all political persuasions into its ranks, but with Communists and Socialists, especially of East European Jewish origin, well to the fore. The job of torturing them when they fell into Nazi hands—often as a result of betrayals—was left to their fellow-citizens in the fascist militia. Those who were condemned to death—rather than the concentration camps—were shot against the wall below the old fort of Mont Valérien above St-Cloud.

As Allied forces drew near to the city in 1944, the FFI (armed Resistance units), determined to play their part in driving the Germans out, called their troops onto the streets—some said, in a leftist attempt to seize political power. To their credit, the Paris police also joined in, holding their Île de la Cité HQ for three days against German attacks. Liberation finally came on August 25, 1944.

POSTWAR PARIS: ONE MORE TRY AT REVOLUTION

Postwar Paris has remained no stranger to **political battles** in its streets. Violent demonstrations accompanied the Communist withdrawal from the coalition government in 1947. In the Fifties the Left took to the streets again in **protest against the colonial wars in Indochina and Algeria**. And in 1961—in an episode that was covered up and completely censored until the 1990s—somewhere between seventy and two hundred Algerians were killed by the police during a civil rights demonstration.

This **"secret massacre,"** which is only now finding its way into French history books, began with a peaceful demonstration by French Algerians, protesting against police powers to impose a curfew on any place in France frequented by North Africans—the result of paranoia during the Algerian war. The demonstration was heralded by headlines in the right wing press such as "Barbarians Advance on Paris" and the police, it seems, went mad—shooting at crowds, clubbing protesters and then throwing their bodies into the Seine. For weeks, corpses were recovered, but the French media itself was silent, in part through censorship, in part perhaps unable to comprehend that such events had happened in their capital.

The state attempted censorship again during the events of **May 1968**, though with rather less success. Through this extraordinary month—*le Mai* as the French still call it—a radical, leftist movement spread from the Paris universities to a general strike by nine million workers—the biggest confrontation that any contemporary Western state has had to deal with. The old-fashioned and reactionary university structures that set off the revolt found reflection in the hierarchical and rigid organizations in every other institution. The position of women, of youth, of culture, and modes of behavior were suddenly highlighted in the general dissatisfaction with a society in which big business ran the state.

This was no revolutionary situation on the 1917, or even 1848, model. The vicious **street battles with the police** instilled fear not inspiration in the peasants and bourgeois outside Paris—as the government cynically exploiting the scenes for TV knew full well. And there was certainly no shared economic or political aim in the ranks of the opposition. The French Communist Party was still stuck with Stalinism and the Socialists were determined at all costs to keep them out of government. Meanwhile right wing demonstrations orchestrated by de Gaulle left public opinion craving stability and peace; and a great many workers were satisfied with a new system for wage agreements. It was not, therefore, surprising that the elections called in June returned the Right to power.

The occupied buildings emptied and the barricades in the Latin Quarter came down. For those who thought they were experiencing The Revolution, the defeat was catastrophic. But French institutions and French society did change, shaken and loosened by the events of May 1968. And most importantly it opened up the debate of a new road to Socialism, one in which no old models would give all the answers.

MODERN DEVELOPMENTS OF THE CITY

Until World War II, Paris remained pretty much as Haussmann had left it. Housing conditions showed little sign of improvement. There was even an outbreak of bubonic plague in Clignancourt in 1921. In 1925 a third of the houses still had no sewage connection. Of the seventeen worst blocks of slums designated for clearance, most were still intact in the 1950s, and even today they have some close rivals in parts of Belleville and elsewhere.

Migration to the suburbs continued, with the creation of **shantytowns** to supplement the hopelessly inadequate housing stock. Post-World War II, these became the exclusive territory of **Algerian** and other **North African immigrants**. In 1966 there were 89 of them, housing 40,000 immigrant workers and their families.

Only in the last thirty years have the authorities begun to grapple with the housing problem, though not by expanding possibilities within Paris, but by siphoning huge numbers of people into a ring of **satellite towns** encircling the greater Paris region.

In **Paris proper** this same period has seen the final breaking of the mold of Haussmann's influence. Intervening architectural fashions, like Art Nouveau, Le Corbusier's International style, and the Neoclassicism of the 1930s, had little more than localized cosmetic effects. It was devotion to the needs of the motorist—a cause unhesitatingly espoused by Pompidou—and the development of the high-rise tower that finally did the trick, starting with the **Tour Maine-Montparnasse** and **La Défense**, the redevelopment of the 13e, and, in the 1970s, projects like **Beaubourg**, the **Front de Seine**, and **Les Halles**. In recent years, new colossal public buildings in a myriad of conflicting styles have been inaugurated at an ever-more astounding rate. At the same time, the fabric of the city—the streets, the métro, and the graffitied walls—have been ignored.

When the Les Halles flower and veg market was dismantled it was not just the nineteenth-century architecture that was mourned. The city's **social mix** has changed more in twenty-five years than in the previous hundred. **Gentrification** of the remaining working-class districts is accelerating, and the population has become essentially middle-class and white-collar.

As a sign posted during the Les Halles redevelopment lamented: "The center of Paris will be beautiful. Luxury will be king. But we will not be here." And now it is not just the center of the city. If those "we" come into Paris at all any more, it is as commuting service workers or weekend shoppers. "Renovation is not for us."

THE POLITICAL PRESENT

In May 1981, people danced in the streets of Paris to celebrate the end of 23 years of right wing rule—and the victory of François Mitterrand's Socialist Party. Five years later, the Socialists conclusively lost their majority in the *Assemblée Nationale* (parliament), while Le Pen's ultra-right *Front National* won a horrifying 35 seats. Mitterrand remained president while the autocratic mayor of Paris, Jacques Chirac, headed the new government. But the return of the Right was not to last. Socialist rule, in drastically diluted centrist form, resumed after the 1988 parliamentary elections.

THE 1980s— THE PARTIES IN POWER

In their first five years in power, the Socialists shifted from partnership with the Communists to somewhere closer to the center under Laurent Fabius's premiership. Their attempts to reform the education system were defeated by mass protests in the streets; ministers were implicated in cover-ups and corruption; unemployment continued to rise. Any idea of peaceful and pro-ecological intent was dashed, as far as international opinion was concerned, by the French Secret Service's murder of the Greenpeace photographer on the Rainbow Warrior in New Zealand.

There were sporadic achievements—in labor laws and women's rights, notably—but there was no cohesive and consistent Socialist line. Their 1986 election slogan was "Help— the Right is coming back," a bizarrely self-fulfilling tactic that they defended on the grounds of humor. For the unemployed and the low-paid, for immigrants and their families, for women wanting the choice of whether to have children, for the young, the old, and all those attached to certain civil liberties, the return of the Right was no laughing matter.

Throughout 1987 the chances of Mitterrand's winning the presidential election in 1988 seemed very slim. But Chirac's economic policies had failed to deliver the goods. Millions of first-time investors in "popular capitalism" lost all their money on Black Monday. Terrorists planted bombs in Paris and took French hostages in Lebanon. Unemployment continued to rise and Chirac made the fatal mistake of flirting with the extreme Right. Leading politicians of the center-right, including Simone Weil, a concentration-camp survivor, denounced Chirac's concessions to Le Pen, and a new alignment of the center started to emerge. Mitterrand, the grand old man of politics, with decades of experience, played off all the groupings of the Right in an all-but-flawless campaign, and won another seven-year mandate.

His party, however, did not fare so well in the parliamentary elections called soon afterwards. The Socialists failed to achieve an absolute majority and Mitterrand's new prime minister, Michel Rocard, went for the centrist coalition, causing friction in the party grass-roots for whom the Communists were the natural partners. The traditional Socialist supporters in the public-service sector were not happy with Rocard's austerity measures. Wage increases were restricted to two percent and nurses, civil servants, teachers, and the like were quick to take industrial action. Though Chirac's programs were halted, they were not reversed, and no alternate vision was given to the populace.

The best news of the election was the collapse, electorally, of the Front National. Le Pen failed to win a seat, only one député was re-elected (for the Invalides constituency), and she has since become an Independent.

THE UNDERLYING POSITION

France is a highly **secretive state**. More so, if anything, than Britain, whose hard-hitting TV documentaries would have difficulty finding airtime across the Channel. And, as in the US and the UK, the truth about such things as nuclear accidents and agreements with foreign powers is not always revealed by the government. That the radioactive cloud from Chernobyl passed over areas of France was admitted very, very belatedly (and no advice given) when too many people had figured out the implausibility of the cloud being deflected by the French–German border. As regards their own **nuclear industry**, the biggest in the world in proportion to their energy needs, almost every French citizen believes that there has never been an accident. A halt to nuclear plant construction and increased investment in renewable sources promised by the Socialists in 1981 was immediately dropped. France has a nuclear reprocessing plant—on the Cotentin peninsula in Normandy—that discharges its waste into the sea. Cotentin also provided some air space for the American bombing raid on Libya in 1986, despite smug protestations that it had been denied.

In all these things it made little difference whether power resided with the Right or the so-called Left, except in **relations with the superpowers**. Contrary to what you might expect, negotiation and trade with the Soviet Union always benefits by a Gaullist government, while Mitterrand was as beloved of Reagan as Margaret Thatcher. The taste for truculence on the Right toward American desires goes back to de Gaulle and represents not anti-Americanism but pro-Frenchness. The independent nuclear arsenal and nonmembership of NATO (for which there has long been cross-party consensus) is one of the major sources of French pride, French glory, and French chauvinism.

When it comes to France's **overseas territories**, there has been a similar consensus on "No" to independence claims, with slight cosmetic differences. When the Kanaks of Nouvelle Calédonie (New Caledonia, an island near New Zealand) began to rebel against the direct, unelected rule by Paris, Mitterrand granted them compensation for their appropriated lands. Chirac reversed this. Mitterrand's "autonomy" measures for the island were not a problem since they kept defense, foreign affairs, control of the television, law and order, and education firmly in the French governor's hands. A massacre of indigenous tribesmen in October 1986 by white settlers was deemed "self defense" and appeals against the judgment prohibited by Paris. Eventually, however, the situation proved to be too much of a headache, and a referendum in November 1988 committed France to granting independence to New Caledonia in ten years.

Both the New Zealand and Australian governments were warned to desist from their support for the island's independence—to stop meddling in French internal affairs as Paris

sees it. Both countries take strong stands against the **nuclear tests at Muroroa** (with the concomitant suppression of information and heavy-arm tactics against protesters). The two secret agents responsible for blowing up the **Rainbow Warrior** had been given ten-year sentences in New Zealand jails. French pressure resulted in a UN-sponsored compromise of a three-year confinement to the French island of Hao. On highly spurious medical grounds, both have found their way back to Paris—leaving New Zealand furious but impotent and French public opinion completely unperturbed. Meanwhile the subjugation of the Polynesian people to French interests, with slum dwellers surviving on subsistence while imported French goods decimate local economies, goes on and will no doubt continue, whether independence becomes a reality or not.

On **the law and order front**, opinion polls suggested that Chirac hit a chord in most Frenchmen and Frenchwomen's hearts even before the Abu Nidal bombing campaign in the capital. The death sentence was not reintroduced—the message seems to have got through that "civilized" European nations don't do that sort of thing. But maximum penalties of thirty years' imprisonment without parole were put on the statute books along with no juries for terrorist offenses, more incentives for turning state's witness, detention without charge increased to a maximum of four days, and police powers of arrest extended.

The practice of **demanding ID papers** more or less randomly (eg from people who are young, black, not wearing suits, etc) was enshrined in law soon after the Right's return to power in 1986. If the police didn't like the look of your passport or ID card, they could take you off to the station, photograph and fingerprint you, refuse you access to a lawyer, and charge you with non-cooperation if you resisted.

The record of the **police** when it comes to "bavures" ("blunders" literally, usually resulting in the death or injury of an innocent person) has long been alarming. After one such incident, which took place a week after the shooting of a policeman in the south, Chirac's Interior Minister made clear his view (shared by the Police Federation) that the one exempted the other and in no event was an individual police officer to blame. The atmosphere in Paris changed noticeably, with agents of the law arrogantly acting out their fantasies of power.

Rocard's government was conscious of the general support Chirac whipped up for his authoritarian approach and has repealed very little. Instead it left the law as it stood while dissuading the police and courts from enforcing it. A declaration of the Rights of Man now hangs by order of the Interior Ministry in every commissariat.

Unemployment never became a key issue during the 1980s. When Chirac came to power in 1986 the official figures stood at 2.4 million. During the election, the comedian Coluche set up thousands of "*restaurants du coeur*" (restaurants of the heart) to hand out soup and food parcels to those living below the poverty line, many of them the long-term unemployed. The money was raised through TV appeals. But if Coluche hoped to bring a point home rather than simply mock the politicians, he failed. Jobs continued to be lost in the mines, shipyards, transport industry, and in the denationalized industries.

Chirac's **privatization program** went considerably further than reversing the preceding Socialists' nationalizations—banks that de Gaulle took into the public sector after 1945 were sold off along with Dassault, the aircraft manufacturer, and Elf-Aquitaine, the biggest French oil company. Monopoly corporatism had a field day with mergers and takeovers ever decreasing the number of independent businesses. The contradiction for French national consciousness was this process opening up French firms to Italian, German, British, or other Common Market members' ownership. That the Americans were kept at bay made little difference to Gallic pride.

The return of the Socialists put an end to further privatizations but Rocard ruled out renationalization. Public spending has been increased, but not enough to compensate for all the jobs lost in the preceding government's manic sell-offs. Where Chirac and his Interior Minister Charles Pasqua (who publicly stated in May 1988 that the aims of the Gaullists and the Front National were the same) came down heavily on **trade unionists**, the Socialists have at least offered amnesty to some of those who were prosecuted. The most famous defendants to benefit were the Renault Ten, accused of conspiring to organize a strike in the car firm's Boulogne Billancourt works. The shock of Chirac's Thatcherite approach to the unions, which in France are mostly organized along political lines rather than by profession, galvanized the usually irreconcilably divided Communist CGT, Socialist CFDT, and Catholic FO unions into finding a common cause. Rocard's centrist program provoked a wave of strikes in the summer and autumn of 1988, but layoffs were not averted.

The most popular minister of the 1981–86 Socialist government, **Jack Lang**, is back as Minister of Culture, after the destructive period of Chirac's appointee, François Léotard, who suppressed all ventures tainted by feminism, gay rights, socialism, etc. Luckily, Lang's work in Paris during his first term was so popular, even with conservative museum curators, that it could not be dismantled at a stroke. Lang's appointment of a Minister for Rock has been the source of major ridicule, but most Parisians are proud of all their new architectural highlights even when they don't particularly like them.

In the culture and politics of the oppressed, the voice of **anti-racism** began to be heard in the 1980s. The racism of the French establishment was trumpeted under the Gaullists. Natality measures and the position of women immigrants brought French feminists into the battle. The strength of the Front National after the 1986 election under proportional representation shocked a broad range of French into recognizing the urgency of taking on and defeating racism. The pedigrees of the Front National deputies were almost ludicrously extreme. They included members of the Moonies, publishers of Hitler's speeches, a defector from the Gaullists for being too soft in the Rainbow Warrior affair, an 86-year-old who as a Paris city council member in 1943 voted full powers for Marshal Pétain's Vichy regime, and the party leader Jean-Marie Le Pen. The fact that they are no longer represented in the parliament (proportional representation has been amended) does not mean that their grassroots support is not still a threat.

The Socialists have always played electoral games with the immigration issue and have yet to prove that they are committed to combating racism. The popular anti-racist movement,

IMMIGRANTS

The **history of immigrants** in France is a familiar one. From the mid-1950s to the mid-1970s a labor shortage led to massive recruitment campaigns in North Africa, Portugal, Spain, Italy, and Greece. People were promised housing, free medical care, trips home, and well-paid jobs. When they arrived in France they found themselves paid half of what their French co-workers earned, accommodated in prison-style hostels, and sometimes poorer than they were at home. They had no vote, no automatic permit renewal, were threatened with deportation at the slightest provocation, were subject to constant racial abuse and assault, and, until 1981, were forbidden to form their own associations.

The Socialist government lifted this ban, gave a ten-year automatic renewal for permits, and even spoke about voting rights. Able to organize for the first time, immigrant workers immediately took on their employers at several car factories on the issue of racism in the selection of workers being laid off. Meanwhile in Paris, Chirac, as mayor of the city, was extending maternity leave to French women who were having a third child, while ensuring that no foreigner would receive the benefit. His line on population growth (a French obsession since 1945 with no basis whatsoever in the new technological age) was that unless French women

were encouraged to reproduce, nothing would stop the hordes south of the Mediterranean from taking over the north. In the context of newly won abortion rights, many women, whether they were concerned with racism or not, began to worry.

Chirac's anti-terrorism and immigration laws provoked unprecedented alliances. The Archbishop of Lyon and the head of the Muslim Institute in Paris together condemned the injustice of their introduction, with the Catholic leader giving his blessing to a hunger-strike protest. Human rights groups, churches, and trade unions joined immigrants' groups in saying that France was on its way to becoming a police state. No idle rhetoric: the measures included the right of the police to expel immigrants without the interference of any courts or any other ministry except their own, ie Mr Pasqua's; the annulment of the right to automatic citizenship for people born in France; the reintroduction of visas for visitors from North Africa, Turkey, and the Middle East; and immediate deportation for any criminal offense. Since the 1986 bomb attacks, visa requirements came into force for all non-Common Market nationals— prompting outraged demands for exemption from Switzerland and Sweden. Now Eastern Europeans who fled their countries years ago are having trouble renewing residency papers.

---

supported by the Communist Party, some sections of the Socialists, and the liberal center, is meanwhile gaining ground, constituting one of the most hopeful developments in French politics. The problem with the government in power is not just that it needs to prove its commitment to crucial issues such as this, but, more generally, to prove its commitment to socialism, or at least to that nineteenth-century formulation: liberty, fraternity, and equality.

THE 1990s

The 1980s ended with the most absurd blowout of public funds ever—the Bicentennial celebrations of the French Revolution. They symbolized a culture industry spinning mindlessly around the vacuum at the center of the French vision for the future. At the same time they highlighted the contrast between the unemployed begging in the Paris métro and the limitless cash available for prestige projects. The crassness of the celebrations also

confirmed the demise of the Parisian intellectual. Left Bank cafés no longer harbor committed theoreticians; the protests over education, unemployment, and the Gulf war have had no Sartres to give them universal credibility.

As he approaches his eleventh year in office, François Mitterrand, "*Tonton* (uncle)" to his people, has perfected the presidential art of upsetting no one, giving sphinx-like speeches in his superbly literary French that place him closer to a pope than to a political leader. **Political parties are dying**, according to many ordinary Parisians. The Right is riven, with even Chirac's Gaullist party facing serious defections; the Left in power has abandoned ideology for centrist pragmatism.

The **political integration of Europe** has found no consensus in the body politic, perhaps because of the realization that Berlin not Paris will be its powerhouse. Instead, the French have settled for second best, maintaining Paris as Europe's most glorious cultural capital.

When compared with Britain, France has certainly **benefited from keeping the Right at bay**: inflation dropped below zero at the end of 1990; interest rates have gone down to ten percent; and the budget deficit has been greatly reduced. In areas such as health, the difference is particularly shocking, with French hospitals able to offer operations like hip replacements to British patients who would wait much longer on their National Health Service. France is weathering the recession well, though the aftermath of the Gulf war may change that.

Perennial problems still persist. **Unemployment** is becoming a crucial issue. The **lycée strikes** of 1990 were not a 1968-style protest but the culmination of years of underfunding in the upkeep of school buildings and an educational bureaucracy that rivaled Soviet standards. Money was soon forthcoming when Mitterrand took the students' side against his education minister, and in 1990 the education budget outstripped defense spending for the first time.

The anger of **third-generation immigrants** from the Paris suburbs has erupted into street battles within the capital which, however, though sensationalized by the media (whipping up more racism), have never reached the scale of similar riots in Miami or D.C. The Bosquets estate in the urban dereliction of Montfermeil 19km east of Paris is a typical breeding ground of justified unrest, with a ninety percent immigrant population, half of whom are under twenty-five. The flats are uninsulated, the elevators don't work, and the chances of youngsters finding legal work are slim. Bernard Tapie, the millionaire entrepreneur with an eye on the next presidentials, has targeted Bosquets for his Citizens' Forum, a capitalism-with-human-face outfit, blessed by Mitterrand but scorned by the people it's supposed to help who say Tapie makes them feel like animals in a zoo.

But **new forces** outside the parliamentary mainstream have emerged and strengthened. **SOS Racisme** has made its mark throughout the country and, though distancing itself from street gangs, has played a major part in the *lycée* strikes and in the anti-Gulf war protests.

It was assumed when Rocard appointed Bruce Lalonde, the leader of the **Greens**, to join his cabinet as environmental minister that this would neutralize *Les Verts*. But Lalonde has stuck to his principles, calling for strict measures on air pollution, water quality, and recycling, the removal of subsidies on fossil fuel production, and a green tax on gas and products using CFCs. He also called for a boycott of Mercedes and BMW as symbols of a car industry gone mad.

The CEA (the Atomic Energy Board, responsible for the lies about the Chernobyl radiation cloud) has been told by the government to mend its ways. This followed an outcry in September 1990, when it was revealed that two **nuclear waste dumps** closed in the Seventies within 40km of Paris were thirty times above the acceptable radioactivity levels. After an initial denial, the CEA were forced to admit the threat to health and the government agreed to Les Verts' demand for an independent inquiry. Politicians and trade unions are beginning to question the safety of nuclear power. The industry minister has criticized the EDF (French Electricity Board) for secrecy and himself leaked critical information to the press.

Civil rights organizations and gays and lesbians joined forces following the discovery of the corpse of Pastor Doucé, director of a gay Christian center, strongly suspected of being murdered by the *Réseignements Généraux*, the internal intelligence services. The interior minister was compelled to order an investigation into the *RG*, the first time French security forces have ever been subjected to such scrutiny.

Other **scandals** in the capital have included phone-tapping of municipal officers in the town hall, and the claim that 24 billion francs (about $4 million) was illegally raised for Mitterrand's re-election campaign in 1988. The campaign treasurer at the time, now minister of justice, first blocked the inquiry then persuaded parliament to grant an amnesty to all involved.

At the outbreak of the **war in the Gulf**, the French defense minister was Jean-Pierre Chevènement, a pacifist on the left of the Socialist Party, who was founder and co-president of the Franco-Iraqi Friendship Society. He led the massive antiwar marches on the eve of the UN deadline and resigned within a week of the war beginning. The French stance on the conflict has revealed all the old contradictions surfacing. Mitterrand's last-minute peace proposals, though admirable in themselves, were motivated by French chauvinism—to show French independence from the US and to claim a leading role in European foreign policy. Once the war began, the prevarication over whether troops would fight in Iraq as well as Kuwait had to do with balancing the future needs of trade and industry with the desire to be a major partner in the West's postwar settlement. And as ever with conflicts in the Middle East, France is handicapped by the guilt still felt for its collaboration with the Germans in World War II, preventing it from ever criticizing Israel.

France in the 1990s is in a state of **political flux**. Old certainties vanished with the swings in government of the preceding decade that put an end to the automatic rule of the Right, and the experiment of *cohabitation* (a Socialist president with a Gaullist prime minister) that forced Mitterrand to distance himself from party politics. The threat of far-right power has been diffused; the French Communist Party has failed to change its Stalin-era leader; and the major parties of the Right and Left both have serious divisions. New movements for new times are needed, and perhaps in 1995, when Mitterrand retires, his successor will usher in a new era of French politics. But only if, and this is a big if, France can finally face up to modern realities and jettison its dearest and most damaging image of itself, as a *Grand Pays* and natural leader of an expanded Europe.

BOOKS

HISTORY

Alfred Cobban, *A History of Modern France* (3 vols: 1715–99, 1799–1871, and 1871–1962; Viking Penguin $6.95 each). Complete and very readable account of the main political, social, and economic strands in French—and inevitably Parisian—history.

Ronald Hamilton, *A Holiday History of France* (UK only; Hogarth Press, 1985; £6.95). Convenient pocket reference book: who's who and what's what.

Christopher Hibbert, *The Days of the French Revolution: The Day-to-Day Story of the Revolution* (Morrow, 1981; $12.95). Good concise popular history of the period and events.

Norman Hampson, *A Social History of the French Revolution* (University of Toronto Press, 1963; $17.95). An analysis that concentrates on the personalities involved. Its particular interest lies in the attention it gives to the *sans-culottes*, the ordinary poor of Paris.

Karl Marx, *Surveys from Exile* (Vintage/Random, 1974); *On the Paris Commune* (Beekman Pubs, 1971; $22.95). *Surveys* includes Marx's speeches and articles at the time of the 1848 revolution and after, including an analysis, riddled with jokes, of Napoléon III's rise to power. *Paris Commune*—more rousing prose—has a history of the Commune by Engels.

Theodore Zeldin, *France, 1845–1945* (OUP, 5 paperback volumes, 1979–80; $10.95 each). Series of thematic volumes on all matters French—all good reads.

Lissagaray, *Paris Commune* (UK only; New Park 1976; £6.95). A highly personal and partisan account of the politics and fighting by a participant. Although Lissagaray himself is reticent about it, history has it that the last solitary Communard on the last barricade—in the rue Ramponneau in Belleville—was in fact himself.

SOCIETY AND POLITICS

John Ardagh, *France in the 1980s* (Viking Penguin, 1988; $7.95). Comprehensive overview up to 1988, covering food, film, education, and holidays as well as politics and education—from a social democrat and journalist position. Good on detail for the urban suburbs (and the shift there from the center) of Paris.

Theodore Zeldin, *The French* (Vintage/Random, 1984; $12.95). A coffee-table book without the pictures, based on the author's conversations with a wide range of people, about money, sex, phobias, parents, and everything else.

D. L. Hanley, **A. P. Kerr**, and **N. H. Waites**, *Contemporary France* (Routledge Chapman & Hall, 1984, $17.95). Well-written and academic textbook, if you want to fathom the practicalities of power in France: the constitution, parties, trade unions etc. Includes an excellent opening chapter on the period since the war.

Claire Duchen, *Feminism in France: From May '68 to Mitterrand* (Routledge Chapman & Hall, 1986; $13.95). Charts the evolution of the women's movement through to the 80s, clarifying the divergent political stances and the feminist theory which informs the various groups.

Simone de Beauvoir, *The Second Sex* (Vintage/Random, 1989; $12.95). One of the prime texts of western feminism, written in 1949, covering women's inferior status in history, literature, mythology, psychoanalysis, philosophy, and everyday life.

Roland Barthes, *Mythologies* (1957; French & European; $9.95); *A Barthes Reader* (Hill & Wang, 1983; $14.95). The first, though dated, is the classic: a brilliant description of how the ideas, prejudices, and contradictions of French thought and behavior manifest themselves, in food, wine, cars, travel guides, and other cultural offerings. Barthes' piece on the Eiffel Tower doesn't appear, but it's included in the *Barthes Reader* (edited by Susan Sontag).

Gisèle Halimi, *Milk for the Orange Tree* (UK only; Quartet Books, 1990; £19.95). Born in Tunisia, daughter of an Orthodox Jewish family; ran away to Paris to become a lawyer; defender of women's rights, Algerian FLN fighters, and all unpopular causes. A gutsy autobiographical story.

ART, ARCHITECTURE, AND PHOTOGRAPHS

Norma Evenson, *Paris: A Century of Change, 1878–1978* (Yale 1981; o/p). A large illustrated volume which makes the development of urban planning and the fabric of Paris an enthralling subject, mainly because the author's concern is always with people, not panoramas.

William Mahder, ed., *Paris Arts: The '80s Renaissance* (Autrement 1984). Illustrated, magazine-style survey of French arts now. The design and photos are reason enough in themselves to look it up. Fortunately, for the English edition now seems to be out of print, the French, *Paris Creation: Une Renaissance* isn't.

Brassai, *Le Paris Secret des Années 30* (Pantheon, 1977; $17.95). Extraordinary photos of the capital's nightlife in the 1930s—brothels, music halls, street cleaners, transvestites, and the underworld—each one a work of art and a familiar world (now long since gone) to Brassai and his mate, Henry Miller, who accompanied him on his night-time expeditions.

Edward Lucie-Smith, *Concise History of French Painting* (Thames & Hudson 1971; o/p). If you're after an art reference book, then this will do as well as any, though there are of course dozens of other books available on particular French artists and art movements.

John James, *Chartres* (Routledge Chapman & Hall, 1982; o/p). The story of Chartres Cathedral with insights into the medieval context, the character and attitudes of the masons, the symbolism, and the advanced mathematics of the building's geometry.

PARIS IN LITERATURE

AMERICAN/BRITISH

Charles Dickens, *A Tale of Two Cities* (1849; Viking Penguin, 1989; $6.95). Paris and London during the 1789 revolution and before. The plot's pure Hollywood, but the streets and at least some of the social backdrop are for real.

George Orwell, *Down and Out in Paris and London* (1933; Harcourt Brace Jovanovich, 1972; $4.95). Breadline living in the 1930s—Orwell at his best.

Ernest Hemingway, *A Moveable Feast* (1960; Collier Macmillan, 1977; $4.95). Hemingway's American-in-Paris account of life in the 1930s with Ezra Pound, F Scott Fitzgerald, Gertrude Stein, etc. Dull, pedestrian stuff, despite the classic and best-seller status.

Henry Miller, *Tropic Of Cancer* (1934; Random, 1987; $7.95); *Quiet Days in Clichy* (1955; Grove Weidenfeld, 1987; $7.95). Again 1930s Paris, though from a more focused angle—sex, essentially. Erratic, wild, self-obsessed writing, but with definite flights of genius.

Robert Ferguson, *Henry Miller: A Biography* (Norton, 1991; $24.95). Very readable biography of the old rogue and his rumbunctious doings, including, of course, his long stint in Paris and affair with Anaïs Nin.

Anaïs Nin, *The Diary of Anaïs Nin 1931–1974* (7 vols; Harcourt Brace Jovanovich, 1978; o/p). Miller's best Parisian pal. Not fiction, but the journals of Anaïs Nin build up a detailed literary narrative of French and US artists and fiction-makers from the first half of this century—not least, Nin herself—in Paris and elsewhere. The more famous *Erotica* (Quartet) was also of course written in Paris—for a local porn connoisseur.

Jack Kerouac, *Sartori in Paris* (1966; Grove Weidenfeld, 1988; $8.95) . . . and in Brittany, too. Uniquely inconsequential Kerouac experiences.

Brion Gysin, *The Last Museum* (Grove Weidenfeld, 1986; $7.95). Setting is the Hotel Bardo, the Beat hotel: co-residents Kerouac, Ginsberg, and Burroughs. Published posthumously, this is Sixties Paris in its most manic mode.

Herbert Lottman, *Colette: A Life* (Little, 1991; $24.95). An interesting if somewhat dry account of the life of this enigmatic Parisian writer.

Paul Rambali, *French Blues* (Trafalgar Square, 1991; $29.95). Movies, sex, down-and-outs, politics, fast food, bikers—a cynical, streetwise look at modern urban France.

FRENCH (IN TRANSLATION)

Baudelaire's Paris, translated by Laurence Kitchen (UK only; Forest Books 1990; £3.95). Gloom and doom by Baudelaire, Gérard de Nerval, Verlaine, and Jiménez—in bilingual edition.

Gustave Flaubert, *Sentimental Education* (1869; OUP, 1990; $4.95). A lively, detailed reconstruction of the life, manners, characters, and politics of Parisians in the 1840s, including the 1848 revolution.

Victor Hugo, *Les Misérables* (1862; Viking Penguin, 1982; $8.95). A racy, eminently readable novel by the French equivalent of Dickens, about the Parisian poor and low-life in the first half of the nineteenth century. Book Four contains an account of the barricade fighting during the 1832 insurrection.

Emile Zola, *Nana* (1880; Viking Penguin, 1972; $6.95). The rise and fall of a courtesan in the decadent times of the Second Empire. Not bad on sex, but confused on sexual politics. A great story nevertheless, which brings mid-nineteenth-century Paris alive, direct, to present-day senses. Paris is also the setting for Zola's *L'Assommoir* (1877; Viking Penguin, 1970; $6.95), *L'Argent* (1891; Schoenhof, 1975; $9.95) and *Thérèse Raquin* (1867; Viking Penguin, 1962; $5.95).

Alexandre Dumas, *The Count of Monte Cristo* (1884; World's Classics, 1991; $9.95). One hell of a good yarn, with Paris and Marseilles locations.

Marcel Proust, *Remembrance of Things Past* (1913–27; Random, 3 vol set; $52.85). Written in and of Paris: absurd but bizarrely addictive.

Georges Simenon, *Maigret at the Crossroads* (1955; Viking Penguin, 1984; $6.95), or any other of the *Maigret* novels. Ostensibly crime thrillers but, of course, Real Literature too. The Montmartre and seedy criminal locations are unbeatable.

André Breton, *Nadja* (1930; Grove Weidenfeld, 1988; $9.95). A surrealist evocation of Paris. Fun.

Jean-Paul Sartre, *Roads to Freedom Trilogy* (1945–49; Vintage/Random; volumes 1 & 2 $6.95 each, volume 3 $9.95). Metaphysics and gloom, despite the title.

Blaise Cendrars, *To the End of the World* (1956; UK only; Peter Owen, 1991; £14.50). An outrageous bawdy tale of a randy septuagenarian Parisian actress, having an affair with a deserter from the Foreign Legion.

Edith Piaf, *My Life* (Dufour, 1991; $30). Piaf's dramatic story told pretty much in her own words.

LANGUAGE

French can be a deceptively familiar language because of the number of words and structures it shares with English. Despite this it's far from easy, though the bare essentials are not difficult to master and can make all the difference. Even just saying *"Bonjour Madame/Monsieur"* and then gesticulating will usually get you a smile and helpful service.

People working in tourist offices, hotels, and so on almost always speak English and tend to use it when you're struggling to speak French—be grateful, not insulted.

FRENCH PRONUNCIATION

One easy rule to remember is that **consonants** at the ends of words are usually silent. *Pas plus tard* (not later) is thus pronounced pa-plu-tarr. But when the following word begins with a vowel, you run the two together: *pas après* (not after) becomes pazapre.

Vowels are the hardest sounds to get right. Roughly:

a	as in h**a**t	*i*	as in mach**i**ne
e	as in g**e**t	*o*	as in h**o**t
é	between g**e**t and ga**te**	*o, au*	as in **o**ver
è	between g**e**t and g**u**t	*ou*	as in f**oo**d
eu	like the **u** in h**u**rt	*u*	as in a pursed-lip version of **u**se

More awkward are the **combinations** in/im, en/em, an/am, on/om, un/um at the ends of words, or followed by consonants other than n or m. Again, roughly:

in/im	like the **an** in **an**xious	*on/om*	like the **don** in **Don**caster said by
an/am, en/em	like the **don** in **Don**caster when		someone with a heavy cold
	said with a nasal accent	*un/um*	like the **u** in **u**nderstand

Consonants are much as in English, except that: ch is always sh, c is s, h is silent, th is the same as t, ll is like the y in yes, w is v, and r is growled (or rolled).

LEARNING MATERIALS

There are any number of French **phrasebooks** around, most of them adequate: *Hugo's French Phrasebook* (Hunter, 1988; $3.25) is one of the most up to date. More complete is *French Keywords: The Basic 2000-word Vocabulary arranged by Frequency* (Oleander Press, 1983; $5.95).

Among **dictionaries**, *Harper and Row* is the standard school dictionary; otherwise pick according to size and price. The *Dictionary of Modern Colloquial French* by Hérail and Lovatt (Routledge, Chapman and Hall, 1987; $14.95) makles great reading—as much for the English expressions as the French. It gives French-to-English only, and includes the language of sex, crime, and drugs—indeed all the words you ever wanted to know.

À Vous La France; Franc Extra; Franc-Parler (BBC Publications; each has a book and two cassettes) are BBC radio courses, running from beginners' to fairly advanced language.

A BRIEF GUIDE TO SPEAKING FRENCH

BASIC WORDS AND PHRASES

French nouns are divided into masculine and feminine. This causes difficulties with adjectives, whose endings have to change to suit the gender of the nouns they qualify. If you know some grammar, you will know what to do. If not, stick to the masculine form, which is the simplest—it's what we have done in this glossary.

today	*aujourd'hui*	that one	*celà*
yesterday	*hier*	open	*ouvert*
tomorrow	*demain*	closed	*fermé*
in the morning	*le matin*	big	*grand*
in the afternoon	*l'après-midi*	small	*petit*
in the evening	*le soir*	more	*plus*
now	*maintenant*	less	*moins*
later	*plus tard*	a little	*un peu*
at one o'clock	*à une heure*	a lot	*beaucoup*
at three o'clock	*à trois heures*	cheap	*bon marché*
at ten-thirty	*à dix heures et demie*	expensive	*cher*
at midday	*à midi*	good	*bon*
man	*un homme*	bad	*mauvais*
woman	*une femme*	hot	*chaud*
here	*ici*	cold	*froid*
there	*là*	with	*avec*
this one	*ceci*	without	*sans*

NUMBERS

1	*un*	11	*onze*	21	*vingt-et-un*	95	*quatre-vingt-quinze*
2	*deux*	12	*douze*	22	*vingt-deux*	100	*cent*
3	*trois*	13	*treize*	30	*trente*	101	*cent-et-un*
4	*quatre*	14	*quatorze*	40	*quarante*	200	*deux cents*
5	*cinq*	15	*quinze*	50	*cinquante*	300	*trois cents*
6	*six*	16	*seize*	60	*soixante*	500	*cinq cents*
7	*sept*	17	*dix-sept*	70	*soixante-dix*	1000	*mille*
8	*huit*	18	*dix-huit*	75	*soixante-quinze*	2000	*deux milles*
9	*neuf*	19	*dix-neuf*	80	*quatre-vingts*	5000	*cinq milles*
10	*dix*	20	*vingt*	90	*quatre-vingt-dix*	1,000,000	*un million*

DAYS AND DATES

January	*janvier*	November	*novembre*	August 1	*le premier août*
February	*février*	December	*décembre*	March 2	*le deux mars*
March	*mars*			July 14	*le quatorze juillet*
April	*avril*	Sunday	*dimanche*	November 23	*le vingt-trois*
May	*mai*	Monday	*lundi*		*novembre*
June	*juin*	Tuesday	*mardi*		
July	*juillet*	Wednesday	*mercredi*	1992	*dix-neuf-cent-*
August	*août*	Thursday	*jeudi*		*quatre-vingt-douze*
September	*septembre*	Friday	*vendredi*	1993	*dix-neuf-cent-*
October	*octobre*	Saturday	*samedi*		*quatre-vingt-treize*

TALKING TO PEOPLE

When addressing people you should always use *Monsieur* for a man, *Madame* for a woman, *Mademoiselle* for a girl. Plain *bonjour* by itself is not enough. This isn't as formal as it seems, and it has its uses when you've forgotten someone's name or want to attract someone's attention.

Excuse me	*Pardon*	please	*s'il vous plaît*
Do you speak English?	*Vous parlez anglais?*	thank you	*merci*
How do you say it in French?	*Comment ça se dit en Français?*	hello	*bonjour*
		goodbye	*au revoir*
What's your name?	*Comment vous appelez-vous?*	good morning/ afternoon	*bonjour*
		good evening	*bonsoir*
My name is . . .	*Je m'appelle . . .*	good night	*bonne nuit*
I'm American/ Canadian/ English/ Irish/Scottish/ Welsh/ Australian/ a New Zealander	*Je suis américain[e]/ canadien[ne]/ anglais[e]/ irlandais[e]/écossais[e]/ gallois[e]/ australien[ne]/ néo-zélandais[e]*	How are you?	*Comment allez-vous? / Ça va?*
		Fine, thanks	*Très bien, merci*
		I don't know	*Je ne sais pas*
		Let's go	*Allons-y*
		See you tomorrow	*À demain*
yes	*oui*	See you soon	*À bientôt*
no	*non*	Sorry	*Pardon, Madame/je m'excuse*
I understand	*Je comprends*		
I don't understand	*Je ne comprends pas*	Leave me alone (aggressive)	*Fichez-moi la paix!*
Can you speak slower?	*S'il vous plaît, parlez moins vite*	Please help me	*Aidez-moi, s'il vous plaît*

FINDING THE WAY

bus	*autobus, bus, car*	hitchhiking	*autostop*
bus station	*gare routière*	on foot	*à pied*
bus stop	*arrêt*	Where are you going?	*Vous allez où ?*
car	*voiture*		
train/taxi/ferry	*train/taxi/ferry*	I'm going to . . .	*Je vais à . . .*
boat	*bâteau*	I want to get off at . . .	*Je voudrais descendre à . . .*
plane	*avion*		
railroad station	*gare*	the road to . . .	*la route pour . . .*
platform	*quai*	near	*près/pas loin*
What time does it leave?	*Il part à quelle heure ?*	far	*loin*
		left	*à gauche*
What time does it arrive?	*Il arrive à quelle heure ?*	right	*à droite*
		straight ahead	*tout droit*
a ticket to . . .	*un billet pour . . .*	on the other side of	*l'autre côté de*
one-way ticket	*aller simple*	on the corner of	*à l'angle de*
round-trip ticket	*aller retour*	next to	*à côté de*
validate your ticket	*compostez votre billet*	behind	*derrière*
		in front of	*devant*
valid for	*valable pour*	before	*avant*
ticket office	*vente de billets*	after	*après*
how many kilometers ?	*combien de kilomètres ?*	under	*sous*
		to cross	*traverser*
how many hours ?	*combien d'heures ?*	bridge	*pont*

QUESTIONS AND REQUESTS

The simplest way of asking a question is to start with *s'il vous plaît* (please), then name the thing you want in an interrogative tone of voice. For example:

Where is there a bakery?	*S'il vous plaît, la boulangerie?*
Which way is it to the Eiffel Tower?	*S'il vous plaît, la route pour la tour Eiffel?*

Similarly with requests:

We'd like a room for two	*S'il vous plaît, une chambre pour deux?*
Can I have a kilo of oranges?	*S'il vous plaît, un kilo d'oranges?*

Question words

where?	*où?*	when?	*quand?*
how?	*comment?*	why?	*pourquoi?*
how many/	*combien?*	at what time?	*à quelle heure?*
how much?		what is/which is?	*quel est?*

ACCOMMODATION

a room for one/two people	*une chambre pour une/deux personnes*	do laundry	*faire la lessive*
a double bed	*un lit double*	sheets	*draps*
a room with a shower	*une chambre avec douche*	blankets	*couvertures*
		quiet	*calme*
a room with a bath	*une chambre avec salle de bain*	noisy	*bruyant*
		hot water	*eau chaude*
For one/two/three nights	*Pour une/deux/trois nuits*	cold water	*eau froide*
		Is breakfast included?	*Est-ce que le petit déjeuner est compris?*
Can I see it?	*Je peux la voir?*	I would like breakfast	*Je voudrais prendre le petit déjeuner*
a room on the courtyard	*une chambre sur la cour*		
a room over the street	*une chambre sur la rue*	I don't want breakfast	*Je ne veux pas le petit déjeuner*
first floor	*premier étage*	Can we camp here?	*On peut camper ici ?*
second floor	*deuxième étage*	campground	*un camping/terrain de camping*
with a view	*avec vue*		
key	*clef*	tent	*une tente*
to iron	*repasser*	tent space	*un emplacement*
		youth hostel	*auberge de jeunesse*

CARS

garage	*garage*	put air in the tires	*gonfler les pneus*
service	*service*	battery	*batterie*
to park the car	*garer la voiture*	the battery is dead	*la batterie est morte*
parking lot	*un parking*	plugs	*bougies*
no parking	*défense de stationner/ stationnement interdit*	to break down	*tomber en panne*
		gas can	*bidon*
gas station	*poste d'essence*	insurance	*assurance*
gas	*essence*	green card	*carte verte*
fill 'er up	*faire le plein*	traffic lights	*feux*
oil	*huile*	red light	*feu rouge*
airline	*ligne à air*	green light	*feu vert*

HEALTH MATTERS

doctor	*médecin*	stomach ache	*mal à l'estomac*
I don't feel well	*Je ne me sens pas bien*	period	*règles*
medicines	*médicaments*	pain	*douleur*
prescription	*ordonnance*	it hurts	*ça fait mal*
I feel sick	*Je suis malade*	pharmacy	*pharmacie*
I have a headache	*J'ai mal à la tête*	hospital	*hôpital*

OTHER NEEDS

bakery	*boulangerie*	bank	*banque*
food shop	*alimentation*	money	*argent*
supermarket	*supermarché*	toilets	*toilettes*
to eat	*manger*	police	*police*
to drink	*boire*	telephone	*téléphone*
camping gas	*camping gaz*	movie theater	*cinéma*
tobacconist	*tabac*	theater	*théâtre*
stamps	*timbres*	to reserve/book	*réserver*

FRENCH AND ARCHITECTURAL TERMS: A GLOSSARY

These are either terms you'll come across in the guide, or come up against on signs, maps, etc, while traveling around. For food items see *Basics*.

ABBAYE abbey

AMBULATORY covered passage around the outer edge of a choir of a church

APSE semicircular termination at the east end of a church

ASSEMBLÉE NATIONALE the French parliament

ARRONDISSEMENT district of a city

AUBERGE DE JEUNESSE (AJ) youth hostel

BAROQUE High Renaissance period of art and architecture, distinguished by extreme ornateness

BASTIDE medieval military settlement, constructed on a grid plan

BEAUX ARTS fine arts museum (and school)

CAR bus

CAROLINGIAN dynasty (and art, sculpture, etc) founded by Charlemagne, late eighth to early tenth centuries

CFDT Socialist trade union

CGT Communist trade union

CHASSE, CHASSE GARDÉE hunting grounds

CHÂTEAU mansion, country house, or castle

CHÂTEAU FORT castle

CHEMIN path

CHEVET end wall of a church

CIJ (*Centre d'Informations Jeunesse*) youth information center

CLASSICAL architectural style incorporating Greek and Roman elements—pillars, domes, colonnades, etc—at its height in France in the seventeenth century and revived in the nineteenth century as **NEOCLASSICAL**

CLERESTORY upper story of a church, incorporating the windows

CODENE the French Campaign for Nuclear Disarmament

CONSIGNE luggage consignment

COURS combination of main square and main street

COUVENT convent, monastery

DÉFENSE DE . . . It is forbidden to . . .

DÉGUSTATION tasting (wine or food)

DÉPARTEMENT county—more or less

DONJON castle keep

ÉGLISE church

EN PANNE out of order

ENTRÉE entrance

FERMETURE closing period

FLAMBOYANT florid form of Gothic (see below)

FN (Front National) fascist party led by Jean-Marie Le Pen

FO Catholic trade union

FRESCO wall painting—durable through application to wet plaster

GALLO-ROMAIN period of Roman occupation of Gaul (first to fourth centuries AD)

GARE station; **ROUTIÈRE**—bus station; **SNCF**—train station

GÎTE D'ÉTAPE basic hostel accommodation primarily for walkers

GOBELINS famous tapestry manufacturers, based in Paris; its most renowned period was in the reign of Louis XIV (seventeenth century)

HALLES covered market

HLM public housing development

HÔTEL a hotel, but also an aristocratic townhouse or mansion

HÔTEL DE VILLE town hall

JOURS FÉRIÉS public holidays

MAIRIE town hall

MARCHÉ market

MEROVINGIAN dynasty (and art, etc), ruling France and parts of Germany from the sixth to mid-eighth centuries

NARTHEX entrance hall of church

NAVE main body of a church

PCF Communist Party of France

PLACE square

PORTE gateway

PS Socialist party

PTT post office

QUARTIER district of a town

RELAIS ROUTIERS truckstop café-restaurants

RENAISSANCE art-architectural style developed in fifteenth-century Italy and imported to France in the early sixteenth century by François 1er (see *Contexts*)

RETABLE altarpiece

REZ DE CHAUSSÉE (RC) ground floor

RN (*Route Nationale*) main road

ROMANESQUE early medieval architecture distinguished by squat, rounded forms and naive sculpture

RPR Gaullist party led by Jacques Chirac

SI (*Syndicat d'Initiative*) tourist information office; also known as OT, OTSI, and MAISON DU TOURISME

SNCF French railroads

SORTIE exit

STUCCO plastic used to embellish ceilings, etc

TABAC bar or shop selling stamps, cigarettes, etc

TOUR tower

TRANSEPT cross arms of a church

TYMPANUM sculpted panel above a church door

UDF center-right party headed by Giscard d'Estaing

VAUBAN seventeenth-century military architect—his fortresses still stand all over France

VIEILLE VILLE old quarter of town

VILLAGE PERCHÉ hilltop village

VOUSSOIR sculpted rings in arch over church door

ZONE BLEUE restricted parking zone

ZONE PIETONNÉ pedestrian mall

INDEX